NEW ORLEANS AFTER THE PROMISES

KENT B. GERMANY

NEW ORLEANS AFTER THE PROMISES

Poverty, Citizenship, and the Search for the Great Society

THE UNIVERSITY OF GEORGIA PRESS   ATHENS AND LONDON

© 2007 by the University of Georgia Press
Athens, Georgia 30602
All rights reserved
Set in New Caledonia by BookComp
Printed and bound by Maple-Vail
The paper in this book meets the guidelines for
permanence and durability of the Committee on
Production Guidelines for Book Longevity of the
Council on Library Resources.
Printed in the United States of America
11   10   09   08   P   5   4   3

Library of Congress Cataloging-in-Publication Data
Germany, Kent B., 1971–
New Orleans after the promises : poverty, citizenship,
and the search for the Great Society / Kent B. Germany.
    p. cm.
Includes bibliographical references and index.
ISBN-13: 978-0-8203-2543-9 (hardcover : alk. paper)
ISBN-10: 0-8203-2543-0 (hardcover : alk. paper)
ISBN-13: 978-0-8203-2900-0 (pbk. : alk. paper)
ISBN-10: 0-8203-2900-2 (pbk. : alk. paper)
1. New Orleans (La.)—Politics and government—20th century.
2. New Orleans (La.)—Social policy.   3. New Orleans (La.)—Economic
conditions—20th century.   4. New Orleans (La.)—Race relations—History—
20th century.   5. African Americans—Civil rights—Louisiana—New Orleans—
History—20th century.   6. Poverty—Louisiana—New Orleans—History—
20th century.   7. Citizenship—Louisiana—New Orleans—History—20th century.
8. Political participation—Louisiana—New Orleans—History—20th century.
9. Liberalism—Louisiana—New Orleans—History—20th century.   I. Title.
F379.N557G47 2007
976.3'35064—dc22   2006031009
British Library Cataloging-in-Publication Data available

To Mary and them

and

To Lovie (1904–1990)

This administration today, here and now, declares unconditional war on poverty in America. . . . [T]he war against poverty will not be won here in Washington. It must be won in the field, in every private home, in every public office, from the courthouse to the White House.

—President Lyndon B. Johnson, State of the Union Address, January 8, 1964

I'm sick of all the people who talk about the things we can't do. Hell, we're the richest country in the world, the most powerful. We can do it all.

—President Lyndon B. Johnson to Speechwriter Richard Goodwin, 1964

All I want, and what the brothers want, is to share in the good life.

—Robert Richardson, Black Power Advocate, New Orleans, 1968

CONTENTS

ACKNOWLEDGMENTS

I was born and raised in Louisiana. Like most people from there, my roots go back several generations—at least four in my case. In August and September 2005, I watched the aftermath of Hurricanes Katrina and Rita from an upscale university town in Virginia and felt like an exile. I want to express my deepest sympathy for the people along the Gulf and my hope that the promises made to them are not forgotten. As for this book, I had essentially completed the final manuscript when Katrina came ashore, and in those weeks after it, I decided not to attempt any significant rewrite. It was too early to assess New Orleans's past through the lens of Katrina. The "Katrina-ing" of New Orleans's history demands an entirely new book because the storm has changed some of the fundamental questions and perspectives. In response, I chose only to revise slightly the introduction and conclusion. I do not know how many people who appear in this book were affected by Katrina, but many were. I did hear about one person who was stranded at the Morial Convention Center. Johnny Jackson Jr., the activist from Desire who became a powerful local politician, was there taking care of his elderly mother and was interviewed on public radio. I hope this book does not do disservice to people like Jackson who labored forty years earlier to make modern New Orleans or to the over one thousand people who died because of the storm or to the many others who endured. I hope that they will forgive me for any inadequacies in telling a complicated story about race, poverty, and inclusion in their city.

Books begin somewhere and end somewhere, and in between, authors rely on a wide range of people and institutions. I am particularly indebted to the archivists and staff members of several research centers. Irene Wainwright and Wayne Everard of the Louisiana Division of the

New Orleans Public Library have been extraordinarily helpful to me. They have fashioned one of the most professional and efficient enterprises I have ever seen in Louisiana government. At the Department of Special Collections at the University of New Orleans's Earl K. Long Library, I want to thank Florence Jumonville and Marie Windell. Most of my work there was with Marie, and I want to commend her for her professionalism and dedication to the study of history. She was delightful and made my research trips enjoyable and productive ventures. At the Special Collections Division of Tulane University's Howard-Tilton Memorial, I want to thank Kevin Fontenot, Wilbur Meneray, Lee Miller, Joan Caldwell, Carole Hampshire, Ann Case, and Robert Sherer. I also want to extend my appreciation to Donald DeVore, Brenda Square, and Rebecca Hankins at the Amistad Research Center in New Orleans; Patricia Lawrence, Alfred Lemann, and John McGill at the Historic New Orleans Collection, Art Carpenter at the Special Collections and Archives department of Loyola University's Monroe Library, and the staff at the Hill Library at Louisiana State University. I wish these institutions the best in their recovery from Katrina and in keeping the city's history alive. Without the rich resources preserved by them, our understanding of New Orleans would be facile and irretrievably commercialized. In addition to those local institutions, I want to note the contributions of the National Archives and Records Administration, particularly the Archives II facility in College Park, Maryland, and the LBJ Library in Austin. The LBJ Library is a model institution, and I express my deepest appreciation to Harry Middleton, Betty Sue Flowers, Tina Houston, Linda Seelke, Allen Fisher, Claudia Anderson, Regina Greenwell, Shannon Jarrett, and Laura Harmon Eggert. I also want to thank Denice Warren of the Greater New Orleans Community Data Center (www.gnocdc.org) for assistance with illustrations and Darlene Fife and Robert Head of the *NOLA Express*, the alternative newspaper published in New Orleans in the late 1960s and early 1970s, for research advice and for help with photographs.

Research and writing for this book was supported by several sources. The Tulane University Graduate School funded my graduate studies and provided a Dissertation Year Fellowship. The Organization of American Historians provided essential research funding through a Horace Samuel and Marion Galbraith Merrill Grant in Twentieth Century Political History. The University of Virginia's Miller Center of Public Affairs provided key assistance and infrastructure.

Many people generously gave time to read all or part of this work and/or to endure long conversations about it. I was fortunate to have been a student at Tulane University with a remarkable group of faculty and graduate students committed to the innovative study of southern history. Patrick J. Maney, Lawrence Powell, Donald DeVore, Bill Malone, and Clarence Mohr helped shape this study and my broader thinking about the South, while Arnold Hirsch of the University of New Orleans offered key advice early in the project. The first parts of this work took shape in Clarence Mohr's southern history seminar, where the insights into the 1960s era provided by Bob Zellner and Malik Ishaan were worth as much as any book I have ever read. Commentary by Jeffrey Turner, Charles Chamberlain, Carolyn Thompson, Michelle Haberland, Kahne Parsons, Michael Andrews, and Mark Souther was invaluable, as were discussions with David Simonelli, Alfredo Mycue, and Mike Redman. The book manuscript was improved by the advice of a number of people. There is not enough space to give them the level of thanks they deserve, but I hope they understand how much I benefited from their efforts. I can only blame myself for errors and for not following all of their advice. They include Gareth Davies, Alice O'Connor, Thomas Jackson, Stephen Webre, John Daly, Felicia Kornbluh, David Carter, Adam Fairclough, Susan Youngblood Ashmore, Timothy Naftali, Guian McKee, Marc Selverstone, David Shreve, Ken Hughes, Brian Balogh, Sidney Milkis, Carl Bon Tempo, Chris Loss, and Andrew Morris. The anonymous peer reviewers for this work also forced me to think about several key issues and saved me from numerous pitfalls. Additionally, I am grateful for Taylor Branch and his generously sharing LBJ material and his vast knowledge of the era and for Tyler and Michal-Jean Storms for their hospitality and wisdom. At the University of Georgia Press, I want to thank Derek Krissoff, Andrew Berzanskis, Nancy Grayson, and Courtney Denney for their skill and expertise—and patience—in moving the book from acquisition through production. Gay Gragson was a superb copy editor.

I owe a great deal to my colleagues at the University of Virginia's Miller Center of Public Affairs, where I spent several years as deputy director of the Presidential Recordings Program. The number of people that I owe there is too numerous to list here, but I want to offer a special "thank you" to Timothy Naftali, David Coleman, Guian McKee, Pat Dunn, Ashley High, Lorraine Settimo, Marc Selverstone, Ken Hughes, and David Shreve. The Miller Center is home to a wonderful scholarly community, and I thank Philip Zelikow, Gene Fife, and Gerald Baliles for their efforts to expand the study of policy and politics. Finally, I cannot overstate my admiration for Kenneth Thompson. He has been a mentor and a friend, and he deserves all of the accolades he has received.

At a personal level, I have many people to thank, but have to keep this short since a mere list of family members in Louisiana would require a chapter-length appendix. My parents, Raymond Dewie and Nelda Sue Germany, and my siblings, Dee Hunt, Ray Germany Jr., and Beth Burns, have indulged me for a long time and have kindly tolerated my seemingly strange opinions. And I thank Hasson and Joe Glasgow for doing the same. Of the people I want to thank the most, one of them is no longer alive to read it. Lovie Irene Wilks Barnett died a half-decade before the first word of this book was ever conceived, but her influence is in every one that followed. She was a southern woman, and she was the smartest person I have ever known. She would have loved my wife, Mary Schumpert, and would have delighted in our children, Elise Irene, Sarah Ruth, and Margaret Holt. They all are the reasons that I do what I do, and I dedicate this book to Mary and them.

NEW ORLEANS AFTER THE PROMISES

Something New for the South?

The attitudes of the Negro populace for a social and community
action project has been stirred due to the Hurricane.
—Robert Warshawsky, a white VISTA volunteer in the Desire
Community Housing Project, December 1965

It took less than a week to end New Orleans as we knew it. The wind
came and the water came and the levees could not keep them away. In
August 2005, the Gulf of Mexico and Lake Pontchartrain returned to
long-ago shores, and people had to head to higher ground. Hurricane Katrina made nomads out of over a half-million people, and it eroded faith
in American progress. Celebrated systems could not keep up. Engineering and technology could not come easily to the rescue. Many thousands
had to wait and wonder. More than one thousand perished in the delay.
This storm was the big one, and it forced a new epoch in New Orleans's
history. Its aftermath revealed tragic flaws in American democracy and
American affluence. Journalists and their audiences were shocked to find
that New Orleans had so much poverty, that so many of the poor were
African American, and that they—along with animals and the elderly—
were left behind in a moment of crisis. The realities of economic inequality and racial privilege could no longer remain hidden by subtleties and
safe distances.

This storm forced a new generation of Americans to ask a generation-
defining question: Is this America? Forty-one years earlier, in August

1

1964, a persecuted Mississippi sharecropper and civil rights leader named Fannie Lou Hamer had posed that question on national television and punctuated the dilemmas of race, poverty, and inequality for baby boomers coming of age. After Katrina, countless citizens asked the same question of themselves and their neighbors. Over the next decade, we will see what their answers are. This book does not attempt to forecast the future, but looks backward to see how New Orleanians and federal officials responded to that question during the last epic transformation of the city's civic culture. It is a history of how local people used local, state, and federal resources to remake their city during the decade after Jim Crow. To understand what kind of New Orleans can emerge after this most recent cataclysm, it may be helpful to examine some of the struggle that produced the New Orleans that existed previously.

To do so, this book explores the legacy of two words uttered by Lyndon Johnson at a college graduation on the eve of summer in 1964. Put together by a gifted speechwriter, the phrase *Great Society* represented the best hopes of a hopeful generation. Those syllables set out visions of American life that were enormous and bold. "We can do it all," President Johnson boasted in private.[1] Over time, the Great Society grew into a diverse set of programs, policies, and laws that touched almost every aspect of American life. The early years produced landmark legislation for health, education, housing, safety, nutrition, recreation, immigration, transportation, consumer rights, land conservation, and air and water quality. Each of those areas was important, but the most ambitious and provocative parts of the Great Society took on two of the most persistent problems in American history—racism and poverty. Those problems were national in scope and required national solutions, but their ultimate resolution had to come locally. This version of the Great Society was not the creation of Lyndon Johnson, his advisors, or some impassioned intellectuals. It bubbled up from pressure on the streets, took form in Washington, D.C., and gained yet another dimension when it returned to the streets. Its impact depended as much on the savvy of local people as it did on the polish of policymakers. Although this Great Society never matched the aspirations of its advocates, the search for it provided a framework for black inclusion that changed the South. By the late 1960s and early

1970s, political pressures, related in part to Vietnam and the urban crisis, diminished dreams about an ideal America, and the words *Great Society* came to represent an often derisive catch phrase for liberal programs and federal regulations. The history of those words in one old southern city offers a story about the slow collapse of civic imagination, the limitations of racial progress, and the evolution of American democracy.

It is not a heroic tale. It is about New Orleans. In 1964, on almost 200 square miles of land and water, approximately 650,000 residents lived in a dilapidated and divided city. Racial segregation, social exclusion, and widespread poverty were as traditional as beignets and bad sewerage. Most white residents believed that black residents were incapable of being equal to whites. They saw race relations as "harmonious," black citizens as satisfied, and the police department as the reason for the lack of disorder. Most black residents, in contrast, viewed race relations as tense, black citizens as restless and agitated, and the police department as a dangerous threat. Three-quarters of all black families earned incomes near the poverty level; almost half were well below the poverty line. More than a quarter of local housing was substandard. Levels of infant mortality, tuberculosis, diphtheria, and venereal disease were among the nation's highest. The city's social welfare services ranked among the worst in the United States, and its private charity system could confront only a fraction of the remaining poverty problems. Yet it could be an achingly beautiful town with its ancient oaks and seemingly ancient people. The grand mansions in the Garden District, along St. Charles Avenue, and in the Tulane University area obscured severe material deprivation and racial inequality. In the 1960s, as a result of the civil rights movement and the search for the Great Society, the city's historically invisible citizens came more plainly into view. New Orleans's 43,000 poor families—approximately 28,000 of them black—had begun to haunt the public sphere, and they revealed that this historic city lacked the ability to solve even the most basic of its problems without substantial outside help.[2]

Of all the southern cities, New Orleans should have been one of the best prepared to adjust to the inclusion demands of the civil rights movement and southern economic modernization. Besides being the most international city in the South and having one of the busiest ports in the world, New Orleans had residents who were accustomed to near-catastrophic change and to coping with forces beyond their control, whether from microbes in their blood, water in their streets, or dictates from higher powers. Hurricanes, floods, epidemics, and wars were all part of the collective memory. Only sixty years earlier, a yellow fever outbreak affected thousands, and in 1947, a massive hurricane devastated the city. Ninety to one hundred and twenty mile-per-hour winds and an almost ten-foot storm surge caused serious flooding in eastern New Orleans and the loss of over one hundred lives along the Gulf Coast. A harbinger of Hurricane Katrina damage, a broken levee allowed the flood waters to continue to rise two days after the storm.[3]

In the past, after the moments of bad blood or bad rain passed, the city's people rebuilt and recovered. In the 1960s, however, blood and water were ambiguous things subject to racial regulation. The state's "one-drop" rule for racial classification meant that a citizen was designated as black if they had "any traceable amount" of "Negro" blood. In 1970, the state legislature defined a drop as $\frac{1}{32}$ of one's ancestry. Attachment to the rule ran so deep that blood supplies stayed segregated in violation of the Civil Rights Act of 1964. In 1970, a white state legislator declared publicly that he would rather see his family "die and go to eternity" than have "one drop of nigger blood in them."[4] In the case of water, political arrangements and land usage patterns meant that gravity actually benefited most white residents more than most black residents. Most often located on the lowest ground in a city where approximately three-fourths of the land was situated below sea level, black neighborhoods tended to lack subsurface drainage systems and had to endure the worst effects of flooding and subsidence. For whites and blacks, blood and rain meant different things.[5]

In 1965, another hurricane—this one named Betsy—brought 160-mile-per-hour coastal wind gusts and a storm surge that swamped the city's Ninth Ward. Water stood stagnant in a three hundred-block area, soaking not only into wood and walls, but into the minds of segregated black residents who realized once again what little power they had to protect their homes and families. Coming at the height of the national civil rights movement—almost exactly one month after the signing of the Voting Rights Act—Betsy hastened a profound democratic moment. The ensuing local search for black power changed the city's civic culture, forcing residents to figure out what they really thought about each other. Over the next decade, this process left a new city with new leaders and new visions. When the reality of Jim Crow's demise hit home, the city's white residents faced a choice. Those who could afford to ignore most public institutions tended to insulate themselves in their own private spheres, while keeping a tight rein on the public purse by appointments to key commissions and boards.[6] Over 200,000 other whites packed up and made a racial *hegira* to the drained swamps of a new suburbia encircling New Orleans. By the turn of the twenty-first century, the city's population was 67 percent black and only 28 percent white, a reversal from the years prior to the modern civil rights movement. As during earlier times of crisis, many residents fled, but some stayed. The remnants adjusted.

One of the key moments in that adjustment came in 1964 when a Texan stood before the nation and declared an "unconditional war on poverty," promising not to "rest until that war is won." Over the next few years, Lyndon Johnson and his allies remade civil rights laws, structured a potentially radical War on Poverty, and set the United States on a course toward what he called "the Great Society."[7] During that time, one of Johnson's most poignant speeches was called "The American Promise." That message, along with several others, set out a vision of an America where racism and poverty and inequality—and in some ways nature itself—were things to be mastered by community action, individual advancement, and unending energy. In New Orleans, the director of the Urban League thought that this search for the Great Society could produce "something new for the South" and turn New Orleans "toward the glittering promise of a great destiny."[8] What follows is a story of race and poverty in New Orleans after the promises.

That story is ultimately about aspirations, and in New Orleans in the 1960s, the city's poverty, racism, and inequality stood starkly against the grand ambitions of Dixie's Sunbelt generation. Southern cities such as Atlanta, Houston, and Dallas became economic growth machines in the post–World War II boom. New Orleans's economy did not keep pace

TABLE 1

New Orleans City Population (Rounded), 1950 to 2000, by Race

Year	Total	Black	White	Black Percentage	White Percentage
1950	570,000	183,400	386,000	32	67
1960	628,000	233,000	393,000	37	62
1970	593,000	276,000	320,000	45	54
1980	558,000	305,000	225,000	55	40
1990	497,000	308,000	173,000	62	35
2000	485,000	326,000	136,000	67	28

Office of Economic Opportunity, "Community Profile Project: Orleans Parish, Louisiana," Box 202, Series E23, Record Group 381 Community Services Administration, National Archives and Records Administration, College Park, Maryland (hereafter cited by folder, box, series, RG 381, NARA); TCA Research Department, "New Orleans," (1969), Folder 4, Box 55, NAACP Field Office Records, ARC.

but still benefited from the region's economic expansion. Local growth advocates wanted New Orleans to emerge as a world-class city replete with glass skyscrapers, endless highways, and professional sports teams; grassroots visionaries favored basics like food, shelter, medicine, jobs, education, paved streets, and indoor toilets. Each group sought to guide integration according to their own version of freedom, dignity, and social order.

The defining local issue in New Orleans was the struggle to tear down the decades-old system of *de jure* racial segregation known as Jim Crow. Sixty or so years earlier, white southerners had pushed policies of racial segregation to preserve regional orthodoxies and promote public stability.[9] Until the post–World War II period, racial segregation persisted because it helped to control labor, regulate behavior, and obscure poverty. Besides being an effective way of keeping black residents "in their place," it kept down the costs of governing and of economic production. By the early 1960s, however, the world had changed around Jim Crow, and the failure of southern leaders to bring the system in line with an increasingly entrepreneurial, world-looking economy helped encourage alternatives. In the era of the Great Society, however, controlling the potential disorder of racial interaction was far less of a problem for local civic leaders and growth advocates than the problems that came from the actual disorder caused by racial segregation. For many whites, the problem with segregation was not that it wrongfully excluded black southerners, but that it was losing its effectiveness at *managing* black southerners.

The most prominent motivation for embracing racial inclusion was the danger posed by alienation—whether of the South from America and the world, of segregated blacks from public life, or of individual selves from society. In that regard, this book tries to answer four brief, seemingly simple questions. What replaced segregation? In the aftermath of Jim Crow, how did black citizens develop power and confront poverty? In a region often obsessed with redemption, did the South finally redeem itself, confront deep inequality, and still remain southern? In short, did the end of Jim Crow mean something new for the South?

In response, this book makes several arguments. First, in the late 1960s and early 1970s, American liberalism seemed to be in decline in presidential politics and in urban areas. But in Dixie, liberalism was renewed by a modification of constituencies and ideas and emerged as a powerful force that offered the best alternatives for governing during the transition from Jim Crow to black power. Second, the struggle for racial equality in New Orleans did not collapse in a crisis of victory after 1964–1965, but instead entered an era of relative progress (although unequally distributed). Black activism, often from women, ensured that social policy distributed rewards to black residents, especially mothers and children and public officials.[10] The local War on Poverty's focus on the family and support of new power networks helped southern liberals remain relevant amid the ascendance of conservatism in the 1980s and the downturn in the local economy. Liberal political organizations from this Great Society era anchored Louisiana's Democratic Party and helped ensure Democratic control over the Governor's mansion for sixteen of the next twenty years and the state's U.S. Senate seats for the next three decades. Third, federal social policy was not merely centralized social engineering imposed from Washington, D.C. Instead it should be viewed more as a fractured set of political and bureaucratic relationships dictated by local conditions and psychological objectives. Locally, activists forced the Great Society to grow. The need to build infrastructure and services in long-neglected black neighborhoods led to the emergence of a public/private governing apparatus that this study calls the "Soft State." It was dependent on soft money from grants, on soft power from private and nonprofit organizations, and on concern about the soft spaces of the human mind. Its growth came from manipulating white fear of black disorder, encouraging social stability through therapeutic solutions, and reshaping the relationships between white and black leaders. In that vein, the delicate interaction between people who wanted to get along may reveal more about 1960s race relations in America than the harsh reactions of white supremacists or the subtlety of people who simply left the city.[11]

This study began as an inquiry into the effects of the War on Poverty on low-income residents in New Orleans. Early in the research, however, it became apparent that the story was, instead, more about how the Great Society's civil rights and antipoverty components became part of the larger local fight for racial inclusion and institutional reform. To explore the process of black inclusion and the evolution of modern liberalism, this book examines nine federal antipoverty programs, a few city government initiatives, and several private efforts. These programs are treated topically within a loose chronological framework. Each chapter explores a different way that black citizens, sometimes subtly and sometimes boldly, sought civic influence after Jim Crow. The first section covers the local War on Poverty and how that initiative turned into a war on racial segregation and personal alienation. It explores the role of community organizing, the various rationales for inclusion, the onset of the urban crisis, and the proliferation of social and economic programs. The second section explores the intense democratic moment produced by community activism, the urban crisis, and the Great Society. It follows several post-1968 grassroots organizations that reshaped the city's civic culture and exposed gender and class tensions that underlay the issues of race and poverty. The interactions between black activists and white civic and business leaders illustrated the potential for success and failure in biracial political relationships. By the early 1970s, the ebullient visions of the mid-1960s had been discarded. The Great Society was no longer an ideal to strive for, but a set of policies that helped accumulate and distribute power.[12] As one activist said, the struggle had come to focus on "politics, not civil rights," and was about getting "the most you can from whoever you can."[13]

Situating Southern Liberalism

Going back at least to John Egerton's work in 1974—and arguably to the works of Howard Odum, Rupert Vance, Wilbur J. Cash, and others in the 1930s and 1940s—modern commentators have been fascinated by the Americanization of the South and the Southernization of America. Journalists, preachers, and scholars have tried feverishly to understand the influence of the region's political conservatism and the migration of its dispossessed.[14] In the 1960s and 1970s, Dixie was becoming more diverse and more professional as it developed into one of the world's busiest banking, transportation, and manufacturing hubs. By the 1980s, southern companies such as Coca-Cola, Delta Airlines, Wal-Mart, Federal Express, and the Cable News Network (CNN) were some of the most visible representations of the United States in the world. The bustle gave rise to the so-called Sunbelt South where southerners produced metropolises, money, and merchandise far faster than they had ever cultivated cotton or cane. Their skyscrapers, strip malls, suburban subdivisions, and occasionally enormous chicken restaurant signs stood as unremitting silhouettes on the new landscape. Their new highways and enterprising universities speeded the transfer of goods and information and guided the expanding professional classes. Eagerly buying into a consumer society, southerners bought up fast food, fad fashion, and fast cars, and, in surprising ways, also bought into popular psychological prescriptions for self-realization. As the South shed the economic backwardness that had skewed its race relations, southerners tried to accommodate remarkable differences involving race and power. In the 1960s, the South boomed, and that boom offered a promise of breaking free from the region's less-than-glorious racial and economic past.[15]

In parts of the South, however, the boom had mixed effects at best. Most people in low-income neighborhoods were left without key economic decision-making power. Although some of them may have helped construct the new southern skyline, very few of them had any real say in its planning and execution. The development of the Sunbelt did not fundamentally redraw routes to economic power or revolutionize the region but adhered to basic socio-economic patterns. Economic expansion tended to reward people who had the education, access, and networks to participate in it. The South's economic progress did not reach urban ghettoes or most rural areas with any deliberate speed. In fact, it encouraged a drain of capital and resources to the suburbs.

This study argues that the South's racial liberals—a diverse group of white and black progressives who gained their first firm grip on public power partly as a result of community activism and the Great Society's civil rights and antipoverty legislation—were almost as important for American politics after 1964 as their much-chronicled conservative counterparts. Several recent works convincingly argue that white southerners have served as prophets, strategists, and constituents for the growth of American conservatism and the transformation of the Republican Party, while black southern émigrés have done much the same for politics in northern cities and the Democratic Party. The story of New Orleans shows that the liberal vision of economic growth and integration offered a formidable challenge to anti-integrationist, anti-elitist, anti-tax whites. Whereas "southern" conservatism transformed national politics under the guidance of George Wallace, Richard Nixon, and Ronald Reagan, southern liberalism took a slower, more incremental path as it snaked through neighborhood organizations, blue-collar and white-collar unions, nonprofit organizations, progressive interest groups, educational institutions, city halls, federal bureaucracies, and federal courts. The reality of southern liberal resurgence stands in contrast to Lyndon Johnson's frequently cited but perhaps misinterpreted private prediction after signing the Civil Rights Act of 1964 that the Democratic Party had lost the South for "a long time to come."[16] Contrary to popular conceptions, the political polarization and fragmentation of the late 1960s did not necessarily signal the disintegration of American liberalism. New Orleans's story shows, instead, that the post-1965 period was a coming of age. From a historical perspective, this seemingly new phase of American liberalism was an extension of its traditional role in integrating economically and politically marginalized people, or as Lyndon Johnson put it, a way to deal with "any bellyache of injustice."[17] In the 1960s, liberalism in Louisiana dramatically turned from its rural, populist, and white-dominated past to become a largely urban, biracial phenomenon whose diverse constituencies coalesced around an inclusion agenda and along the federal funding pipeline.

Before Jim Crow ended, the South had been home to few racial liberals. Before the 1960s era, their stories usually involved a process of alienation followed by submission, exodus, or death, with some version of Wilbur J. Cash's "savage ideal" guiding the narratives. For this reason, many historians of the region have had to turn to literary figures, philosophers, preachers, theorists, and radicals to find a recognizable liberal tradition. They have tended to explore the nuances of gradualism, offer caveats about regional exceptionalism, and lament lost opportunities. Defining terminology has been tricky; commentators have had to carefully separate out racial liberalism from cultural liberalism from economic liberalism.[18] Beset by antimodernist, anti-intellectual tendencies, the American South has historically had little room for movements that challenged orthodoxies on race, much less on gender, spirituality, sexuality, family, or biology. Before the post–World War II civil rights era, economic populists and/or growth advocates were some of the few people capable of confronting political and economic inequality in southern civic life; a few intellectuals insulated at universities were able to insert important ideas into the mix.[19] Southern attempts to expand the power of the state had to preserve social and cultural traditions, not challenge them.

In the late 1960s and early 1970s, the South developed its first long-term, clearly legitimate political liberalism in which cultural tolerance, intellectual openness, and racial inclusiveness were guiding themes. The historical background to the rise of southern liberalism in the 1960s is long and complicated. There is no easy trajectory from Populism to Progressivism to the New Deal to the Great Society. All of those moments were responses to demands for economic modernization that required changes in the regulation of work, consumption, and market growth. At their heart, they were products of profound on-the-ground cultural and political crises that forced extraordinary adjustments in the relationship between the individual, the market, and the government. The Great Society on the streets of New Orleans stood out as something new, somewhat resembling the late-nineteenth-century Populist movement. Disgruntled by the concentration of power and the obstacles presented by corporate capitalism, bands of locals, like their Populist predecessors, formed political cells and linked them into a larger framework. Building power meant reaching across the color line and forming tricky biracial coalitions, though black participants in the 1960s had much more power than those in the 1890s. In the end, both movements dissipated, and corporations ended up in some ways in stronger positions than before. As consolation, the populists of each era got some leaders in long-term positions of power and forced the nation to deal with their issues.

Some of the clearest historical similarities are between the local Great Society and the Progressive movement of the late nineteenth and early twentieth centuries. Both were products of cultural and intellectual movements as much as political ones. Both involved adjustments to cultural and economic shocks—the Progressive Era to new immigration and corporate abuse and the Great Society to corporate abuse, the end of Jim Crow, and the dilemma of poverty. People in each period pursued social order and individual assimilation as means to better and happier citizens, workers, and consumers. Solutions in each era focused on increasing democracy, empowering more individuals, and rationalizing social and political institutions. Not surprisingly, two local organizations leading the early War on Poverty in New Orleans were founded in the Progressive Era. For a half-century, one, the Social Welfare Planning Council, offered the city's most consolidated response to poverty and social disorder. The other, the Kingsley House, was a church-sponsored settlement house that dominated social work in a white ethnic area known as the Irish Channel.

The New Deal and World War II directly benefited racial liberals in terms of economic growth and institutional development. Progressives had begun the work of shifting the classic liberal emphasis on free trade, individual rights, and relatively small governments to an emphasis on state responsibility for creating equal opportunity, protecting workers, regulating corporations, and safeguarding people on the economic and civic margins. New Dealers built on this, centralizing power in public bureaucracies and in the hands of professionals and expanding the idea that the state had a collective responsibility for the welfare of individuals. In the South, this state-based power shift eroded the control of the local courthouse, and federal economic policy enabled the South's economy to become less of a problem for the rest of the U.S. economy.[20] Lyndon Johnson's

Great Society antipoverty efforts were rooted in New Deal jobs programs and infrastructure development.[21] The New Deal welfare state addressed southern poverty through market reform and economic growth strategies, particularly through new labor rules and outright federal subsidies. Just as important, politically potent social welfare bureaucracies offered social stability and created a partial safety net that continued to expand during the Great Society. For some historians the 1930s and 1940s were days of hope when a loose coalition of interests labored to facilitate more equal political participation and a more just economy. With the rise of the Cold War, the room for such leftist activity narrowed considerably. Afterwards, the region's liberalism made an arduous migration from a movement to improve the region's economic standing to one more focused on improving its racial standing.[22]

Although Populism, Progressivism, and the New Deal were historical turning points for liberalism, none of them adequately confronted racial inequality. From the 1930s to the early 1960s, prominent political leaders closely linked to the New Deal expressed the South's liberalism, but they rarely critiqued the color line directly.[23] A few white southern journalists (Jonathan Daniels, Ralph McGill, and Hodding Carter) and isolated white racial liberals (Clark Foreman, Clifford and Virginia Durr, Anne Braden, James Dombrowski, Leslie Dunbar, Lillian Smith, Myles Horton, and student activists at several southern universities) were willing to risk ostracism or death to do so. Institutional bulwarks such as the Southern Regional Council, the Southern Conference movement, and the Highlander Folk School bolstered the liberal periphery. But the front lines of the war against racial inequality were manned primarily by black citizens: some black ministers, union officials, students, teachers, and a variety of local activists. In the late 1950s and early 1960s, the black-inspired and largely black-led civil rights movement built organizations like the Congress of Racial Equality (CORE), the Student Nonviolent Coordinating Committee, the Southern Christian Leadership Conference, and the NAACP, organizations that became the leading edge of black insurgency and were capable of sustaining long-term resistance to white supremacy and white privilege. These pioneers set the broad objectives for a southern search for the Great Society.

The Great Society, the Civil Rights Movement, and the Local Soft State

The Civil Rights Act of 1964, the Economic Opportunity Act of 1964, and the Voting Rights Act of 1965 represented a shift in governmental policies regarding black citizenship, political participation, and economic opportunity. Built on a century of struggle on the streets and in the courts, those pieces of legislation changed the civil rights movement. A traditional historical interpretation holds that this period after 1964–1965 embodied a "crisis of victory" in which conflicts over economic inequality and racial identity fragmented the national civil rights agenda and led to the decline of several key organizations. Violence, disillusionment, and disorder seemed to replace visions of brotherhood, idealism, and harmony. But if the historian turns away from the internal dynamics of civil rights organizations and national-level policy battles, and instead focuses on the local struggle against economic inequality, the civil rights narrative takes a different trajectory. The story in New Orleans suggests that federal policy did not necessarily take the life out of the civil rights movement, that in fact the movement pressed on, though in ways more incremental, less dramatic, and harder to quantify. Although federal War-on-Poverty funding effectively curtailed some radicalism, the community organizing that it supported gave medium-term structure and stability to community activism, ultimately building power. With no tight federal control over community action, local activists turned parts of the War on Poverty into a bureaucratic extension of the freedom movement.[24]

The local civil rights movement in New Orleans was a decades-old enterprise grounded in labor unions such as the International Longshoreman's Association, a few churches, some affiliates of national organizations, and some black-controlled local institutions. Direct action protests throughout the early 1960s were led by the local branch of the NAACP, the Urban League, CORE, and several other local groups.[25] In 1964, these organizations were joined by the multi-layered organizational presence of the War on Poverty. The earliest "layer" derived from the Economic Opportunity Act of 1964 (EOA) and its administrative arm known as the Office of Economic Opportunity (OEO).[26] Although the EOA was contemporarily viewed as the foundation of the War on Poverty, the "War efforts" extended well beyond that legislation and arguably included the presidential drive to stimulate economic growth (manifested in the $11 billion 1964 tax cut), the Medicare/Medicaid programs, the Food Stamp program, the Elementary and Secondary Education Act, the creation of the Department of Housing and Urban Development, the Model Cities program, Urban Renewal projects, and several job training programs. Additionally, the Civil Rights Act of 1964 and the Voting Rights Act of 1965 affected antipoverty efforts by changing the rules about civic and market participation.

Great Society legislation and spending helped cushion the impact of racial inclusion. In the early years, the OEO led the War on Poverty. Designed as a flexible bureaucracy capable of bypassing traditional federal offices and entrenched powers, the OEO pursued an aggressive, innovative, and experimental agenda premised on empowering the poor and giving local people significant authority in fighting poverty. Envisioned by OEO administrators as an attack on the causes of poverty more than the symptoms, the War on Poverty was an ambitious effort to reform the psychology of the poor, the institutions of the ghetto, the systems necessary for upward mobility, and the patterns of black political participation. The War on Poverty in New Orleans served three primary functions: to encourage economic growth, to offer compensation to historically excluded citizens, and to promote competition as the chief way to achieve inclusion. The Great Society kept the welfare state fragmented and decentralized, which happened to make it much harder for opponents to dismantle.

As local, state, and federal policymakers and activists began to implement the War on Poverty, what this study calls the "Soft State" began to develop. The Soft State consisted of a loose set of short-term political and bureaucratic arrangements that linked together federal bureaucracies, neighborhood groups, nonprofit organizations, semipublic political organizations, social agencies, and, primarily after 1970, local government to distribute (occasionally in an ad hoc manner) upward of $100 million in federal funding (over $512 million in 2006 dollars) in predominantly black neighborhoods.[27] The broadly defined War on Poverty helped to fill in some of the soft spaces, particularly those regarding race, of the New

Deal-constructed welfare state. Much of the funding for that filling-in process was soft as well, coming primarily from grants to local nonprofits and local government. To secure that money, local people had to take the initiative, and their efforts resulted in new local political structures.[28]

For nearly a decade, the programs and networks of this Soft State helped expand a public sector marketplace that compensated for private sector discrimination.[29] Because a vast majority of New Orleans employers and financiers in the private marketplace continued to resist black inclusion, the Great Society-driven Soft State accommodated the insurgency of ambitious, civic-minded African Americans. The resulting arrangements gave structure to the rights revolution and coherence to new communities of liberal leadership. The Soft State, however, was precarious. Funding sources were unstable, and the leaders and constituencies were equally fragmented. It helped build power for some and produced benefits for many, but there was a price: Those who would partake had to adhere to the demands of state-building, to the rigidity of bureaucratization, and to the political compromises necessary to preserve power.

In New Orleans, the Soft State grew from experimental federal antipoverty programs, from the turmoil surrounding the urban crisis, and from the network of neighborhood-based organizations that fostered black power after 1965.[30] This growth process provided an institutional base for New Orleans progressives to pry power away from traditional white leaders. It also offered a fairly cheap way to cope with urban protest and to improve dismal infrastructure in poor black areas. By the 1970s, low-income, predominantly African American neighborhoods had the votes, the organizations, and the access to government to have a historic impact on elections and policy. Leaders of three largely black political groups with close ties to the Great Society—known by their acronyms as SOUL, BOLD, and COUP—wedged themselves into positions as power brokers. By the early 1970s, the Acronyms, as this study refers to them collectively, controlled this Soft State, although most of them were private organizations. After the electoral triumphs of racially liberal local leaders in 1970 and 1971, these soft arrangements hardened into a more formal part of local government. New Orleans's story rebuts the contemporary assessment of federally funded community action as a sham.[31] One commentator has argued that it stymied true grassroots development.[32] Instead, the history of New Orleans suggests that Great Society programs may have been the only public turf that the grassroots could ever really influence.

Inclusion through Therapy

In New Orleans, America's urban crisis merged with the South's cultural crisis. Set against the struggle to tear down the South's racial system, the local welfare state was not simply a means to distribute benefits, to manage the economy, and to buy off discontent, but was something that reshaped ideas about civic life and broadened the reach of social policy. By examining the political thought of southern Great Society participants, this study attempts a partial, street-level intellectual history of inclusion. Inclusion advocates borrowed heavily from Judeo-Christian theology, from popular trends in psychological analysis, and from post–World War II hyperindividualism. Local thinkers frequently argued that community stability, social justice, and economic growth depended on a righteous, community-centered nurturing of individuals who had been politically and psychologically segregated for almost all of their lives. The most widely used inclusion strategy revolved around the idea that one earned citizenship through personal responsibility and beneficial contribution to society. Local social politics consisted of much more than lining up votes and mobilizing constituencies; they involved serious debates about who deserved to participate in the good life.

Those debates drew their symbols, language, and logic from southern culture and social science. In particular, locals persistently invoked psychological theory to argue for inclusion. An emphasis on psychic uplift guided attempts to make the poor more like other people and the ghetto less threatening to the rest of society. To street-level activists and policy professionals, full inclusion started from within. Liberals labored to define the psychological impact of poverty and to reshape the rationale for combating alienation. In New Orleans, being okay and feeling fine were a core part of the political process. In some ways, the local Great Society was an extension of John Dewey's conception of the democratic individual as "society concentrated" and democracy as "the idea of a personality."[33] Personal pride became a civic virtue, and social scientific knowledge forced a reinterpretation of American individualism. Considering the South's legacy of defeat and the gothic traditions in the region's literature, it is ironic, perhaps, that the newest South arose partly from a pervasive pressure to feel good.

The growing role of the therapeutic in American social policy in the 1960s cannot be dismissed simply as misguided managerial policymaking.[34] Grounded in what was believed to be the best science and the best hope for America, the politics of psychological uplift was more than therapy for a disturbed, egocentric culture. It reflected how Americans viewed the republic's problems, its cities, and its citizenry and how it had begun to probe the causes of its alleged pathologies. The flowering of identity politics in the late 1960s, therefore, did not erupt simply from Black Power or women's liberation, but emerged from a much deeper post-World War II fixation on the inner world of the self and from the emptiness of the era's celebrated materialism.

During the 1960s, New Orleans struggled with how to include the excluded. What emerged, however, was not the beloved community dreamed by Martin Luther King Jr. or by activists with the Student Non-Violent Coordinating Committee or the "way of life beyond our realm of experience" envisioned by Lyndon Johnson.[35] Divisions of race, class, gender, geography, economic inequality, and political competition—as well as from radicalism, alienation, and bureaucratization—raised the question of whether a great society could rise from a sunken city on a southern bend of a river called Father of Waters. From the early 1960s through the mid-1970s, the civil rights movement and the Great Society led to the rise of racial liberalism and caused many to see the city as a model of race relations after Jim Crow. New Orleans seemed to be on its way to being that glittering city of great destiny envisioned by the Urban League. Had New Orleans become something new for the South?

PART ONE

A WAR ON POVERTY, SEGREGATION, AND ALIENATION, 1964–1974

Locally, the politics of the Great Society became a matter of calculating black potential and black peril. There are many examples of both, but two instances stand out, serving as the symbolic opening and closing of this history. One involved a little black girl named Ruby Bridges, the other a young black man named Mark Essex.

In mid-November 1960, Bridges and three other black girls tried to go to white schools in New Orleans. The white reaction was fierce and disturbing. People around the world saw those first-graders endure gauntlets of screaming white working-class mothers who cursed, spit, and threw eggs. John Steinbeck immortalized one of these mornings in his book *Travels with Charley*, describing the scene as "insensate beastliness" akin to a "witch's Sabbath." He found the chants and screams of the "Cheerladies" to be "vomitings of demoniac people."[1] Norman Rockwell produced a famous painting, *The Problem We All Live With*, that depicted the pony-tailed Bridges being escorted to school by federal marshals, with splattered tomatoes and the word *Nigger* scrawled along the wall behind her.[2] Downtown not far from City Hall, approximately two thousand white protestors raged against integration, with some breaking into mobs in search of black targets, belying the carefully crafted image of an open, hospitable, progressive New Orleans.[3]

A little over twelve years later, in January 1973, another set of images of New Orleans flashed across the world: A downtown hotel with broken windows and curtains blowing in the wind, smoke rising above the skyline, people dying on the street, crowds of angry black Americans yelling at reporters, a Marine helicopter cruising just above rooftops, and the body of a twenty-three-year-old black man—Mark "Jimmy" Essex—bloody on some gravel surrounded by police officers. Although viewers of live national television or the next day's newspapers could not see the estimated one hundred bullet holes in Essex, they would learn that this homicidal, self-styled revolutionary had just shot and killed nine people, burned a new building, and exposed the fragile state of race in the City That Care Forgot.

A few days after that—although not directly related—Lyndon Johnson died of a heart attack, Richard Nixon was inaugurated for a second time, and the United States agreed to get out of Vietnam. The time for the Great Society and the 1960s had come to an end. It may have also been time for the end of Dixie.

CHAPTER ONE

A European-African-Caribbean-American-Southern City

> The best way for a person to become a community leader is to
> arrange to have had his grandfather born here.
> —Anonymous New Orleans Business Executive, 1972, quoted in Chai,
> "Who Rules New Orleans"

New Orleans began in 1718 as a gamble made by French aristocrats. In time, the decision to create a European community in a subtropical river delta devastated thousands, perhaps millions, of lives, but built a civilization that guided the growth of the New World. In a pattern repeated throughout the city's history, mercantile dreams beat out the inconveniences of early death and frequent flooding. Over the next century, the city's proximity to river and sea helped it become a bustling port that grafted bits of France, Spain, and western Africa onto the end of the Mississippi River. From its founding forward, New Orleans filtered the world through the Louisiana coast. Traders, bankers, and royal bureaucrats mixed with sailors, slaves, and nuns to create a conspicuous Creole society. By the time the United States took ownership in 1803, the city had become a chief funnel for middle American commerce, and it had become a depot for visionaries, gamblers, and scoundrels. Those residents created a diverse, dynamic culture and gave New Orleans and Louisiana reputations for wildness in both public and private life.

In the Sunbelt era, New Orleans's vivid history evolved into an economic development tool as local marketers strove to distinguish the city from other, more dowdy American places. Atlanta became the "City Too Busy to Hate." New Orleans held on as the "City That Care Forgot," becoming best known for being like nowhere else. Boosters hyped New Orleans and much of modern Louisiana as places crafted by the indulgences of the Mediterranean, the sophistication of continental Europe, the commercial capacity of the United States, and the mystery of Africa and the Caribbean. Writers and movie directors proved adept at casting the area as a bizarre bayou frontier stained by politics and voodoo and passion.

New Orleans might have been the birthplace of Jazz and the place where good times rolled, but beneath those slogans, its residents lived most of their lives according to the quiet rhythms of work, family, and faith. Most people who died in New Orleans were born there. Contrary to some stereotypes, most New Orleanians—like, arguably, most Americans—preferred social stability and civic order, but they liked to make it happen in their own way. Surrounded on all sides by water, most locals knew firsthand the insignificance of their own lives in the face of nature. Flood and hurricane levees formed veritable mountains that kept out river and sea. Massive pumps emptied drainage canals. Ocean-going ships often passed by above rooftops. Survival depended on faith, whether in God or man or both, and it led to a veneration of the past unequaled in perhaps any other American city. In no place did the dead live as well and, as the joke goes, vote as frequently.

In New Orleans, the political was so personal that it was often difficult to separate the two. Well before racial radicals and feminist theorists in the late 1960s and 1970s articulated the phenomenon known as "personal politics," many citizens in New Orleans and Louisiana lived lives defined by it. Part of the reason was deep family roots: in tightly knit communities where economic power was concentrated in few hands, almost every act was politicized. According to the 1960 U.S. Census, 82 percent of the state's citizens had been born in the state and 78 percent of Orleans Parish residents were lifelong residents. Black and white, rich and poor, and boss and worker understood the political consequences of their personal choices, which were subtly regulated by family, church, and government. Residents in New Orleans and in Louisiana were quite willing to accept state regulation of racial interaction, sexual practices, and the behavior of welfare recipients, teachers, and other beneficiaries of state funding. The church, too, wielded considerable power, and the line between the state and the church, like the line between the political and the personal, was often blurred. Churches were cohesive local communities that taxed themselves and shared control over often expensive property. Parishioners had close relationships with their leaders and looked to them for guidance on both public and personal matters. This fact helps explain the conundrum of why citizens who ostensibly distrusted authority would empower the state to extensively regulate parts of their lives: they expected it and, in some ways, hardly recognized the intrusion.

Economy

New Orleans was not Atlanta or Houston or Charlotte. For that matter, it was not Dallas or San Antonio or Phoenix or Las Vegas. Other major Sunbelt cities tended to have better transportation systems, better education systems, fewer arcane social rituals, and, maybe most important, more room to grow. During the Sunbelt boom, these cities became engines of a new economy, their growth dwarfing that of New Orleans. The New Orleans economy was limited by heavy dependence upon the federal government, the Mississippi River, and the extraction, processing, and marketing of the region's natural resources. Under the leadership of Mayor DeLesseps S. "Chep" Morrison in the late 1940s and 1950s, the local economy fared well. He improved governing structures, commissioned dozens of reports from the Bureau of Governmental Research, and formed a powerful City Planning Commission. Morrison fought corruption, reducing patronage jobs, centralizing purchasing, and confronting vice. During his watch, international trade boomed, growing from $300 million in 1940 to $1.3 billion by the late 1940s. In one year alone, from 1951–1952, eleven new industries found new homes in town. Beyond public relations, Morrison's greatest skill was raising vast sums of money for construction projects. His administration built several bridges, a new railroad terminal, a new civic center complex, several thousand units of public housing, and numerous playgrounds and swimming pools—occasionally for black residents.[1] At the end of the 1950s, just as Morrison seemed to have New Orleans primed to be an international leader, scandals in his police department erupted and, most damaging, a crisis developed over school desegregation. The 1960 school showdown in the Ninth Ward showed that governmental efficiency and economic progress were no match for the deeply rooted desire of white New Orleanians to maintain white privilege. The entry of four black girls into white schools changed the local economy as much as any vision of progressive capitalism. The city's finances never quite recovered from the ensuing exodus of white residents and their tax revenue.

Most of New Orleans's problems were bigger than Morrison or any other politician. Its physical infrastructure barely surpassed that of some cities in the nineteenth century. Perhaps half of the roads were unpaved, and the inadequate sewage system kept the city fragrant and fluid-filled. Its school system was in an unparalleled downward slide. Its tax base was withering but its undervalued property tax assessments were enshrined as virtual entitlements. Compared to the residents of Dallas, Houston, and Atlanta, New Orleanians paid fewer taxes, but earned less money, were unemployed more often, and paid more for housing. Wealth was also more concentrated in New Orleans. The top fifth in New Orleans earned 44 percent of the city's income, compared to 39 percent for Atlanta, 41 percent for Dallas, and 40 percent for Houston. The poorest fifth in New Orleans took in 4 percent of the city's income, compared to 5.5 percent in the other three cities. The local government's ability to raise bond money was tightly controlled by a coterie of gentlemen from old families. City Hall was virtually all white—except at the "mop and broom" level as Moon Landrieu described—and primarily served the city's corporate interests and, to a declining extent, ward bosses.[2] The most important sectors of the economy were the Port of New Orleans and the petroleum industry. The city did well when oil prices were stable, but over time Houston proved to be the more attractive venue for major energy companies. The Port of New Orleans did well in the 1950s, but it did not keep up with trends in mechanization and would later fall behind the shift toward modular containers. The airport was small and the victim of turf battles among several local governments. Goods coming into the city by road had to cross large bodies of water and were limited to fewer than twenty lanes of traffic. Unless one were coming by boat, the city was hard to get into and to get out of.

As entrepreneurs, New Orleans's financial elite had the reputation of being overly cautious and lukewarm. As a local joke went, the local Whitney Bank and Hibernia Bank were better known as the "Whitless" and the "Hibernation." Many of those leaders were accused, perhaps unfairly, of having more interest in jousting with their social peers over such things as whose daughter would reign over Mardi Gras. Contemporary sociological studies found that genealogy often determined social status.[3] According to the arguments of social scientists in the early 1970s, the closed social circles of the white New Orleans social elite hampered economic progress partly because major corporations were reluctant to locate in a city whose socialites refused to admit their best and brightest managers. Houston, Atlanta, and Miami offered more opportunities for the emerging managerial and professional class.

Segregation and social exclusivity deeply affected economic options. With a few exceptions for professionals and small business owners, black residents usually represented a low-cost labor force that served others, rarely with access to the real sources of economic, and therefore political, power. Black citizens were not the only locals to feel the burden of exclusion. A number of business leaders were troubled by the social veil that curtailed entrepreneurism. An official for the Urban League asserted that "things happen or don't happen in the city based on the decisions of a group of five, six or eight men." Ben Toledano, the Republican candidate for New Orleans mayor in 1970, claimed that the "so-called establishment has strangled this city over the years" and "has so co-ordinated the social and business affairs over the years that a person must be a blue-blood before he can participate in major economic decisions."[4]

Although only a few of these elite leaders held political office, they wielded enormous influence through control over local capital, support of politicians who did their bidding, and membership on important boards and commissions. According to sociologist Phyllis Raabe, upper-class men dominated the boards of directors of the major New Orleans banks. The

Hibernia Bank and the Whitney Bank controlled almost half of all bank assets in the city. Eighty-five percent of Hibernia's board were defined by Raabe as upper-class men, and the Whitney had 62 percent. Two critical public boards with high percentages of upper-class men were the Liquidation Board, which determined the city's borrowing capacity, and the Dock Board of the Port of New Orleans, which oversaw the most important part of the local economy. In 1971, 77 percent of the Liquidation Board were members of the Boston Club, with 88 percent of the board considered upper class. Seventy-six percent of the Dock Board belonged to either the Boston or Pickwick Clubs.[5] The importance of personal networks made it difficult to establish the institutional reform required by the inclusion struggle. The blurring of things private and public presented a daunting dilemma for racial liberals. How could they confront segregation—even in light of court decrees and civil rights legislation in 1964–1965—without a substantial amount of personal power? How could they develop that power in a relatively short span of time without being corrupted by it?

Politics

Louisiana's political culture did not produce the sanitized efficiency celebrated in some Midwestern states or the idealized civility of the rural New England town hall. Political life was rowdy, dirty, and dominated by a few men. The most successful leaders were skilled at displaying down-home ingenuity, artfully managing informal economic arrangements, and leveraging the interests of petroleum companies, all while appealing to God, honor, and manhood. Several state and local politicians lived up to the state's reputation for eccentricity and chicanery. Among them were a man who wanted every man to be king, another who liked to hang out at a shabby farm known as the Pea Patch, and another who some people likened to a modern incarnation of the French Sun King.

The state's three best-known politicians—Huey Pierce Long, Earl K. "Uncle Earl" Long, and Edwin Washington Edwards—are almost as famous for their defiance of behavioral norms as for their seemingly magical command of power. Huey Long met foreign dignitaries in his pajamas and, at least once, urinated on a gangster in Long Island. He died after being gunned down in the marble corridors of his beloved state capitol by the son-in-law of a political enemy.[6] His brother Earl—while governor for the third time in the late 1950s—frequented brothels, cavorted with a stripper, and spent time in two mental hospitals. Edwin Edwards, for his part after 1971, acquired a legendary status as a playboy and high-stakes gambler. So confident about his prospects in the 1983 gubernatorial campaign, he prophesied that he could lose only if he were caught in bed with a dead girl or a live boy. In the 1991 gubernatorial runoff against David Duke, the Republican candidate who had once been a Grand Wizard of the Ku Klux Klan, one pro-Edwards bumper sticker read: "Vote for the Crook. It's Important." Eleven years later, in October 2002, Edwards began serving a ten-year sentence in federal prison for conspiracy and racketeering in the distribution of riverboat casino licenses. In the late 1960s, racial liberals joined a long line of people who had tried to challenge the so-called Louisiana way.

In some ways, New Orleans was different from the rest of Louisiana, particularly the Protestant-dominated hill country and delta lands of northern Louisiana. The city's reputation for vice and sin made it a popular stop for many Louisianans, but others avoided it with equal passion. The historian Edward Haas has written that Louisiana's "common folk" believed "New Orleans was the enemy." Those rural-urban antagonisms had historically defined the city's relationship with the state government. In the late 1920s and early 1930s, Huey Long battled ferociously to seize governing functions from the city's blue bloods. His brother Earl kept up the fight in legendary duels with Chep Morrison. Earl Long's attempt in 1948 to put more control over New Orleans into the hands of state government was so fierce that it became known as the "rape of New Orleans." As a result, the city enacted a home-rule charter and shifted to a more powerful mayor-council arrangement in 1954.[7]

Southern Louisiana was one of the most ethnically diverse places in America, and New Orleans was home to the richest fusion of international influences in the South. This diversity created serious social problems and political divisions. Cultural and ethnic cleavages had long been parts of New Orleans society. Splits between Catholics and Protestants and between Creoles and Americans provided local political fault lines for much of the city's first two centuries. In 1975, black Catholics were still a dominant force in New Orleans, accounting for almost 22 percent of the local black population.[8] In the mid-nineteenth century, an influx of Irish and German immigrants highlighted class divisions. In later decades, the addition of settlers from southern and eastern Europe introduced new cultural issues and aggravated traditional ones. Black leaders enjoyed more influence in the city than in most other southern places, especially during Reconstruction, but they had weak positions that grew weaker with the onset of Jim Crow.[9] Historian Edward Haas argues that the basic continuity in New Orleans politics from the late 1870s until 1946 was the perennial struggle between politicians associated with the Regular Democratic Organization (RDO)—also known as the Old Regulars—and the "commercial-civic elite." Immigrants and workers provided the base of support for the Old Regulars who struggled with the business-dominated Citizens League. The RDO was the dominant force in most of the late nineteenth century and the central power in local politics in the twentieth century. From 1897 to 1926, the Old Regulars, often lumped together with a group known as the Choctaws, provided the political muscle for Mayor Martin Berhman.[10] Others led the Old Regulars until 1936, when Mayor T. Semmes Walmsley resigned under pressure Huey Long had applied prior to his assassination. The next boss of New Orleans was Robert S. Maestri, who led an organization linked to the Long legacy.

Ten years later, Chep Morrison, the polished progressive newcomer, upset the Maestri-Long machine with promises of good government and economic progress. He went on to formulate an almost equally powerful organization known as the Crescent City Democratic Association (CCDA). The CCDA continued to battle with the RDO. Morrison's position was solidified by his relationship with various black leaders, particularly Reverend A.L. Davis and the Orleans Parish Progressive Voters League. Although Morrison remained an avowed segregationist, he was a moderate who eventually consented to the desegregation of parks and public transportation.[11] Morrison's departure in 1961 to serve as President John Kennedy's ambassador to the Organization of American States put the CCDA into the hands of Victor Hugo Schiro, an affable insurance executive and Morrison ally who had served on the City Council since 1950. Schiro lost Morrison's support when he failed to hold the CCDA machine together, and in 1962, he failed to gain the endorsement of the CCDA. But he proved to have electoral legs of his own and defeated Adrian Duplantier, the candidate supported by Morrison's legendary Cold Water Committee. In 1965 Schiro beat city councilman James Fitzmorris. Lyndon Johnson liked the diminutive Schiro and nicknamed him the "Little Mayor." While in office, the Little Mayor gained a reputation as a political lightweight, a smiling Italian man with a famous moustache who liked cutting ribbons and consorting with celebrities. That image, however, obscured his well-honed political skills, and he made a career out of defeating opponents who made the mistake of underestimating him.[12]

Class

Southerners like to know who belongs, and they have exquisite rituals to establish an individual's social worth, often making it big business to know other people's business. In New Orleans in the 1950s and 1960s it was pretty clear who belonged to the upper class. The top group comprised well-established (pre-1920s) wealthy families who, according to contemporary studies, included only about 2 percent of the city's population. Their lifestyles diverged demonstrably from all others in the city and typically revolved around their own schools, social events, and lunch clubs. In particular, the celebration of Mardi Gras and the Carnival season solidified their social networks and affirmed a sense of ownership of what was good about the city. At the center of the city's economic and civic power were groups of men organized into clubs known as "krewes." Just before the Lenten season, these krewes held public Carnival parades in which the captains dressed in white hooded costumes frightfully similar in design to outfits worn by Ku Klux Klan night riders. Members rode on opulent floats, throwing trinkets to the grasping crowds below. The four dominant upper-class parading krewes were called Comus, Momus, Proteus, and Rex. Their members generally were also members in the Boston, Louisiana, and Pickwick clubs. They allowed no black members and relatively few Jewish members; as late as 1992 all but Rex chose to stop parading on public streets rather than desegregate.[13]

The other 98 percent of New Orleans society was a jumble of people, most of whom believed that their part of New Orleans was the "real" New Orleans. Some divisions came from religion. Conflicts between Protestants and Catholics were traditional to local culture, as was the isolation of a powerful Jewish minority.[14] The local Jewish community was one of the most prominent in the South and was home to some of the most powerful capitalists in the country, including the heirs to the Sears, Roebuck & Company. A few ornate synagogues and private schools catered to Jewish families. Being segregated from parts of the dominant local culture and society caused many members of Jewish families to become active in civil rights and antipoverty work. Without their involvement, the struggle for racial liberalism would likely have succumbed to segregationist opposition. Other splits involved class and geography. Residential patterns in New Orleans are hard to generalize because there is mixed-income settlement throughout the city, but some of the heaviest concentration of working class whites tended to be in the neighborhoods known as Mid-City, the Irish Channel, and parts of the Ninth Ward. Plenty of others lived interspersed in the wealthy Uptown and Garden District sections. On the Pontchartrain lakefront, many middle- and upper-class subdivisions were being developed, often in conjunction with the Orleans Levee Board. One of them, Pontchartrain Park, was being developed for middle class black residents. New Orleans middle- and working-class residents sent their children primarily to public and parochial schools. An overwhelming majority of white residents favored segregation and wanted to maintain privileges accrued from it. Their voting power made them the chief cogs to a ward-based, patronage-dependent political system. They were also the major demographic leaving Orleans Parish for the suburbs.[15]

Black society was as stratified as white society. Oretha Castle, perhaps the city's best-known civil rights activist, told *New Yorker* magazine in 1964 that "we're split in so many different ways. We don't have just Negroes. We have our Catholic Negroes and our Protestant Negroes, our downtown Negroes and our uptown Negroes, our light Negroes and our dark Negroes. And we have too many Negroes who don't think they're

Negroes."[16] The findings of one local group of social scientists offer insight into that stratification. They identified three "distinct cultural traditions" that underlay class divisions in the black community: the Creole, the Middle Class, and the Lower Class. A 1960 study concluded that between the black middle class and lower class there existed dramatic differences "in terms of education, occupation, religious participation, family structure, neighborhoods, political activity and associational memberships."[17] In particular, the line between Creole blacks and American blacks was a long-standing feature of New Orleans society. Most Creole families were Catholic, with historical links to the city's European heritage and to free people of color. They had a distinct culture with privileged social and economic institutions. They tended to go to their own schools, marry within their own circles, and occupy the most powerful positions in the black community. In the 1950s and 1960s, both the NAACP and the Urban League were led by Creoles. Later, the city's first three black mayors all had Creole backgrounds. These distinctions created deep antagonism within the larger black community, and as the freedom movement progressed, Creole superiority was viewed almost as unfavorably as white supremacy. Black militants in the late 1960s raged against Creoles for their air of aristocracy and for not fully accepting their blackness. Although the lines between Creole and non-Creole were blurred during the 1960s, the divisions remained major points of tension.

Race

In the early 1960s, Protestants, Catholics, Jews, Italians, Germans, Hungarians, Irish, blue-blood whites, newly rich whites, middle-class whites, poor whites, black Creoles, American blacks, middle-class blacks, and low-income blacks were all trying to figure out what they thought about sharing their city with each other. Although the situation had improved dramatically by 1964, New Orleanians of color still could not access many places to which they had a right as citizens. Perhaps more detrimentally, they did not benefit equally from advances in health, education, employment, or housing. Even leisure time continued to be largely segregated, despite the token desegregation of public parks. Only two of forty-six movie theaters in the city were integrated, and six were black-only.[18] The venerable New Orleans Athletic Club denied entry to African Americans at least until the middle 1980s; likewise the Audubon Park Golf Club until 1983.[19]

Most black areas had grossly inadequate street lighting, drainage, schools, public transportation, health facilities, police protection, and political influence—if any at all. Infant mortality rates in these areas were twice as high as the rest of the city. One-half of the residents of those areas had less than an eighth grade education, compared to one-third of other New Orleanians. Sixty-one percent of streets in predominantly black sections lacked adequate paving and drainage, with that percentage rising to 86 in the Lower Ninth Ward. Outdoor toilets were common. For outdoor recreation, children in those areas typically had to use public roads and vacant lots. Combined, the three largest African American areas had a mere sixteen acres of recreational space. The minimum recommended standard for such an area was 202 acres. In the Desire area, one public park served over seventeen thousand children.[20] Employment opportunities for African Americans were equally limited. A particularly stark example of job segregation was in the supposedly more liberal field of social work. In a 1964 study, the Social Welfare Planning Council surveyed 87 of the 120 social service agencies in New Orleans. They found that, despite the absence of any laws supporting segregation practices, black applicants were hired almost exclusively as custodians. In fact, 90 percent of agencies were not willing to consider an African American for a professional position, and 5 percent of the agencies refused to serve black clients at any level.[21] Educational opportunities were at least as constricted. White elementary schools in Orleans Parish averaged 495 students, while black schools averaged 892.[22] For white males aged 25–44 years, 29 percent had an elementary education or less. For black males of the same age, the percentage was an astounding 69 percent. New Orleans had so few skilled workers that the National Aeronautic and Space Administration (NASA)–funded Michoud facility in eastern New Orleans had to recruit out of state for workers.[23]

Housing was woefully inadequate. The local Urban League identified it as "the No. 1 social problem in New Orleans."[24] The *Louisiana Statisti-*

cal Abstract indicated that, in 1960, 28 percent of the city's 202,643 housing units were "deteriorating or dilapidated," and the subtropical climate ate away at the rest.[25] The Housing Authority of New Orleans (HANO) estimated that over fifty thousand black families were living in substandard housing, which included "gross overcrowding," several families sharing one outdoor toilet, multiple families using one kitchen, constant leaks, poor lighting, unsafe stairs, and rats. The rent for such amenities averaged from ten to sixteen dollars per week. The relocations required by Downtown construction of a new Civic Center, Union Railroad Terminal, and a massive Mississippi River bridge had aggravated an already troubled housing situation. Mayor Morrison attempted to solve these problems by seeking more federal housing money, encouraging individuals to rehabilitate their properties, and creating the Department of Housing Improvement and Slum Prevention. Of these, the public housing efforts were the most productive. According to HANO's tenant relations advisor in March 1964, the only recent construction of new housing for the poor was nine thousand public units.[26]

Local black leaders' fight for improvements laid the foundation for racial liberalism. In the early twentieth century, social aid clubs, Marcus Garvey's Negro Improvement Association movement, and the NAACP led the agitation against white supremacy. The NAACP, under the direction of A. P. Tureaud, with later help from Dutch Morial and others, instituted a long-term legal battle against Jim Crow. In 1935, the Urban League began its quiet crusade. During and after World War II, black activism expanded under labor organizers like Ernest Wright and a number of ministers and neighborhood leaders. In the 1950s, the NAACP weathered severe attacks from segregationists. In this climate, the United Clubs, a Mardi Gras organization led by Urban League president Leonard Burns, twice initiated black boycotts of Mardi Gras. In 1960, the school crisis provided a high-profile beginning to a period of very intense effort to desegregate white institutions, white jobs, and white commerce. White resistance encouraged black activism and galvanized black groups with often disparate interests.

After the school crisis, the direct action protests against segregated public accommodations were the most public efforts of the local civil rights movement. The Reverend Avery Alexander's Consumer's League targeted the Dryades Street corridor. In 1961 and 1962 the NAACP Youth Council, led by Raphael Cassimere Jr., and young activists with the Congress of Racial Equality (CORE) focused efforts in the Canal Street district and elsewhere. Mayor Morrison quickly acted to stop sit-ins. While the legal wrangling continued for two years, young activists were turning up the intensity. During that time, the Youth Council angered NAACP leader Arthur Chapital for pushing too fast, and CORE, initially a biracial organization of local students, forced out white members in 1962. The New Orleans CORE members were some of the most aggressive and legendary activists in the entire civil rights movement, including Jerome Smith, Rudy Lombard, Matteo "Flukie" Suarez, Oretha Castle (later Haley), Doris Jean Castle, Richard Haley, Dave Dennis, and Isaac Reynolds. While these groups supplied shock troops for direct action, the chief negotiators came from an older generation of black leadership. Black attorneys Lolis Elie, Robert Collins, and Nils Douglas administered vital legal services. In 1961 Lolis Elie helped to form a black Citizens Committee, the key figures of which were President Albert Dent of Dillard University, Reverend Abraham Lincoln Davis of the Interdenominational Ministerial Alliance (IMA), Dutch Morial of the NAACP, Norman Francis of Xavier University, Leonard Burns of the Urban League, and labor attorney and lead negotiator Revius Ortique. This committee negotiated with a similarly organized white Citizens Committee. In early 1962, downtown merchants agreed to desegregate their lunch counters and other public accommodations, although City Hall held out. While the Citizens Committees negotiated, Daniel Thompson of the historically black Dillard University and Virginia Collins of the Southern Conference Education Fund (SCEF) led voter registration efforts under the auspices of the Coordinating Committee of Greater New Orleans.[27]

There were also white leaders who provided black activists with critical help. Members of SCEF endured severe pressure from federal, state, and local officials and became the subject of a major civil liberties case.[28] The League of Women Voters provided leadership on voting and other political issues, and many of the League women were key mobilizers in the Save Our Schools (SOS) organization that tried to promote school desegregation in the crisis of 1960. Helen Mervis, a prominent civic activist and political bankroller, used the Community Relations Council to bring leaders of both races together. She was later a key backer of Moon Landrieu. Betty Wisdom, a League of Women Voters leader, and Rosa Keller, the local Coca-Cola bottler's daughter who shocked Uptown society by marrying a Jewish man, offered consistent support for integrationists. Two socially prominent attorneys, Harry Kelleher and Harry McCall, helped form the white Citizens Committee and became its chief negotiators. Several other white lawyers offered more radical assistance, including John Nelson Jr., who helped Dutch Morial form the New Orleans Legal Assistance Corporation (NOLAC) in the later 1960s.[29]

Most white citizens, however, were dedicated to preserving the color line. Segregationists clung to white privilege by manipulating the law, engaging in violent intimidation, and stoking white fears of black power. In 1960 alone the state legislature passed forty-three new Jim Crow statutes.[30] In Louisiana's 1959 gubernatorial election, at the height of white massive resistance, all serious candidates were segregationists. One of the most ardent was Willie Rainach, a Citizens Council leader and state senator from Summerfield who tried to purge black voters from the rolls. Rainach incensed then-governor Earl K. Long, who lashed out at him before the state legislature. Uncle Earl told Rainach, "When you [get back to Summerfield after the elections], you got to recognize that niggers is human beings!" Governor Long was troubled by the "grass-eaters"—his term for arch segregationists—who seemed to be taking over Louisiana politics. The winner of the 1959–1960 governor's race was Jimmie Davis, a country music star and actor whose master's thesis in education argued that black children were intellectually inferior to white children.[31] He played a key role in inflaming the New Orleans school crisis in 1960.

On the street, violent intimidation became the most noticeable technique for preserving segregation. In May 1965, one of the first black families moved into an Irish Channel residence near the all-white St. Thomas housing project. Shortly thereafter, at least three young white men firebombed the residence. In the ensuing months at least eleven more bombs exploded in places such as the car of the director of the Louisiana Civil Liberties Union, the Unitarian Universalist Church, and the law offices of civil rights attorneys Robert Collins, Nils Douglas, and Lolis Elie. In August, a young black man was shot twice while waiting for his food at a Royal Castle Hamburger stand. The assailant, a white 49-year-old convict, was angry that the young African American had used the window traditionally reserved for white customers.[32]

In the seats of leadership, the struggle for racial equality was addressed in differing, though perhaps equally damaging, ways. Louisiana Senator Russell Long, Huey's son and Earl's nephew, fought change. Long called the Civil Rights Act an "obnoxious piece of legislation," and he defended the fight against the bill on the basis of preserving white privilege. If the bill passed, he warned, it might "very well shift the political power in Southern States to the side of the bloc minority voters" and "create havoc with Southern customs and businesses." He worried that it could produce a situation in which "white secretaries" might have to work "under Negro executives."[33] On the other hand, Mayor Victor Schiro's office—the primary representation of public power in New Orleans—denied the existence of racial divisions. "Racially," the city's public relations department explained, "we now have and always had a stable situation here." There was "no continuing history of serious disturbances." To these apologists for the current civic order, New Orleans' easygoing culture had blended social differences into a formula for stability. "Three or four generations of all races, mellowed by time," they expressed with sincerity, "have been associating in an atmosphere of mutual understanding." New Orleans was special, they claimed, because of the close relationship that its whites had with blacks. In fact, "they worked in our homes and office, hospitals, restaurants and other public places," Mayor Schiro's public relations aides declared proudly. "Thus, we knew and understood each other more fully" than did others in other cities.[34]

City Hall apologists also clamed that black residents wanted to remain separate. They asserted that the African American's economic advancement in recent years had "enabled him to move into better homes in better neighborhoods mostly near his own people, which is what he naturally wanted." They claimed, for instance, that although public buses and streetcars had been desegregated six years earlier, many blacks continued to avoid the "mutual embarrassment" of sitting next to a white person.

Black New Orleanians preferred to stand out of politeness. Schiro's office did admit that the city had a long way to go to become a fully integrated society. Revealing a belief that segregation was a natural and not a socially constructed phenomenon, they explained that it would be resolved through a long-term evolutionary process. Like thousands of other southerners during this period, they echoed the refrain that the "habits and prejudices 100 years in the making aren't easily overcome. . . . It should be remembered that all peoples everywhere create and foster their own little communities. This basic instinct can be traced back to the caveman." In their final anthropological assessment, city officials explained: "You cannot successfully coerce your belief into another man's heart. In the whole of recorded history there hasn't been a single instance of a large-scale successful forced integration."[35]

The administration's actions belied their rosy prose. In August 1963, Schiro agreed to desegregate public accommodations and forbid discrimination in the civil service, yet a month later it had not been implemented. In an unprecedented show of unity, black leaders organized a Freedom March, and the white members of the Citizens' Committee obtained permits for them. Between ten and fifteen thousand black residents and a reported three hundred whites marched from the Central City neighborhood to City Hall. A. L. Davis, Dutch Morial, Oretha Castle, Arthur Chapital, and Central City leader Milton Upton were out front. Schiro did not show up to meet them. Four days later, however, the New Orleans Police Department raided the offices of SCEF and even seized an autographed picture of Eleanor Roosevelt. Four weeks later, on Halloween Day, several activists went to City Hall to desegregate the cafeteria and meet with Mayor Schiro. As the police dispersed them, photographers captured two remarkably symbolic images. Officers dragged Avery Alexander, a highly respected black minister, out of City Hall by his feet. Others carried away Doris Jean Castle, a local CORE activist outfitted in a nice dress, still seated in her chair. Twenty-two others were arrested. Their crime was refusing to leave the center of their government.[36]

CHAPTER TWO

Establishing the Early War on Poverty

> Our party has always been a group that you could come to
> with any bellyache of injustice. . . . It thrives and exists as long
> as the poor and the downtrodden and the bended know that
> they can come to us and be heard. And that's what we're doing:
> we're hearing them.
>
> —President Lyndon B. Johnson to Walter Reuther and
> Hubert Humphrey, August 25, 1964

In the 1960s, Louisiana was home to some of the least educated, most poorly paid, and most persistently violent citizens in the United States. The Bayou State led the nation in overall illiteracy and had the fourth highest black illiteracy rate.[1] In New Orleans, 35 percent of residents had less than an eighth grade education.[2] Statewide, infants died at a rate almost 30 percent higher than the national average. Louisiana also experienced almost twice as much violent crime per capita than the national average. In 1947, the state's murder rate was 12.6 per 100,000, compared to a 6.1 national average. By 1963, the ratio was only slightly better. Interestingly, Louisiana fell well below national averages in nonviolent crime. Louisiana residents were less likely to steal, but more likely to kill. In 1964, the average per capita income was $1,864, almost $700 below the national average of $2,550, but slightly higher than neighboring states of Alabama ($1,737), Mississippi ($1,444), and Arkansas ($1,633).[3]

Like other cities in the Deep South, New Orleans was ill-prepared to fight a War on Poverty. Until the early twentieth century, state obligations to the poor in the United States were minimal. Compared to other industrial nations, the United States' response to poverty was hesitant, inconsistent, and grudging, and it reflected racial and ethnic cleavages in American society. Historian Michael B. Katz characterized the American welfare state as a "semi-welfare state." That welfare state originated in federal efforts to provide pensions to Civil War veterans and in state efforts to provide pensions to widowed mothers. During the Progressive Era, legislation designed to aid women, children, and workers added form to the welfare state. Its chief formative moment came with the New Deal, especially the 1935 Economic Security Act that created contributory social insurance programs mainly for white male workers and state assistance for others.[4] In Louisiana, until the Poor Law of 1880, private charity was the only recourse for the unemployed. During Reconstruction, New Orleans Republicans allowed poor people to shelter in police stations, but once the Democrats took power again, relief efforts declined dramatically. From 1880 until 1933, the Poor Law called upon parish police juries to take care of their needy citizens. Churches and charitable agencies bore responsibility for supplementing the typically insufficient aid police juries provided to the poor. During the Progressive Era, the Regular Democratic Organization's hope that economic growth would relieve poverty was reflected in the addition of bureaucracies that included the ineffectual Board of Charities and Corrections, the Sewerage and Water Board, the Board of Commissioners of the Port of New Orleans, and the New Orleans Public Belt Railroad Commission. Another development was the Charitable Organization Society movement, which led to the professionalization of social work and relief efforts.[5]

Prior to 1933, Louisiana's social welfare efforts were limited to charity hospitals, prisons (which often sold labor to private firms), and asylums for the mentally insane.[6] In 1932, New Orleans ranked last among 31 American cities for spending for public relief. Most telling, it offered no relief at all for poor black residents, something that even Birmingham, Atlanta, Charleston, and Memphis provided.[7] Private organizations helped fill this gap, and one of the most important was the Kingsley House in the Irish Channel; founded in 1896 by the Episcopal Church and rooted in the Social Gospel, it was the first settlement house in the region. Another product of the Progressive Era was the Council of Social Agencies, called the Social Welfare Planning Council by the 1960s. Organized in 1925, it coordinated a growing number of social service agencies in the city. Other important groups included the Associated Catholic Charities, the United Fund, and the Urban League of New Orleans (ULGNO). Formed in 1935, the Urban League was one of the primary organizations serving the needs of the black poor. The United Fund, a product of the Community Chest movement, raised and distributed private funds to local charities, but by the 1960s it found the Urban League too controversial to fund.[8]

In 1930s Louisiana's state government finally made serious efforts to address the institutional problems affecting the poor, but it relied over-whelmingly on the federal government for funds. According to one study, the federal government provided 98.5 percent of public relief funding in Louisiana from 1933–1934. During the rest of the 1930s, the New Deal provided jobs, established critical social insurance programs (primarily for whites), created need-based social welfare programs, poured millions into the city for public works, and generally helped reform the south-ern economy. The impetus of federal involvement led New Orleans to create its first Department of Public Welfare in 1934.[9] The Federal Eco-nomic Security Act of 1935 created programs for social security pensions, unemployment insurance, and other aid and public health programs. In response, in 1936 a state-level Department of Public Welfare was estab-lished. While these organizations did improve the state's ability to serve its needy citizens, they were not comprehensive and they adhered to Jim Crow requirements.

Thus in early 1964, the starting point for the War on Poverty was a decentralized morass of private and federal agencies operating in a sys-tem that was lethargic, inefficient, and hemmed in by local racial politics. As poverty gained national attention as an important social issue, New Orleans's Urban League sought local solutions to black poverty.[10] The Social Welfare Planning Council, on the other hand, had tended to shift social service concerns for black populations to the periphery. Although still controlled by white leaders in the mid-1960s and wrestling with a Jim Crow past, the SWPC added more African Americans to its board, complementing the social workers, publishers, labor union officials, church representatives, leaders of local universities, and socially conscious members of the local business community. Poverty and substandard living conditions offered this diverse group a civic issue around which to organize. The SWPC pushed for a new Citizens Housing Council to help initiate Neighborhood Improvement Associations, coordinate housing improvement efforts, conduct surveys, and lobby for housing code compliance.[11] The Council sought to create oversight of local agencies operating at the Guste Homes, an almost one thousand unit public housing development for the elderly that opened in 1964. Most controversially, the SWPC tried to build a community center for the massive Desire housing project.

While the private Urban League and the SWPC were engaging in small-scale organizing in New Orleans, federal policymakers were contemplating grander schemes. John Kennedy's administration had established the President's Committee on Juvenile Delinquency and Youth Crime (PCJD), a pet project of his brother and attorney general Robert Kennedy. Building on the opportunity theory of Lloyd Ohlin and Richard Cloward and on the efforts of the Ford Foundation's Gray Areas Program, the PCJD laid the conceptual foundation for the Community Action Program. It drew heavily from the "community competence" idea of Leonard Cottrell of the so-called Chicago School that argued for improving the community's capacity to incorporate individuals in society. A few days before his death, President John Kennedy indicated definite support for expanding these experimental efforts and instructed Walter Heller, chair of the President's Council of Economic Advisers (CEA), to "keep your boys at work, and come back to me in a couple of weeks." A few days after the assassination, President Johnson held his first meeting with Heller and affirmed his support for Kennedy's initiatives, telling the CEA chair, "That's my kind of program. I'll find money for it one way or another. If I have to, I'll take away money from things to get money for people." While on Christmas vacation at his Texas ranch, Johnson met with Heller and others and hammered out a vision.[12]

Two weeks later, Johnson used his first State of the Union Address to declare an "unconditional war on poverty" in America. A few weeks after that, he appointed Sargent Shriver, the director of the highly successful Peace Corps and the brother-in-law to the slain president, to direct War on Poverty efforts.[13] Shriver began putting together a poverty task force that devised programs and political strategies. The President's official launch called for an unprecedented effort at the local and national levels. Called by one historian "Big Daddy" for his expansive paternalism, Johnson gave a post–World War II voice to a continued crusade for, in Johnson's words, a "more perfect union."[14]

Johnson's Great Society vision reflected the chief liberal dilemma of the 1960s. Premised upon a faith in economic and technological progress, liberalism required abundant national—and individual—growth to preserve social and political equilibrium. Millions of Americans, however, lived with obvious limits and persistent privation. Those "Other Americans," as Michael Harrington labeled them, were unsettling evidence of a dangerously imperfect union. Intellectually, Johnson's solution involved pleading for more soul-searching and refining national myths about progress and belonging.[15] In a keynote speech at the University of Michigan—written mostly by Richard Goodwin, the chief architect of Johnson's public vision—Johnson outlined a need to make "progress" a "servant of our needs" to prevent "old values and new visions" from being "buried under unbridled growth." As Johnson explained in an October 1964 speech in New Orleans, material abundance needed to account for more than physical satisfaction; it had to offer self-fulfillment to all Americans and, by so doing, reshape the national "purpose."[16] Richard Goodwin later explained that he purposefully grounded Johnson's Great Society vision in "distinctively American values," that the vision was not a "utopian construct," but a "response to the discontents" in American society—the activists in the civil rights movement, the environmental movement, the consumer protection movement, and the New Left. Goodwin claimed those speeches were products of a "time when public service, the turbulent energies of a whole nation, seemed bursting with possibilities—conquer poverty, walk on the moon, build a Great Society."[17]

Lyndon Johnson's public vision undoubtedly helped to shape thoughts in New Orleans's poor neighborhoods, but it also reflected intellectual influences already prominent in those places. The sophisticated packaging of the Great Society as a means to reinforce individualism, self-responsibility, hard work, and communal bonds made it possible to link the politically risky mission of the War on Poverty to the nation's reverence for entrepreneurial risk and reward. His vision tweaked some of the most enduring national values and defined inclusion as an almost patriotic act.[18] In his 1965 State of the Union Address, for example, the President explained that America was a community of individuals reaping the rewards of "unbounded invention and untiring industry." Seeking a Great Society that was more compassionate and inclusive would keep America from being "condemned to a soulless wealth." Great Society programs and regulations offered the chance to align racial inequality solutions with American intellectual and cultural traditions.[19]

In the president's War on Poverty speech on March 16, 1964, he proposed broadening the role of the state beyond providing services and protection to "enrich" the personal lives of every American. His administration promised to extend the Good Life to everyone. He argued that "our history has proved that each time we broaden the base of abundance, giving more people the chance to produce and consume, we create new industry, higher production, increased earnings and better income for all." After all, he explained in prevalent liberal logic, "giving new opportunity to those who have little will enrich the lives of all the rest."[20] However, in less public settings, Johnson explained his vision for the War on Poverty in saltier language. "I'm going to try to teach these nigras that don't know anything how to work for themselves, instead of just breeding," he told the editor-in-chief of the Scripps-Howard newspaper chain in early 1964. "I'm going to try to teach these Mexicans [that] can't talk English to learn it, so they can work for themselves. I'm going to try to build a road in eastern Kentucky and northern West Virginia and a few of these places so they can get down and go to school, and get off of our taxpayers' back."[21] He defended the war to Henry Luce, the head of *Time*, Inc., as a way "to give a little bit on our social consciousness." Johnson planned to "try to have some adult education, teaching people to read and write, taking the illiterates and trying to prepare them to hold a job instead of just stay on the tax rolls."[22]

Johnson drew upon the memory of Franklin Roosevelt when he explained poverty plans to Elliot Bell, the editor of *Business Week* magazine. "Roosevelt talked about the one-third that's ill-clad, and it's still one-fifth 30 years later," Johnson lamented. "But I hope, someday, it'll be one-tenth. But I'm going to start it, and try to get the states to do something, and the localities to do something, and the foundations to do something."[23] During the preliminary planning for antipoverty legislation, Johnson described the political advantage of the War on Poverty to Richard Daley, the powerful Democratic mayor of Chicago. "I wish you'd get your local people together through local initiative," the President lobbied, "and let us cooperate and establish the coordinating mechanisms, the planning and developing, what you think ought to be done for it there in Chicago." Most important, then, when his administration passed the poverty bill, "we can drop a hunk of it in there and do it."[24]

In April 1964, the Economic Opportunity Act was introduced in the House, and Sargent Shriver, President Johnson, Hubert Humphrey, and several other leaders, including the House floor leader Phil Landrum of Georgia, began shepherding the legislation through. The Senate passed it 64–31 on July 23, and the House passed an amended version 226–185 on August 8, with the Senate concurring with this version three days later. President Johnson signed it into law on August 20 in a Rose Garden ceremony.[25]

While antipoverty warriors in Washington wrangled with Congress over the Economic Opportunity Act, progressive New Orleanians were establishing linkages between private and public interests. In addition to the Urban League and the SWPC, the Stern Family Fund (a philanthropy controlled by local heirs of the Sears and Roebuck Company) provided leadership and seed money, and the recently formed New Orleans Mayor's Youth Committee served as the liaison between City Hall and local reformers.[26] In April, David Hunter, the New York-based director of the Stern Fund, inquired locally about creating an antipoverty structure focused on education programs. Initially, Mayor Victor Schiro's office seemed to be cooperative since his administration had supported efforts to create a citizen's housing advisory committee and a City Hall-based committee to study juvenile delinquency. As word of the early efforts to organize a War on Poverty reached influential members of the business community, however, the mayor's interest in a federal-linked effort dwindled, and conservative leaders lost the chance to harness the Great Society for their own interests.

With Schiro abstaining from planning and implementation, local reformers bypassed the traditional sources of approval and power and cultivated new constituencies on their own terms. Leading the local effort
from April to June was a loose collection of white and black liberals associated with the Stern Fund, the ULGNO, the SWPC, and, to a lesser extent,
City Hall. In May and June, local antipoverty leaders encountered resistance from racial conservatives and opponents of federal involvement,
forcing them to appeal to enough sympathetic business leaders to "prevent the strong, overt opposition of [the] Chamber of Commerce." By
July, progressive antipoverty leaders had lined up support from key individuals in the labor unions, the universities, the Catholic archdiocese, and
the social welfare bureaucracies. Added to this mix, according to Clark
Corliss, were sympathetic representatives from City Hall and "carefully
selected" businesspeople "whose point of view was fairly well known."[27]

Mindful of the power of the mayor, the Chamber of Commerce, and a
segregationist-dominated electorate, Clark Corliss and the early leaders
of the War on Poverty struggled to neutralize these potentially volatile
forces. The first substantial conflict between the nascent liberal coalition
and local conservatives occurred in middle May. On May 14, members
of the SWPC, the Urban League, the AFL-CIO, the Chamber of Commerce, the Orleans Parish School Board, and the Mayor's Youth Committee met in Schiro's office to discuss the possibility of developing a
federally-funded War on Poverty in New Orleans, contingent on the passage of the Economic Opportunity Act. This group tentatively agreed to
invite Sargent Shriver to speak in New Orleans. They hoped to use this
seemingly innocuous visit to expand the Mayor's Youth Committee and
the SWPC efforts on youth problems into a full-fledged antipoverty fight.
At this point, the group planned to create a nonprofit organization to
serve as the coordinating agency. Corliss reported that Schiro "expressed
wholehearted support of any effort of this kind" as a way to secure a "share
of the funds."[28]

Schiro did not anticipate the extensive protest. Throughout the next
day, members of the Chamber of Commerce and the local business community phoned demands that he reconsider the invitation to Shriver.
Schiro backed away from his commitment, instructing his Youth Commit-

tee chair to write to Shriver asking him to consider speaking if the EOA passed.[29] To the SWPC's Clark Corliss, this was another incident of the "old economic power structure saying no, and that settling the issue."[30] This time, however, that pattern was temporary.

On June 2, Darwin Fenner, a longtime civic leader and partner in the investment firm of Merrill, Lynch, Pierce, Fenner, & Smith, agreed to organize a luncheon at the Royal Orleans Hotel to discuss the possibility of the War on Poverty.[31] Expectedly, business leaders continued to resist. The biggest resistance, however, came from school board members who were facing elections in December and feared the wrath of constituents opposed to desegregation, which would likely be required by federal education programs. Despite the seeming setback, the local War on Poverty planners moved ahead. The meeting at the Royal Orleans Hotel merely indicated to them the need to "neutralize" the conservative business forces and to avoid dealing with the public bureaucracies such as the school board in official capacities. The most successful way to deal with hesitant leaders, they concluded, was to approach them as individuals, not as representatives of their organizations. Lawrence Merrigan, a local bank executive; Matthew Sutherland, an insurance attorney and school board member who figured prominently in the struggle to desegregate Orleans schools in 1960; and Thomas Godchaux, prominent head of a major local department store, led most of the organizing through August. The Stern Fund offered a $15,000 grant for seed money.[32]

Although initially these early organizational efforts were kept quiet, in mid-June the affected public bureaucracies had to be included when word trickled down to the SWPC that Louisiana would likely be eligible for $5.7 million from the Economic Opportunity Act. The nationwide competition for those funds was expected to be fierce, so New Orleans had to be ready to move once the bill was passed.[33] In late June, the antipoverty fight became public began when Clark Corliss outlined the agenda to a public SWPC meeting filled with media representatives.[34] A few days later, in July, the New Orleans Committee for the Economic Opportunity Program (NOCEOP) began holding meetings. As the official committee chosen to oversee the mobilization of a local War on Poverty, the NOCEOP continued the basic strategy of coalescing the city's liberal groups and attempting to allay concerns about the War on Poverty encroaching on the territory of existing social welfare agencies. Two divisions shared responsibility. Providing political support was a "Leadership Group" of sympathetic figures from the business community, the Jewish community, labor unions, universities, the United Fund, City Hall, and the clergy. A "Consultants Group" of social workers and experts began developing possible programs, devising implementation strategies, and maintaining close contacts with government agencies and private foundations.[35] According to Congressman Hale Boggs, these were "men and women of dedication and not people who are corrupt or scheming or graspy or greedy and who try to live as octopuses on the body politic."[36] Ironically, neither the leadership group nor the consultant's group included low-income members (see appendix 1).

Reflecting the spirit of the Economic Opportunity Act before Congress and the civil rights movement unfolding on the streets, the committee emphasized the need to have projects "carried out not *for* the community, but rather *by* the community—with external financial assistance." Local progressives hoped their programs would be strong enough to survive on their own after the cessation of federal funding.[37] New Orleans's poverty committee intensified its efforts after the Economic Opportunity Act (EOA) passed in August 1964. Among other things, the legislation created the Office of Economic Opportunity (OEO), the Community Action Program, Head Start, Job Corps, Volunteers in Service to America (VISTA), and Legal Services for the poor. The OEO had an initial appropriation of almost $1 billion and was able to bypass some traditional structural constraints.[38] The Community Action Program was particularly important for southern political reform and racial politics. It offered a means to expand black political participation because most OEO grants sidestepped existing city and state governments, typically funneling money to newly created nonprofit organizations. Although this system made it through the legislative deliberations, it concerned President Johnson, who wanted community action to flow through existing state and local structures. He told his close aides Bill Moyers and Walter Jenkins that he thought it would be "awful dangerous" to have money flowing through "organizations like YMCA and YWCA and Urban League and

NAACP." "I'd a whole lot rather [Chicago Mayor] Dick Daley do it," he instructed, "than the Urban League."[39]

In the months after the Economic Opportunity Act passed, the New Orleans Committee for the Economic Opportunity Program took its agenda to the public. President Johnson and Sargent Shriver came to town to support NOCEOP's efforts.[40] Local forces shared the vision of NOCEOP through high profile public meetings. In late October, the NO-CEOP held its first major organizational meeting to explain the possibilities of the EOA to over forty-one local agencies. The first foray into the community came a few days later with a meeting examining "The Face of Poverty in New Orleans!" There, Gillis Long, the assistant director of OEO and one-time gubernatorial candidate, gave a keynote address outlining the benefits of a federal War on Poverty.[41] Local antipoverty officials met with the Johnson administration's task force and made exploratory trips to Community Action Agencies in Harlem, Boston, and North Carolina. Over the next several years, local antipoverty leaders would attempt to implement some of the more famous antipoverty strategies, such as Richard Cloward and Lloyd Ohlin's Mobilization for Youth project and Saul Alinsky's focus on teaching local people the skills to challenge institutions.[42]

In November 1964, the NOCEOP changed its name to Total Community Action (TCA), and in December it was incorporated as the city's Community Action Agency. Headed by leading progressives with substantial participation from prominent Jewish families, Total Community Action, Inc., became the chief bureaucracy overseeing the New Orleans antipoverty experiment. In the preamble to TCA's articles of incorporation, the founders assured the public that appeals to action from local people in the past had never festered an inappropriate radicalism. Instead, community involvement had, over the past decade, improved the transportation system, attracted industry, and reformed City Hall. In striking poverty "at its source," the War on Poverty's highest function, they claimed, would be helping the underprivileged become full citizens and better economic contributors.[43] Fighting poverty, for many progressives, had become serious civic business. A blend of boosterism and fear cloaked in humanitarianism and righteousness, TCA represented a much larger agenda, namely to make New Orleans richer and more productive. To them, poverty was holding it back.

For a time in 1964 and 1965, New Orleans liberals had enough intellectual finesse and moral momentum to establish a formidable political foundation. Touting the Great Society programs gave them, momentarily, the political high ground, but the future struggle lay in Louisiana politics. The Great Society would have to be forged on the streets of a city whose politics, though mystical in appearance and seemingly open to emotional appeals, rested on a *realpolitik* of favors and spoils and brothers-in-law.

Louisiana Frankenstein

In Louisiana, the early War on Poverty tested how well the liberal integrationist agenda would fare under pressure. Formulators of the local Great Society had to contend with resistance from within the city as well as from powerful state government leaders. Louisiana governor John McKeithen was elected in early 1964 as a segregationist Democrat who raised the specter of the "bloc vote" to smear his chief Democratic opponent, former New Orleans mayor DeLesseps S. Morrison.[44] Although McKeithen's inaugural address focused on a more positive message, his actions regarding the War on Poverty showed his willingness to play to the state's segregationists and to reward his political friends.[45] In June 1965, McKeithen made public comments that segregation was the best system for Louisiana and that African Americans only needed the vote to be equal. The black-owned *Louisiana Weekly* responded that the governor needed to consider "the myriad injustices, the years of suffering, the job denials, the franchise limitation and other evils inflicted upon the up-to now helpless Negro minority in Louisiana by this vicious system."[46]

On the other hand, local liberals backed by federal antipoverty bureaucracies enjoyed the growing political influence of the Great Society. Germinal "Jimmy" Messina, director of the New Orleans office of the Louisiana State Employment Service, believed that the real value of the Economic Opportunity Act would be "the effect of the organization laid down to implement it."[47] William J. Dodd, Louisiana's State Superintendent of Education, warned prominent politicians Congressman Hale

Boggs and Senator Russell Long not to let Governor McKeithen get control over War on Poverty funds and staff the state's antipoverty bureaucracy with cronies who could "form both the nucleus and the organization to fight you folks at the polls." The staff positions at the Louisiana OEO technical office were plum patronage positions because they paid handsome salaries, required no formal education or training, and fell outside the civil service system. "Instead of creating a Frankenstein to destroy you," Superintendent Dodd instructed, "you could be building up an organization that would help you."[48]

Dodd was correct in perceiving that McKeithen was trying to use the War on Poverty to build support for himself. Governor John McKeithen was a segregationist who had to balance an economy at the mercy of worldwide trade against the volatile, racially conservative coalition that had placed him in the governor's mansion. McKeithen's handling of the federal antipoverty fight demonstrates the protection the OEO provided the War on Poverty progressives. The Louisiana OEO was an extension of the governor's office that provided "technical assistance" for rural projects, coordinated OEO efforts with state agencies, reviewed all grants within the state, and advised the governor on the approval or veto of OEO programs.[49] Although funded primarily by OEO, the technical office gave the governor a contact point from which he could influence community action projects that otherwise bypassed him. His most important source of authority in the War on Poverty was his power to veto certain OEO programs. Perhaps only Governor Ronald Reagan in California and Governors George and Lurleen Wallace in Alabama had a more publicly acrimonious relationship with the OEO, as their actions accounted for 60 percent of all gubernatorial vetoes.[50]

The governor's most controversial act was appointing several archsegregationists, in particular giving the position of deputy director to Shelby Jackson, a former Superintendent of Education who had obstructed the desegregation of New Orleans public schools in 1960 and had run for governor in 1963 as a vitriolic segregationist.[51] When McKeithen initially refused to rescind his appointments, the national OEO withheld funding, forcing a showdown. The confrontation was a critical turning point because it helped galvanize the War on Poverty coalition and demonstrated the capacity of federal influence to counteract the forces of segregation. It also showed that the rules of governance had changed. The Louisiana Human Relations Committee, a body McKeithen had appointed, strongly opposed Jackson's appointment, and their main argument against him was the danger he posed to the state's ability to attract outside capital.[52] At a time when southern governors had to redefine their positions on race, federalism, and economic development, he was learning the delicate requirements of bureaucratic management. The editors of the *Louisiana Weekly* warned that "federal program or not, it is beginning to be the same old soup warmed over."

African American leaders in New Orleans also intensely opposed McKeithen's appointments. Several of New Orleans's most influential black leaders, including Dutch Morial and Arthur Chapital, lobbied to have Shelby Jackson and others removed from the Louisiana OEO and to have African Americans appointed to their places. Several black ministers and members of the New Orleans branch of the National Association for the Advancement of Colored People (NAACP) supported OEO's decision to withhold funding until McKeithen rescinded the appointments.[53] Officials at the OEO would later remark that the Jackson appointment issue generated more complaints through the mail than "all the other states combined."[54]

For the first five months of 1965, Governor McKeithen and Louisiana OEO Director Champ Baker continued to dismiss the requests from black leaders and to resist compliance with the OEO's demand for an integrated Louisiana OEO. Baker claimed that the Louisiana OEO was working hard to "overcome" the early criticism and the "unwarranted action" of withholding funds.[55] Baker defended the McKeithen appointees as "conscientious, hard working people who are doing their best to develop this program in the state." Finding little support from other congressional members, he turned to arch-segregationist Congressman F. Edward Hébert of New Orleans.[56]

By March, McKeithen had wearied of the confrontation. According to Baker, McKeithen promised to crush the War on Poverty in Louisiana if "harassment" over the Jackson appointment continued and the $131,000 for administration of the Louisiana OEO was not released. McKeithen reasoned that Jackson should not "be disqualified just because he is a segregationist."[57] Gus Weill, McKeithen's executive secretary, was equally blunt. "It would be rather difficult in this state to find anyone of any note in public life," he stated, "who is not an avowed segregationist, including the governor." Not eager to support the War on Poverty but desperate for clear economic stimulus, McKeithen argued that federal antipoverty money would be "better spent on other worthwhile projects, such as road-building."[58]

When McKeithen eventually realized that he could not win the show-down with the OEO, he decided to make the most of situation. McKeithen was quite skilled in appealing to the pride of his constituents and their distrust of outsiders—especially highly privileged northern liberals.[59] He offered an inflammatory account of a tension-filled meeting in March 1965 with Sargent Shriver, the OEO director and husband to John and Robert Kennedy's sister Eunice Kennedy Shriver.[60] He told reporters that he had never known any two people who disliked each other more than he and Shriver, and the two realized their "mutual" dislike "within 30 seconds." Shriver's attitude was a result of "his obvious dislike for me and for the State of Louisiana." McKeithen excoriated the OEO director for having arrived ten minutes late. When Shriver finally made it, McKeithen howled indignantly to the press, "he started looking down his nose at me as if he were trying to shut out some odor that was offensive to him." McKeithen blamed Shriver entirely for the delay in funding, not OEO assistant director Gillis Long, a Louisiana native and political enemy of McKeithen.[61]

McKeithen capitulated to OEO's demands for new appointments to the Louisiana OEO in early May 1965. In return, OEO released the funds to operate the Louisiana technical assistance office.[62] The only remaining McKeithen appointee was the political operative Fred Dent. The most notable new appointee was Kacellious Bridges, a former Congress of Racial Equality (CORE) worker and a Orleans Parish School Board teacher. One of the first black appointments to a non-civil service position in Louisiana's state bureaucracy, he became the Louisiana OEO's specialist in education.[63] The tension between OEO and the governor's office did not stop, however. Champ Baker continued to defend the Louisiana OEO from what he viewed as attacks on Louisiana's control over its own affairs. The Jackson affair had resulted in their being "misunderstood" and was mostly due to a poor "public relations effort." In another instance in July 1965, Baker complained to Jules Sugarman, assistant director of the Community Action Program for OEO, about OEO officials coming to Louisiana without notifying the state office. Baker claimed that OEO representatives were not "aware of conditions existing here in Louisiana" and could throw off a delicate racial balance by coming in unannounced. At a "critical" time in Louisiana, Baker pleaded, "all races" needed "much patience and understanding" in getting programs underway.[64]

This episode is notable because of its implications for the development of liberalism in Louisiana. It was an obvious victory for integrationists, who were able to apply pressure for change from sources immune to traditional Louisiana political tactics. It also marked an important transition for Governor McKeithen and for the governor's office he represented. A leader who shifted from qualified segregationist to qualified integrationist during his eight years in office, McKeithen witnessed a changing reality in the wielding of power in the state. He had to accommodate black power. In a broad historical view, maybe the most important development involved the future of the welfare state in Louisiana. Unlike the programs of the New Deal, the Great Society would not have to answer as directly to the segregationists. The Shelby Jackson affair demonstrated clearly that federal social welfare policies could be effective in confronting white supremacy.

As a result of this showdown, the Louisiana OEO technical office had only minor influence in the War on Poverty in the Crescent City. While the governor and the OEO haggled, the Great Society policymakers in New Orleans pressed on. Walter Barnett, a civic leader and HANO president, called their efforts "a very inspiring thing" that would "hit at the roots of those things which impede the progress of the city."[65] In February 1965, Mayor Victor Schiro announced his support for TCA as the official local representative of OEO, and he made Orleans Parish one of fifty-seven parishes (out of sixty-four) seeking OEO funds.[66] Shortly thereafter, news of approved grants became a staple of local reporting. Officials with Total Community Action, the local arm of the Office of Economic Opportunity, worked with the Social Welfare Planning Council to apply for health and welfare grants and with the Orleans Parish School Board for education proposals, hurriedly putting together successful grant applications for programs that began later in the spring.[67]

By the fall of 1965, TCA's core leadership for the next two years was in place. Winston Lill, a Tulane-educated protégé of former New Orleans Mayor Chep Morrison, was the director. Thomas Godchaux, a local department store executive, served as president of the board of directors. Among the other executives only one, Clarence Jupiter, was black. Jupiter was an associate director who was an Xavier University graduate and former public relations director at Flint-Goodridge hospital, the major health center for black residents who did not go to Charity Hospital. Other key staffers were Joseph Marchese, an associate director who was an alumnus of the Tulane University School of Social Work and former director of the United Fund of New Orleans; Iris Kelso, the education specialist who was a local journalist; and A. P. "Pat" Stoddard, the manpower specialist who was a former New Orleans AFL-CIO president, former TCA board member and treasurer, and local journalist.[68] The primary function of the administrators was to funnel federal grant money to the various agencies that operated as TCA's delegates (see appendix 2).

Early Programs

TCA employed a three-pronged approach in the early War on Poverty: (1) organize the residents of low income neighborhoods, (2) develop more educational opportunity for children and adults, and (3) improve the employability of poor people. The most notable programs funded in the early Great Society were Head Start, the Job Corps, the Women in Career Services (WICS), and the Neighborhood Youth Corps, but there were others. Projects Score and Upgrade were adult education ventures that had success in teaching reading and other skills, but ultimately became lost in funding battles or fell under the control of the state board of education.[69] Upward Bound began at Dillard University and offered remedial education for high school students. It proved popular and spread to Loyola University and Xavier University. Project Enable was an innovative and ambitious program to help parents solve problems, but it did not progress beyond the early Great Society.[70] In New Orleans, it received funding in February 1966 and was operated by the Urban League and the Family Service Society, a social work agency that specialized in juvenile services and counseling. With a heavy focus on psychological uplift and on increasing parental participation in the larger community, the Family Service Society ran four parental discussion groups and reached almost 130 families; a consumer education component reached almost 400 more. Early on, the Family Service Society administrators found a "prevailing mood of hopelessness in these parents." As the discussion groups continued, however, "their mood changed to hope," as they articulated ways for "setting limits, teaching self-responsibility, assigning chores."[71] Although Project Enable's reach was shortened by funding prerogatives and policy priorities, some of its parental education and psychological rehabilitation functions also were part of Head Start.

Head Start has been arguably the most successful and politically acceptable component of the War on Poverty. Although assessments of it vary, its staying power has resulted from the perception that it has helped make poor children into better students, workers, and citizens. Equally important was the control given to local school boards.[72] Designed to upgrade the educational preparation of low-income children before they reached the early primary grades, Head Start was a comprehensive program. Although it varied from place to place, the program generally offered instruction in basic skills to preschoolers in addition to rudimentary health services. In Louisiana, Head Start was one of the most controversial antipoverty programs because of desegregation requirements. Particularly in rural areas, these programs posed a serious threat to white hegemony and caused some of the most violent resistance to Great Society programs altogether. In 1965, the Acadiana Neuf Community Action Program in south-central Louisiana encountered stiff opposition to their Head Start programs, and as late as 1967, white segregationists firebombed Head Start centers in northern Louisiana.[73]

In New Orleans, Head Start programs enjoyed only token integration due to the use of neighborhood schools, the reluctance of TCA officials to antagonize white residents, and the general refusal of white parents to participate. That first summer's program was operated by the Orleans Parish School Board. After submitting their application in May 1965, the

OPSB received almost $400,000 to operate a summer program for approximately 3,500 children in 44 schools and received another grant for the fall term. Of the forty-four Head Start schools in Orleans Parish, thirty-four of them had only black students and nine were virtually all-white. By August 1965, New Orleans's Head Start program had 3,381 African American students, but only 118 white students. The criteria for enrollment included being eligible for first grade in the upcoming fall term, being within walking distance of the school, and having no "major physical handicaps." Students needed parental permission and an escort to the school. Their parents had to attend at least four classes. Children received instruction in music, art, play, and reading and had access to hot meals, field trips, medical examinations, and immunizations. At least two of their field trips included going to City Park (usually the first time for many of the students) and to see the Houston Astros play the New York Mets. Louis Riecke, president of the school board, stated that the board wanted to give these children the attention that "higher income parents provide for their own children."[74]

Statewide, Head Start accounted for $3.5 million in grants in 1965 and over $5 million for 1966. That money helped to do more than teach children to read and write. In the words of the Louisiana OEO, it was preparing poor children for "responsible citizenship."[75] An attempt to remedy deficiencies in the market, Head Start expanded the *in loco parentis* role of the state in the lives of the poor. Iris Kelso, the education specialist for TCA, explained that she and her community contacts agreed that "citizenship starts with education. And that's what Project Headstart is all about." Daniel Kelly, a New Orleans city council member, defended Head Start to its critics by asking, "How are you going to have good citizens and a good city if you refuse to work an entire segment of the population?"[76] In a later assessment, New Orleans Congressman Hale Boggs described Head Start as a program "where we brought them [poor children] in and taught them and in a matter of several years made them a part of the community where they could function."[77]

The rationale used by local school officials to justify Head Start was in line with Great Society inclusion thinking. Local education leaders hoped that Head Start could "reduce some negative influences on children who derive from depressed enviorments [*sic*] and to offset the lack of home training skills" that often were responsible for good performance in the early school years. They argued that the pre-Kindergarten program would be an "effective vehicle for the socialization of children in that it will help them to maximize their potential for intellectual, academic, social, and cultural development." Like other Great Society programs, Head Start targeted the psyche of the supposedly alienated. Designed to "broaden the horizons" of children, the program encouraged "self-confidence, self-expression, self-discipline and curiosity, and . . . the development of a positive self-image." After its first year of operation, Head Start in New Orleans continued to serve that psychological role and became one of the least controversial programs of the Great Society. Administered initially by local reporter Iris Kelso, Head Start and the other education components of TCA became the long-term projects of Pearlie Elloie, the wife of budding politician Charles Elloie. Eventually, Total Community Action took over Head Start classes from the local school board, and prior to Hurricane Katrina, the program was TCA's most substantial, serving approximately 2,500 students in 35 centers.[78]

Complementing Head Start during the early Great Society were three jobs programs. One was the Urban League's Youth Adjustment and Development Project, the goal of which was to make black youth more qualified for jobs. Adhering to the therapeutic tendencies of social policy, its practitioners claimed that they were targeting the unemployed and the "emotionally unstable." They wanted to "develop motivation and confidence" that could help them compete.[79] A second jobs program was the WICS program, led by women from the National Council of Jewish Women and the New Orleans Council of Negro Women. Serving as a female Job Corps service, the WICS program placed young women living in urban areas into job training facilities. It was a small program that placed only twelve local women in Job Corps in its first few months of operation.[80]

The major jobs program of the early Great Society was the Neighborhood Youth Corps (NYC), an effort designed to help teenagers remain in school. In New Orleans the NYC provided jobs for students in school, for dropouts, and for young people during emergencies. Because of these opportunities, TCA officials in 2002 considered the NYC to have been "revolutionary."[81] The goal of the NYC in New Orleans was for young people to "do something with their lives" and to "develop responsibilities as good citizens while learning a trade."[82] Local officials lauded its effects. Young men who held NYC jobs cleaning up after Hurricane Betsy in the fall of 1965 (approximately 1,500 in-school and 1,500 unemployed dropouts) were praised by a state official for "being willing and eager to work." Charles B. Rousseve, principal of Booker T. Washington high school in New Orleans, asserted that the jobs helped many stay in school by helping them with "clothes, lunch and car fare."[83] Despite some praise for the program, it made few inroads with most of the private employers in the city. One example of that problem occurred in the fall of 1965. Leaders proposed a version of the NYC in which TCA was to pay two thousand youths to hold jobs in the city's private sector for ten hours per week at $1.25 an hour. Beyond on-the-job training, little was required of potential employers; TCA was to provide payroll services, the Louisiana State Employment Services to provide counseling, and local agencies to supervise. The catch, however, was that it forbade racial discrimination in hiring. The local Chamber of Commerce replied that they were "not interested."[84]

The other major Great Society job-provision and job-training initiative was the Concentrated Employment Program (CEP). Since the CEP was a massive $11 million operation that began in 1967 and operated during a different stage of the War on Poverty, it is examined in chapter seven of this book. Another program—the Community Action Program—was not specifically designed as a jobs-provision program, but quickly took on the task of offering needed employment in black neighborhoods. During the formulation of the Economic Opportunity Act, many policymakers wanted community action to expand the political participation and policy planning of the poor, thus, the hope was, empowering marginalized constituencies. Lyndon Johnson, however, wanted the Economic Opportunity Act to be less incendiary in its outcome and to focus on distributing jobs. In New Orleans, and elsewhere, the Community Action Program did both, serving as a major source of funding, patronage, and political opportunities for thousands of locals.

CHAPTER THREE

Building Community Action

What happens to a community that is economically deprived, where housing is deplorable, education is scarce, streets are mud-holes and yards are garbage pits—what do people do? . . . Do they wait for a miracle or a hand-out; or do they wake up and live?

—*Central City Areascope*, April 1968

Community action was supposed to empower the supposedly powerless. One of the drafters of the Economic Opportunity Act, William B. Cannon, intended it to be "a method of organizing local political action," not just a means of repackaging social services. Adam Yarmolinsky, one of the chief architects of the poverty legislation and a speechwriter for Johnson's War on Poverty message, believed that community action was to be "partly a means of ensuring black participation in the south." Jack T. Conway, a former labor leader who headed up the national Community Action Program for the Office of Economic Opportunity (OEO) in 1964 and 1965, claimed that "a big part" of community organization was to encourage the political mobilization of black southerners. In New Orleans, War on Poverty organizers wanted to encourage the "promotion of untapped leadership" and wanted community action to turn the poor into "positive social forces."[1] Local community action improved social services, but its most lasting legacy came from the mobilization of progressive constituencies.

President Lyndon B. Johnson apparently had a narrow understanding of community action and later became irritated when it did not resemble the New Deal's National Youth Administration program that he had administered as a twenty-six-year-old in Texas. His secretly recorded telephone calls reveal that he did not want community action to challenge local politicians or to fund nonprofit agencies. Instead, he generally favored community action as a way for local governments to sponsor projects that could provide jobs, especially for unemployed black youth. To him, community action projects would pay young men to "work for the library or sweep the floors or work in the shrubs or pick the rocks." In particular, he hoped it could "take a bunch of these young, strapping boys out of these damn rioting squads" and "put them to work." Offering a slightly different interpretation, a local New Orleans activist wanted community action to inspire ghetto residents to "wake up and live."[2]

Community action gave power and money to local leaders desperate for money and power. From December 1964 to early 1968, organizers expanded a neighborhood leadership core that had been roused by the civil rights movement. Leading efforts on the streets was a wide variety of professionals, activists, and common citizens.[3] Organizers used federal policy to bring more power, more services, more money, and better living conditions to the target areas, particularly for children. They articulated visions of community and civic duty, drawing from traditional cultural values, and appealing to Christian symbolism, a populist-infused Americanism, and a devotion to place. They also appealed to shame, duty, outrage, and hope, implementing what TCA officials described as a "walking and talking" strategy in bars, schools, churches, anywhere people gathered. By 1967, black assertiveness—and what organizers called "community unrest"—had grown and been cultivated by organizers, many of whom used confrontational tactics taught by the legendary activist Saul Alinsky. Coupled with increased political sway from the Voting Rights Act, that unrest forced well-meaning white progressives to cede control over community action to a new generation of black leaders.[4]

To shape the newest meanings of freedom in the modern South, these committed activists had to seek answers to questions about feeding the hungry and caring for those on the margins. What services mattered most to families? What could improve streets, drainage, utilities, water, sewerage, sanitation, and housing stock? What could force action from public institutions? What new institutions were needed, and how should existing ones be improved? The most frequent answer began with hands-on control over governing institutions. Black activists wanted the power to change the rules governing who could parade, who could run for office, who could influence influential boards and commissions, and who could get government contracts. At a deeper level, they also wanted to affect who could complain and be heard, who could talk back to the police, and who could sit and shop wherever they wanted. What started out as a warm-hearted exercise in civic uplift turned into a lesson in post-Jim Crow black power.

The Community Action Program's emphasis on localism meant that the architecture for a more inclusive state would be created as much on the streets of New Orleans as in the offices of the nation's capital. The first community action leaders tended to be from liberal white interest groups influenced heavily by social work professionals. Their work sparked meetings, rallies, conversations, and new neighborhood newspapers that clarified what black citizens wanted after Jim Crow. By the summer of 1966 and certainly by 1967, black citizens made it clear that what they wanted most was to be in charge of their community. Two-thirds of target-area organizations identified their number one objective as creating or changing economic and social institutions. This chapter explores the local structuring of community action and the ineffective attempts to create a racially integrated antipoverty movement. The next chapter examines specific ways that community action challenged white authority and led to black leaders taking over the multi-million dollar enterprise.

By the end of President Johnson's term in office, almost one thousand local Community Action Programs (CAPs) were operating throughout the United States. Those organizations were not easily controlled from Washington, and oversight of local CAPs was not extensive. Unless a CAP became a source of controversy or complaints, it typically received only occasional field inspections from the OEO in Washington, D.C. The minimal federal oversight and the emphasis on local CAP planning led to notorious program variations from place to place. Although most Community Action Programs served as the quiet tools of local politicos as Lyndon Johnson had foreseen, a significant number became the source of serious political conflict as black activists and neighborhood leaders answered calls "to wake up and live." Heavy controversy resulted in such places as Chicago, San Francisco, Newark, and several Deep South states.[5]

The New Orleans Community Action Program clearly challenged existing local political power, but it proved less controversial than in other places because it was supported by Johnson's ally, House Majority Whip and New Orleans congressman Hale Boggs. Locally, community action expanded black power through programs for jobs, education, and social services overseen by Total Community Action (TCA). The most dynamic movement came through the Neighborhood Development Program, TCA's community organization component. In the city's black areas, this program was coordinated by the venerable Social Welfare Planning Council (SWPC). In the span of three years, over eighty neighborhood-based councils and committees arose, with perhaps five thousand residents directly involved (see appendix 3). Ninety-seven percent of those participants were black. Fifty-one percent were female. Although the residents involved in community organizing accounted for slightly less than 10 percent of low-income people in the target area, their numbers were massive and unprecedented when compared to previous attempts. Hundreds got jobs, and many others began finding a civic voice.[6] But although these federally subsidized programs enabled more of the poor to become involved in politics and policy, gaining real control of the civic decision-making process in New Orleans was a frustratingly slow process of building formal institutions in a notoriously informal political culture.

The development of the Community Action Program coincided with the implementation of the Civil Rights Act of 1964 and the Voting Rights Act of 1965. In the standard narrative of the civil rights movement, the fragmentation and chaos that followed this legislation were considered a "crisis of victory," a time when the ideals of tactical nonviolence and interracial and interfaith cooperation tended to give way to disillusionment, self-defense, black separatism, and urban civil disorder. From a national perspective, this crisis-of-victory story line generally holds up. From a lo-

TABLE 2

Participation of Low-Income Residents in Community Organization in Predominantly Black Target Areas, 1965–1968

Target Area	Low-Income Residents Involved in Community Organization	Percentage of Low-Income Population of Target Areas	Number of Neighborhood Groups Involved in Community Organization	Low-Income Residents in Neighborhood Groups
Desire	1,111	15%	25	227
Central City	459	2%	13	179
Lower Ninth Ward	876	15%	9	280
Algiers-Fischer	911	32%	17	789
St. Bernard	799	15%	13	759

Office of Economic Opportunity, "Community Profile Project: Orleans Parish, Louisiana," Box 202, Series E23, Record Group 381 Community Services Administration, National Archives and Records Administration, College Park, Maryland (hereafter cited by folder, box, series, RG 381, NARA); TCA Research Department, "New Orleans," (1969), Folder 4, Box 55, NAACP Field Office Records, ARC.

cal viewpoint, however, the most expansive part of the civil rights movement began after the legislative victories of 1964 and 1965 as activists, bureaucrats, politicians, and constituents had to work out what kind of power black southerners really had. In New Orleans, community action encouraged a shift in focus from seeking access to institutions to seeking control over institutions. The result was another stage in the local struggle for black inclusion, albeit with some significant strings attached.

Many problems plagued community action. The poorest rarely participated. Vague objectives made success hard to judge and, therefore, hard to sell to a broader public. Bureaucratic demands and the annual uncertainty of federal funding prolonged program deficiencies, muted spontaneity at the grassroots, and sapped the emotional energy to make change. Vastly differing class assumptions and expectations among administrators, organizers, and target area residents offered narrow ground for building a common political identity, forcing many coalitions to develop around specific projects or protests. Radical organizers wanted to create a sweeping revolution, but in an era of heightened concern for urban civil disorder, cautious representatives of the Social Welfare Planning Council preferred a slower and safer course. The biggest problem was race. Early hopes for the integration of the white and black poor into a dynamic movement diminished as white residents generally refused to work with black participants.

Reconstructing the story of these community organizing efforts is difficult because the people involved had little time to keep extensive written records, and local politicians were notorious for their reluctance to write things down. However, the documentary fragments that do exist for New Orleans show that community action depended on fledgling councils and bureaucracies influenced by the interests and savvy of leaders in seven different neighborhoods, which often had competing needs. Finding unifying elements requires generalizing about attitudes, ideas, and actions, but two themes emerge: Community action helped channel the voices and interests of poor and segregated people into a politically vibrant framework of local organizations, and it showed that federal War on Poverty policies were almost meaningless until tested at the neighborhood level.

Target Areas and Community Organizations

In 1965 and 1966, Total Community Action designated seven target areas: the Irish Channel and Florida were majority white areas, and Desire, the Lower Ninth Ward, Central City, Algiers-Fischer, and St. Bernard were largely black or black Creole areas. Statistically, the residents in these areas were the least educated, least healthy, least affluent, most violent, and most prone to criminal activity in New Orleans. These areas accounted for approximately 150,000 of the city's almost 700,000 residents (estimated in 1966). Of the 150,000, about 115,000 were African Americans. Civic leaders chose these areas for attention because of the racial problems they posed and the perceived level of social despair, as well as the presence of significant social welfare efforts and the potential for political activism.[7] Desire and the Irish Channel received the most attention during the first year.

Throughout 1965 and early 1966, TCA and SWPC leaders focused on establishing Neighborhood Development Centers that provided meeting spaces for the community, offices for organizers, and, under liberal mayor Moon Landrieu in the 1970s, contacts with City Hall. They also served as hubs for social services, over time also housing health services and voter registration substations. Initially, several TCA board members viewed these centers as a possible waste of resources and time, but black leaders in the target areas successfully applied pressure to accept the proposals. Moon Landrieu worried about "putting an awful lot of money in a physical structure," but forty years later he recalled those centers as one of the best legacies of community action. The input from black areas helped Landrieu to understand things that he "didn't necessarily see at the time," and to learn that he was "at least smart enough to know that I didn't know everything."[8]

The neighborhood centers augmented traditional ways of bringing community residents together.[9] Historians have shown clearly in the last forty years that ghettoes were not merely barren enclaves saturated with despair, and the poor were not entirely powerless.[10] The power of the neighborhood institutions cannot be ignored in examining the culture of New Orleans. Bars, for example, were a primary location for information exchange and coalition forming; where one drank was often as important as where one prayed, played, and bought insurance. Churches offered spiritual rest and rejuvenation, but they also provided social welfare relief, recreation, and, often, avenues to political influence.[11] Churches and schools complemented recently organized homeowner's associations, improvement and civic associations, and community councils. For community continuity in black New Orleans, few organizations were as vital as the social aid and pleasure clubs of Mardi Gras, mutual aid societies, and funeral homes and life insurance groups. Institutions like the Quakers' American Friends Service Committee connected target areas to the larger world. After Hurricane Betsy, for example, sixteen college students, most of them with civil rights experience, lived in the Lower Ninth Ward "in a communal arrangement" while working in their own Community Development Project.[12]

Janet Moore, a reporter for the Free Southern Theater's *The Plain Truth* newspaper, described the richness of community life in the ghetto and the subtle power residing in its informality. She describes it as "a place where people know each other and look out for the well-being of their fellow man if only because no one else will." Through "brotherhood,"

TABLE 3

Comparison of New Orleans's War on Poverty Target Areas, Ca. 1960

	Population	White	Black	Families Below Poverty Line	Unemployed Males	25 years old, less than Eighth Grade (Male or Female)	AFDC Recipients (families)	Disease Cases per 1,000 Residents
New Orleans	627,525	63%	37%	28%	6%	35%	2%	4.7
Central City	54,252	15%	83%	54%	10%	38%	16%	10.5
Lower Ninth Ward	33,001	18%	82%	32%	8%	48%	5%	5.9
Irish Channel	23,655	87%	13%	35%	8%	47%	7%	7.5
Desire	17,033	9%	91%	61%	10%	52%	17%	6.7
St. Bernard	10,972	5%	95%	58%	15%	46%	9%	2.6
Florida	10,678	56%	44%	44%	9%	24%	9%	3.1
Algiers-Fischer	9,177	40%	60%	38%	6%	29%	14%	9.5

The percentages are rounded figures. TCA, "Demographic Information By Target Area," [taken from 1960 Census Tract surveys], Folder 18, Box 5, Community Relations Council of Greater New Orleans Collection, ARC; Office of Economic Opportunity, "Community Profile Project: Orleans Parish, Louisiana," Box 202, Series E23, RG 381, NARA; TCA, "Quick Facts: TCA Target Areas," in Gordon Wilcox, "Inspector's Field Report," 23 July 1966, Folder New Orleans, Box 102, Series E75, RG 381, NARA; TCA Research Department, "New Orleans," [1969], Folder 4, Box 55, NAACP Field Office Records, ARC.

she asserted, "the bondage can change from ghetto to community." She praised "the little old ladies" who sat on their stoops watching everyone in the neighborhood, and she claimed that "the brothers who hand [hang] out on the corner of the white owned bar room" belonged to "a fraternity of the highest order."[13]

Organizers had to understand these pre-existing neighborhood institutions, and they often had to become master bureaucrats as well, balancing paperwork and politics. Arthur Cooper, a white Neighborhood Development coordinator for the Irish Channel, described the slow, time-consuming managerial tasks—finessing personnel matters, setting up phone lines—around which he squeezed in meetings with local merchants, smoothed over potential problems with the Catholic Church, and reassured wary white Irish Channel residents.[14] Cooper and other organizers had to fit into the well-defined hierarchy of the Neighborhood Development Program. In the majority black areas, the SWPC was the delegate agency in charge of community organization and the Volunteers in Service to America (VISTA) program. Other groups led majority white areas, especially the Irish Channel.[15] Each SWPC target area was led by a team chief who supervised all organization efforts in that area and answered to the Neighborhood Development director. The team chief was supposed to have prior community organization experience and be able to talk easily with the poor. One of their main functions was to link target area councils and the SWPC staff. In New Orleans, all but one of the team chiefs possessed a college degree. The next level of employment was the community worker, a position that required either a college degree or comparable work experience. The third level was that of community aide, for which the SWPC had "no hard and fast qualifications" except that low-income, target-area residents had priority in hiring. According to a report by the director of the SWPC, target hiring requirements were inadequate in 1965, but nevertheless had been followed "religiously" in 1966 and 1967.[16]

These staff members trained neighborhood activists in topics that varied from how to run meetings to understanding the political power structures in New Orleans. Of New Orleans's almost 80 neighborhood organizations, two-thirds employed "cooperative" tactics such as holding rallies, writing letters, and circulating petitions, while the other third were more aggressive, opting for boycotts, direct action, and litigation. Perhaps the most influential director was Richard Haley, who served from November 1966 to January 1968, directing the thirty-five paid employees organizing black target areas. TCA Director Winston Lill called Haley, the former southern director of the Congress of Racial Equality (CORE), "without question, the best [community organizer] I've ever seen."[17]

Each target area had unique characteristics, but they shared common problems. Central City was the largest area in terms of population and square mileage. One of the oldest black sections of the city, it had earlier been known as "back of town." In the post–World War II era, it was one of the city's most stable low-income areas. A mix of private and public housing, it was home to over fifty thousand residents, twenty thousand of whom were under twenty-one years old.[18] Central City had three public housing projects: the new Guste Homes for the elderly complemented the pre–World War II Magnolia and Calliope projects.[19] Like other poor sections in New Orleans, Central City had a reputation for despair. A Tulane University graduate in history and a future editor of the *New Orleans States-Item* claimed that although the city's bustling tourist and business district was only a few blocks away, they "might as well be two million because it's in another world." He referred to Central City and similar areas as "prisons" where people were "serving time." According to him, "civil rights don't mean much to these residents."[20] The primary War on Poverty organization in Central City was the Central City Economic Opportunity Committee, and it produced several prominent black politicians.

Another major target area was the Lower Ninth Ward. The official target area had 19,000 residents, but the general area had 53,000.[21] A reporter described it as an area that "looks like the wrong side of the tracks in any small rural southern town." The area was notable for "dirt roads, ramschackle homes, cement block buildings, abandoned automobiles, and overgrown vacant lots."[22] The area had at least thirty-two churches, including the strongest presence of spiritualist churches, which, according to a local journalist, combined "Catholicism, Protestanism [*sic*], and voodoo."[23] Although comprised of 414 city blocks, the Lower Ninth Ward had no hospitals, public clinics, library branches, bank branches, high schools, police stations, pawnshops, or department stores. Public recreation space consisted of only three acres, not counting 866 thirty-foot-wide, privately owned vacant lots. Eleven blocks had over 67 percent blight. Over five hundred buildings were designated as dilapidated and over eight hundred as deteriorating. The average family income was half of the Louisiana average.[24] The situation worsened in August 1965, when Hurricane Betsy wrecked much of the area.[25] According to Urban League reports, the storm directly affected over forty thousand black residents and caused an estimated $1.6 billion damage. About 22,000 blacks and 8,000 whites were evacuated. Many residents from hard-hit Plaquemines Parish came to New Orleans for relief. The worst flooding occurred in the Lower Ninth Ward from the Industrial Canal to the St. Bernard Parish line and from Florida Avenue to St. Claude Avenue. The agencies involved in recovery efforts included the Urban League, the Red Cross, the Small Business Administration, the Office of Emergency Planning, and the Social Welfare Planning Council.[26]

Neighboring the Lower Ninth Ward target area was the Desire area, and for locals who cared, it was the archetype of despair. Geographically, it was an urban island isolated from the rest of the city by canals, railroads, trash dumps, and an industrial corridor. One neighborhood leader described Desire as a place where residents were "confined from birth and struggle and death." According to another, people inside and outside of Desire thought of the area "as a ghetto whose inhabitants are isolated socially, economically and physically from the mainstream of community life."[27] Its roughly twenty thousand residents occupied a major portion of a demographic crescent consisting of predominantly black, low-income neighborhoods that followed a basin formed by the natural slope of the Mississippi River's natural levee. The basin was considerably below sea level and historically had been marginal land.[28] Desire's population density of over six people per household was the highest in the city. Approximately two-thirds of the area's population fell below the poverty line. Average annual family income hovered around $1,900. Average educational attainment stopped at the eighth grade, with the dropout rate over 50 percent.[29] Like other black areas, the public support services were deficient and suffered from a lack of planning. Desire had no indoor public recreation areas, unless, according to the SWPC, one counted "beer joints" operating out of "dilapidated shacks." A single flood-prone public park was supposed to serve over seventeen thousand minors. A massive rural immigration after World War II had swelled the area's population, but the city had made few adjustments in services.[30] Playwrights for the Free Southern Theater wrote in the summer of 1966 that "no one speaks for the Ghetto of Desire. The situation parallels, almost as if planned, precisely that of Watts in Los Angeles before last summer's riots."[31]

The Desire area was dominated by a housing project that was a distinctly post–World War II development. Unlike the nineteenth century origins of neighborhoods in the Irish Channel and Central City, Desire was an outgrowth of architectural, political, and planning trends of the middle twentieth century. It provided homes for well over ten thousand people, ranking it as one of the nation's largest. The local Free Southern Theater, in a broadcast designed for CBS television, mused that it had been "dreamed up by a city planner at Auschwitz" and was the "center in New Orleans of every social ill."[32] During the city's postwar population expansion, the Desire project offered a fast solution to a serious housing problem. It was an experiment in modern community-building by the state. Located on roughly one hundred acres of veritable swamp land, the seemingly endless blocks of cheap brick buildings severely lacked open space for the community to gather in. Within twenty years of completion, Desire's speedily built buildings revealed the shoddy nature of their construction, the decomposition emphasized by lack of repair. By the mid-1960s, the experiment was unraveling.

The location and design of the Desire project proved inadequate for the long-term needs of the community.[33] The project was too far away from places of employment, and trains occupying the tracks surrounding Desire often choked off ground transportation for half an hour at a time. Health services were a thirty-minute bus ride away. Schools were overflowing and often operated on a double-shift system. The police department was often hostile. Not surprisingly, it was the least popular public housing project in the HANO system.[34] Perhaps surprisingly, the Desire area was home to many who were not in poverty. A group of black professionals—administrators, teachers, nurses, social workers—served as important leaders. Until the War on Poverty, however, they were largely excluded from meaningful decisions about the area and had to broker concessions from segregationists.

The Irish Channel was the largest white target area, a historic working-class neighborhood undergoing rapid demographic changes. The out-migration of white residents (primarily of Irish and German descent) and the in-migration of African Americans and Latinos created a socially combustible environment. According to an Irish Channel leader, the area represented "the city in microcosm."[35] An area large enough to qualify as one of the ten largest cities in Louisiana, the Irish Channel was tucked between downtown, the opulent Garden District, Louisiana Avenue, and the Mississippi River wharves.[36] The Irish Channel's St. Thomas Housing Project—all-white until 1965 when HANO ended its policy of seg-regation—sheltered approximately five thousand residents.[37] Most Irish Channel residents had low incomes, but in contrast to Desire, almost half of the private housing was owner-occupied.[38] Over half of the housing stock was substandard. One contemporary report by Carolyn Kolb de-scribed it as "hardly a slum, but neither is it impressive. The houses are large, Victorian, and run-down. The stores are small, dark, and jammed up. The streets are narrow, the bars noisy, and the children seem to multi-ply block by block." Police officers worried about its high rate of juvenile delinquency. Racial tension, cheap land in neighboring parishes, vanish-ing local jobs (especially political patronage positions which had fallen from 1,900 in 1946 to 290 in 1966), and deteriorating neighborhood hous-ing were scattering the Channel's inhabitants to the suburbs.[39] Despite claims by its residents that the Irish Channel was "the last real neighbor-hood in the city," tourism marketers and the Chamber of Commerce did not tout the area.[40]

Such were the target areas in which community organizations carried on the War on Poverty. Twelve of these community organizations rose to prominence. Eight were located in predominantly black target areas and helped foster cadres of rising political talent. Most of the following analysis focuses on the organizing efforts in five of those areas, leaving out Algiers-Fischer and St. Bernard, where the documentation was espe-cially sparse. In the beginning, the neighborhood councils were intended to serve as clearinghouses for community complaints and reform ideas. In addition, they were to coordinate community organizing. One neighborhood activist explained that they did not want "to fight" but to "organize, talk, and work together to improve our community."[41] Attempts by these community organizations to establish more control over civic space, to refine the quality of that space for the poor, and to mobilize community sentiment in the target areas resulted in an unsteady, but increasingly assertive, African American civic presence in New Orleans.

The leaders of the Central City Economic Opportunity Committee (CCEOC) claimed that their objectives were to "insure" achievement of the OEO's goal of maximum feasible participation of target area residents and to direct War on Poverty money to the poor. The CCEOC hoped to "unite the citizens of the area" and to help them "help themselves." They endorsed the underlying psychological mission of the Great Society, explaining that they wanted to help "in creating pride, dignity, self-identification and community spirit" among young people.[42] Richard Haley credited community organizations like the CCEOC for their pioneering role in black civic participation. "Their primary importance is not the problems they choose, or even the successes they have," he declared, "it is their being, their actual existence, that is important." While "white middle-class society" had been accustomed to neighborhood councils, the War on Poverty "introduced this social tool to the ghetto."[43]

In Desire, the SWPC, the Desire Area Community Council (DACC), and the Desire Economic Opportunity Council led the way. The DACC was a new group of community activists and leaders that began organizing twelve-block units in February 1965.[44] The Desire EOC served as TCA's citizen-participation group and began operations in May 1965. Both groups had a majority female membership. One of the first tasks of the DACC block units was to develop a list of pressing problems in Desire. The group came up with sixty-one, including the need for a bridge over a dangerous canal, improving the area's only playground, providing child care, preventing school dropouts, and broadening opportunities for children.[45] Over the next several months, the DACC oversaw public meetings with War on Poverty officials and local agencies, lobbied city hall for improvements, and mounted a voter registration drive. The DACC focused efforts on getting the attention of bureaucracies and convincing residents that pressure from the neighborhood could bring it about. The DACC stressed that the residents "do the talking" and the bureaucrats "do the listening."[46] Most of the residents' concerns were about jobs, job training, and recreation.[47] In May 1965, the DACC planned a major voter registration drive to complement the expected passage of the Voting Rights Act. Led by teachers, students, principals, and neighborhood leaders, this successful drive showed the influence of the DACC and the block-oriented groups. According to the *Desire Digest*, a neighborhood newspaper, if the community-led bureaucracies could not "do the job, it probably can't be done."[48]

Among the chief tasks of Desire organizers was to improve services from City Hall. Moweaner Mauldin, a middle-aged woman and civic leader, worried about the atmosphere created by the area's weeds, trash, bad lighting, empty buildings, and old cars.[49] She looked to TCA to fund a "face-lifting project" that would be critical for "morale building."[50] Others complained intensely about the area's dangerous drainage canals that many locals linked to the high incidence of disease in the area, especially tuberculosis. Requests to the city accomplished little, and the DACC turned to the Community Action Program, asking SWPC leader Clark Corliss to use his influence with white civic leaders. In turn, he pressed the SWPC board of directors to use their contacts to help because "this is the type of situation which angers people and which could erupt, particularly if small children are harmed."[51] Other groups in Desire and the neighboring Lower Ninth Ward continually asked Mayor Schiro for paved streets, streetlights, slower speed limits, healthcare centers, and other services.[52]

In the majority-white Irish Channel, organizing efforts were filtered through a well-established, though still meager, network of institutions providing social services, including the Catholic Church, the Kingsley House settlement, and the St. Thomas Neighborhood Council (formed in November 1964 in response to the Economic Opportunity Act). Kingsley House, since its beginning in 1896, was one of the major social services suppliers for the poor whites living there. The Irish Channel Action Foundation (ICAF), a group with close ties to the Catholic Church, began in

1962 to help teachers deal with emotionally troubled children. Its leader, Father John Vaughan, developed programs to help school dropouts, created a Parents Institute to offer advice to parents with troubled children, and conducted a housing and church survey of the area. In December 1964, the ICAF expanded when it began an aggressive community organizing campaign through the War on Poverty.[53]

Like most community groups in the Irish Channel, the ICAF was a heavily religious organization. Its leaders were skilled at attracting residents to Catholic mass and other services, and they used those skills to organize during the War on Poverty. The leaders of the ICAF believed that many of the poor in the Channel were "church-less and evidently alienated." The War on Poverty offered the opportunity to help tie them to the community by improving their job skills and helping them earn more money. The ICAF declared an "all-out" effort to lift up the Channel "morally, culturally, socially, physically and economically." The leadership wanted to use OEO funds for a comprehensive socio-economic survey, a housing survey, a community newspaper, and family counseling. Their primary goals were to improve housing stock and develop block leadership.[54] Despite some support from the Catholic Church, the ICAF came under bitter attack from Father William Miller. Father Miller resented "the Government moving in on the Church," and "the 'do-gooders,'" and he threatened litigation to expel War on Poverty programs from a Catholic-owned building. According to one eyewitness, he put "the curse of god on the program."[55]

Nevertheless, organizing efforts continued in the Irish Channel. In fact, the rejuvenated ICAF attracted so many key leaders from the area that some critics labeled it as the group representing the "Establishment."[56] By June 1965, ICAF and Kingsley House had arranged to share organizing responsibilities. ICAF worked with established business and civic interests and Kingsley House expanded its community action effort in the St. Thomas project. In October 1968, Kingsley House and ICAF merged, and Kingsley took over all community organizing.[57]

In the Lower Ninth Ward, a group of well-informed and ambitious civic leaders dominated community organizing. The Lower Nine, as many locals referred to it, eventually became the most tightly organized area of the city, due largely to the Great Society and the emergence of the Southern Organization for Unified Leadership (SOUL) political organization in the late 1960s. After 1964, black power in the Lower Ninth Ward coalesced around efforts to deal with bad public services, bad topography, and bad weather. Throughout 1966 and 1967, residents in the Lower Ninth Ward held numerous meetings about housing and health reform, tried to expand the target area boundaries, and lobbied for a Legal Services program. The Ninth Ward Civic Improvement League organized a boycott of a supermarket until the grocer hired blacks as "cashiers or in other responsible positions."[58] Perhaps the central focus of community action concerned Urban Renewal. Since their neighborhood lay largely below sea level but lacked subsurface drainage, Lower Ninth Ward leaders hoped federal funds could support infrastructural improvements and put more residents to work.[59]

In September 1965, New Orleans was hit by Hurricane Betsy, a massive Gulf of Mexico storm that brought 110 mile-per-hour winds, heavy rain, and a ten-foot storm surge. In some parts of the Ninth Ward, water reached into the second story. In 1966, debris still remained in Desire and the Lower Ninth Ward. Mayor Schiro and the city's department heads told Lower Nine complainants that there was little that the city could do. Only after what the Desire Area Community Council called "persistent and forceful citizen action" did Schiro trouble himself to make a special fact-finding visit to the area.[60] A few months after that visit, little had changed. A group of Lower Ninth Ward residents calling themselves the "Betsy Flood Victims" proclaimed that they were "shocked to find our Mayor so powerless." Not only were they disillusioned with the mayor, they were disgruntled with a city council that met their requests with "undignified howls and subterfuges." Believing that their elected local representatives would "never move for the people unless pushed hard," residents of Lower Nine took their pleas to Congress and to the local administrators of the War on Poverty.[61]

The aftermath of Betsy also strained relations between the Community Action Program and the Catholic Church in the Lower Ninth Ward. Father Mulligan of St. David's Church was particularly concerned about the role of the Ninth Ward Civic Improvement League and the Social

Welfare Planning Council. He disliked the "attitudes" of Richard Aronson and Tom Dent, two community organizers employed by the SWPC who had allied with the NWCIL during Hurricane Betsy relief efforts. Along with Desire team chief Bettye Pope and local civic activist Paul Sanzenbach, they set up a disaster center at St. Philips School, informed residents of services, recruited teenagers for the Neighborhood Youth Corps clean-up effort, and coordinated volunteers. Aronson held a master's degree in social work from Columbia University with a specialization in community organization. Dent was a graduate of Morehouse College, a civil rights activist, and son of the well-known president of New Orleans's Dillard University. Father Mulligan, who was prone to tell Ninth Ward residents to keep "their minds open and their mouths shut," accused them of favoring friends of the NWCIL, a black group that Mulligan claimed was off-limits to whites in the Lower Ninth Ward.[62]

In the process of pushing for the area's physical reconstruction, community activists helped to shift neighborhood influence away from more traditional, church-based leadership to growth-oriented business leaders and newly created, War on Poverty–linked organizations. In particular, the Lower Ninth Ward Neighborhood Council, a group that functioned as part of the War on Poverty framework, overshadowed the Ninth Ward Civic Improvement League, a good-Samaritan group founded twenty years earlier. Although the NWCIL and its chief leader, the longtime NAACP leader and civil rights advocate Leontine Luke, remained influential, Neighborhood Council leaders took over most of the negotiations with federal bureaucrats. They were particularly involved in lobbying the U.S. Department of Housing and Urban Development to find a way to get around Louisiana's lack of Urban Renewal enabling legislation.[63] The efforts of Lower Ninth Ward leaders eventually led to several million dollars in federal funding for streets and drainage projects and formed the core of the movement to overturn state legislation that had prevented Urban Renewal funding since 1954. During this process, local people tested the concept known as "maximum feasible participation."

The Economic Opportunity Act's demand for the "maximum feasible participation" of area residents is perhaps the single-most addressed issue in the history of the Community Action Program (CAP). This scholarly fascination with MFP, as it was called, stems from its potential to restructure social welfare policy and politics. Depending on one's perspective, the citizen participation requirement of the CAP can appear to be another lost moment in American progressive politics or can look more like what the social policy bureaucrat and future U.S. senator Daniel Patrick Moynihan disparaged as "maximum feasible misunderstanding."[64] He was correct that its definition was unclear, but local activists were able to use that vagueness to define MFP in ways that fit local struggles. In fighting Jim Crow in New Orleans, black activists had long been trying to create their own maximum feasible participation. The policy of the Office of Economic Opportunity added another opportunity. The leaders of New Orleans's Social Welfare Planning Council believed that target area residents would learn enough to take over community organizing in five years. Target area leaders, however, gained control faster than expected.[65]

Early on, MFP levels in New Orleans were inadequate by almost any standard, and one problem was that the War on Poverty could not overcome the pressures of family and work. A large number of women, for example, noted that their lack of childcare kept them from participating. Others expressed concern about "reprisals" from the white-controlled local housing authority or the local Department of Public Welfare.[66] Winifred Anderson, president of the Central City Economic Opportunity Committee, had a different take. She observed that a "large following" had grown in mid-1965, but had "dwindled to a faithful few" by late 1966. She suggested that numbers fell when residents learned that the War on Poverty was a "self-help" program and not one of "bread lines and soup kitchens."[67] Mr. L. C. Brass of Central City may have been representative of most target area residents when in 1966 he admitted, "I have not heard of the Poverty Program, but I would like to have a job to help myself because I'm having a rough time."[68] The failure of people such as Mr. Brass to get involved caused several leaders to blame target area residents. Malcolm Barnes, a leader in Algiers-Fischer, contended that if the antipoverty movement failed, fault should lie with residents who did not participate. For too many residents in the area, self-help "meant they could help themselves to a lot of free government money."[69] Another problem was linked to the composition of TCA's early board of directors.

One contemporary study found that the vast majority of its members were white and had "high class" values. That is, 60 percent of the board believed that the poor were not capable of holding positions of authority, and almost 40 percent explained that poverty was the fault of the individual. During 1966, TCA addressed these problems.[70] By 1967, however, political power in black neighborhoods was so strong that MFP concerns became moot. A more pressing issue was the level of racial integration in community organizing.

The Limits of God and Community

For decades, most white southerners had denied the existence of any serious racial problems and assumed their black neighbors to be happy and well-fed. In the middle 1950s and early 1960s, the civil rights movement delegitimized that perception, and the War on Poverty intensified the threat to segregationists. The New Orleans Community Relations Council concluded that most local whites perceived community action to be undermining "traditional values, i.e., that the Negro community is not equal to the white."[71] A number of activists involved with Total Community Action tried to confront the issue of white prejudice head-on. They dreamed of hearty individuals, white and black, working together to ensure justice and governmental responsibility. A wide range of target area activists celebrated the belief that one could make a difference if one would sacrifice for the good of the whole, for something higher than oneself. Their hope for the Great Society resembled Lyndon Johnson's public vision for inclusion and reflected countless themes preached from local pulpits. They embraced the Progressive Era philosopher John Dewey's suggestion that "democracy is a form of government only because it is a form of moral and spiritual association."[72] They found, however, that racial integration would remain mostly a dream. Community organizing in the Irish Channel and Florida were racially integrated to a small degree, but for the most part, efforts were segregated.

Despite the frequent conservative criticism of CAP as something that undermined authority and eroded American values, community activists—black and white—often used community action as a way to promote hard work, personal responsibility, and patriotism. In New Orleans, CAP participants helped reinforce allegiance to an American civic ideal. In the Algiers-Fischer area, neighborhood leaders claimed that a federally funded Boy Scout program stressed "proper respect to the Flag of the U.S.A." and "taught" the young boys "that a citizen's duties begin at home today."[73] James Gayle, principal of McDonogh School No. 36 in the Central City neighborhood, blamed the existence of poverty for impeding "the nation's effort to mature." The War on Poverty, he perceived, was encouraging a "growing concern for others, the exercise of selfless interest in social change for the good of the community and the spirit of cooperative effort to cure social pathologies."[74] Louis King, a Central City leader, urged, "What we are trying to do, with the help of Uncle Sam, is make a better life for ourselves, family, relatives, friends and neighbors."[75]

The writings of a wide range of neighborhood activists held that compassion for the alienated and sacrifice for the good of the community multiplied individual rewards. If, in the United States, the individual's efforts provided the community's strength, then that community needed to be structured to fully develop the individual's potential. One activist from the Algiers-Fischer neighborhood argued that through the War on Poverty, the federal government was pursuing the will of the Almighty by "sharing the wealth of its accumulated treasure with those who have practically nothing." According to her, "you start with what you have and God will do the rest," but most important, "God helps those who help themselves."[76]

Situating the relationship between the self and society and between God and man was a major enterprise. According to a leader in the Lower Ninth Ward, the search for community and power required participation not only by "the sober, the well scrubbed, the well fed, the solvent, but also by the intoxicated, the tattered, the hungry, and the alienated."[77] The Ninth Ward Civic Improvement League declared that "A little help from someone who cares can bring many out of the deplorable condition they live in. It will also give them the courage and initiative to help themselves and to take an active part in community problems that benefits them as well as others."[78] In the winter of 1966, a spokesperson for the Clouet and People's Improvement Group in the Desire area articulated an all-important faith in the collective action of individuals. "We know that we are little people," they admitted, "but by working together we cease to be little people." They wanted and needed "everybody's hand in the pie."[79] In language quite similar to that used by President Johnson in his May 1964 Great Society speech, Reverend George Simon of the Irish Channel warned, "Our enormous increase in material power will poison our lives unless we speedily share what we have with others." In a blending of religious instruction and social activism characteristic in the target areas, he concluded, " 'unto whomsoever much is given, of him shall much be required.' "[80]

In May 1964 at the University of Michigan, Lyndon Johnson called for a movement "upward to the Great Society" that would "ennoble" American wealth and materialism. Submerging one's self within a greater collective purpose was one way to achieve that goal. For Johnson, this situation would produce a community "where the city of man serves not only the needs of the body and the demands of commerce but the desire for beauty and the hunger for community." With some slight alterations, an activist in Desire concurred, stating that "the individual may stand out to lead and inspire, but alone he can do little." Accordingly, the heroic and unfettered individual had no room in community action because "no man can live to himself alone." The best "organization" was one "in which each man shoulders the responsibility of all."[81] Another activist articulated the sentiment in another way by warning, "none of us are safe when our neighbors are neglected."[82]

In the Irish Channel, the War on Poverty prompted a struggle over church and state, righteousness and racial identity.[83] "Our community will prosper," pleaded Alex Benz, the chairperson of the St. Thomas Housing Project Council in the Irish Channel, "if all of us will try to have an honest and valid intellectual humility that will allow each of us to accept what all other members of the community have to give."[84] Another Irish Channel activist echoed those sentiments of unity. "In these days when racial tensions are high and some people of both races waste a lot of time and energy on fear and hatred," this person offered, "some neighbors are living the simple truth that a person cannot be judged by the color of his skin. Some of us are showing that a Good Neighbor—is a Good Neighbor, period!" Calling upon a sense of progress inherent in a conception of Christian stewardship, this activist admonished that a "human being can only live their highest and best when they live for others; that the person who lives for others will receive for himself ten times what he gave because he makes himself a better person by doing so."[85] To plead for community cohesion, another Irish Channel activist compared Channel residents to Jonah, the Old Testament figure who avoided God's command to serve the settlement at Nineveh because he found its people offensive. "We forget that God is the God of all people—the person on the bottom rung of the socio-economic ladder on up to the man of means," she reminded her audience. "He is the God of white-collar workers and the God of Laborers too. He is the God of upright citizens, but also the God of the skid row character. He is God of both the white and negro races. There is only one God for all the people of the universe."[86] In hindsight, however, the idealism of these activists paled next to the deep influences of racial bigotry, the decline of longshoreman's jobs, the transformation of political patronage, and the lure of low taxes and cheap land in neighboring parishes. The attempts to integrate community organizing in the Channel caused friction and slowed the growth of antipoverty programs.[87]

War on Poverty officials and community organizers could not overcome the color line. Black residents were wary of white organizers and white organizations. White residents rebuked black organizers and rejected organizations with any substantial black involvement. From 1965 to late 1967, community organization progressed largely as a segregated process. Of the seven target areas, only the majority-white Irish Channel had substantial white participation. The Florida target area also had some white participation, but mostly from women from outside the neighborhood who were associated with the National Council of Jewish Women. In the summer of 1967, the SWPC tried a last-ditch effort to operate an integrated program. According to Richard Haley, "white residents" had not "as a whole responded positively to Negro workers, nor have the workers made a continuing effort to draw in white participants." Because the SWPC had found it extremely difficult to hire white workers, they looked to the VISTA program to help with the "re-integration" of the community organization staff. Haley recognized the dilemma posed by seeking race-based appointments, but believed that white organizers in black areas could "'evangelize' the similarity of problems of the poor" in attempts to build class consciousness.[88] With little hesitation, VISTA officials denied the SWPC request, citing their policy against the proposal's principal aim of getting more whites involved in the program simply because of their race. Upon receiving this news, Haley abandoned his plan and the hope of integrating community action to any significant degree.[89] In this instance, VISTA officials' adherence to a strict colorblind liberalism undercut grander goals. This challenge to national VISTA policy was an outgrowth of the most significant trend in the local War on Poverty—using community action to confront the color line and what activists commonly called "the establishment."

CHAPTER FOUR

Challenging the Establishment and the Color Line

> You have been exposed, through the community organization
> program, to racial attitudes of the sixties, an experience that has
> forever, let us hope, shattered any idyllic or sentimental
> nonsense about a happy people principally endowed by nature
> with songs, sex and a childlike simplicity.
> —Richard Haley, Director of Community Organization Program,
> February 1968

In 1966 and 1967, local organizers used community action to build political power, and they turned the social policy process into an extension of civil rights activism. Challenges to the "establishment" helped to shift bureaucratic influence from white progressives to black neighborhood leaders. At the forefront were neighborhood women who wanted better living conditions for their families, student activists who wanted to reform the American Way, and residents who wanted to control their own affairs and improve their economic status. Many of the direct challenges failed in the short run because of racial prejudice, economic inequality, bureaucratic conflict, and racial and class privilege. Some activists, however, had successes that sent renewed energy to other efforts. This chapter focuses on three episodes. One small but important expression of black power was the Target Areas Recreation Committee (TARC), which brought together activists from four predominantly black neighborhoods to focus attention on the city government's inadequate commitment to black children. The other two were efforts by VISTA volunteers and by longtime black activist Virginia Collins to push for more radical objectives and to confront police brutality. Although less successful than the recreation movement, they revealed some of the potential of and the limits to community action.

In most black areas, there were few recreation programs. Despite former mayor DeLesseps Morrison's campaign in the prior decade to equalize white and black facilities, public parks were absent or in poor condition.[1] Children had to hold ball games in vacant lots, and in one park available to black residents—the Edith Sampson Playground in the Desire area—the basketball court turned to mud in the rain. At night, public recreation space was limited largely to streets and sidewalks.[2] For several months in the spring of 1966, the Target Areas Recreation Committee, assisted by the Social Welfare Planning Council, led a fight to give black parents more control over public recreation. When those efforts largely failed, they turned to TCA to create a multimillion dollar parallel program essentially for black children. The TARC included several men but was led by two women, Oretha Castle Haley and Dorothy Mae Taylor. Haley was a formidable civil rights activist and was married to Richard Haley, the director of the SWPC's community organizing efforts. One of the busiest thoroughfares in Central City is now named in her honor. Dorothy Mae Taylor was a young mother who would emerge from the War on Poverty to become the first black woman elected to the Louisiana legislature (in 1971) and then to the New Orleans city council (in 1986).[3]

The struggle against the New Orleans Recreation Department (NORD) was not new. The Desire Area Community Council had led a revolt against NORD the previous summer, resulting in the swift creation of a temporary, TCA-administered recreation program.[4] Some of the same Desire activists continued to apply pressure to NORD in 1966 through the TARC. In April 1966, TARC leaders cautiously noted that "a strong feeling of defeatism" had disappeared.[5] By May, they had forced a meeting with city officials. Representing NORD was executive Buck Seever, who reportedly brought along a body guard for protection. Standing in for an absent Mayor Schiro was future New Orleans mayor Maurice "Moon" Landrieu, a sympathetic city councilman and an advocate for racial integration. Outside the NORD office, according to activists, a "very orderly" group of fifty target area residents held protest placards and sang songs. Inside, Dorothy Mae Taylor led a group of four women and two men who demanded the integration of all city departments, the removal of any vestiges of a "Negro division" in NORD, and the opening of all swimming pools that had been closed rather than integrated. Seever, the NORD representative, denied the existence of any segregated division and claimed that any child could attend any activity. Landrieu, the city's most visible white liberal and a dedicated reformer in the Catholic Jesuit tradition, agreed that more steps needed to be taken to ensure black participation, but he wanted the TARC to work within NORD. He also promised that ten pools would open in the summer, or he would get "on somebody's back."[6] Landrieu's assurances were of little consolation. Taylor later declared that the city representatives had failed to satisfy her group's demands.

After the disappointing meeting with city leaders, TARC intensified its protests against what they termed NORD's "conscious policy of racial discrimination." They drew upon escalating white fear of black civil disorder, warning Mayor Victor Schiro about "growing unrest of our Negro citizens through-out the entire city of New Orleans because of the consistent abuses by NORD." Tokenism would not suffice. "One integrated tennis tournament or two Negroes in a Derby contest is not integration," TARC leaders informed Mayor Schiro.[7] A few days later, energized by the apparent rebuff by City Hall, approximately two hundred target area residents, urged in part by Parent Teacher Association councils, crammed into the chambers of the City Council, an all-male, all-white entity that conducted the city's business literally under the Confederate flag. Surrounded by two male members of TARC, Dorothy Taylor read the group's demands, finishing with sharp language that would become a hallmark of her political career: "A segregated recreation program is as out of place in these times as the confederate flag that flies in these council chambers."[8]

The City Council was reluctant to act, so TARC leaders bypassed NORD. Over the summer of 1966, TARC implemented a recreation program through Total Community Action that provided jobs for 150 neighborhood residents and new recreation opportunities for an estimated 30,000 predominantly African American children. During the negotiations with TCA, Taylor wanted written commitment that the neighborhood would hire all of the employees of the recreation program except the Program Director. One TARC member claimed it was "perhaps the only program in New Orleans in which there was truly 'maximum feasible participation' both in planning and in administration."[9] Such end-runs around local government created new Soft State layers and revealed a developing pattern of black political and organizational activism that used the fear of civil disorder to encourage institutional changes. A year later, the TARC redoubled its efforts against NORD, pushing TCA for control over recreation funds to combat "mounting racial tension" and "great unrest throughout the city." In recommending more support for these recreation efforts, a leader of the Metropolitan Area Committee, a group of the city's most powerful business leaders, argued that "when a Negro mother sees a filthy child playing in the dirt, or hurt playing in the street and then takes a look at a white baseball team going to Pennsylvania, she gets to hate." By 1969, concern about the rage of black mothers led TCA to seek a nearly $1 million OEO grant for a recreation program to be administered primarily through neighborhood councils.[10]

With the 1966 summer program, the TARC demonstrated that a black citywide organization with a unified front and access to federal money and influence could successfully fight city hall. They showed that the Great Society poverty programs were shifting power to the neighborhoods, among other things providing localized control of War on Poverty jobs, which numbered over five hundred by 1968. And City Hall leaders learned a valuable lesson about getting the federal government to pay for services for black constituents.

Although TARC had successfully leveraged TCA, other activists found the TCA structure itself to be another form of the establishment, too middle class and thus too resistant to innovation. Their criticism reflected the widespread conservative charge that the War on Poverty served the self-interest of its employees and not the truly poor. In February 1966, fifteen months after TCA was created, civil rights advocate Leontine Luke severely criticized the organization's lack of maximum feasible participation. She informed TCA officials that the Ninth Ward Civic Improvement League was "disturbed" by the TCA's failure to adequately communicate with "working mothers and those who are in the most need." "Citizen participation," she complained, "means more than saying thank-you once a program is in the area."[11] A year later, according to a report by the OEO, the situation had improved. Almost two-thirds of the 114 employees of the War on Poverty in the Lower Ninth Ward were identified as poor. Most of them worked in child development (thirty low-income employees) or in recreation (twenty-three low-income employees). Of six administrators, five were from the target area.[12]

Many Central City residents agreed with Leontine Luke, complaining that employees of War on Poverty programs were getting too much of the money. "I'll tell you honey," Mrs. R. Jones, a domestic worker, explained with resignation. "The poor people who should be getting help from it ain't. Nobody but the upper dogs getting all the money." Mr. E. Valdary, a man working in real estate, offered a plan to change the War on Poverty. He proposed taking people off of welfare rolls and giving them federal poverty jobs. "That way," he explained, "they are at least doing something for the money they are receiving. Stop giving [money to] the directors and other subordinated officials and spread the money out more among the poor people."[13]

In the neighborhoods, the War on Poverty was commonly criticized for being too much like the establishment. Central City community worker Virginia Collins reported that members of the TCA's Central City Economic Opportunity Committee "seemed to have the 'those people' attitude which is very common among the Middle Class."[14] Even at a mass community rally, Collins complained, the agenda was "too structured" with too little participation from the "real poverty stricken people."[15] A Central City newspaper reported that "with a great deal of noise," the War on Poverty was exposing poverty problems, but it had done nothing profound for the poor. In short, without better representation of those it claimed to serve, the War on Poverty would not be "a radical departure from traditional welfare programs where the poor are assisted meagerly on a day-to-day or week-to-week handout basis."[16]

There was, however, one group of organizers dedicated to making community action a radical departure from traditional social policy. Some of the most aggressive, well-trained activists in New Orleans were sent by the Volunteers in Service to America, Inc. (VISTA) program. Between 1965 and 1967 almost twenty Vistas—all of them apparently were white— operated in the New Orleans target areas, staying with target area families while organizing neighborhoods, improving housing, and conducting surveys. According to the SWPC, their main job was to help residents "play effective roles in community affairs" and to raise their "self-esteem."[17]

The chief complaint among New Orleans's VISTA volunteers was TCA's and SWPC's cautious adherence to the local bases of political support for the War on Poverty. Winston Lill, director of TCA, purposely shaped the TCA board of directors to represent specific interests within the city so that they could have a better chance of getting things done. The first contingent of VISTA volunteers contained several organizers who preferred a much more confrontational approach. Disgust ran so high among those early VISTA volunteers that only four chose to complete their terms, despite a deep reluctance about leaving their new friends in the target areas. One volunteer, Vincent Bonacci, claimed that he and others had "found total dissatisfaction" in their service during part of 1965 and 1966, and they were incredulous that SWPC officials had told them that "Vista meant three social workers at no cost."[18] The volunteers were also seriously disillusioned by a philosophical conflict with leaders in the SWPC. Charles Langley, a folk singer and University of Texas philosophy major from suburban Dallas, resigned his appointment because he could no longer work with the SWPC team chief in Desire, a man with an impeccable résumé. Langley labeled him an "unimaginative administrator" who had "little idea about what community organization is" and identified "with the Desire population as little as possible." When he left, he thanked the SWPC "for the role you played in the invaluable education in community organization, egotistical professionalism and the 'Establishment's' self-defeating goodwill."[19]

These disgruntled VISTA volunteers had wanted, in Langley's words, "radical" change, and they had wanted it quickly. When it did not materialize, they blamed the "middle class leadership" in the target areas. Langley argued that SWPC's decision to work with such leaders made sense early on but had begun to undercut the mission of involving the poor.[20] Robert Warshawsky, another vocal VISTA volunteer, contended that "working with the establishment" did "more harm than good." This former student activist from North Carolina informed the SWPC that Desire residents had "no respect for agencies, private, state, or federal" because they were perceived to be "in total conflict" with their own "needs, desires, and aspirations."[21] In his estimation the War on Poverty was continuing traditional American social policy that served the political interests of the middle class instead of the real needs of the poor.[22]

This conflict between the TCA-SWPC leadership and the more radical Vistas reflected differing strategies for increasing the power of low-income residents. TCA sought established powers to build coalitions that could endure political attacks. The Vistas dismissed that tactic as propping up a corrupted social order. The white Vistas preferred to build the trust of black target area residents through close contact and street-level coalitions. The SWPC and TCA did not officially discourage radicalism. In instances involving the civil liberties of employees, the SWPC board (and then the TCA board after December 31, 1967) followed a policy that allowed neighborhood workers to participate in potentially controversial incidents such as "selective buying campaigns" as long as they were not illegal and met OEO guidelines.[23] Three examples illustrate the dilemmas that aggressive organizers presented to the SWPC-TCA leadership and vice versa.

Robert Warshawsky, a 1966 VISTA volunteer in Desire, revealed the mammoth task faced by organizers who tried to build a movement person by person, especially when custom and local law enforcement were against it. He focused his efforts on intense social interaction, dedicating many hours to what he called "working in the bars." After several unsuccessful attempts to organize meetings in his first month, he finally convinced several Desire residents to hold an informal meeting. The group bought a bottle of wine and then strolled around the housing project "drinking wine in the rain." Making their way to another bar, the burgeoning activists "talked with some other cats." The next day Warshawsky continued to build friendships by playing a "fast ball" game with project residents, but he claimed that New Orleans police officers came by and hassled him.[24] Warshawsky continued trying to coalition-build in this manner for another three months until he resigned in frustration. He told his superiors that he could not "organize in the Desire Area," and that it was "wrong that I should have been there in the first place."[25] His strategy was admirable. He forced residents to interact on equal footing with a college-educated white male doing the work of the white progressive civic leadership. Unfortunately, there were not enough people like him to build coalitions among the poor, and if his reports are to be believed, too many bureaucrats willing to sanction his loose style of organizing.

Warshawsky claimed that the SWPC forced policy onto the neighborhoods and left neighborhood residents "dismayed and bewildered" by keeping them out of the policy-making process. He also claimed that the SWPC leaders curtailed his activities because they believed that ideas from the neighborhood were "too extreme." He was particularly disgruntled when they denied his proposal to rent a house near the Desire project where he could serve drinks to and socialize with neighborhood people. The agency, he grumbled, was ensuring that the War on Poverty would perpetuate "our liberal ways, that of mediocrity."[26] Nevertheless, Warshawsky remained in New Orleans to attend the Tulane University School of Social Work. Ironically, a year later the SWPC rehired him as a community worker in Central City, earning $4,800 a year (approximately $26,000 in 2003 dollars) at twenty-three years of age.[27]

Two of Warshawsky's VISTA colleagues, Peter Friedberg and Gary Sledge, brought to light another dilemma in the Community Action Program: What role should the community worker play during controversial incidents? In the summer of 1966, the SWPC leadership was particularly concerned that a "major public confrontation" would erupt between neighborhood residents and the police. SWPC president Philip James noted a "disturbing sense of frustration in the community." In June, Friedberg and Sledge sought a confrontation over the issue of police brutality. In response, the SWPC consented to have several staff members put under the surveillance of the Federal Bureau of Investigation and the New Orleans Police Department.[28]

Fear of racial disorder in the summer of 1966 was prevalent nationwide. Outbreaks occurred at least forty-three times in U.S. cities, with the most intense occurring in Los Angeles, Chicago, and Cleveland. The bad relationship between police departments and the black community was the most frequently cited cause. An incident in New Orleans on June 11 demonstrated the new role for the War on Poverty in expanding the policing power of the government to black areas. On this Saturday night in Central City, about one hundred residents and ten policemen gathered around an automobile accident on Third Street near the Garden District. Supposedly, as the crowd grew, a black man and his wife tried to cross the street to get to their car to go home, but police officers asked them to stop. The couple kept going. According to several witnesses, when an officer grabbed the man's shirt, the man attempted to remove the officer's hands. At that point two other officers entered the scuffle and beat him with their clubs. They then pushed him into a police car, shoving his wife aside.[29]

The next day, Freidberg, Sledge, and several members of the Central City Economic Opportunity Committee organized a meeting to take action and distribute a controversial flyer they had produced. The SWPC leadership was not happy. Afraid that the flyer could encourage a riot, the SWPC censured the pair and forced them to shelve the brochure. The Central City team chief Allie Mae Williams, who was also the wife of a prominent minister and had been a long-time supervisor at the New Orleans Health Department, described the young men as "very headstrong" and correctly predicted that they would "launch out on their own." Unable to pass out their flyer, the men relied on word-of-mouth publicity and attracted thirty-two residents to a meeting at the People's Methodist Community Center (HANO refused them access to a public housing center). In response, the SWPC brought in Richard Haley, who used his expertise to move the meeting toward productive action. Like the Vistas, he wanted to use the incident to stir activism city-wide, but in a less inflammatory manner. At this initial meeting, Central City residents decided to push harder to increase the number of racially integrated police patrols and to require more education for officers and to establish a civilian review board. These suggestions won out over others that ranged from "petitions to marches to 'jacking up a couple of cops.' "[30]

The end of the story for Sledge and Friedberg sent a repressive message to other would-be radical volunteers. The NOPD watched the two Vistas closely and concluded they were communist sympathizers or "at least trouble-makers." Special agents with the Federal Bureau of Investigation warned Central City team chief Allie Mae Williams that "if these boys keep up, they will jeopardize the whole Poverty Program."[31] Under pressure from law enforcement, the SWPC had them transferred away from New Orleans. A year later, the OEO ruled that community workers employed by OEO could plan and participate in direct action demonstrations as long as those demonstrations were "lawful."

Virginia Collins, a fifty-one-year-old Central City community worker, was involved in another sticky administrative issue that developed out of the June police brutality protest. Before joining the SWPC in 1965, she had been a follower of Marcus Garvey and the Universal Negro Improvement Association, a civil rights activist, president of the McDonogh No. 35 High School Parent Teacher Association, and a community worker with the Voter Education and Registration Project. In 1962, she organized three hundred students as part of the Youth Voter Crusader Corps who tried to get more local black residents registered to vote.[32] Most troubling for the local establishment, she also belonged to the board of the controversial Southern Conference Education Fund (SCEF), a civil rights organization that had been branded a communist front organization by the State of Louisiana's Joint Legislative Committee on Un-American Activities (LUAC). Collins had also been active in organizing protests of the Vietnam War and had refused to tone down her rhetoric in support of black liberation and for socialism. Also, her son, Walter Collins, refused to obey his draft board and fought induction into the military.

Virginia Collins began working for the War on Poverty in December 1965, but on June 15, 1966, a few days after the Sledge-Friedberg police brutality protest, the SWPC fired her for "an accumulation of negative factors." As former Louisiana governor "Uncle" Earl Long might have said, her dismissal undoubtedly resulted from her "political halitosis."[33] As a result of her radical activism, Collins became a target of one of the most intense assaults upon the War on Poverty in Louisiana. The LUAC engaged in a widely publicized quest to purge Collins and two other supposedly "communist" organizers, two workers for the Community Action Program in southwest Louisiana.[34] The director of the state's OEO office, Champ Baker, claimed that he had New Orleans's officials terminate her because she was "associated with communists." Her confrontational style—one SWPC evaluation described her as "radical without Oretha's [Castle Haley] finesse"—had made her a liability. Collins unsuccessfully appealed her dismissal well into 1967. She then became a leader in an even more radical cause. In September 1969, she was the regional president of the Republic of New Africa, a group that demanded a new black nation be carved out of land in the American South. A year after that, in November 1970, her son Walter Collins, an activist for the Southern Conference Education Fund, was arrested for draft evasion after exhausting his appeals to avoid the draft. He defended his evasion because there were no black members of his draft board and four of the five members lived outside New Orleans. The U.S. Supreme Court denied his appeal.[35]

Despite the fact the SWPC cited inadequate reporting as a major flaw in Collins's work, the reports she wrote during 1966 show a committed community worker with the interests of the poor and the dispossessed as her primary mission. Her job in Central City entailed three interrelated tasks—publicizing and promoting meetings, making community contacts, and organizing program planning meetings—revolving around establishing personal connections with civic-minded residents. This time in the community showed Collins what residents wanted most—stability and a sense of belonging. According to Collins, her contacts—most of them female—sought programs that could improve healthcare, housing, credit, streets, juvenile delinquency, and out-of-wedlock births. On a more controversial level, they pushed for planned parenthood services, voter registration, family counseling, school truancy programs, and better legal representation for youth under arrest. At the top of the list was a "crying need" for child care for working mothers. Speaking to the larger mission to alleviate alienation, Collins believed that day care programs would help "to awaken those with large numbers of children to the realization that someone cares enough to help them help themselves."[36]

Besides helping residents identify problems, she tried to create politically active organizations and coordinate political rallies. She organized "block captains" who got out the word about community meetings. Collins organized a "Mammoth Rally" in April 1966 that, she claimed, allowed the poor to express "the needs of their community as seen through their eyes—which may present quite a different perspective of the problems of poverty than the one which is seen by those who are on the outside looking in." That massive gathering was part political rally, part pep rally, and part carnival. "The time is now for Central City," announced a truck rolling through the neighborhoods. "You can be heard. Your voice is your key. Break the chains of Poverty. Come to the Mammoth Rally on the War on Poverty." In a nod to local traditions, organizers promised that there would be bands, parades, and cash prizes.[37]

Collins's vision for political organization went beyond carnival tactics, however. One month before her dismissal, she organized what she called a "voter-education" meeting to build on the momentum of the rally. Participants pushed for the creation of "machinery" comprised of volunteers and War on Poverty workers. To create the widest participation, she advised local War on Poverty administrators to "make every effort to involve all churches, all Negro businesses, bar rooms, barbershops, beauty salons, etc., within the target area." She wanted business owners to support the creation of "Voter Registration Committees," and for churches to hold registration classes. Her plan reflected some of the structure of the city's successful white political machines of former Mayor DeLesseps S. "Chep" Morrison and current Mayor Victor Hugo Schiro. She wanted a hierarchy of block workers, zone workers, precinct captains, ward captains, church coordinators, and business coordinators.[38] But Virginia Collins would not see her vision through.

The actions of the aggressive VISTA volunteers and of organizers like Collins did not lead to a radicalized antipoverty bureaucracy, but they did show neighborhood leaders the value of controlling the bureaucratic machinery behind programs, whether formally or informally. Clark Corliss, the director of the Social Welfare Planning Council, got the message. "We can not and must not attempt to control neighborhood actions," he advised. "The moment our staff loses its identification with neighborhood residents, as seen by neighborhood people, it has destroyed its possible effectiveness." By 1967, however, leaders of the national Office of Economic Opportunity realized that a change in leadership was needed.[39] All along, the intent of the SWPC had been to turn over the administration of the Neighborhood Development Program to target area leaders.

The rapid growth of black influence and neighborhood activism, however, speeded that transfer. The end of SWPC's control began in May 1967 when the OEO recommended that TCA take over all community organization and transfer all SWPC coordinators to the new neighborhood-controlled structure. The SWPC leadership accepted the decision, but it tried unsuccessfully to stretch the transfer out over a longer period of time.[40]

In 1967, during the protracted negotiations about control over community action, participants at all levels realized that the governing boards were too disconnected from the citizens in the neighborhoods. In early November 1967, the TCA board of directors voted to take control away from SWPC and eventually to turn community organizing over to neighborhood councils. Beginning January 1, 1968, TCA took over all community organization efforts, absorbing SWPC's existing neighborhood staffers. A year later, the neighborhood committees took outright control, and a year after that, in 1970, the War on Poverty neighborhood councils took charge of the management of TCA altogether. Clark Corliss recognized the attempts to adhere to maximum feasible participation, affirming that "the principles of citizen participation, particularly at the neighborhood level, have proven to be sound." Signing off with a bit of melancholy, Corliss expressed the importance of the Great Society in his career and declared that it had given him "more personal satisfaction than anything else attempted in over thirty years of social work practice."[41]

In the end, the boards governing the local War on Poverty gave up on creating racial balance in community action, and by implication so did the national OEO. Energetic activists, Bible-centered inclusion rationales, and passionate protests by mothers and fathers could not overcome the fact that a vast majority of poor whites declined to interact in a politically meaningful way with black organizers or residents. That was not unexpected. A bigger problem was that the color line thwarted even the efforts of those who were eager to get along. The overwhelmingly white, wealthy, and highly educated members of the SWPC often took courageous risks to be involved in community action and the War on Poverty, but they were unable to satisfy the demands rising from the streets. Gary Lloyd, professor of social work at Tulane University, charged that the influence over the SWPC had been "notoriously white, middle class or elite" and overly susceptible to "the power structure of the community."[42] As the experiences of several VISTA volunteers and Virginia Collins revealed, the SWPC's board was reluctant to openly challenge the city's racial customs. Some activists claimed they were hostages of their own cultural expectations and class values.

On January 4, 1968, Richard Haley officially ended the SWPC role when he took the records of SWPC's Neighborhood Development Program to TCA.[43] That the former southern director for the Congress of Racial Equality (CORE) was overseeing the transfer of a multi-million dollar enterprise from a white-dominated agency to one increasingly controlled by the black community was evidence of a historic shift. Haley was eminently qualified to preside over the transfer. His home was New Orleans and he knew it well. Perhaps as clearly as anyone in the city, he understood the divisions between white civic altruists and poor blacks.

Shortly after moving to TCA, in a powerful assessment of New Orleans's racial divisions, Haley assured the mostly white SWPC board members that their involvement in community organization had helped to develop "a direct line to the ghetto." [44] He proudly maintained that target area residents had not been on a "one-way street" where War on Poverty bureaucrats simply handed down instructions. Instead, white civic leaders had "established firm, direct connection with a mass of people previously invisible." Haley advised them to keep believing that the poor were "a part of that mystic body called the 'Power structure.'" Most important to Haley, the War on Poverty had exposed the SWPC "to racial attitudes of the sixties, an experience that has forever, let us hope, shattered any idyllic or sentimental nonsense about a happy people principally endowed by nature with songs, sex and a childlike simplicity."[45] Then he informed these civic altruists that "this board room, your comfortable office, your lily-white Lake Vista—these are one and the same: insulation, not involvement." He condemned them for limiting their activities mostly to listening. "By that very symbolic act, repeated hundreds of times by thousands of boards across the country," he added with an impassioned and ironic flourish, "you yourselves created Black Power—and I want to thank you." He chastised them for being unable to step over the cultural lines laid down by their peers. He accused them of not knowing the people and implied that, deep down, they probably did not want to really know them. According to Haley's reasoning, Black Power was a product of segregation, but not simply the virulent kind. It was also a product of segregation unwittingly endorsed by white liberals who had helped to solidify the sense of alienation that they were trying to eliminate.[46]

Haley offered the SWPC board powerful advice. He pleaded with them to maintain personal relationships with target-area residents in order to reduce the friction of race and class. They needed to do this "to learn the unique nature—and believe me, it is unique—of these seventh generation strangers. Do it to get a first-hand picture of the impact of social work and workers; to get some fresh new indigenous ideas on social planning; to get some inkling of the tension in that community, of its hostility to you." His parting words complimented the community organization effort for identifying the problems, but emphasized the need for cross-class, bi-racial exchange. "The neighborhood residents need your help," he offered, "and you'd better believe it—you certainly need theirs."[47]

Conclusion: Assessing Community Action

Although Richard Haley frankly found fault with white civic leaders, he also believed that community action had been beneficial. Plenty of his white contemporaries, however, argued differently. Predictably, many local segregationists found community action to be an example of liberal excess that sacrificed local authority in the interests of an expensive, multiracial outside agenda. They believed the Community Action Program (and the Great Society) hurt local people, especially whites, and rewarded people who were not needy, especially the bureaucrats who answered to federal as well as local bosses. A devotee of Senator Russell Long—a politician who led the congressional effort to enact punitive measures in the federal Aid to Families with Dependent Children program—was willing to fight another Civil War if it would bring an end to the War on Poverty.[48] One constituent of moderate Congressman Hale Boggs charged that the Office of Economic Opportunity was "a subversive outfit riddled with revolutionaries, communists, beatniks, hippies, etc., ad nauseum, who are doing their utmost to undermine the whole American system."[49] A citizen from northern Louisiana claimed that the War on Poverty was designed "to make jobs for a few bureaucrats with the pretense of helping the poor and poverty stricken masses."[50] An Acadian lady, who claimed to be a former employee of the War on Poverty, explained that the antipoverty fight was the "biggest waste I've ever seen." The "poor" were "being cheated," she cried, "and the taxpayer robbed."[51] Senator Long replied to a flood of similar complaints with a form letter in which he agreed that there were "many abuses and substantial waste in the poverty program." It was "extravagant and poorly administered," and "most of its projects have been of little or no value." Too much of it, he charged, aided "persons and groups who should not be helped."[52] In 1967 during a heated political fight over funding for the War on Poverty, New Orleans's arch-segregationist Congressman F. Edward Hébert promised to vote "millions for guns, but not a cent for butter . . . a tax raise for the war—yes; a tax raise to promote the fraudulent Poverty Program—No."[53]

Community action was not a failure despite criticism from people like Eddie Hébert and Russell Long. Its influence was too widespread to dismiss it so easily. In the first three years, progress combined with uncertainty. Liberal leaders thought community action was a positive stride forward. Beneficiaries liked their new power and status and saw the limited success as an essential first step. Of course, antipoverty bureaucrats negotiated precarious political terrain. They had to balance the need for support from moderate white civic and business leaders with the escalating assertiveness of residents in the target areas. But their caution was not necessarily counterproductive. The timidity may have allowed the leadership of the antipoverty movement to remain in liberal hands instead of being seized by less progressive interests. In 1967, Congress changed the rules governing community action programs to facilitate control by City Hall. Nationally, mayors had more authority to take over community action agencies, but they did so rarely. According to one study, of 900 community action agencies, only 48 were taken over by mayors' offices. Robert Levine, a researcher for OEO, claimed that the agencies often were too unwieldy for mayors to want control of them. In New Orleans, a more radical early organizing effort may have forced Mayor Victor Schiro to exercise more control and rein in antipoverty activists.[54] Instead, TCA's and SWPC's activities remained in cautious liberal hands.

Many of the early problems with maximum feasible participation were not the fault of SWPC or TCA. Low participation percentages were common nationwide, and TCA's effort brought out more people in a sustained enterprise than any previous local civil rights organizing efforts. The tendency of the more fortunate to participate more fully was a reflection of the lives of the poor. More money and stability meant one had more time to contribute. The participation that did occur was an important step in local leadership development and served as a nexus of liberal politics. In the fifteen-year period after 1964, War on Poverty programs counted among their former employees or board members many dozen influential business people and politicians, including at least nine state representatives or senators, four city council members, and four mayors (three of New Orleans). Total Community Action's own list of alumni— defined by them as people "affiliated" with TCA for at least ninety days— who later achieved positions of "leadership" ran to over two hundred people. TCA leaders in 1984 did not exaggerate when they claimed that TCA's former employees comprised a " 'who's who' of the City of New Orleans" [see Appendix 4]. Some of those leaders were already wealthy and powerful and would likely have continued their roles regardless of TCA and the War on Poverty, but TCA did offer opportunities for many neighborhood leaders who would have otherwise been sidelined.[55]

The initial years of community action in New Orleans raise questions about the confusing history of the CAP at large. Despite a remarkable amount of scholarly interest in it, especially from social scientists in the 1960s and 1970s, there is little clarity about what the program was supposed to do, what it did, or what it has meant for American history. Contemporary opinions of the program were mixed. Conservatives, particularly racial conservatives, saw community action as a way to help rabble-rousing radicals undermine American democracy, foment riots, finance race-mixing, and foster communism. Office of Economic Opportunity policymakers saw it as a way to streamline social services and give more power to the people. Many activists also saw it as an opportunity to build power, while others saw it as the federal government co-opting the civil rights movement and curbing the potential for radical social change.[56] Lyndon Johnson liked that it shifted resources to local people, but he may not have understood the full implications of what policymakers were developing. He was especially uncomfortable when it challenged friendly Democratic regimes. Shortly after its creation, he began to see it as a political liability. "It's not worth it," he declared to budget advisors in an August 1965 Oval Office conversation. "I think somebody ought to veto these damn fool community action [programs]," he continued with increasing agitation, "Don't you put any money into community action. Just cut it down. You hear that? Just *cut that down.*"[57]

Most Community Action Program assessments focus on the period between 1964 and 1967 and emphasize controversial episodes in a few cities where local activists used the program to challenge existing urban political regimes. The problem these challenges posed was resolved with the passage of the Green Amendment to the Economic Opportunity Act in late 1967. Proposed by Congresswoman Edith Green of Oregon, the legislation gave local governments the option to take over community action, although few did so. The legislation bolstered congressional support for the OEO and led to a funding boost of over $100 million, but it also curtailed radical challenges to existing political machines.[58]

Assessment of community action's role should take into account the historic struggle for black power and community development, the migration of capital, and the population shift away from cities. Viewed from this perspective, the years of community action become less about teeth-gnashing among established urban politicians and new challengers and more about a historic reaction to deep social and economic problems. The period from late 1964 to early 1968 was not the high-point of community action, but merely another formative moment in the modern American struggle over race, poverty, and democratic values. After all, by the late 1960s, there were almost one thousand Community Action Agencies in operation. By 1999, the U.S. Department of Health and Human Services reported over three thousand in operation, with one agency in 96 percent of all U.S. counties—albeit in fairly benign service delivery roles.[59]

Determining the impact of the War on Poverty depends on one's interpretation of the subtleties of political change, especially when considering the relationship of the Community Action Program and the civil rights movement. The CAP in New Orleans built on local movements for black equality. Clearly, the War on Poverty siphoned off many activists from established civil rights organizations, and bureaucratic structures stifled many impulses from the street. The events in New Orleans affirm that the CAP hired away good organizers and also hampered some of their efforts, but viewed against larger forces propelling the movement after 1964 and 1965, a strong argument can be made that the CAP actually provided long-term structure to the fight for equality and access. Where would activists have been able to go after 1965? From where would the funding have come? Could the local CORE chapter have expanded its presence considering the turmoil of 1962 when its membership split apart over the participation of white organizers?[60] New Orleans's situation suggests that the War on Poverty likely furthered the movement's deeper agenda for jobs and opportunity and power by injecting those activists into the Great Society framework. Without those voices, professional social workers would likely have dictated the direction of community action and left political mobilization with fewer structures and far less funding.

Most of the neighborhood organizers in New Orleans had not been civil rights leaders, but many of those who led those organizers were. Four vital members of the CORE became major leaders in the local War on Poverty. Perhaps the most important was Richard Haley as director of the organizing effort. His wife, Oretha Castle Haley, served as a community development worker and led the target area movement to reform children's recreation. Isaac "Ike" Reynolds was the team chief for the Lower Ninth Ward, and Doris Jean Castle, sister of Oretha Castle Haley and a well-known activist, was an important community organizer in Central City (and later in Monroe, Louisiana). Mateo Suarez served as a powerful lobbyist for more aggressive tactics and later was a community worker with the War on Poverty. Although less involved with TCA, Jerome Smith, a legendary activist in the southern freedom movement, did establish a long-running youth program in 1971 in the Tremé area known as Tambourine and Fan.[61]

The War on Poverty helped to broaden the methods of the civil rights movement and expand the base of active participants. The Community Action Program encouraged the less-bold to take to the streets, or at least to push their leaders for better streets. Total Community Action and the Social Welfare Planning Council gave essential cover and insulation for black leaders to push for civic reform without the threat of white backlash, and in some cases in the later 1960s and 1970s this actually encouraged more radicalism and pushed state and local governments to provide even more services. Political shelter through the War on Poverty provided one of the major, and often overlooked, contributions of the Great Society to the freedom movement: it limited the impact of white retribution in the South. White violence, both legal and extralegal, was shifted to the political periphery for a number of reasons, but perhaps the major reason was the fact that African Americans had the moral and political power not to have to endure it. Although the War on Poverty reduced the thunder of the civil rights movement—partly because it facilitated the entry of less radical, but often more powerful bureaucratic leaders—the efforts that spun outward from federal social welfare legislation did bring some of the economic goals of that movement closer to reality, at least for some. Community action created institutions capable of a longer-lasting, if less bold, struggle for African American inclusion.

Through Total Community Action, civil rights and neighborhood leaders got in on the ground floor of an unprecedented state-building effort. In 1969 alone, the Office of Economic Opportunity brought $11 million to New Orleans (equivalent to nearly $60 million in 2006 spending), and the CAP structure distributed $5.2 million of it.[62] To secure control over that growing state apparatus for low-income neighborhoods, local Great Society leaders had begun cultivating a liberal political base. When conservative white leaders balked at supporting Total Community Action in 1964 and 1965, they left an important vehicle available for racial liberals and pro-growth progressives. TCA mediated between demands from the streets and rules from the federal government and encouraged the development of bureaucratic expertise and organizational experience among black and poor leaders who previously had been shunted to the public margins. The War on Poverty ensured that local control over federal influence went through political institutions whose ultimate authority lay in the neighborhoods, instead of through entities controlled by racially and fiscally conservative whites. Working through the War on Poverty, community organizers experimented with political ideas and organizing techniques that would help to define black participation in the emerging biracial political world. Those programs, however, did not overcome the problems of race. In New Orleans, the War on Poverty became a means of coping with the legacies of segregation and alienation. Intellectually, it became an exercise in making better and happier citizens.

CHAPTER FIVE

Making Better and Happier Citizens

> Until the citizens in the neighborhood are better and happier
> citizens, we cannot have a better state or nation or world.
> —Kingsley House, New Orleans, May 1965

While community action was helping to build structures for black political inclusion after Jim Crow, an equally important question was being
worked out at an intellectual level: *Why* should black residents be included as full citizens? The answer, judging from the ideas of local progressives, was that alienated and segregated people reduced productivity, constrained consumption, and threatened tranquility.[1] To discourage
disorder and expand the economy, local progressives pushed for black
psychological transformation and civic assimilation, focusing arguments
for inclusion on improving the way black citizens learned, worked, purchased, and, most important, believed in themselves. Self-esteem and
self-realization took on key economic and political functions. As the administrators of Kingsley House explained, "Until the citizens in the neighborhood are better and happier citizens, we cannot have a better state or
nation or world."[2] Sister Kathleen M. Hensgen, a Head Start administrator in Louisiana, explained the economic and psychological value of her
program to an audience of business leaders. "In 1967," she acknowledged,
"there is a dream to spend $1.7 million to help people find themselves
and to be somebody." Great Society money would help people find "an

identity within themselves that they had never possessed before" and help them "take their place" in society.[3] In the aftermath of the Voting Rights Act, local citizens did not have to pass tests to register to vote, but they still had to fulfill plenty of other requirements if they wanted to take their place at the mythical American table. In the local dialogue about those requirements, one theme seemed to gain widespread acceptance: One did not merely receive full citizenship, but one earned it by being a stable, productive contributor to the economy and the society.

Viewed in retrospect, the process of racial inclusion involved applying psychological solutions to political problems. The objective common to each of the early War on Poverty programs was to transform the identity of the poor. Great Society advocates looked first to the individual in trying to overcome what were ultimately the institutional legacies of segregation—including low wages, union discrimination, inadequate city services, ineffective public schools, discriminatory credit practices, an almost exclusively white and wealthy corporate culture, restricted access to higher learning and skills development, and racialized housing opportunities. During the middle 1960s, many reformers saw that the best way to remake the ghetto was from the inside out, one American at a time. At a time when southerners were trying to figure out how they were going to live without Jim Crow, the War on Poverty was a grand experiment in psychological policymaking and civic redefinition.

The experiment was so grand because so many thought the problem of alienation was so deep. "The poor are not like everyone else," wrote Michael Harrington, a socialist intellectual whose book *The Other America* refocused attention on American poverty. "They are a different kind of people. They think and feel differently; they look upon a different America than the middle class looks upon." The U.S. Labor Department's August 1965 Moynihan Report, named after principal author Daniel Patrick Moynihan, contended that the poor, especially the black poor, were caught in a "tangle of pathology" and blamed much of that tangling on the disintegration of the black family. Critics excoriated Moynihan for blaming the victim and for misguidedly blaming the black family, but in retrospect, many of the report's assumptions were not out of the mainstream and parroted thinking about poverty by theorists and by people on the street.[4] Reverend Morris A. Edwards, a black Baptist minister from New Orleans's Desire area, added a variation of that sentiment. The poor "can climb the ladder," he predicted. "They can be like other people."[5] Similarly, a community action-sponsored group of teens in the Desire area, the Students for Human Advancement and Community (SHAC), explained that "lack of one's identity usually results in a person not adequately knowing his role in our society which can further lead to an inability to relate to the American way of life."[6] As Jim Crow was torn down, the local War on Poverty attempted to make the black poor more like other people, but as some of their responses showed, many of the poor and alienated thought they were already like other people. In fact, a growing number of them thought that the problem was not with them or their minds, but with the systems that ruled them. On the streets of New Orleans, there was a profound desire to establish what the Reverend Dr. Martin Luther King Jr. called a sense of "your worth and your own somebodiness."[7] Some target-area residents sought "somebodiness" in ways preferred by white progressives—by producing, consuming, and feeling better about themselves in orderly fashion—but a growing number grew impatient and began experimenting with the power of disorder.

The Threat of Alienation and Disorder

One prominent theme in local progressive thinking was the desire to keep individuals from abandoning the community. Of special concern were black individuals who had few ties to key civic institutions, and, it was feared, inadequate self-awareness and personal pride to be integrated into the mainstream. Reflecting trends in the social sciences and in popular opinion, local progressives characterized poverty, and by extension segregation, as a problem of the mind rather than the economy. Circumscribing the much-feared Karl Marx, their thinking reflected the influences of thinkers such as Sigmund Freud, Erik Erikson, Oscar Lewis, and John Dewey. To close the gap between a life of poverty and the American Good Life, local leaders searched for ways to assimilate supposedly alienated area residents.

The appeal of the War on Poverty lay more in its capacity to diminish the problems that the poor posed for the rest of the community than in actually solving the problems of the poor. As researchers for Total Community Action explained, "While killer diseases may get started among lower-income families, epidemics . . . are no respectors [sic] of zoning ordinances or income levels."[8] While those TCA researchers were specifically concerned about diseases of the body, others were more focused on pathologies of the mind. The alienation of the poor frightened Maurice Anderson, chairman of the Social Welfare Planning Council's Youth Committee and one-time president of the SWPC Board of Directors. He worried about "disenfranchised individuals, condemned to personal dissatisfaction, who do not have a stake in our society as full-fledged, functioning citizens." Those citizens posed "not only an economic loss and burden, but also a physical danger to our society. . . . Large numbers of alienated persons . . . trapped in poverty for lack of education, without a stake in society and without a sense of belonging," he warned, "can obviously jeopardize the welfare and future of our community and the physical safety of the population."[9]

The concern for the minds of the poor was not merely a product of fears within the white professional class, but also was an outgrowth of widespread thinking that prized individualism in the process of civic inclusion. Local progressives drew heavily from the traditional liberal American ideal of the individual as an independent, hard-working, intelligent, and logical being whose capacity to contribute to society sustained public life.[10] This vision simultaneously held that the community had to nurture all of its individuals. Many of the city's antipoverty administrators were not merely participating in an age-old paternalism. They were tied into this worldview by their training. Many had backgrounds in therapeutic social work and were healers trained to diagnose and treat individual problems.[11] These leaders were also operating in an intellectual context framed by the civil rights movement and the Cold War that left little room, either in imagination or in action, to assault the structure of America's political economy. In this regard, as in so many other areas, the antipoverty movement followed the path cleared by the civil rights movement.[12]

Two specific influences on the thinking of local progressives stand out. One was the culture-of-poverty theory that grew out of anthropological studies of the 1930s and 1940s, but is most closely associated with 1960s studies by the anthropologist Oscar Lewis. The theory was reflected in Michael Harrington's work and by many of the shapers of the Economic Opportunity Act. Lewis's study of a poor family living in Mexico City argued that their poverty stemmed from cultural determinants passed down from their ancestors. This culture of poverty actually provided stability in their lives.[13] A second influence was the pronounced national fixation on psychological therapy. Programmatic emphasis on the therapeutic was not original to the War on Poverty. Social Security Amendments in 1956 pushed the Aid to Dependent Children program toward a more rehabilitative mission. Ten years later, the prevalence of therapeutic thought at almost all levels of New Orleans's early Great Society suggests that the shift to rehabilitation ran deeper than a mere policy initiative and reflected popular understandings of poverty and disorder.[14]

Local examples of both influences abound, but two documents offer particularly good illustrations. One was an evaluation of an adult literacy program by a social science student at the predominantly black Southern University at New Orleans (SUNO). The other was an Office of Economic Opportunity (OEO) grant proposal by the New Orleans branch of the National Association of Collegiate Women (NACW). In her assessment of the adult literacy program known as Operation Upgrade, Mary Balthazar of SUNO argued that the program's value was in preventing poverty from warping one's personality. Adult illiterates lacked "dignity" and were not able to "represent themselves." They were "forgotten people who have been driven like animals into the slums . . . unable to make their silent cries heard because of their inability to verbalize their desires, their frustrations, and their fears in a hostile world." They had "bruised" souls, "naked" minds, and hearts "hungry for kindness and recognition." Endorsing theories about the culture of poverty and the debilitating impact of exclusion, she explained that "offsprings [sic] become trapped in the ongoing vicious circle, become virtual slaves to a society which isolates them in an alien world outside the mainstream of life."[15]

The NACW grant proposal described the black, single mother as the most alienated. In clinician's language, they deemed her a "victim" and a "social problem" who was "too often unproductive, unacceptable and a social outcast from the mainstream of our modern day society." Society had deformed her personality and her capacity to fit in; her distorted sense of self came from the "triple jeopardy" of being black, poor, and socially deviant. She suffered from "racial bias" and, most debilitating in postwar America, from "insufficient class mobility." That triple jeopardy had limited her opportunities and had made her "ill-prepared to participate productively in an affluent society—let alone be acceptable to the masses." The NACW offered a textbook analysis of these single mothers as lacking "motivations, expectations, and abilities because of all-ready defective family, peer group, cultural and sub-cultural preparation to fulfill acceptable adult or pre-adult roles in this society."[16]

A broad assortment of other social welfare professionals and activists endorsed the belief that racial prejudice and poverty had made the poor (again, particularly the black poor) different from the rest of society. The director of the New Orleans Department of Welfare explained to the OEO that the poor were "sullen, suspicious, ignorant, and resentful" people who lived in a "constant state of crisis" and were rarely able to keep up "even the minimum standards expected by the larger cultural group in hygiene, health-care, child rearing and education."[17] According to the SWPC, a group whose leaders worried about the dangers of stigmatizing the poor, New Orleans's target-area residents "feel forgotten, bitter and helpless." Many residents had "given up—they no longer believe life could be better."[18] A community organization supervisor for Kingsley House stated that "feelings of isolation, hopelessness and defensiveness" pervaded the residents of public housing in his area.[19] Proponents of the Volunteers in Service to America (VISTA) program believed that desolation and racial segregation in the target areas had encouraged "defeatist attitudes," "lack of 'self-esteem,'" and "hostility toward society, its representatives and spokesmen."[20] One social worker saw "a climate of hostility and distrust on the part of residents toward the wider community and the representatives of its institutions and agencies." In one example, one worker reported that "adults systematically drill into the minds of their children not to trust 'others—they are only out to harm you.'"[21] Similarly, the coordinator of the Irish Channel Neighborhood Development Center contended that poverty had a "demeaning effect on human character." Poverty tended to make the poor "either thoughtlessly aggressive or submissively passive."[22] The local Urban League explained that historical neglect from city government had caused many residents to feel "rejection, suspicion and isolation."[23]

Administrators argued that solutions to poverty and alienation called for a better-organized community, a better-integrated individual, and a better-realized self. Clark Corliss, the SWPC director, explained the vital need to treat the psyche of the poor in order to preserve social stability. He wanted to relieve "personality stresses" that created "maladaptive coping mechanisms."[24] The "poverty stricken for some time often feels defeated. He may withdraw from normal contacts, or become ill, or take to flight, or turn to alcohol or narcotics or steal or do any one of the many things defeated people do to protect the little ego they have left. From a therapeutic standpoint, the problem then is one of helping to restore self-respect."[25] The SWPC planned to provide services to "create a social climate more conducive to better individual and group functioning." Corliss envisioned community organizing as a way to "reorient perceptions, attitudes and behaviors."[26] Above all, according to Corliss, the SWPC would "instill confidence." They wanted citizen participation in their programs to result in "better self-images" in addition to material and health benefits.[27] A Kingsley House organizer provided his interpretation of the objectives of the antipoverty movement. Programs needed to help target area residents "maintain and build upon an attitude of self-respect and independence, while at the same time, demonstrating that they are members of this community and do have a role to play and a responsibility."[28] The NACW wanted to use their program for unmarried mothers to contribute to "the more productive and economic aspects of their communities." The collegiate women hoped that "perhaps a few attitudes might be changed in the process from negative and punative [sic] to positive and constructive."[29]

Although compassion motivated many depictions of the poor as civic risks, they constructed a sense that exclusion had turned the poor, especially the African American poor, into ineffective Americans who were, perhaps, unworthy of the full benefits of American life. This "politics of personal despair" forced the War on Poverty—and the broader inclusion struggle—to highlight the dangers of desperation. Ironically in an age of optimism, much of the Great Society's political appeal ultimately lay in pessimism. The participation of the poor was essential for Great Society liberalism in New Orleans, but, ironically, the inclusion tactics of local liberals cast the poor as people who might not ever be like other people.

Earning Citizenship through Pride and Productivity

Productivity and economic growth were perhaps the most powerful arguments for making better and happier citizens. "Hopefully," mused Norman Francis, a prominent black leader who was the executive vice president of the historically black Xavier University and close friend of Moon Landrieu, "the South is beginning to wake up and harness its last untapped natural resource—a human one—the Negro man."[30] In harsher language, Louisiana congressman Gillis Long, a distant cousin of Huey and Earl Long, argued that "Negroes are certainly not the only poor, but they are the most costly . . . in terms of crime[,] disease, illiteracy . . . and most important of all, productivity."[31] John J. Stretch, a social work professor at Tulane University, contended that as a national problem, poverty was most dangerous because it manifested itself in the personalities of the poor. Poverty, professor Stretch explained, "surely and steadily robs a nation of its full productive power."[32]

The marketplace became the ultimate proving ground for inclusion. For many business progressives, the Great Society provided a chance for black Louisianans to help the economy. Edward Steimel, the executive director of the Louisiana Public Affairs Research Council (LA-PAR) and future director of a major probusiness lobbying group (the Louisiana Association of Business and Industry, or LABI), put it bluntly. "The Negro," Steimel explained, was the "biggest problem that stands in the way of economic growth in Louisiana and the South." "Uneducated," the LA-PAR director continued, "he has been only marginally productive; he has been a heavy drag on the economy to say nothing of his personal plight."[33] His words echoed sentiments from New Orleans congressman Hale Boggs, who explained that the idealism of "charity and brotherhood" was nice, but the real reason to be concerned about poverty was its effect on "your pocketbook and mine."[34] Using different language, a local African American college student worried that the poor were not helping to "strengthen the state." They were "not producing" enough and "not consuming enough."[35]

Steimel's organization, LA-PAR, was founded in 1950 and was comprised of leading businesspeople and civic progressives from New Orleans and the rest of the state. The LA-PAR wanted to minimize political corruption and make public institutions more efficient, thus making Louisiana more attractive to investors. In the mid to late 1960s, they made the issue of black inclusion and economic productivity the centerpiece of their research agenda.[36] Speaking at a public LA-PAR meeting, Ramon S. Scruggs, public relations manager for AT&T, complained about the inefficiency of alienation. "Today we are faced nationwide with the necessity of including *everybody* in a productive society," he insisted. "We simply cannot afford," he continued, "to have a large segment of our society, such as the American Negro, looking in from the outside, and not fully contributing to, or sharing in, the harvest of the nation."[37] In a similar appeal, a LA-PAR-affiliated black political scientist, Earl M. Lewis, called for a massive national commitment to educating poor black children because otherwise "our society cannot hope to compete efficiently in the struggle for survival against atheistic and totalitarian international forces." Continuing the present course meant that the "economic growth of our communities, our states and the nation at large will be substantially crippled and, in some cases, ultimately nullified." Without "adequate education," black children would be denied "the capacity to live the 'good life.' "[38] Eugene McManus, a white priest and teacher linked to LA-PAR, claimed that the state would be unable to "fulfill its potential for progress as long as a substantial segment of its population is deprived of the skills and the opportunities to share equally in the profits and the responsibilities of such progress."[39]

The reward for accelerating black inclusion would be the exponential economic growth resulting from expanded consumerism. Purchasing power also offered the almost uncontestable benefit of black inclusion.[40] Victor Bussie, president of Louisiana's AFL-CIO and one of the most powerful men in state politics, cited the President's Council of Economic

Advisers on the need for improving black productivity in order to improve American productivity. If black workers received wages equal to their white counterparts, Bussie claimed, the United States would add $12.8 billion in personal income. If education levels were equal for African Americans, then that amount would be $20.6 billion.[41] Congressman Hale Boggs argued that the War on Poverty would dramatically help the United States because it could include people who had been wastefully excluded from the marketplace and, most important, because it would increase "PURCHASING POWER."[42]

The solutions progressive leaders—and to a large degree community activists—recommended usually centered on making the individual more competitive. The community, of course, had some responsibilities, but the ultimate success of integration lay with the capacity of individuals to claim their citizenship. As explained by Victor Bussie, "[S]ociety owes him [the black male] the educational and work opportunities but he must furnish the motivation." He proclaimed that "Negroes themselves must realize that this is a competitive world, in employment—in opportunities—in education—in social standing—and in acceptability."[43] Competing in that world was not easy, recognized Ramon Scruggs of AT&T. Echoing themes from Lyndon Johnson's June 1965 Howard University address, Scruggs contended that it was not enough to "open the gates and say, 'Let's be equal.'" "The Negro," he explained, "as any other individual, must be prepared by training and experience for his place in society if he is to be productive."[44]

Thus, education offered the most promising solution to black alienation and economic productivity. Locally, there were plenty of platitudes. The Desire target area's newspaper, *Our Paper*, proclaimed that education was "one asset that no one can do without." It was the "chance to improve the community, but most of all your self, in this forever changing world."[45] SWPC director Clark Corliss, again in near-textbook analysis, explained that "high grade public education is a primary key to good citizenship, to realization of the individual's maximum potential for productive and constructive labor, and to a healthy economic climate, to improving the quality of urban life."[46]

An insight into white perceptions about the mythical black mind came from Father McManus of New Orleans's elite black St. Augustine High School. He assured white audiences that black individuals did actually have pride and ambition, did possess the tools to earn citizenship, and did desperately want to use them. He encouraged civic leaders to stop seeking "some magic that will motivate Negro youth" at the same level as "white youth" because "beneath the skin we are all the same." A young black man needed what a young white man needed—"belief in himself." According to Father McManus, the best way to encourage productivity from a young black male was to show "him that America is for him, too, and mean it. Before too long you'll see more motivation than you ever dreamed possible." "Pride," the priest assured, was not a vice, but "more often a virtue."[47] Father Philip Berrigan, who became known for pouring blood over draft records in protest of the Vietnam War, admitted being "a racist" when he began teaching at St. Augustine, but his students there had helped him by "gently, but firmly healing my blindness" and by showing him how racial discrimination and poverty poisoned "hopes" and killed "dreams."[48]

The push to improve the competitiveness of alienated and segregated individuals was prevalent at all levels in the War on Poverty. Writing in the *Algiers Sentinel*, a community newspaper for the Algiers-Fischer target area, one anonymous activist argued that the fault for poverty lay with the individual's inability to compete. Blaming circumstances and environment was wrong. The problems did not lie with the "weaknesses and sins" of one's family or with "the stars or fate or the Creator." Individuals could overcome poverty with "courage and fortitude" and the "strength to control our lives."[49] Emelda Washington also celebrated the resilience of the rugged individual. Living in the St. Bernard area, she claimed that she had made her son a better competitor by teaching him to "earn his way in the world" by "hard work, hard study and scarificing [*sic*] some of the pleasures and ease his friends may get." She affirmed how important it was for him to have been "proud" to work odd jobs for money, "to be clean and neat and decent," saying "sir" and "ma'am," and love the American flag.[50]

Individual-centered inclusion strategies in the target areas allowed reform efforts to adhere to politically acceptable traditions and values, while channeling the growing energy of black southern neighborhoods into a governable phenomenon. Locally, social politics of the early Great Society drifted away from questions of wealth distribution towards questions of personal identity and citizenship. Progressives recognized that the effectiveness of including the excluded could not be fully measured in income transfer tables, by cost-benefit ratios, or through racial balance formulas. The soft spaces of the government, the market, and the psyche became proving grounds for racial liberalism. Progressive concern about alienation and productivity, though, were only one part of the process. The reaction in the target areas held clues for the future of inclusion.

"Somebodiness" and the War on Poverty

In 1964, U.S. attorney general Robert Kennedy told President Johnson in a secretly recorded phone call that one of the chief goals of the War on Poverty should be to give young low-income people a "feeling that there's some hope . . . that there are people in government and important places that are interested in them."[51] In New Orleans, some local people were very clear on that point. Participants in a variety of programs identified personal improvement as critical for ensuring citizenship. In the target areas, a number of program participants expressed confidence that the federal government, with local help, could make a difference in individual lives, particularly since few alternatives existed.

Despite the prevalence of theories about the warping nature of poverty, low-income blacks were not simply "other" Americans. Their civic objectives were rooted in the same core values and assumptions held by most Americans. For many participants, the War on Poverty reaffirmed a faith in American individualism, a belief in opportunity, and a need for personal responsibility. By 1967, the early Great Society's antipoverty components were offering some participants a wedge into a new world—more money, more rights, more political power, more ways to take one's place in society, and a more sophisticated sense of self. One of those components was the Neighborhood Youth Corps (NYC). Designed to provide part-time jobs to low-income youth, the NYC program received one of the largest appropriations in the local War on Poverty.[52] Teenagers employed through the program defended the Great Society as essential for preparing them for full citizenship. Foremost, they argued that the NYC helped them to earn money for consumer goods and to save money for their anticipated college education, typically stating a preference for the historically segregated Tulane University. Second, they expressed that the NYC helped them to ease burdens on their parents, to assimilate into the adult culture of work, and to learn to work better with others.

Linda Adams, an Algiers youth, credited the programs for reducing juvenile delinquency, promoting a sense of self-worth, and for instilling national pride. "Really all children need is a chance to know that some-one cares enough about them," she wrote to Hale Boggs. "They take over a great responsibility and it makes them feel wanted." She hoped that Boggs and his colleagues would continue to allow "others like me a chance to show they can strive for a better America."[53] Another NYC student, Karina Gracia, wrote that the War on Poverty encouraged self-realization. The program had given her and her friends a "chance to express ourselves" and ways to avoid "being frustrated with ourselves." She and others lauded the NYC for teaching responsibility, offering a "taste of independence," and stimulating an "understanding of values."[54]

The comments of these NYC participants also reveal a trait inherent to successful participation in America's consumer culture: they wanted more. The students defined their connections to mainstream society by their clothing and appearance and their ability to acquire goods. They sought status and self-satisfaction like other teenagers. Sixteen-year-old Betty Newsome captured the meaning of the War on Poverty for local teenagers, writing that the programs were "helping them to finish school, to buy cloths [sic], and to help them go places." Several other participants focused on being able to purchase things such as school yearbooks and clothing.[55] One young target area resident, Loria C. Jordan, described the NYC program as "an opportunity for young people to earn money," to "engage in work which could help us choose a vacation [vocation]," and to "become contributing member[s] in society." She credited the program for teaching her how to find and keep a job.[56]

The search for more goods and status accelerated students' growth of confidence and a sense of belonging. In Central City, Alma M. Cottles, a mother of several successful children, exemplified the search for some-bodiness. On her own, she developed a lengthy plan for a War on Poverty-funded public works program that called for young poor children to train as social workers in their own neighborhoods. So confident was Mrs. Cottles in the success of her plan, she informed Congressman Boggs that, if Democratic leaders would use it, they would not have to "worry about being re-elected" or about making "so many speaches [sic]." Holding together her plan was an intellectual commitment to the genius of the individual free from the constraints of class and race. Regardless of their backgrounds, she argued, American children had "great creative minds" and just needed "half a chance." Her plan also revealed the extent to which fashion reflected status. She required participants in her proposed program to wear suits, ties, and nice dresses and to make themselves "pleasurable."[57]

Like Mrs. Cottles, other antipoverty participants wanted the War on Poverty to encourage social advancement, particularly for their children. They longed to have someone care about their situations. To many of them, the government was finally standing in for people facing a marketplace that had already rendered them almost irrelevant. Such sentiment is clear in several participants' appeals for continued funding for an adult education program. In seeking increased federal help, they sought recognition as citizens. Alma Chester, an elderly woman just learning how to read and write, asked, "What is and will become of us? do any one care? [sic]"[58]

Some activists hoped that compassion would improve competitiveness. According to Miss E. Gardner, a teacher at Booker T. Washington High School, the War on Poverty proved that "helping to build, rebuild, and equip communities encourages the people to seek worthwhile and effective goals." In the process, it helped to "make them better citizens."[59] A mother with children in some of the Total Community Action (TCA) programs believed that without the War on Poverty, target-area residents would "be at a lost [sic] as of just what else to do to help our kids."[60] TCA community worker Lavada Jefferson, a key organizer of the Keystone Terrace Improvement Group in the Desire area who represented one hundred families, professed that the War on Poverty fostered "security and contentment" and solidified a sense of belonging to America. The programs made it easier for "fathers" to leave home and "fight in the Viet Nam [*sic*] war to save our country." As a result of the poverty war, she wrote, "The children who ate from garbage cans are eating at a table; the children who played in derelict cars and broken glass are now able" to participate in organized recreation. Although her statements contain ample hyperbole, her verbal extravagance points to her faith in the power of government to affect individual lives. To her, the practical benefits were preventing drop-outs, making better citizens, and encouraging more contact with government officials. She wrote excitedly that "people who never had a chance before are acquainted with City and State officials . . . even writing letters to them."[61] In another instance, investigators of an OEO-funded Boy Scouts program in Algiers-Fischer noted the possibilities offered by status. "Uniforms, which have been provided after the boy has given evidence of his worthiness, have added immeasurably to the 'feeling of belonging,'" explained the investigator. "The boys take great pride in their appearance and their records of achievements." Parents and scout leaders wholeheartedly believed that the program had improved "the conduct and morals of the boys."[62]

After 1967, black residents in the target areas seized more official control over the local War on Poverty and pushed it in more aggressive, and occasionally radical, directions. This transfer of administrative authority, however, did not dampen the psychological mission. Instead, the focus on improving the mentalities of the poor and alienated seemed to intensify. A growing number of radicals were becoming astute at blending depictions of despair with their advocacy for racial pride and black power. Father Jerome Ledoux, a Catholic priest writing for the radical Free Southern Theater's *The Plain Truth* newspaper, argued that "for many, being Black means alternately shivering and roasting in a rat-infested tenement, watching babies grow up undernourished and spiritless, trying to impress upon adolescents that they should have the initiative and ambition of which they see little in the squalid environment of the ghetto."[63] In 1969, the Lower Ninth Ward Neighborhood Council explained that "changing the attitudes of impoverished individuals" was one of their top priorities. Accordingly, the "most important single task" was to create a "sense of pride, dignity and individual worth as a human being."[64] The St. Bernard Community Council put the redefinition of black identity at the forefront. "The historic racial identity of black people has been almost totally obliterated from the socio-cultural patterns of thought of all Americans particularly black Americans in poverty settings," explained the Council's leaders in early 1969. "Consequently, their image of themselves is demoralizing, self-effacing, and lends itself to distorted beliefs relating to racial inferiority, second-class citizenship, and other elements of socio-economic compromise." The St. Bernard Council planned to concentrate its community action efforts on helping black residents to develop "functional, aggressive self-esteem." The council wanted to "elevate the economic, social, and spiritual status of community residents to a level of competitive adjustment in the American society."[65]

"Hurry Up before I Slap You"

In addition to inclusion thinking and Great Society programs, another group of psychological prescriptions were being shaped in New Orleans's low-income neighborhoods. Radicals of varying perspectives used self-reliance and race-pride to push for black economic growth and political power, and they were willing to use any means available to fight for it. These militants represented the local version of the national Black Power phenomenon. In retrospect, Black Power was primarily a unifying slogan and call for action that borrowed from a culture-wide fascination with personal identity, group solidarity, and social mobility. It was a powerful, yet plastic, phenomenon that lacked a coherent ideology or leadership, and in Louisiana, an overwhelming majority of black residents rejected the slogan.[66] Within five years of emerging as a rallying cry during the 1966 March Against Fear in Mississippi, though, its meaning had become vague enough for President Richard Nixon to appropriate part of it to underscore his agenda for black capitalism.[67]

In New Orleans, a small but vibrant black radicalism developed after 1967, and it shifted the focus of socio-economic reform—and accelerated white flight. Locally, black militancy was complex, with ideas ranging from the outlandish to the mainstream. Sam Bell, an early leader of the Ninth Ward political organization known as SOUL, advised that "All blacks should learn to hate all whites." Bell believed that only when black Americans found their true selves could they be free enough from hatred and from white people. In a staunchly anticommunist, antileftist Louisiana, Bell's most inflammatory statement was that "communism would be the best form of government for this country." Lloyd Lazard, an activist from the Gert Town area who operated an Afro-centric shop called the House of Wisdom, cautioned black citizens not to let "demagogue" black and white politicians continue "jiving you and me" with "their trickery and their treachery." It would take "culture revolution," he claimed, "to unbrainwash an entire people" and that process would have to be violent. Leaders of the local branch of the Republic of New Africa were more extreme, and in terms of political possibility, unrealistic. Representing a fringe of the black liberation struggle that disregarded political realities, they called for the confiscation of land in the southern United States to be used to create a new nation for people of color. Ulugbolo Mboya (formerly Bobby Brooks) informed whites that "You're things of evil. Germs. Contagion! You're worse than leprosy." He and his group were anticipating a white-led genocide of African Americans. "We know you," he declared. "You're going to try to kill all blacks." In one protest action, a Louisiana member of the Republic of New Africa actually hijacked a commercial airliner at the New Orleans airport and forced it to Cuba.[68]

Black Power was a product of time and place. In New Orleans in the middle to late 1960s, its expression came from multiple sources, both white and black. A variety of proponents pushed black capitalism, black consumerism, black self-sufficiency, black pride, and black defiance. Despite a controversial rhetoric of separatism invoked by some activists, the strength of local Black Power thinking was its rooting in conceptions of American individualism. Complementing, and often complicating, the Great Society framework of programs and ideas were aggressive, identity-based demands for political access that came from street-level radicals who articulated their own homegrown interpretations of social democracy. The emphasis on earning citizenship through personal responsibility, moral idealism, and individual competitiveness had long been a part of African American political thought.[69] For almost a century, leaders had preached the need for individuals to forge their own places in the marketplace and to sacrifice for the community, reflected most starkly in the willingness of African Americans to serve in the military. To secure more of a role in the marketplace, African Americans in Louisiana historically pursued a variety of such institutional wedges as the International Longshoreman's Association, benevolent societies, and recently, politically active civic organizations. The civil rights movement enabled black leaders to force the federal government to join them in confronting inequality. The most politically successful black leaders shaped those components into formulae for attracting white support.

The local growth of black power owed much to a set of ideas that can be described as Black Power populism. Many radical leaders on the streets steeped their search for inclusion and citizenship in the therapeutic, competitive individualism of the War on Poverty. As expressed locally, many black militants called for the expansion of self-pride and drew from populist traditions that celebrated keeping the fruits of labor and the products of consumption under control of laborers and consumers.[70] Activists fought against corporate domination and to preserve conditions conducive to individual competition. Although local militants made appeals to collective racial identity, ultimately, their primary goals focused on opening access to the market. An activist with the Free Southern Theater lamented that black citizens "work for the white man, receive our salaries from him, live in our own community, and spend our money in his businesses." Involved in a "white american [sic] cycle of exploitation," blacks were "both a source of labor and a gigantic market for white business products."[71] Like the disaffected farmers of the late nineteenth century, Black Power advocates tried to force the market—and the political apparatus controlling it—to better serve their own interests. One interpretive difference was that the turn-of-the-century agrarians protested to avoid becoming alienated, while Black Power advocates did so to overcome their long-term alienation.

In late 1968, Robert Richardson was a spokesman for Dillard University's "Afro-Americans for Progress," a group of self-proclaimed "young militant New Orleans Negroes" who defined Black Power as "the search for identification as a race and as individual men." Crucial to that identification was the opportunity to prove one's "merit" in the "big arena."[72] Richardson's emphasis on cultural identity developed partly from inequity he observed in his parents' lives and the lives of others in his neighborhood. Central to black identity, according to Richardson, was the fact that "we've always been without, or what we've had has been the leavings." Black residents needed sources of personal pride because "when you've grown up watching your Daddy go to the hospital and make maybe $40 a week and your Ma scrub floors, or maybe not scrub floors, but wash dishes and iron clothes to get a few dollars, you wonder 'What the hell do I have to look forward to?'" His life experiences had caused him to think that "this is a great affluent society," but he knew too many people who could not afford transportation to their jobs and children who lacked enough clothes or lunch money to go to school. In that environment, one's self-esteem became fused with the need to "scrounge for a few bucks, one way or the other, and you learn how to steal, and you get in trouble." Richardson wanted inclusion to bring about opportunities to be productive, not to join the "white culture" and wear "black, narrow-shouldered suits and imitate all of the success we see." Donning Dashikis instead of double-breasted suits did not completely separate one from the community. What mattered were the values of self-reliance and industriousness. "Values," he informed his readers, were "what produce habits, and good habits are what produce hard work." He abhorred welfare and advocated the fruits of competitive inclusion. Echoing arguments by LA-PAR director Ed Steimel, labor leader Victor Bussie, and several others, Richardson encouraged the "white man" to see that "in the long run, it's better to compete with the black brothers than have to support them, just because they've never been given a chance to be productive." What "brothers" needed were programs that provided "education, values and foundation to get out and be taxpayers themselves." His strategy for getting support for those programs, however, diverged from those of progressives. "If violence and looting is the only way," he warned, "then that's the white man's decision, and we don't have any other choice." He did not "want to stop the white folks from enjoying life and having a good time." Like other populists before him, he wanted his people to enjoy the fruits of their labor. "All I want, and what the brothers want," he declared, "is to share in the good life."[73]

Those ideas took economic form in efforts to exert more black control over black business development and black consumer choices. A conservative white New Orleans businessman argued that the best way to solve poverty was not through federal programs but by getting "negroes . . . involved" in "free enterprise," particularly by owning small businesses.[74] Lee Green, a leader of TCA's Resources and Development Department, led a crusade to encourage black-controlled commerce in black areas, claiming it was the "*only* technique which will *ever* result in the reasonable independence from the white Establishment." Several organizations sprouted up to do just that. The Interracial Council for Black Opportunities began in 1967 and was followed by Model Cities-related organizations such as the Amalgamated Builders and Contractors of Louisiana (ABCOL) and Taking Care of Business, Inc., which received a $50,000 seed grant from the Stern Family Fund.[75] Another group, the Brothers in Economic Action Movement (BEAM), summed up the objective of black capitalism: "To help the poor, Negroes especially, find an identity as consumers and producers and to help them act as a community in the economic sphere."[76] Even the more radical groups like the Thugs United, Inc., and the Black Panthers put small business development at the top of their priorities.

One example of a grassroots fight for more economic control involved members of the Central City area who organized a boycott against a grocery chain known as *The Opportunity Food Store*. Owned by a white businessman in Baton Rouge, Louisiana, the grocery chain offered black entrepreneurs the opportunity to manage grocery stores, with the hope it would make the businesses more attractive to black shoppers. The owners hoped to sell products by appealing to opportunity and upward mobility. Unfortunately for its ownership, the high prices at New Orleans's Central City store at Galvez and Melpomene streets proved too much for residents, who protested in public for nearly half a year. Many residents viewed the store as a fiendish manipulation of racial goodwill, especially when community residents realized that the markets would not be owned by the community, but by absentee white capitalists. Community activists offered to stop protests if the company sold the Central City store to them. A writer for *The Plain Truth* explained the protest as a means to thwart subtle attempts by the "white man" and his corporations to use black fronts and franchises to control the black community.[77]

Radical black voices offered a stinging critique of American corporate capitalism. "The real outlaws are the people who run this system," explained Val Ferdinand (now Kalamu ya Salaam), a health worker in the Lower Ninth Ward and a student activist at SUNO. "Black tools of white men," he continued, "are the weapons of the system used to oppress the black people."[78] Another activist pointed to some serious shortcomings in the radical movements themselves. Black capitalism was hampered by insufficient capital, and militant groups lacked the organizational power to "bargain for Black People."[79] Ronald Walton of *The Plain Truth* called into question the validity of appeals to the "American" work ethic. "Who," he asked, "has worked harder than black people?" Ideas such as "rugged individualism, green power, free enterprise and all them other good things" were just "white bull." Next, he asked, "Who's [sic] blood are Black people going to suck? There is no one left beneath us on America's social ladder whose labor we can exploit, no one out of whom we can make a market, no one we can charge exorbitant prices to; we would have to misuse each other." The problem, he noted, was that black Americans had been excluded for so long that "black capitalism could never catch up to white capitalism." Liberation had come too late. The best economic opportunity for black Americans was through small business development, but the large corporations were squeezing out the small businessman. "Production and control are what count in capitalism," he instructed, "and there's nothing left that black people can produce exclusively in this country in order to give us a voice in how this place is run. Some popcorn negro store owner doesn't count 2 cents in america's [sic] monopoly capitalistic system."[80]

On the surface, the intense words of Ronald Walton and other radicals stood in contrast to the hopeful visions of Alma Cottles and those like her. Beneath the words, however, were key similarities. These people all were looking for ways to reshape the future of the black individual and to alter the systems that managed that individual. They were all pushing for more black power, and ideas from each perspective would factor into the politics of race and poverty in the late 1960s. Some developments were encouraging. Locally, the black middle class was growing. According to one report, the percentage of local African Americans who could be considered part of the typical American middle class had grown from 5 percent in 1955 to around 20 percent in 1968, and many black workers had risen to higher paying jobs previously available only to whites. The gains were relative, however. One black hotel manager argued that progress was being made because he had been called "nigger" by "a white man" only once during the past year.[81] For many black activists, however, a modest expansion of the black middle class and the decline of public disrespect hardly constituted adequate progress. The language of Black Power was a product of black frustration, and frustration rose dramatically in the next few years. Amid the chaos of racial disturbances, antiwar protest, and white flight, the expansion of black influence brought the city into a different political age. According to SOUL leader Sam Bell, "A new era" had "been born." The "tired and longtime forgotten" had come together and were producing a "spirited, informed, amalgamated black people."[82] Charles Carter, another Lower Ninth Ward activist, offered a simpler assessment. White America, he claimed, had years before stolen his freedom. "Why don't you give it back?" he demanded. "And I say hurry up before I slap you."[83] From the late 1960s into the early 1970s, black assertiveness would alter the politics of inclusion and expand the Soft State. How would the South respond to this new "urban crisis"? With the Jim Crow system becoming history and black citizens seizing power in its wake, what new ways would the region's people use to manage race and inequality? By 1967–1968, calls for compassionate inclusion were declining and more credence was given to demands that African Americans earn their citizenship. The fight against poverty and exclusion was refocused on defusing the southern powder keg.

CHAPTER SIX

Defusing the Southern Powder Keg

Failure to act could result in New Orleans becoming
a powder keg.
—Study of Racial Attitudes in Louisiana, Fall 1966

Between 1963 and 1968, the United States experienced an urban crisis. In over 250 American cities, at least 334 episodes of urban unrest erupted, nearly 90 percent of them between 1967 and 1968.[1] During those six years, approximately 250 African Americans were killed, 8,000 were injured, and 50,000 were arrested. A sizeable portion of the injuries and deaths came from fires or from actions taken by state or federal authorities. Cities suffered property damage estimated in the hundreds of millions, but the most damage was caused in Los Angeles in August 1965, Newark and Detroit in July 1967, and in several cities in April 1968 after the assassination of Martin Luther King Jr. These riots or rebellions or whatever one chooses to call them sparked an intense search for solutions to urban and racial problems.[2]

Amid the supposed triumph of the civil rights movement, these disorders incensed many Americans, who saw them as evidence of black Americans being shiftless, criminal, and dangerous. Reactionary white leaders characterized the disturbances as destructive mercantile rampages by lawless thugs and expressions of sinister Communist plotting, often implicating federal programs as the root of the problem. Diehard New Orleans segregationist congressman F. Edward Hébert, who led the 1948

Louisiana Dixiecrat movement, blamed the disorders on a "complete disregard for proper authority" and worried they were part of a Communist takeover funded by the War on Poverty.[3] Alabama governor George Wallace insinuated that the disorders were part of a conspiracy hatched at a "conference of world guerilla chieftains" in Cuba. According to opinion polls, almost half of all Americans were willing to believe at least part of these claims.[4] In the presidential campaign of 1968, Republican nominee Richard Nixon and his running mate Spiro Agnew pressed the issues of law and order.[5]

The strongest rebuttal to these assertions came from the National Advisory Committee on Civil Disorders, better known as the Kerner Commission. The *Kerner Report* rebuffed claims that the typical "rioter" was a "hoodlum, habitual criminal, or riffraff." Instead, their evidence indicated that the typical person was a young man between 15 and 36 years old (over half under the age of 24), a long-time resident of the community, and a high-school dropout who was still better educated and more politically aware than most of his neighbors. Additionally, the *Kerner Report* contended that most urban black residents did not participate in civil disorder. In fact, a sizeable number of them were "counterrioters" who worked diligently to reduce community tensions. Those counterrioters were generally better educated and more affluent than the typical "rioter" and were often linked to the federal War on Poverty.[6]

Civil disorders, particularly race riots, have been a part of American history since the colonial period. The Kerner Commission noted, however, that the traditional pattern has been one of white mobs carrying out attacks on African Americans. The violent protests of the 1960s, however, involved black Americans lashing out against "symbols of white American society."[7] Perhaps more than any other domestic events of the post-World War II period, they changed America's political culture and led to what resembled a domestic containment policy carried out by federal, state, and local governments. For the Great Society and its War on Poverty, the protests clouded the early vision of individual and community uplift, gave symbols and issues to a so-called white backlash, and, most important, shifted race and citizenship debates from liberty and equality to law and order.

Urban unrest did not bypass the American South, although the numerous episodes in northern cities and West Coast enclaves have attracted more scholarly attention. For the most intense year of disorder, 1967, the Kerner Commission found that 22 of 164 disorders nationwide occurred in southern cities. Kerner commissioners defined "Major Disorders" as lasting longer than two days and involving large mobs, numerous fires, "intensive looting," "reports of snipers," and National Guard or Army soldiers. Of eight such disorders, one occurred in Tampa, Florida. "Serious Disorders" spanned one to two days, had small groups, "isolated looting," fires, rock throwing, and involved primarily state and local police. Of thirty-three such episodes, six were southern: Atlanta, Birmingham, Houston, Jackson, Nashville, and Riviera Beach, Florida. The most frequent were "Minor Disorders," action from small groups that lasted less than a day, with a few fires or broken windows. Fifteen of one hundred twenty-three minor disorders nationwide happened in southern towns. In the South, the legacies of segregation created a different context for disturbances otherwise similar to those in other parts of the country. Historian Thomas Sugrue has stretched the time frame for the northern urban crisis back into the 1940s and 1950s, linking it to white racism and deindustrialization patterns in the American economy. The unique history of the South creates a much longer historical arc.[8]

In Dixie, the urban crisis went well beyond riots, calling into question the rules and structures of a disorderly society that had been constructed since the Civil War. In 1987, former New York Mayor John Lindsay coined the phrase "slow motion riot" to describe life for many urban African Americans after the 1960s.[9] To modify his phrase slightly, black southerners had long been experiencing a "slow motion" crisis perpetuated by white supremacy. From the turn of the twentieth century, a regional tendency toward extreme violence, a semi-colonial economy, and a concentration of power among a few citizens had combined to keep black residents segregated and subordinated. In the late 1960s, the decline of legal segregation meant that African Americans had more tools to turn the reaction to the long-term crisis into a politically potent new phenomenon. As explicitly discriminatory legal barriers were overturned and extralegal white violence condemned, political leaders had to manage the new black presence through the state and through expansions in the soft spaces of the War on Poverty. In New Orleans, the urban crisis became a test of the Great Society and the inclusion agenda.

In July 1966, one New Orleans group spoke for many when it predicted that "some day, possibly very soon, the city of New Orleans will hear an explosion" when an arrest or a train blocking the street or another child drowning in an unprotected canal would "trigger the fuse."[10] But New Orleans did not join the list of cities where the metaphorical powder keg blew. The potential was certainly there: New Orleans was one of the poorest, most violent, most racially prejudiced, and most corrupt cities in one of the poorest, most violent, most racially prejudiced, and most corrupt states in the United States. Why, then, did New Orleans not explode?

Historically, political disputes in New Orleans had turned explosive at regular intervals, especially when race was an issue. In 1866, white attacks on a constitutional convention held by Radical Republicans and African Americans led to a race riot known as the "Absolute Massacre," which left forty-eight people dead and over two hundred injured. Twelve years later at the Battle for Liberty Place, the White League, which was led by men from some of the city's most prominent white families, routed the pro-Republican state militia in a downtown street battle. Thirty-eight died. Seventy-nine were wounded. In 1891, rioting whites lynched eleven Italian Americans in the infamous "Who Killa Da Chief" episode when the suspected murderer of the New Orleans police chief was not brought to justice. In late July 1900, in a stark aberration of the usual pattern of white-on-black or white-on-ethnic political violence, black migrant Robert Charles shot twenty-four white people, killing at least seven before being killed himself by several dozen bullets near a Central City apartment house. Sixty years later, the white reaction to the school-integration crisis set a tone for the modern era. In 1965, the year after the passage of the Civil Rights Act, white supremacists set off twelve bombs in attempts to quell civil rights activities. By the late 1960s, though, overt, massive white violence had diminished, although white violence against black residents continued at a more private level. Instead, the politics of inclusion were dominated by the threat of African American rebellion.[11]

In New Orleans in the late 1960s, local leaders had good reason to worry that poverty and racial tension could escalate into a destructive riot. Larry Odom of the national Office of Economic Opportunity (OEO) recommended sending an "Advance-Man" to cities "to find out what the 'gig' *really* is" before sending in task forces to open dialogue with local leaders.[12] Had they sent an "advance-man" to New Orleans, the Johnson administration would have found a city in full simmer. Although neither the OEO nor the Kerner Commission exhaustively investigated New Orleans, several local academics and journalists found that conditions for African Americans were as troubling as in any city in America. A series of articles published by the relatively moderate *New Orleans States-Item* concluded that conditions for local black residents were as bad as anywhere in the United States.[13] In another report, nationally prominent sociologist Daniel C. Thompson, a professor at Dillard University, found that the Crescent City had serious problems in all of the evaluation categories used by the Kerner Commission. Foremost among the many volatile problems were joblessness among African American workers (over one-third were unemployed at some point during the year), the black community's severe housing problem (second only to Pittsburgh), and its meager, 12-percent high-school completion rate. Thompson explained that New Orleans's discriminatory political system and the "*lack of official communication between the Negro poor in New Orleans and the local government*" had left a "*dangerous, potentially explosive vacuum*" (emphasis in original). In the summer of 1968, another major problem was the absence of black leaders among the city's elected officials, despite African Americans accounting for approximately 40 percent of the population. That gap caused Thompson to warn that "when a powerless people cannot express their needs through traditional, legitimate channels they may be expected, sooner or later, to attempt to influence government through illegal, destructive channels."[14]

The city's police force and its black communities were dangerously at odds. According to Thompson, black New Orleanians almost unanimously agreed that their neighborhoods got the police department's "most impolite, brutal, racist" officers.[15] A few protests against alleged police brutality required quick action by local officials. In the spring of 1966, the public beating and arrest of a young man from a large and respected Lower Ninth Ward family caused a community organizer to warn that it was "very obvious to us all that if this situation continues severe violence will result from it."[16] In May 1967, black leaders severely criticized the city's recent "Stop and Frisk" ordinance that allowed the police to stop and search anyone they deemed suspicious. African Americans were often the targets, and one group claimed that the police department provided files to the City Council on anyone who complained about the ordinance.[17]

The *NOLA Express*, an underground newspaper, described what it termed a "typical" account of police brutality. On a late summer Saturday morning, police officers approached a porch occupied by Joseph Lee Reynolds, a twenty-five-year-old longshoreman in the St. Bernard area whose brother was wanted for questioning by burglary detectives. Reynolds allegedly told an officer not to "put that f—— pistol in my mouth!" The officers then allegedly held his arms and beat him on the porch swing, resulting in broken ribs and an injured eye. Reynolds claimed most of the beating came after being handcuffed. He remained the subject of what he called "routine harassment," with the same officers telling him, "This is our project [St. Bernard], and we're going to keep running it the way we want, you hear!"[18]

One of the most inflammatory incidents between police and citizens involved a highly respected community leader. The unlikely target of police attention was Elizabeth "Bettye" Pope, a War on Poverty target area team chief who held a master's degree from Atlanta University and had done graduate work at the Tulane University School of Social Work. Twice she was cited for allegedly interfering with police officers. The August 1965 incident took place a few days before the L.A. Watts civil disorders and was little more than a controversial traffic stop, but it is instructive of the attitude of local officers. One night, Pope was awaiting her turn at a stop sign near the Desire housing project. As she waited, she witnessed several officers shining flashlights on the arms of youths, apparently searching for signs of heroin usage. The words "coon" and "nigs" casually floated by. When an officer knocked off a boy's cap and hit him with his night stick, she exclaimed, "Good gracious!" Hearing her through her open window, one of the officers asked her if she was "one of those smart nigger bitches?" He then instructed her to "move on" and not to let him "catch you around this neighborhood anymore." During the ensuing exchange, the officer learned that she worked for the Community Action Program in Desire. Pope said the officer then turned "rather sheepish and delivered an eloquent speech on the 'problems we policeman have in this area with dope, delinquents, etc.'" and admitted often making "mistakes." She took her ticket for improper stopping and insubordination of a police officer and told him she would see him in court. The officer failed to show for the court date and the charges were dropped. Local War on Poverty officials, however, began requiring staff members to carry identification badges.[19]

Pope's second run-in with the NOPD was more serious. On July 27, 1967—the day that OEO director Sargent Shriver testified before a House committee about civil disorders and, effectively, the final day of the almost week-long Detroit eruption—Pope was arrested after a confrontation with Desire area patrolmen. While Pope was being held in isolation at the local precinct station, community leaders led a protest. They were particularly upset that the arresting officer defended his actions by claiming that he had to "prevent damage to his 'image' by this 'colored woman.'" After the incident, Desire leaders warned city officials that "tactless and overbearing" officers "might trigger civilian violence."[20] A local group known as the Concerned Parents of Desire reported that police crowd-control tactics gave "impetus for creation of a riot."[21] Frank Bivens, president of the Desire Area Community Council, charged that the "intemperate action" of white police officers had "nearly spawned civil commotion."[22]

To temper emotions, the NOPD quickly reprimanded the officers in question and transferred them to another part of the city. Councilmen Philip Ciaccio, John Petre, and Maurice "Moon" Landrieu defended Pope, which helped to alleviate tension, and Pope thanked them for their support. She proudly stated that "Many of us will not go down in the 'annuals' [sic] of New Orleans History for our dedication, for our convictions, nor for our concern for the right of all people to be treated with dignity, respect and justice." Nevertheless, most Desire activists would "continue to strive toward this goal and for peace and harmony among all men."[23] Moweaner Mauldin of the Desire Area Community Council was less congenial when she informed City Hall that the "anger" of Desire was not just going to "blow over" because "Things don't really blow over. We hold them inside." The "mistreatment of another person" and the "brutality of another year," she explained, had shaped the "image" of the police, and the result was not "a pretty one."[24]

Shortly after the Pope arrest, a serious rumor of a planned riot sent local War on Poverty officials scurrying. In mid-August, TCA Manpower Specialist and former labor leader A. P. "Pat" Stoddard received information about a possible riot from sources that he considered reliable. Allegedly, antagonists were to light several stores on fire in Algiers, an old neighborhood on the West Bank of the Mississippi River across from the French Quarter. The smoke and flames were to signal to compatriots in Central City on the East Bank to begin. Whether the conspirators lost heart or the rumor proved a hoax is unknown. What is certain is that nothing unusual was lit that night.[25] In the summer that Newark and Detroit exploded, New Orleans seemed to escape. Seven months later in the spring of 1968, two incidents caused the New Orleans powder keg to come close to igniting. One was the shooting of a young black man by the New Orleans Police Department; the other, ten days before Easter, was the murder of Martin Luther King Jr.[26]

April 1968

In 1968, the NAACP held a "March of Truth" from Shakespeare Park in Central City—the same route as the October 1963 civil rights march that attracted ten to fifteen thousand people—to the downtown branch of the Louisiana governor's office to rebut John McKeithen's claim that "racial harmony" existed in Louisiana. Key speaker NAACP state president Emmitt Douglass told a reporter, "The uneducated, unemployed, and hopeless blacks standing on street corners and sitting on the steps of slum dwellings know their governor is lying. The black living in forgotten areas where dirt streets are not cleaned or lighted listens to his governor, and inside him the bitterness grows. Unchecked it will burst into violence." Douglass warned that McKeithen was "playing Russian roulette with riots; he is gambling glibly with some future day of disaster." On the day of the march, the governor toured the city and met with black leaders, most of whom were intricately involved with War on Poverty programs. In this turnaround from his public efforts in 1964 and 1965 to limit liberal influence over the War on Poverty, he sympathized with residents living in what he described as the worst conditions he had ever seen. In 1968 on the day of the march, he pledged his support for a local option referendum to allow New Orleans to receive Urban Renewal funds.[27] The goodwill of this visit was tested in the next week as many black residents seethed about the police shooting of Robert Lee Boyd.

Almost two weeks later on April 4, Martin Luther King Jr. was assassinated four hundred miles upriver from New Orleans. In the week or so that it took the dirty liquid of the Mississippi River to roll southward from Memphis to the sea, the United States experienced unprecedented black protest. According to estimates, civil disorders occurred in 125 cities. "There was chaos all over this city the night that Dr. King was murdered," reported Robert Richardson, Dillard University student activist. "This city came damn near exploding." He conceded that the incidents were not like the riots that had shaken Detroit or Newark seven months earlier, but "it was here, man, right here in New Orleans, and this old city came close to being in flames, and there were some black leaders who said that they were not going to tell their brothers not to burn."[28] The local NBC affiliate reported that "rumors of the wildest sort" had given "rise to further rumors" and had "served only to heighten tensions."[29]

Those tensions remained high for several days. On the night of April 5, twenty-two firebombs were set off. Two nights later nineteen more exploded across the city, many of them aimed at corner grocery stores, liquor stores, and parked cars. During several nights of sporadic looting, rock-throwing, and firebombing, over thirty people were arrested. The St. Bernard area near Bayou St. John experienced some of the heaviest activity. In the most prolonged outbreak of violence, a group of "irresponsible youths," as the *New Orleans States-Item* described them, began throwing bricks at authorities around 10:35 p.m. on Sunday, April 7, and continued for a couple of hours. After projectiles damaged a fire truck and a police cruiser, police chief Joseph Giarrusso sealed off the area. Officers armed with shotguns then swept in and cleared the streets. The next day, Catholic archbishop Philip Hannan, Dillard University president Albert Dent (the Dillard campus was near St. Bernard), and other ministers worked to restore calm and order.[30] That night in the Desire area, approximately twenty police officers, two of whom were black, broke up an agitated group of about one hundred residents. One witness claimed that white officers used rifle butts to control the largely black crowd.[31]

Although the injuries, arrests, and property damage were less than in other cities, the early April incidents showed that—in politics and race relations—New Orleans could no longer be the same town. One St. Bernard youth proclaimed that the disorder in his neighborhood had come "out of eyes being opened. . . . It came out of this hell we've been living in." To that end, Dillard activist Richardson warned cryptically, "there maybe could be bad nights, and maybe we would all suffer, but maybe we would accomplish our objectives."[32]

Prevention of "bad" nights became a priority of black and white civic leaders. In one example, a peaceful work stoppage by six thousand white and black longshoremen shut down the Port of New Orleans to honor Reverend King. In another, two days after King's death, the New Orleans Negro Summit Conference, a group of sixteen civic organizations, urged local black residents not to riot because it would only worsen already poor conditions. Along with the local branch of the NAACP and the Central City Economic Opportunity Committee, the Summit Conference pushed for more constructive ways to demonstrate that African Americans had "not shared in the economic fruits" of United States citizenship. On Tuesday, April 9, in New Orleans's largest public demonstration, eight hundred citizens marched silently downtown to mourn Reverend King and to protest the lack of black power. Three days later another more vocal group of a few hundred marched.[33] At City Hall, Mayor Schiro put the finishing touches on the city's Human Relations Committee and hurried the appointment of the city's first black mayoral aide. That aide, Philip Baptiste, later claimed that Schiro "just wanted me as a showpiece" during the "long hot summer." In another action linked to a process well underway, Sherman Copelin, a recent graduate of Dillard University and former student body president, was named the assistant to the director of the Ninth Ward Rehabilitation Survey office, the chief forerunner to Urban Renewal.[34]

Several organizations praised the city's leaders and its residents for avoiding serious violence. WDSU television, a relatively progressive voice in the New Orleans media, admitted that some "racial incidents" had transpired, but lauded the "overwhelming majority" of both races who had "acted with dignity and responsibility in trying times." They felt secure that the police could handle anything that arose. The *Vieux Carré Courier*, a progressive weekly newspaper that had sprung from the alternative press movement of the 1960s, deplored the violence surrounding King's assassination as something that "violate[d] his grave," and they explained that rioters were "not avenging his death but rather extending its violence for ego's sake and proving their own unworthiness to enjoy human freedom." Reverend Zebadee Bridges, an African American minister who led the influential Seventh Ward Interdenominational Ministerial Alliance, commended the city for the "superb way in which the riot situation was handled." He credited the police for a "splendid job" and promised his group's continued support.[35] For the next several months along the banks of the lower Mississippi River, as one local commentator explained, New Orleans became a "city searching for the formula to a peaceful summer."[36]

Searching for a Peaceful Summer

According to the Kerner Commission's criteria for civil disorders, the early April events in New Orleans qualified only as "minor disorders." New Orleans remained peaceful in the late 1960s, at least according to New Orleans standards. There is no clear explanation, however, why a society filled with violence, poverty, and racial injustice did not experience a dramatically violent mass reaction against poverty and racial injustice. Chance, timing, local ethnic diversity, and the scarcity of adequate private-market housing all played roles, but the three common local explanations for the lack of major civil disorder were the city's supposedly easygoing culture, the actions of the local police, and the influence of the antipoverty movement.

Although the city's fatalism cannot stand alone as a reason for its lack of serious rioting, the sense of hopelessness expressed by some target area residents may have lowered expectations and cushioned their reaction to slow progress. TCA director Winston Lill has argued that the city had plenty of provocative incidents, but they did not escalate because "there was no urge to get out and fan" the flames.[37] Future mayor Ernest "Dutch" Morial cited a "conditioned apathy among blacks" that derived from decades of "White Power."[38] Although that analysis assumes too much about the muted passions of the city's population, it does reflect a commonly espoused conviction that New Orleans was different from the rest of America. In general, white residents tended to think their friendships with black residents helped to disperse tension. Such sentiment caused Revius Ortique, an attorney and black civic leader, to warn members of the New Orleans National Council of Jewish Women not to expect their maid or chauffeur "to tell you how Negroes really feel."[39]

Some aspects of local life probably did buffer discontent. First, black residents' bad economic situation was not a recent trend, but a fixture of New Orleans history. Whereas residents of Detroit, Los Angeles, or Newark were suffering from loss of industrial jobs due to capital migration and technological innovation, these changes had a limited impact on New Orleans's small manufacturing sector. Second, the tension between the city's Creole class of African Americans and its non-Creole African Americans likely helped to fragment momentum that could have led to disorder—or to a more unified black political response.[40] A prevalent perception of black Creole social superiority certainly caused resentment among young black radicals in the target areas. Third, the comparatively integrated housing patterns in Central City and the Ninth Ward might have tempered outbreaks, and the physical isolation of such places as Desire, St. Bernard, and Algiers-Fischer may have made it easier to seal off trouble spots and concentrate police resources.

The actions of the police department and the influence of antipoverty policies are also offered as explanations for New Orleans's relative nonviolence. Unquestionably, relations between black residents and white police officers were strained and often inflammatory, but many people on both sides praised outreach efforts by the police department. Under police superintendent Joseph Giarrusso, the New Orleans Police Department (NOPD) had taken steps to develop a less threatening presence in black target areas. Mayor Schiro, the Housing Authority of New Orleans, and WDSU-TV credited the NOPD's "Getting To Know You" program for the lack of civil disorder. During the summer of 1966, the police department tried to provide various housing projects with free concerts that included a police singer, a local speaker, horse shoes, and free Coca-Cola. The program also offered safe driving lessons and stationed an officer in the housing projects whose duties included serving as an "athletic promoter."[41] Giarrusso stated that black residents needed more than membership on a few committees and boards. They needed a sincere and "direct display" by business and governmental leaders that conditions could improve. *The Louisiana Weekly*, New Orleans's major black-owned and operated newspaper, applauded Chief Giarrusso for realizing that "positive community action is the best antidote to violence." WDSU television commended Giarrusso for trying to move beyond "tokenism." Professor Daniel Thompson believed that entreaties by Giarrusso had broken down at least some of the wall separating the people from the police.[42]

Ultimately, the tactics used by police in tense situations likely had more influence than Coca-Cola and jazz.[43] The dramatic use of force often dissuaded mass action. In tense situations such the St. Bernard housing project after the King assassination, the NOPD erred on the side of caution by cordoning off the area to reduce confrontation until adequate force could be used. It is also possible that officers' yearly involvement with Mardi Gras crowds meant the NOPD was better trained at handling large and potentially unruly crowds than police forces in other cities.

If the police department was the state's most immediate response to disorder, the Housing Authority of New Orleans (HANO) and the War on Poverty were less direct but perhaps equally effective deterrents. On the one hand, a critical but often-overlooked factor was the appeal of public housing for black residents who had limited private market choices. Demand for HANO homes was high. Estimates of the waiting list of families wanting to rent one of HANO's 12,270 units ran from 10,000 to 20,000.[44] Rioting could have damaged people's homes, and getting arrested for insurrection could have been grounds for eviction. The most volatile projects were Desire and St. Bernard; they were also two of the least desired projects in the city and had some of the highest proportions of young people.

On the other hand, the War on Poverty offered programs that either provided financial opportunities or contributed to a more intense response by African Americans. The public-private apparatus that this book labels the Soft State was becoming effectively controlled by African American target area leaders and was offering unprecedented alternatives for black communities to receive more public attention. In June 1967, Total Community Action (TCA) and City Hall tapped federal funds to operate a joint summer jobs program "aimed at cutting down on unrest in the community this summer." A mostly white minister's group congratulated Mayor Schiro on his efforts to "avoid the possibility of upheaval" through employment and recreation.[45]

Although most commentators in the late 1960s paid too little attention to them, probably the most influential factor in the city's lack of severe disorder were the networks of authority and influence in black neighborhoods. Local War on Poverty leaders played a crucial role in identifying and cultivating those networks. Despite their depictions in the media as enclaves of fratricidal violence, uncontrolled passion, and funky rhythms, black neighborhoods were richly developed communities with complicated and often informal sources of authority and support such as extended families, neighborhood leaders, churches, and community organizations. Those informal networks, in combination with concentrated organizing efforts by War on Poverty activists, helped to build an administrative presence in black areas. Judging from other civil disorder-torn cities, New Orleans's five black target areas were the most likely places to experience disturbances. In 1966 and 1967, and certainly by 1968, those areas had a substantial organizational presence funded by the War on Poverty. Total Community Action, the Social Welfare Planning Council, and the Urban League of Greater New Orleans established vital connections with neighborhood leaders and showed new paths to power for people who previously had very few. Additionally, the establishment of a City Hall-based Human Relations Committee offered a chance for black and white leaders to meet.

At the time, the federal Office of Economic Opportunity took much credit for calming situations in cities that experienced riots and for preventing disturbances in cities that had none. Nationally, OEO officials spent much of their time defending their role in peacekeeping activities and rebutting critics who charged that employees of Community Action Programs (CAP) instigated many riots. Sargent Shriver asserted that "once the riots began, OEO smothered, not fanned, the flames." After all, the OEO had "taught the poor to build up, not tear down."[46] Shriver explained to New Orleans congressman Hale Boggs that Community Action Programs in many cities had plans in place to deal with riots and often worked in concert with local police. He estimated that, for 1967 alone, the civil disorders had caused over $300 million in damages, but the only damage inflicted on OEO property were seven sets of broken windows in one CAP building that cost $1,840 to replace. In his most strident rebuttal to his critics, he observed that only 16 of over 30,000 CAP employees had been arrested, and no one was convicted.[47]

Locally, OEO efforts had a role in reducing racial tension. An OEO report on "Southern Peacekeeping Activities" stated that the prevention of riots was the "acid test" of southern Community Action Agencies. New Orleans's TCA seems to have passed with high marks. Winston Lill, the director of TCA from 1964 until 1969, claimed that he "shut up" a group of influential white executives who were upset with the War on Poverty's community organization activities by telling them, "Look, the only reason we haven't had a riot is because of what [the organizers are] doing out there." Because of TCA, the "people who would have nudged the crowd into the street . . . were either on our staff or working for our staff."[48] Other federal officials and local leaders concurred. Sargent Shriver claimed that TCA's community workers were "a very effective civilian force in helping bring peace, order and hope" to New Orleans. He credited the city's leaders for having the police department work with TCA in joint anti-riot efforts. Mayor Schiro and Orleans Parish school superintendent Carl Dolce solidly supported TCA's labors. Police superintendent Joseph Giarrusso thought that TCA had "helped prevent violence," and TCA president Thomas Godchaux praised the recreation program for "reducing tensions."[49]

Expanding the Soft State

New Orleans in 1968 was a much different place than New Orleans in 1960. Black neighborhood leaders had taken over the multi-million dollar community action effort, and their political influence was growing exponentially.[50] Nevertheless, the urban crisis showed the inadequacies of the state apparatus response to demands coming from predominantly black neighborhoods. Local and national leaders scrambled to establish bureaucracies, programs, and public-private institutional linkages. Their actions set out a framework for the post–Jim Crow state.

The national urban crisis produced an outpouring of federal expenditures, although the federal government did not create a Civil Disorders Bureau equivalent to the Children's Bureau of the Progressive Era, the War and Industries Board for World War I, or the War Production Board for World War II, or the National Security Council for the Cold War. Political scientist James Button has provided compelling evidence that the federal government unquestionably boosted social spending because of the urban disturbances of the 1960s. The quickest response came from the Office of Economic Opportunity, which instituted what Button labeled a "'Fire Brigade' Approach." OEO jobs programs such as the Concentrated Employment Program, Job Opportunities in the Business Sector (JOBS), and Neighborhood Youth Corps were the major tools used by antipoverty bureaucrats to combat conditions that they believed had bred the riots. Despite their denials, OEO leaders did follow recommendations from the controversial *Kerner Report* until 1971, when Richard Nixon tried to remove all but emergency jobs programs. The responses of the Department of Housing and Urban Development (HUD) and the Department of Health, Education, and Welfare (HEW) were more moderate because they were open to more political pressures. The HEW mostly boosted welfare payments and funding for compensatory education. The HUD was only slightly more innovative. Model Cities programs offered some new approaches, but Urban Renewal's development agenda represented the primary response. The executive department that changed the most was the Department of Justice. It shifted from a strategy based on preventing civil disorder to one that encouraged active interdiction.

Advocates for the law-and-order approach pushed for more police officers, more jails, more crime-fighting technology, and harsher sentencing. From 1968 to 1972, the Nixon administration poured money into troubled police departments through Law Enforcement Assistance Administration grants. They also used the United States military to process information on ghetto activities. The Pentagon monitored disturbances on a twenty-four-hour basis and sent over a thousand Army personnel to investigate civilians. Public pressure caused them to lessen their role after 1970. The Justice Department also funded a massive database program known as the System for Electronic Analysis and Retrieval of Criminal Histories (SEARCH) in hopes of speeding reaction to disorders.[51] Locally, Mayor Schiro began beefing up the firepower of the police through anti-riot grants to fund preparation for crowd control.[52]

In New Orleans, the desire to prevent disorder prompted substantially more participation from conservative and moderate white civic leaders. One white resident of New Orleans's affluent Garden District called for more attention to the social and economic needs of residents in the neighboring Central City target area because "selfishly, too, I don't want to *see a Watts here*."[53] The urban crisis had awakened many other white New Orleanians to the realities of life for fellow citizens often living only blocks away. The local press took a greater interest in the black community, and several civic groups stepped up their involvement in establishing better relations between black citizens and the local government. The Metropolitan Area Committee, a group of some of the city's wealthiest and most powerful business and civic leaders, sought to improve recreation programs, job opportunities, and interracial communication. The Greater New Orleans Chamber of Commerce overcame internal opposition from conservative members to contribute to a jobs program, a recreation program, and a fundraising campaign for a local black self-help group known as the Thugs United. At City Hall, the New Orleans Human Relations Committee eventually became one of the city's premier biracial institutions.

In one symbolically important effort, a private biracial group known as the Committee for Open Pools (COP) sought to honor Reverend King by forcing the city to reopen the Audubon Park swimming pool, which

Mayor Schiro had closed to prevent its integration. After almost a year and a half of labor, a group of about fifteen newly inspired civic activists from wealthy white Uptown neighborhoods finally succeeded. One of the group's leaders was a civic-minded Jewish housewife who was deeply troubled by the King assassination. Norma Freiberg described the ways that her participation empowered her. "I was scared all the time," she explained. "I had never done anything before that public, that controversial." Before her involvement, she claimed that she "had never had a real friendship with a black" and had "never worked with black people on a joint project." To her, the Audubon Pool experience was a "wonderful lesson" that made her "hunger to get more into the real life of the community . . . to know more black people." In a city that remained starkly divided by race, the biracial experiments in political action gave some hope for future change.[54]

Some of the city's most influential citizens were trying to give black residents a larger stake in public life. Perhaps the most influential civic group in New Orleans in the late 1960s was the Metropolitan Area Committee, comprised of some of the city's wealthiest and most powerful business and civic leaders. The MAC occasionally wielded power nearly equal to that of City Hall. Its goal was to help provide black residents with more jobs, to coordinate meetings, and to lobby the state legislature for Urban Renewal legislation. In one instance, the MAC and the Chamber of Commerce held a fundraising drive that gathered $125,000 for summer recreation programs (over $700,000 in 2006 dollars) and encouraged City Hall to pump in an extra $100,000. Reducing racial tension was their motivation. Its members took the advice of the *Kerner Report* and tried to find spokespeople for "blighted areas" to develop "grievance lists" and looked into creating a "Neighborhood City Hall." They also created a Civil Disorders Committee that included Chief Giarrusso and five of the leading businessmen in the city.[55] One of the most influential members of the MAC was Charles Keller Jr., the husband of longtime civic activist Rosa Keller and a prominent Jewish businessman. Keller praised local leaders for the "relative calm" after the King assassination. Local black leaders, some of them affiliated with the MAC, had arranged a meeting with white MAC leaders to address "the greatest social crisis our urban areas have ever faced." King's murder had worsened black "frustration, despair and restlessness." Keller was thankful that those local black leaders "displayed a rare quality of true leadership by their ability to retain the confidence of local militant groups" and of the MAC. The MAC showed that "New Orleans *does care.*"[56]

The New Orleans Human Relations Committee was another effort to structure public responses. New Orleans already had one semi-public Community Relations Council (CRC) that had functioned since 1962. Made up of leading black moderates and white civic altruists, it was one of the few biracial voices in the city, but it operated as a private organization.[57] The Human Relations Committee of New Orleans (HRC) was a result of over ten years of lobbying by local liberals. In the heat of 1967, New Orleans's Mayor Schiro finally began to act, although he lagged behind not only progressives in New Orleans, but also leaders in all other south Louisiana cities and in the governor's mansion. Governor McKeithen's tortuously conceived Louisiana HRC had twenty-one white and twenty-one black members whose primary job was to find issues "before they reach the streets." By the end of 1967, eight other Louisiana cities also had HRC commissions in place.[58]

In August 1967, shortly after the Detroit and Newark disturbances, Mayor Schiro began rounding up acceptable church liberals, social welfare liberals, business progressives, and a few black leaders to begin discussions. Many of the same leaders who had negotiated the outcomes of the civil rights demonstrations in the early 1960s mapped out the structure of the HRC.[59] In 1967 and 1968, they were trying to solve the enigmas of employment, housing, education, and recreation.[60] The group functioned as an independent city agency that received funding from public and private sources. The leaders wanted to move quickly and carefully to avoid being what one member termed "just another piece of window dressing."[61] In September 1967, the City Council passed an ordinance allowing the committee, and by January 1968 they had set the criteria for membership. There were to be twenty-eight members equally divided by race. Eight were to be nominated by groups, and six were to be elected from specially drawn districts. The mayor had final authority to approve all appointments.[62] The HRC election came in March, and according to Monsignor A. T. Screen, the first coordinator of the New

Orleans HRC, more than eighteen thousand residents voted in fifty-seven polling places. In April, Schiro made his appointments and the HRC became a functioning arm of city government.[63] In December, John Pecoul Jr., a religious leader who would later serve as an assistant to Norman Francis at Xavier University, was chosen as the full-time staff director.[64]

Although the HRC accomplished no fundamental reform of the city's socio-economic structure, it did demonstrate how far city government had come on the issue of race. In a dramatic step away from the politics that had dominated city government until the middle 1960s, leaders of the HRC defined their organization as a means "to resist, oppose, circumscribe and ultimately end white racism and oppression." Although hampered by weak enforcement powers and budgets, the HRC leadership wanted to make the city "an open community" that celebrated "individual, ethnic, religious, and racial diversity." The "prerequisite" to reforming the situation was "the emergence of pride, power and self-determination in the black community."[65] The Committee's leaders outlined their four basic functions: "to take sides, to stand for something, to risk mistakes, to be an ombudsman for the unorganized and the unrepresented." Holding to the Great Society vision of inclusion, they believed "community demand" was the only thing that could "produce the many other changes that New Orleans needs to become a truly just and open city." In the following years, the HRC became institutionalized at City Hall. For the next decade, it served as a public voice for equality and diversity. Its *Help Desk*, which was begun by Margery Stich, leader of the local National Council of Jewish Women, and made permanent by Norma Frieberg, temporarily bridged some of the distance between the poor and City Hall.[66]

Another example of changing civic attitude was revealed in a series of articles on black poverty in the *New Orleans States-Item*. This moderate New Orleans daily newspaper—where the right-wing congressman Eddie Hébert had gained notoriety as the political editor in the 1930s—had come to accept the War on Poverty and much of its inclusion agenda, both programmatically and intellectually. The paper's editors advised their readers to recognize that the "Negro's problems go much deeper than previously believed." Reciting a mantra of War on Poverty advocates, they declared that the difficulties of African Americans were "the problems of all Americans," and finding solutions was the "right and decent" thing to do. After interviewing scores of overworked and under-paid mothers, fathers, grandmothers, and children who wanted to succeed, but lacked opportunities, one reporter began to sound like a War on Poverty leader. She called for the delivery of self-respect and dignity through the growth of the individual and the economy. Jobs, training, and education were the devices that she designated to elevate black self-worth. "Unemployment and poverty," she wrote, "put self-respect out of reach and eat away at the last shreds of even the simple dignity of being a human being."[67]

The civil unrest of the late 1960s also focused the attention of several national antipoverty figures on issues of alienation and the "softness" of the human psyche. OEO director Sargent Shriver saw the urban crisis as a result of deficient communal bonds and wavering national compassion. On July 27, 1967, a few days after the worst of the Detroit riots, Shriver appeared before the U.S. House of Representative's Committee on Education and Labor. Although no single piece of evidence can serve as the point where liberals made their last best stand for a massive expansion of the Great Society, perhaps Shriver's lament to Congressman Adam Clayton Powell's committee was close. Shriver blamed racial "isolation" for breeding "distrust and hatred." Americans did not "know" or "care" about each other, and this disconnect was destructive.[68] Relying on a vision of reform rooted in changing ideas and attitudes, he argued that affluent Americans had to escape from "an interior ghetto of the mind where we seal off parts of democracy that don't suit us, where we box off our obligations to justice and shut out our commitment to fairness. This ghetto of the mind is no less stinking and rotten than the ghetto of the city."[69]

Several other OEO officials saw urban unrest as a result of psychological alienation that supposedly resulted from material deprivation. One internal report reveals the political weight being placed on the supposedly wide psychological gap between ghetto residents and the rest of society. The poor needed a "new respect for authority," and governmental representatives at all levels needed to foster a new attitude by convincing the poor that the government was not out to get them, but was there to help them. Of course, the poor associated the word "Authority" with "handouts, welfare, jail," and "people in the ghetto look upon the 'Authority' with disgust and hatred."[70] Theodore "Ted" Berry, a black Cincinnati attorney and politician who directed the OEO's Community Action Program, explained that the disturbances were the "final culmination of years of neglect."[71] Larry Sylvester Odom of the OEO's Technical Assistance Office contended that the secret to creating an "inclusive society" was to help the individual "find a meaningful and relevant role for himself and his children." He explained that in 1967, "Negro" was "no longer afraid," but believed "he has the moral advantage" and "now views himself in a new light." The OEO needed to "structure a social climate" that could help resolve the conditions behind the riots and perpetuate the "self-directed reversal" of the "demeaning trend" caused by years of oppression. Odom asserted that those years had impeded the development of a sense of dignity necessary for full citizenship.[72]

The most famous analysis of civil unrest and civic alienation came from the *Kerner Report*, commissioned in 1967 by President Johnson to find out "What happened? Why did it happen? What can be done to prevent it from happening again?" He instructed its members to "find the truth and express it," unsullied by political consideration.[73] Released in March 1968, it contained one of the most devastating critiques of American society ever produced by a government-supported body. A stunning document that forced a much more sophisticated approach to America's urban problems, the Kerner Commission set the standard by which future political discussions about race, poverty, and progress would proceed. Its scope and impact were analogous to that caused by the 1944 publication of *An American Dilemma* by Swedish economist Gunnar Myrdal.[74] Like Myrdal, the Commission identified race relations as America's chief dilemma. Whereas Myrdal implicated white American identity as preventing the republic from achieving its core ideal of liberty and equality, the *Kerner Report* focused on the deeply ingrained segmentation of America's public life. Myrdal found a nation divided over the moral dilemmas of individual inequality. The Kerner investigators found a nation with racial divisions permeating virtually every institution and every mechanism for upward mobility.

In their oft-cited epigram about the state of the nation, the authors of the *Kerner Report* declared that America was "moving toward two societies, one black, one white—separate and unequal." Plodding the "present course," they warned, meant "the continuing polarization of the American community and, ultimately, the destruction of basic democratic values." In perhaps their most controversial pronouncement about American society, the Commissioners asserted that "What white Americans have never fully understood—but what the Negro can never forget—is that white society is deeply implicated in the ghetto. White institutions created it, white institutions maintain it, and white society condones it." The *Report* so enraged Lyndon Johnson that he canceled a ceremony to mark its public release and refused to extend the life of the Commission. Senator Fred R. Harris of Oklahoma, a member of the Commission, blamed Johnson's actions on misinformation. Gary Orfield, a social scientist, and John Herbers, a reporter for the *New York Times*, argue that a deeper reason was that Johnson did not want his acceptance of the report to make the Democratic Party soft on law-and-order issues in future elections. Rejecting the Commission was part of an attempt to salvage Great Society programs and to retain white Democratic support.[75]

The Kerner Commission gained enormous attention for blaming white America for the problems of the ghetto. Its wordsmiths rested their recommendations on the same intellectual elements of unity, growth, and compassion that dominated Great Society inclusion thought. They declared their "major goal" to be the "creation of a true union—a single society and a single American identity." As Lyndon Johnson had asked in 1964 when he unveiled the Great Society, Americans needed "new attitudes, new understanding, and above all, new will." Kerner Commission members' program recommendations relied primarily on expanding existing Great Society initiatives in education, job training, and housing, as well as boosting welfare transfer payments and relaxing qualifications. In what amounted almost to an admission of the impossibility of their designs, they also encouraged ghetto residents to leave the inner-city and integrate into the "society outside the ghetto."[76] The Kerner Commission's conclusions were politically profound, but analytically vague, placing much weight on inexact notions of race and linking the ultimate cause for disorder not necessarily with white actions, but, ultimately, on black internalization of white oppression. Instead of blaming the victims of poverty and discrimination for racial disorder, as segregationists commonly did, they blamed the psychological and economic influences that shaped the thoughts and actions of the supposed victims.

The local and federal searches for a peaceful summer provided a turning point for the city and the nation. In few other thirteen-month periods since World War II have so many profound—and often profoundly violent—events transfixed the nation. The events from July 1967 to August 1968 were stunning, especially in an age when television news coverage was redefining national moments. The shock of the Vietnam War, political assassination, and smoky city streets instantly transformed America's political culture. The shortcomings of liberal foreign policy and the dilemmas of race and poverty in America's cities were threatening to undo the liberal regime that had dominated America since the 1930s. In New Orleans, however, the result was an expansion of the Soft State and a solidification of liberal political power.

In the Crescent City, four programs solidified post-Jim Crow liberalism and coincided with a second stage of the War on Poverty that ran roughly from 1967 to 1974.[77] Food Stamps, the Concentrated Employment Program, Urban Renewal, and Model Cities were direct programmatic answers to black assertiveness and also extended the rehabilitative mission of the Great Society. Although their immediate goal was often to reduce racial disturbances, their long-range objective was to remake the disadvantaged individual into a contributing and productive producer and consumer. Each of these programs adhered to three requirements for social welfare policy in the post-Jim Crow world: they had to build human capital through improving skills, self-esteem, or consumption; they had to potentially enable participants to give back more to the economy and the society than they received; and finally, and perhaps most important, they needed to encourage economic growth and, more specifically, to reward constituencies beyond the poor.[78] Orville Freeman, the Secretary of the U.S. Department of Agriculture, summed up the sentiment in a statement to President Johnson in 1966 that extolled the value of the Food Stamp program: "The homemaker is able to buy more and better food, retail food sales improve, farm markets are strengthened, and the entire economy of the community benefits from the stimulus provided by the increase in food purchasing power."[79] The demands for growth and for rewards for all fit well with the Louisiana way. During this phase of the War on Poverty, grocers, butchers, farmers, teachers, social workers, contractors, developers, and consultants had to get their share of benefits. Historian Allen Matusow called this a process where policymakers had to "buy off vested interests and call it consensus."[80] Viewed against the stark realities of Louisiana politics, for progress to be made at a programmatic level, key groups had to be rewarded. The negotiation surrounding these programs helped form a pattern for working through the clash of interests. Holding to tradition in Louisiana politics, the government served as a source of opportunity and in this case helped to expand the Great Society marketplace. White reluctance to accept blacks as equals guaranteed that black political power came through public bureaucracies and political hardball. In the late 1960s, the Great Society metamorphosed according to black power and white compromise, backroom bullying and public grandstanding. In the process, the War on Poverty made racial progress a central reason for state expansion, instead of a by-product.

CHAPTER SEVEN

Making Workers and Jobs

The crying demand from neighborhood people was for jobs.
—SWPC Report, December 1968

In the middle and late 1960s, the unemployment rate in the United States was at one of its lowest points in history. Roughly 3.5 percent of Americans were reported to be out of work. In New Orleans that number was only slightly higher at 4.2 percent. For New Orleans's black neighborhoods, however, the rate hovered near 10 percent, and the *under*employment rate in those areas approached 45 percent for men and nearly 70 percent for women.[1] Local target-area organizations cited the lack of jobs as the most pressing limitation of residents.[2] To combat this serious problem in an otherwise prosperous nation, major parts of the Great Society were focused on improving prospects for black workers. In New Orleans, Great Society job-training programs anchored strategies to improve the employability of low-income residents and to better prepare black citizens to earn citizenship.

Throughout the twentieth century, manpower had been a central concern of economic policymakers. During the New Deal, the federal government openly manipulated the labor market. The Fair Labor Standards Act and the Fair Labor Relations Act recast the relationship between employee and employer by providing workers with friendlier rules governing wages and benefits. Those acts continued to regulate employment in the 1960s. Although they had disappeared by 1943, the Civilian Conservation Corps, the Works Progress Administration, and the Public Works Administration were unprecedented New Deal direct-jobs programs that created public jobs primarily to stimulate economic demand and alleviate high unemployment. After World War II, especially under the John Kennedy and Lyndon Johnson administrations, the state's role in manpower changed from assuaging panic and poverty to promoting precision and growth. Although the largest expenditures continued to be benefits to unemployed workers administered for the most part by state governmental agencies, the major focus was on helping trainees integrate themselves into the skilled workplace. Hoping to create full employment and stimulate the economy, Kennedy- and Johnson-era policymakers designed programs to improve productivity and by the later 1960s to maintain urban stability.

The first important Kennedy-Johnson era manpower program was the Manpower Development and Training Act of 1962 (MDTA). Designed partly to help workers who had been displaced by technology, the MDTA emphasized skills replacement. In Louisiana in 1964, it was headed by State Education Superintendent William Dodd, and it had no black members on its board. The Johnson administration developed the Neighborhood Youth Corps (NYC), the Job Corps, the Concentrated Employment Program (CEP), New Careers, Operation Mainstream, the Work Incentive Program of the Aid to Families with Dependent Children program (AFDC), and Job Opportunities in the Business Sector (JOBS) with the National Alliance of Business. They were neither comprehensive nor unified. The manpower division of OEO labeled MDTA, Neighborhood Youth Corps, New Careers, and state-level employment services as "largely discrete programs" that lacked effective interconnections.[3]

During the first four years of the Great Society in New Orleans, the Neighborhood Youth Corps, the Job Corps (including the Women in Community Service recruitment component), New Careers, and, especially, the CEP were the mainstays. The NYC provided jobs for low-income high school students and dropouts, while New Careers tried to facilitate access to clerical jobs. The Job Corps brought disadvantaged youth to centralized job-training facilities, which some contemporaries likened to a 1960s version of the New Deal's Civilian Conservation Corps. Job Corps was one of the most controversial manpower programs, but after addressing some initial discipline problems, it became one of the longest lasting programs of the Great Society. In New Orleans, Job Corps had little initial impact since most of the trainees went to facilities elsewhere.

The most important training program in New Orleans was the Concentrated Employment Program. One of twenty-two CEPs nationwide, the local version was an ambitious enterprise with an initial appropriation of $4.6 million out of a total national appropriation of $97.5 million. Through centers to be located in the target areas of Central City, Desire, the Irish Channel, and the Lower Ninth Ward, the CEP was supposed to provide training and placement assistance. According to the OEO, the program drew most of its funds from existing entities in an effort to streamline manpower approaches and to focus resources on target areas. In a complicated arrangement, the U.S. Department of Labor monitored each CEP. Total Community Action (TCA) conducted the work-training program in conjunction with the Metropolitan Area Committee (MAC), the Urban League of Greater New Orleans, and the Louisiana Division of Employment Security (LDES). The MAC was the liaison between the program and private employers. The Urban League, along with Loyola University, operated two-week orientation sessions in which enrollees learned how to interview, how to maintain "good grooming," and how to fill out forms. The LDES was responsible for placing graduates into jobs. Other contributors were social service agencies, neighborhood advisory committees that offered policy suggestions, and neighborhood residents who were hired to recruit other residents into the program.[4] Local organizations offering counseling and case-work services included Tulane University, the City Department of Welfare, Orleans Parish Department of Welfare, and the Family Service Society. To qualify for the program one had to have low income, lack an adequate job, and live in a target area.[5]

In some ways the Concentrated Employment Program was similar to an adult Head Start program. Like Head Start, it embodied a so-called comprehensive approach to integrating the poor, and the black poor in particular, into the larger community. CEP policymakers wanted the program to manage enrollees from "recruitment through assessment, counseling, physical examination, orientation, remedial education, training, work experience, necessary social services (including day care) referral, placement, coaching and follow-up."[6] Also like Head Start, it focused heavily on building the self-esteem of participants and making them more productive. The CEP's stated purpose was to train "undereducated and unskilled people to work in a job that offers dignity and satisfactory remuneration." Instead of Head Start room mothers, the CEP employed "coaches or helpers" who oversaw twenty-five enrollees. According to TCA, the coaches offered "visible proof of our recognition of his importance as an individual."[7] As the program developed, it tended to operate primarily as a placement service. Within the first year, many critics realized that the program offered little real training for skilled positions. Almost half of the placements went into other Great Society programs. Beyond superficial behavioral instruction, most of the CEP trainees learned on the job. CEP's federal grant usually paid the salaries for the few CEP enrollees hired by participating local businesses.

Local officials hoped CEP could help thousands of previously unskilled workers. From 1967 to 1970, the CEP brought almost $11 million into New Orleans (approximately $55 million in 2003 dollars). Neighborhood activists, local political leaders, War on Poverty officials, and various business organizations initially extolled its virtues. Business and government leaders were collaborating on a project that could provide real hope, "self-confidence," and opportunity for the poor. They thought it could encourage the poor to "perform a useful role in society as a family breadwinner."[8] Enthusiasm quickly faded. When it became obvious that the CEP could not place even half of an anticipated five thousand enrollees, the program began a slide from which it never recovered. The orientation sessions were the centerpiece of the training component, but they failed to prepare many for the job market. One fifty-six-year-old ex-longshoreman enrolled in the Loyola University orientation declared, "I need a job, but you are all crazy as Hell!" in response to the instructors' modernist dresses and the feel-good curricula.[9]

In addition to the limits of the orientation program, the CEP suffered from the reluctance of local businesses to hire black workers and an insufficient bureaucratic framework. Although the CEP seemed to have the support of key constituencies, it did not have the capacity to force changes from white employers. One analyst of the local CEP placed much of the blame for the shortcomings on the involvement of the Metropolitan Area Committee, charging that "perhaps MAC overestimated its ability to open doors."[10] The demise of the CEP showed that the MAC and the Chamber of Commerce either lacked the will or the ability to reform the local labor market.

In the late 1960s, the CEP in New Orleans operated under three separate grants known as CEP I, CEP II, and CEP III, each funded through Title V of the Economic Opportunity Act of 1964. CEP I was the most controversial. Running from July 1967 to December 1968 at a cost of $4.6 million (over $25 million in 2003 dollars), CEP I placed fewer than half of its initial enrollees. Over the next three years, disillusionment plagued CEP as placements remained low and the cost per enrollee remained high. CEP II ran from December 1968 to September 1969 at a cost of $3.2 million. According to one estimate, each placement cost $3,500 per month. CEP III operated in 1969 and 1970 at an approximate cost of $3.4 million. One grant worth $516,000 went to the Chrysler Corporation for a training program, which placed 108 people at a cost of $4,777 per person. The New Careers program, a component begun to develop careers in clerical jobs, averaged $4,800 per placement per year.[11]

In the beginning, the CEP received enthusiastic endorsement. According to one source, enrollees were "flocking to the program."[12] Harry Kelleher, president of MAC and one of the city's leading business progressives, backed CEP because "competent businessmen, not [the] government" were paying for the MAC's participation.[13] The local media presented CEP as a promising way to manage public and private economic resources. In their best boosterism, the editors of the *New Orleans States-Item* asserted that New Orleans had "vast potential," and "given its great natural assets, it is not utopian to believe it has the capacity to provide an adequate standard of living for all its citizens."[14] Using a metaphor that United Auto Workers president Walther Reuther used to explain his support for Model Cities programs, another local journalist called the CEP a "new type of conservation program." She argued that instead of conserving rivers, trees, and wilderness, it would offer sanctuary for human potential. Engaging in the despair mythologies so prevalent among progressive journalists, this reporter claimed that the CEP would be a "big step toward helping break what can only be called the vicious cycle of poverty and wasted human lives."[15]

As motivations for local leaders to support CEP, however, altruism and civic boosterism paled in comparison to preventing racial disorder. At a national level, the OEO noted that "the urban and racial crisis" had encouraged a "new receptiveness on the part of local government to get involved in human resource programs."[16] During the summer of 1967, religious, labor, governmental, and business leaders aggressively pushed for a CEP in New Orleans.[17] Police Chief Joseph Giarrusso hoped that involvement in the CEP would improve the image of the police department in the target areas, while Mayor Schiro wanted help for a "desperate situation." The "inertia of chronic unemployment," he lamented, had led to a higher crime rate and posed a threat to the community at large.[18]

When the New Orleans CEP began, a reporter for the *New Orleans States-Item* asked a question that haunted the program for its duration: Would its enrollees get jobs?[19] The answer was no, or at least not enough of them. TCA officials never reached any of their hiring goals. Given the rate of job placement at the beginning of 1968, reaching their initial goal would have taken fifteen years. By middle November 1967, only 1,295 enrollees had finished orientation. Of those, 108 had found jobs, 136 were engaged in remedial education, and 293 were in training programs that paid wages. Clarence Jupiter, associate director of TCA and director of CEP, put a positive spin on these numbers. He praised a jump in weekly job placements, which he claimed had recently doubled from 25 to 50. At the end of November, he lauded the program as a success.

The numbers did not support him. After four months of orientation, 237 enrollees were working in neighborhood Great Society programs. Only 69 enrollees worked in private businesses. In the following months, CEP officials sent letters to 3,150 businesses notifying them that TCA would pay them twenty dollars per week for every enrollee. A mere fifty companies accepted the offer. Overall in the first six months of the program, officials spent $714,076 for 817 placements in NYC and New Careers and 316 placements in more permanent jobs.[20]

The difficulties in New Orleans were not unique. According to a high-ranking OEO manpower specialist, every CEP in the United States experienced a "rough time" because "The 'Feds,'" he explained, "expected too much too soon." In over half of the twenty-two CEP programs across the nation, the most persistent problem was the lack of "meaningful jobs." The OEO determined that the lack of job commitments "by the private sector" was the "chief operational problem for all CEPs." Nationwide, only 3,332 enrollees had been hired, and only 1,651 private companies participated. By April 1968, 59,400 people had enrolled in CEP nationally. Only 16,000 (approximately 28 percent) had been placed in jobs, while 7,600 were dropouts, 10,900 were in a "holding status," and 24,900 were in some type of training.[21]

When the jobs did not appear in New Orleans, enrollment plummeted and outrage spiked. In the first three months, 2,417 low-income citizens had enrolled, but for the next four months, the number dwindled to only 428.[22] According to Jupiter, orientation courses had a 40 percent dropout rate. Neighborhood activists were furious. One protest group, the Soul Go-Getters, challenged the truth of any positive news emanating from the TCA camp. As evidence, they claimed that in their Central City area CEP officials had predicted 250 placements in the first twelve months. After the first six months, there had been only 44 placements, with only 110 expected for the entire year.[23] In early October, the Soul Go-Getters held a mass protest meeting at Booker T. Washington High School. The audience greeted TCA and City Hall representatives with boos and catcalls. One critic expressed a sense of disillusionment because they thought the CEP was a signal that the "national power structure and the local community realized that what poor people really need are jobs that would help us support our families."[24] At another time Miss Barbara Davis, a spokesperson for the Soul Go-Getters, announced that they were "promised jobs and we are going to raise hell until we get them." Hurling criticism at the MAC, TCA, and Louisiana Division of Employment Security, she lamented that the CEP was another instance of money going "down the drain." In response, TCA officials asked for patience and tried to explain that CEP was not a "make-work" program.[25]

At an Irish Channel Action Foundation meeting in late October, the simmering tension underlying the program burst forth in a public confrontation between neighborhood activists and the CEP leadership. In front of approximately seventy residents, CEP director Jupiter admitted the program was progressing slowly. Despite having placed only about one-third of enrollees in permanent jobs, he promised the future was bright. Germinal Messina of the Louisiana Division of Employment Security (LDES) and Henry Wirth of the U.S. Department of Labor both concurred. In a voice that local reporters described as "practically shouting," Philip M. Baptiste, director of the Urban League CEP Center No. 6 and soon-to-be the first African American aide to a New Orleans mayor, offered a dramatic challenge to their optimism. "I may lose my job for what I'm going to say," he chided, "but I'm tired of hearing all these so-called rabble-rousing speeches you've heard tonight. All that you're hearing is hogwash . . . the same hogwash you've been hearing since the poverty programs began." Continuing, he complained, "You came here to hear what job you could get with CEP and you've heard nothing." At one point he received an ovation for telling Germinal Messina, "Listen, Mr. Messina, SHUT UP." Jupiter yelled back, "As a staff person you seem to think you're born to lead these people to the promisedland," and he warned Baptiste not to "promise them jobs" and not to expect "fussing and ranting" to improve the situation.[26]

Fussing and ranting did, however, focus attention on the problems of the program. Charles Keller, a vital member of the MAC, was admittedly influenced by the "protest meetings and picketing." He cautioned that many target-area residents thought "that the program is a snare and a delusion, and that they've been had again."[27] Excuses for the program's inadequacies were plentiful. Germinal Messina blamed the inadequate manufacturing core in the area. Several officials blamed the problem on the failure of policymakers to account for the needs of local business owners. Ray Diamond, the successor to Clarence Jupiter as CEP director, cited the difficulty in trying to get businesses to lower their entrance standards to "hire Negro, poverty-stricken, school dropouts [who were] reading on a fifth-grade level, doing math on a fourth grade level, usually have a public record, [and] often have a history of drug use." Regarding CEP II, he insinuated that the local unemployment office and the

National Alliance for Business were to blame for placement problems because they were the only agencies with authority to contact business owners.[28] General Ellsworth I. Davis, vice president of the MAC, argued that the local CEP was too ambitious. Officials were wrong to expect employers to lower their hiring standards.[29]

Two influences permeated all of the reasons for CEP's poor performance and provided the core cause of the CEP's inadequacies. One was the city's color line. Harry Kelleher of the MAC tried to circumvent it by emphasizing that the CEP was "open to all citizens." Nevertheless, the Concentrated Employment Program was widely perceived as a program to help black workers. White residents were as reluctant to participate in it as white employers were to hire black graduates from it. The *Times-Picayune* admitted that CEP was "for white people as well as Negroes," but they "assumed that untrained Negroes are in most need of it." In addition, locating the training centers in target areas ensured that white residents would not participate in the program.[30] The Free Southern Theater's *The Plain Truth* newspaper offered a revealing interpretation of the situation. "The bitter truth of the matter is," they insisted, "that despite the Civil Rights Act" and other equal opportunity measures, "many jobs are still closed to black people." Accordingly, "culturally biased tests, unrealistic entry level requirements, 'quota' systems, and outright prejudice" had made the "systematic exclusion of Black people" part of the city's institutions.[31]

A second source of CEP's pervasive inadequacies was the differing vision of CEP held by participants, policymakers, and business people. The poor wanted jobs and higher incomes. The government offered a hastily planned program that focused on self-esteem and image. While CEP taught black workers the etiquette of pleasing white interviewers, they largely ignored the racial cleavages of the local job market. In failing to offer institutional wedges into traditionally white job markets, federal officials hobbled the CEP from the start. Black neighborhood leaders, in addition to wanting jobs with good wages, hoped to use manpower programs to help black participants understand themselves and the value of political power. They wanted to go beyond CEP's behavioral training to include a much more radical political instruction about the forces that made their position in the marketplace so precarious. Program bureaucrats resisted this tactic. White employers pursued different racial and political agendas altogether.

White racial prejudice toward African Americans proved too deep to overcome in a short period of time. An OEO investigation of CEP nationally found that "racial discrimination and prejudice" were the "dominant influences" in every program they examined. It was "blatant" in Birmingham and "subtle" in Boston. Potential white enrollees tended to refuse to consider entering the "mostly black" CEP, and white businessmen often refused to hire blacks in good jobs. Black participants, they discovered, often felt CEP helped them to get only traditional "Negro" jobs that were "dead-end, low status, and low pay." They tended to see the program as another example of "white tokenism."[32] The OEO's conclusions fit the situation in New Orleans. The vast majority of local CEP enrollees were African American, yet most jobs in New Orleans beyond low-skill, labor-intensive positions were closed to African Americans. One example of the difficulty was the skewed civil service system. In a city where black residents comprised approximately 40 percent of the population, they held only 16 percent of its civil service jobs, and then usually in the lowest echelon. Jefferson Parish, a white-flight suburb of New Orleans, was surprisingly better, with blacks comprising 27 percent of its civil service sector—although still in low-scale positions.[33] General Davis of the MAC blamed "just plain racial discrimination in most cases." His plea for improving the situation involved the MAC going "into the woods and beat[ing] in the customers, who feel rebuffed and reluctant to come forward."[34]

From the summer of 1968 through the next several years, Great Society manpower programs were in a crisis mode. Bureaucratic uncertainty, placement dilemmas, and racial divisions were causing bewilderment among officials from Washington, D.C., to New Orleans. The many problems and the slow progress of the CEP in New Orleans caused Department of Labor officials to warn that they were "beginning to seriously question the capability" of the local CEP officials to operate the program. Labor officials criticized what they saw as a "floundering approach" to manpower problems. Their evaluation of TCA's operation of the CEP found serious problems in coordination, in the coaching program, and in the number of participants in a "holding status." They were especially disturbed by the division of the duties of the CEP director and by unrest in the neighborhoods. To continue their role in the CEP, warned Labor officials, TCA had to make "radical changes" that included giving the director "full authority," instructing staff on the nature of the program, and establishing better follow-up procedures for enrollees.[35]

New Orleans was not alone. Internal assessments of manpower policy by the Office of Economic Opportunity found that nationwide MDTA, NYC, CEP, and New Careers programs were not having a "meaningful impact." Analysts viewed the CEP mostly as a "holding corporation" that doled out subcontracts to other agencies and as merely a "drop in the bucket" compared to manpower needs. The OEO evaluation recommended significant reforms in CEP's placement procedures, antidiscrimination strategies, and in its bureaucratic organization. OEO analysts advocated reducing the number of CEPs but maintaining the same level of funding. The ultimate solution was in increased public-sector employment for enrollees and in shifting more decision-making power to the local level. With rising inflation and growing economic uncertainty, an OEO administrator warned, CEP was poised to become "a disaster." Although their evaluation stressed that CEP had improved the manpower system by unifying the manpower process, the CEP was still the victim of bureaucratic territorialism. OEO analysts believed the future of CEP depended on local unemployment offices taking the lead in placing graduates instead of viewing the CEP as a threat. As the CEP continued to unravel, its critics in the OEO interpreted it "as a transitional mechanism" that required "further experimentation with alternate structures and methods of operation."[36]

As with most of the Great Society, local concerns dominated the Concentrated Employment Program. According to the OEO, "local conditions" dictated each CEP grant, causing each one to vary "widely—in almost every dimension—from project to project." Local influences subverted federal design almost every way. Throughout the CEP nationwide, the phrase "local conditions" was a euphemism for racial conditions. In many cases, OEO officials wanted to shift more control to local authorities in an attempt to placate "militant" black leaders. The lack of a unified federal effort in target areas—despite the original intention to do so—encouraged a "fragmentation of support." That fragmentation was the chief reason that OEO officials recommended that the CEP develop a "mechanism" to involve target-area residents in every aspect of the program.[37]

Federal policy makers were clearly reacting to the escalating assertiveness of black neighborhood leaders. In New Orleans, the rising power of target-area activists was forcing changes in the manpower programs, and black leaders were successful in getting African Americans hired to lead them. By the end of 1968, the tensions forcing revisions in the city's original War on Poverty leadership structure were also affecting the CEP. The New Orleans branch of the NAACP asked for the dismissal of CEP director Raymond Diamond, who had replaced Clarence Jupiter, for "lack of insight and feeling for the community." They also wanted longtime TCA director Winston Lill removed for allegedly making decisions without approval from the agency's board of directors.[38] Too often, the NAACP claimed, CEP officials bypassed the black-dominated neighborhood advisory council, and the TCA officials made the key decisions without seeking their sanction.[39]

Differences between local black leaders' aims and the colorblind policies of federal bureaucrats weakened the local program and underscored the power of the color line. Foremost, local African Americans involved in the jobs programs wanted economic stability. They also wanted to use the programs to promote black cultural awareness. Influenced by Black Power thinking, several program developers tried to use black heritage to both insulate trainees against the vicissitudes of the marketplace and to cushion their entry into it. The orientation program of the Urban League of Greater New Orleans was the best example of the tension between federal colorblindness and the personal and cultural politics of local African American leaders. The Department of Labor wanted the Urban League to gear its efforts to white and black residents alike. The Urban League, however, customized its program almost exclusively to address the concerns of the local black community. It included discussions meant to help the enrollees better comprehend how the structures of their society influenced their status. Federal representatives objected to the topics of "the

System, the Negro, Entrepreneurism, and Cooperatives" and chastised the Urban League for including material on civil rights, urban life, and "Black Heritage."[40]

Despite the problems associated with CEP I and CEP II, in 1969 Total Community Action received funding for CEP III, although with one-fourth less money. The funding was granted in part because TCA agreed to make several changes in the CEP organization. Under CEP III, CEP funds and leadership would be separated from TCA, which gave the CEP director more authority over the program. CEP III continued the basic design of its first two versions, but put more emphasis on skills training and providing jobs for participants, especially through New Careers and the Neighborhood Youth Corps. TCA received almost $640,000 of the $3,426,000 grant to operate a "job conditioning" component that involved education and counseling. The Louisiana Division of Employment Security received $330,000 to conduct outreach and recruitment, and almost $640,000 went for skills-training for two hundred participants in "exploratory work experience." The New Careers program received a little over $540,000 to place between 100 and 150 participants in "sub-professional jobs," and the NYC received almost $530,000 to hire around 175 students.[41] The Chief Administrative Officer for City Hall recommended the city not take over the CEP, but take more interest in it.[42]

Contemporary assessments of the Concentrated Employment Program in New Orleans were necessarily harsh.[43] It was poorly planned and executed. It was disorganized, and its structure was too weak to overcome the problems of inadequately trained participants and racially prejudiced employers. The program proved particularly hard to defend because critics could easily perform simple cost-benefit analyses to judge the program. A popular tactic compared the cost of one year manpower training to one year at Harvard. There were clearly not enough jobs in the local private sector to accommodate the demand created by the program. However, like many other Great Society programs, the inadequacies of CEP were perhaps most notable for what they revealed about the problems afflicting the society as a whole. The problems arising from CEP forced some citizens to ask why jobs were not available for the trainees and focused attention on the poor preparation provided by the city's educational system. The development of CEP showed that low-income workers in New Orleans needed institutions that could better prepare them for the marketplace. Attitude adjustment could only go so far. CEP also showed that without adequate federal funding to sustain them, private sector efforts were as ineffective as any part of the program. Finally, the program revealed how precarious reform could be when confronting an increasingly complicated color line with an uncertain strategy. In the end, the problems with the CEP led to changes in federal jobs programs. The 1971 Emergency Employment Act funded direct jobs in 1972 ($1 billion) and 1973 ($1.25 billion). The 1973 Comprehensive Employment and Training Act (CETA) tried to streamline manpower efforts and focus on public employment. CETA was operated by the Department of Labor, and it became the repository of the OEO job training components such as Job Corps and NYC. In 1982, CETA was replaced by the Job Training and Partnership Act.

One of the major reasons that racial divisions limited the success of the Concentrated Employment Program was that the program did not offer enough financial and political incentives to white employers. Initially, a similar fate seemed to await the Food Stamp program. In the end, however, New Orleans's Food Stamp program became operational because it offered clear rewards to area merchants, farmers, and politicians. The fact it overcame the obstacles of race and bureaucracy was important because, of all of the Great Society's antipoverty programs, perhaps none touched the lives of the poor more directly.

CHAPTER EIGHT

Making Groceries

> We are sure that no civic minded individual or public official
> could be so short sighted not to raise the $65,000 needed to
> impliment [*sic*] this plan.
> —Frank Meydrich, Louisiana Supermarket Association, 1967

They came for groceries. In August 1969, a reported three hundred welfare recipients, most of whom were female African Americans, made their
way over land and water to the New Orleans Civic Center complex to
collect on an offer of free food and shoes. At least, that is how the day
started. The rest of the story is a bit cloudy, but, after a short while, the
congregants realized that the promises of bread and footwear were, at
best, a mistake or, at worst, a malicious hoax. The August heat and humidity intensified. Some grew surly. In the end, the event turned into
what some analysts might characterize as a modern bread riot, a 1960s
expression of ancient politics of desperation. In downtown New Orleans,
protestors smashed windows and rushed the building that housed state
government offices, making it to the third floor before being repulsed.
Outside, a typical late-summer Louisiana thunderstorm helped to scat-
ter the remaining crowd and defuse a potentially serious incident. In all,
the police carted off three women, and workers cleaned up. Later in the
day, the New Orleans Welfare Rights Organization (NOWRO) handed
out thirty-five bags of groceries to compensate the food-seekers for their
troubles.[1]

165

The people who had come for free food frequently had a hard time "making groceries," a French-derived term to describe shopping for food.[2] Besides having little money, low-income black citizens were caught between clean, well-stocked "white" grocery stores that were usually too far away and too hostile and ghetto markets that often charged exorbitantly for sub-par goods. By August 1969, however, the burden of making groceries was becoming slightly less onerous for eligible poor families. Six months earlier, the city had begun participating in the Food Stamp program run by the United States Department of Agriculture. In those six months, participation had grown to almost 38,000 people. The downtown disturbance demonstrated, however, that the program was no panacea. During the six years it took to fully establish New Orleans's Food Stamp program, the program worked modestly to help reduce hunger—or food insecurity as some now define it—and bolster a fledgling regional liberal coalition.[3] In the early 1970s, low-income families in New Orleans did not find themselves seated—metaphorically or literally—with gentry at the city's famous Creole restaurants like Antoine's, Arnaud's, or Gallatoire's, but they did find themselves able to bargain for more food at the local checkout counter.

The August incident was, at one level, about bread, shoes, and the limitations of African American consumption. At a much broader political level, these low-income women were trying to find out where they stood in the post–Jim Crow South, to test revised meanings of freedom in a supposedly desegregated public world. The story of how New Orleans's Food Stamp program developed is in part a story of how the American welfare state rewarded the people who controlled it at the local level. If small government advocates were in control locally—typically the case in Louisiana if policies were targeted to black citizens—the welfare state reaffirmed existing power relationships. If control was in the hands of motivated progressives who wanted to redistribute power and distribute goods and services to marginalized citizens, the welfare state could empower alienated constituencies. The New Orleans Food Stamp program developed in a convoluted, hesitating, and occasionally bizarre fashion, but it left racial liberals solidly in control of the agenda. From the outset the local program was a response to black assertiveness. Radicalized, poor black women provided the pressure that led to its founding, and once in operation a black director administered it, black-led neighborhood councils oversaw it, and over forty black workers, primarily women from impoverished target-area neighborhoods, staffed it. Black target areas housed the program's four offices. Compared to New Orleans almost ten years earlier—when the city had ground to a halt over four little black girls going to first grade at two white schools—the transformation was startling. Locally, the Food Stamp program served a largely black clientele and, according to local estimates, expanded purchasing power of the poor by $25 million.

And then something strange happened. A year and a half after the program began, at the height of black-power radicalism when white leaders nationwide were often eagerly buying off black discontent, the program's black director agreed to shift control to a white mayor. The reason was that New Orleans had experienced a profound political shift, and for the first time in modern history, black leaders were reasonably certain that the local political apparatus would move beyond tokenism and reward their constituencies with effective services.[4]

Between 1965 and 1971, the politics of the Food Stamp program helped re-order black influence, and its history demonstrates how black activists and leaders negotiated benefits for the city's low-income population. Those benefits almost always had to come through formal and informal arrangements with white leaders, whether liberal, moderate, or conservative. In the early 1960s, the process of pressuring white business elites had contributed to the desegregation of schools and lunch counters. In the late 1960s, those delicately constructed black and white relationships changed in nature as African Americans increasingly wielded essential electoral and bureaucratic influence.

The Food Stamp program's policy roots stretch from the New Deal through the late Great Society. Food Stamp scholars have provided compelling evidence that, by the late 1960s, the New Deal program's primary focus on creating demand for agricultural surplus had shifted to a Great Society focus on alleviating food insecurity among the urban and rural poor, albeit while benefiting food growers and sellers. In 1939, the United States Department of Agriculture (USDA) began the first Food

Stamp program, allowing qualified poor families to buy food coupons that could be redeemed at far higher values for certain food items. Nearly four million people participated, but the range of items was limited, and the demand for the program was minimal. The program ended in 1943 as wartime economic expansion and agricultural scarcity rendered it unnecessary. Throughout the 1940s and 1950s unsuccessful efforts to revive the program were made by Senator George Aiken of Vermont, Congresswoman Leonor Sullivan of Missouri, and a core group within the USDA. One minor legislative success in 1959 withered when Secretary of Agriculture Ezra Taft Benson refused to act on it.[5] The modern era of Food Stamp policy began in January 1961 with President John F. Kennedy's Executive Order 10914, which expanded the commodities program, and his economic message announcing eight new Food Stamp pilot programs. Those programs retained many of the New Deal program's procedures, particularly the requirement that participants purchase stamps with their own money. This requirement captured conservative support for the program because it forced recipients into the labor market. A year and a half later, the Kennedy administration expanded the pilot programs to twenty-five. All but one of them were initiated in congressional districts represented by Democrats. Ted Sorensen, one of President Kennedy's chief advisers, told the President, "It's a very popular program, both on the Hill and in the communities where it's taken."[6]

In August 1964, the passage of the Food Stamp Act formalized the program, and it was a feat of legislative maneuvering. A strange coalition of conservative agricultural interests and liberal antipoverty advocates negotiated the passage of the final bill.[7] To gain support for the Food Stamp Act, proponents leveraged their votes for agricultural subsidies, especially for southern tobacco. One of the behind-the-scenes bureaucrats who helped to shape the bill explained that many in the antipoverty bureaucracy were initially wary of the legislation because of its support from southern and southwestern farmers and their representatives. "It was very much a farmer's [program] really," this official said. "Farmers were wanting to sell more food, even if they had to sell it to poor people."[8] The Act expanded the reach of the program, but adhered to the design of existing projects, particularly the USDA and state-level welfare departments. The federal government did not have the power to impose the program on local governments. Local leaders had to seek it out, and state officials set eligibility criteria. Additionally, the legislation forced local leaders to choose between joining the stamp program or continuing to receive surplus agricultural commodities. This choice was partly responsible for some of the early criticism of the program and for low participation rates. In East Carroll Parish, one of the poorest counties in the impoverished Mississippi River delta of north Louisiana, participation dropped sharply in one month from almost 5,200 people in the commodities program to barely 700 in the Food Stamp program.[9]

The first attempts to build a Food Stamp program in New Orleans began in 1965. The first stamps, however, were not sold until February 1969—purchased at a staged event by a Mrs. Shirley Collins. In the intervening years, thirty-five other Food Stamp programs had become operational in Louisiana.[10] At the national level, program development during those years was also slow but steady, and the total number of projects grew from 43 in 1964 to 2,225 in 1973.[11] In most southern states, Food Stamp programs were controlled by conservatives, who kept eligibility standards high and controversies low and generally liked having the federal government pay for the benefits while leaving implementation to the states. By the late 1960s, for example, Mississippi was one of only six states in America that had a food assistance program operating in each county.[12] In part because of local control, Mississippi became the site of the infamous 1967 hunger tour by Senator Robert F. Kennedy and others and the symbol of America's failure to adequately address hunger. In Louisiana, the Department of Public Welfare had enormous control over determining a family's eligibility and over which parishes (the Louisiana equivalent of a county) could operate a program. This department had become famous in the early 1960s for midnight raids on welfare recipients and for purging thousands of children from the Aid to Families with Dependent Children (AFDC) program.

The federal Food Stamp program generally fell under the jurisdiction of southern-dominated congressional agriculture committees, and it required poor people to have enough money to meet purchase requirements.[13] Most of the criticism of the program in the 1960s came from people worried about hunger; the stories about steak-eating, Cadillac-driving welfare mothers did not become a staple of conservative critics and outraged journalists until after the middle 1970s. The rediscovery of hunger in 1967 and 1968 by the media, the Citizens' Board of Inquiry into Malnutrition and Hunger, and several politicians built public awareness and created an informal "hunger lobby." Several studies support the claim that the resulting political pressure led to administrative changes in 1969 and then to legislative amendments to the 1964 Act in December 1970. Two other major reforms in the program occurred later. In 1973, amendments required all counties in the nation to have a program and set eligibility standards at the national level instead of by locale. In 1977, amendments eliminated the food stamp purchase price.[14]

Considered from a broad perspective, the Food Stamp program did not differ greatly from other parts of the American welfare state. It was an underfunded, noncomprehensive program controlled by a select number of congressional committees, policy professionals, and bureaucrats.[15] Local administrators, rules, and politics guided its implementation, and demands for profit, peace, humanitarianism, and inclusion complicated the process. The food fight in New Orleans indicates that America's responses to hunger involved far more than distributing fat and flour to country folk or devising structures to reward America's most influential farmers. In the post–Jim Crow southern city, the response to hunger involved realigning rights, reordering civic power, and integrating marginalized citizens into the state. Confounding New Orleans's welfare-rights advocates and emerging liberal leaders were white Louisianians reluctant to do anything to benefit their fellow black citizens unless it clearly satisfied their self-interest as well.

By not forcing state and local governments to develop food-stamp programs, the 1964 Food Stamp Act encouraged a hesitant approach. New Orleans's political leadership proved to be in no hurry to seek a meaningful program until 1967. Then they bickered for two more years over who would control it.[16] Between 1965 and 1969, the motley contingent of Food Stamp lobbyists—welfare rights activists, members of the Louisiana Supermarket Association, and labor unions, to name a few—struggled to reshape the way poor New Orleanians bought food. The policies followed by the USDA (which distributed the food coupons) and the Louisiana Department of Public Welfare (whose caseworkers determined eligibility) were enormous stumbling blocks to lobbyists' efforts. Lobby groups wanted the up-and-running Total Community Action (TCA) to administer the program locally and wanted the OEO to foot the bill. Consistently, USDA and the Louisiana Department of Public Welfare administrators rejected proposals to operate through TCA's Neighborhood Development framework on the grounds that the USDA was forbidden by law to contract with nongovernmental agencies. TCA was technically a private nonprofit corporation, and local leaders floundered for several years before finding an acceptable way around USDA rules. However, by early 1971, TCA had to give control of the program to the city because the program's massive growth quickly outdistanced TCA's structural capacity and its appropriations.

Early lobbying for a food-stamp program began in March 1965 and was led by A. P. "Pat" Stoddard, a local AFL-CIO leader and manpower specialist for TCA.[17] Two years later in April 1967, he had made little headway. Eventually, he and other advocates proposed that the state government bear most of the clerical costs of a program for six months until a more permanent structure (their choice was TCA) could take over. Two hurdles stood in the way. First, the Southwest Regional Office of the OEO had to approve TCA's operation of the program. Second, they had to convince Governor John McKeithen and Secretary of the Louisiana Department of Public Welfare Garland Bonin to provide operating funds and to make necessary requests to the OEO.[18] Both men had a history of confrontation with the OEO.[19] Although there is scant evidence that the governor opposed the Food Stamp proposal, Pat Stoddard took no chances, lining up a formidable cast of lobbyists. He arranged for New Orleans mayor Victor Schiro, Catholic archbishop Philip Hannan, and Louisiana AFL-CIO president Victor Bussie to lobby McKeithen for a $65,000 appropriation to operate a temporary program from January 1968 to June 1968. Confident of the plan's approval, the president of the Louisiana Supermarket Association informed a TCA administrator, "We are sure that no civic minded individual or public official could be so short sighted not to raise the $65,000 needed to impliment [sic] this plan."[20]

To bolster their position, program proponents had nurtured the support of the USDA, the Louisiana Department of Welfare, the City of New

Orleans, and Total Community Action. In a common but politically astute argument, they emphasized the low cost of the program compared to the benefits, claiming that the city would have to contribute only $1,500 and the cost of police protection for transporting the stamps.[21] According to them, a combined investment of less than $67,000 by the city and state would translate into over $225,000 in local and state tax revenues and a $5 million increase in retail sales for the first half of 1968. Proponents also argued that the arrangement would reduce "disease and hunger," provide "nutrition and consumer education," and help stabilize Neighborhood Development Centers amid budget cuts.[22] In early October 1967, McKeithen found their arguments acceptable and agreed to provide the state's share. One TCA official summarized the reason for the program's political appeal. Its "special merit" was that it "benefits not only the hungry, but our state's farmers and New Orleans' businessmen."[23] For their part, Louisiana's grocers offered a compelling political rationale that rivaled the appeal of economic growth even as it exposed a fear of civil disorder. They endorsed the program as a way to "help end the slum areas and ghettos which are the birthplace of much crime and many other evils and diseases." If the New Orleans stamp plan were in place "sufficiently before the hot summer" of 1968, they forecasted, it could save the city "many times the cost it would have taken for the Food Plan." They implored state and city officials to "see the handwriting on the walls."[24]

The local group doing most of the handwriting was the New Orleans Welfare Rights Organization (NOWRO). Where Louisiana's grocers and farmers applied pressure to the state through their deep pockets and their political networks, the NOWRO applied pressure from local housing projects. Led by Shirley Lampton, Eartha St. Ann, Monica Hunter, Audrey Delair, and Clementine Brumfield, this group had emerged with the help of the TCA Neighborhood Development Program. Delair was a member of the TCA board of directors, and St. Ann was employed as a community worker's aide for SWPC and then TCA. Among their activities, they organized residents of several federal housing projects, and they orchestrated a city-wide rent strike, a poor people's march to the state capitol, and several protests. Perhaps most important, they lobbied policymakers and legislators. They encountered tenacious adversaries, in particular Louisiana Welfare Secretary Garland Bonin. He openly refused to meet with the NOWRO because it was, in his words, one of several "outside militant groups"; this despite the fact that almost all of its members resided in New Orleans target areas. To Bonin, these women "were attempting to stir up trouble" and "intended to embarrass, harass, and disrupt welfare operations in the city."[25] In contrast to this view, NOWRO leaders characterized their group merely as "city-wide organization working to protect the rights and improve the living conditions of families living on welfare." Their major structure consisted of four committees in local target areas, not a far-flung, conspiratorial web of remote revolutionaries.[26]

In the autumn of 1967—despite the tensions between welfare rights activists and state welfare bureaucrats—fear, compassion, and profit seemed to have triumphed. The Food Stamp program for New Orleans was signed, sealed, and almost delivered. The OEO, the governor, and City Hall followed through on their commitments. Mayor Schiro welcomed a program that he thought would bring relief to what he estimated as 2,500 families in "dire need."[27] In October, the all-white city council attempted to institutionalize his sentiment by approving a resolution.[28] By the end of 1967, however, the city still had no Food Stamp program, and the NOWRO was still lobbying state officials for action.[29] The delay continued for another year and a half. The delay resulted from a combination of procedural uncertainty, inconsistent funding, and bureaucratic territorialism. The blame centered on Secretary Bonin, who contributed to three more delays in December 1967, June 1968, and December 1968, and on the USDA's regulations preventing program delegation to non-public agencies. Bonin deflected much of the criticism directed at him by citing legal restrictions and the rules of the USDA.[30] A New Orleans television station accused Secretary Bonin of putting New Orleans's application last among other Louisiana applications. Bonin admitted reluctance to push New Orleans's application and shrugged off his critics by claiming that the city was in less need than other Louisiana municipalities and that it lacked adequate staff.[31] In the months following the December 1967 delay, New Orleans officials produced two additional plans. The first plan failed, but the second one finally proved acceptable to all parties. In the first scheme, the city replaced the state as the primary funding agent for clerical costs, agreeing to pay $28,900 in start-up costs in order for the program to begin in June 1968. TCA, for its part, agreed to pitch in $25,000 to administer the proposed $2 million program.[32] Like the previous plan, it was stopped largely because of Bonin's reluctance.[33]

The final, successful food-stamp plan emerged from yet another TCA proposal to OEO. This version called for four distribution centers to be located in neighborhoods of Desire, Central City, St. Bernard, and Algiers-Fischer and overseen by neighborhood advisory committees. At a total cost of $194,003, of which $58,000 would come from OEO, TCA would initiate programs designed to reach 25,000 families the Department of Public Welfare determined eligible.[34] This new plan circumvented the rule against contracting with nongovernmental bodies by making the city the holder of the contract with TCA. In an arrangement finalized in early January 1969, the city council approved TCA's operation of the program and contributed $48,000 for operating costs. As a sop to agri-business interests, policymakers agreed to allow grocers to accept stamps only for domestically grown food items.[35] Over the two-year process, the state government's investment had dropped from $65,000 to no direct cost. The city government's part had risen from a little less than $2,000 to $48,000. OEO's contribution had gone from TCA's administrative costs to almost $60,000.

The criteria to qualify for food stamps were fairly straightforward, unlike the process of funding the program. To keep the program from being too closely identified with the recipients of AFDC, qualifications were designed to include many of the poor who did not receive public assistance.[36] Food-stamp purchasers—assumed by TCA to be women—had to reside in Orleans Parish, have cooking facilities in their home, and have incomes that fell below established limits. All families receiving public assistance qualified. In a nod to the notion that the male was the head of the household, women could apply only if there was no man in the home, but TCA used the pronouns "she" or "her" to refer to purchasers. In addition, program officials required proof of citizenship and proof of income, which required applicants to produce a valid social security card and a combination of rent or mortgage receipts and payroll, unemployment, and/or banking records. The qualifying and registration processes were not overly easy, but any participant who believed his or her civil rights had been violated at any point in the process was encouraged to file a complaint.[37]

From the beginning, participation in the program and sales tax revenue were encouraging. The first year and a half of operation, however, were not without problems. When the Nixon administration liberalized eligibility rules in late 1969, local administrators found themselves in a bind. The number of households purchasing food stamps jumped from approximately 3,400 (13,863 participants) in February 1969 to over 9,400 (37,186) by the end of August 1969. The city provided $300,000 for distribution and the federal government approximately $20 million for the stamps.[38] In the next year, the number of participants jumped to seventy thousand people, with children accounting for approximately fifty thousand of them. By January 1971, program officials expected over one hundred thousand local participants.[39] The Food Stamp program became one of the largest social welfare programs in New Orleans, expanding the purchasing power of the poor by an estimated $25 million.[40] This growth required TCA to hire a staff of forty-four full-time employees that included eighteen tellers and sixteen receptionists (as of August 1970). In 1969, administrative costs averaged about $20,000 a month. Sales tax revenue projections for 1970 predicted that food coupons would add $490,260 to the city budget and $326,836 to the state's coffers. Officials expected those figures to double in 1971 with city revenue from sales taxes on goods bought with food stamps accounting for $971,013 and state revenue coming to $647,341.[41]

Ironically, this massive participation hobbled the implementation of the program. Long lines and long waits at the distribution centers caused alarm, at one point nearly causing a riot. The wait at some facilities was reported to be as long as six hours.[42] In addition, procedural entanglements plagued the program. An evaluation of the first two months of operation uncovered several policy violations in TCA's four target-area offices. The Louisiana Department of Public Welfare and the USDA expressed concern over a "general lack of courtesy" and the competence of some employees. Supervisors at Algiers-Fischer and Central City were allegedly not following "the Federal manual for operation." An example of a more serious violation was keeping over $1,000 in a safe overnight because the armored car pick-up had been missed. A Food Stamp official at TCA defended those occurrences because unexpected lines required keeping the offices open beyond the stated hours, resulting in missed pick-up times. The USDA was particularly distressed by TCA's apparent policy of hiring only "Negroes" in the four offices. [43]

Other criticisms dogged the program. Advocates for the poor contended that eligibility standards excluded too many of the needy. Recipients thought that the coupons cost too much. Others bristled that commodities stopped being distributed once the Food Stamp program got underway. [44] An evaluation later in 1969 noted some improvement, but found that TCA was overwhelmed. On the upside, an in-house investigator found the neighborhood offices "operating routinely and efficiently." On the downside, many purchasers had to travel long distances to reach the centers, and too few non-AFDC recipients were in the program. In a subtle rebuff of critics who claimed that the true root of the hunger problem was not access to food, but rather poor people's ignorance about food and lack of self-discipline, TCA stopped its consumer and nutritional education component because they could not maintain the personnel to implement it. [45] Another in-house TCA evaluation in April 1970 revealed some of the problems that led to TCA handing over operation of the program to the city. On a positive note, it claimed that New Orleans's program was the most efficient in Louisiana and better than comparable ones in Houston and San Antonio, Texas. In part, the target-area distribution system presented a good opportunity to bring residents in for medical examinations and inoculations. However, the program had become a victim of its own success. Predicting doubled participation in the next year, the analysts recommended using a projected $505,359 boost in sales tax revenue to improve the delivery system. [46]

By the spring of 1970, TCA officials realized that the Food Stamp program needed new management. In mid-April, Food Stamp workers went on strike to bargain for overtime pay. In an incident disturbing to TCA leaders, a reported three hundred women workers allegedly stormed TCA's downtown offices, where they forced a meeting with Daniel Vincent, an African American logistics engineer who had succeeded the original director of TCA one year earlier. Vincent and Food Stamp clerical workers walked a few blocks to City Hall to procure $5 payments to "tide them over," and the women agreed to return to work. A few days later, Vincent suggested transferring administration of the program to another agency.[47] Louisiana Welfare Secretary Bonin blamed the problems on TCA's policy of hiring neighborhood workers. With little vested in antipoverty leaders' concern for maximum feasible participation of the poor, Bonin declared it a mistake to hire what he called incompetent staff from the "welfare roles" to operate the distribution centers. He believed the quickest solution was in hiring more workers, but demanded that those workers not have allegiances within the War on Poverty neighborhood framework.[48] Vincent strongly disagreed with Bonin's assessment of his workers' competence, but he did agree that the program was "near collapse."[49]

One of the reasons TCA was willing to give up direct control over the Food Stamp program was that they were handing it to a key Great Society liberal. Mayor Maurice "Moon" Landrieu, a young and energetic political leader who represented the new technocratic trend in southern politics, had been elected a few months earlier by a coalition of African American voters and relatively affluent Uptown whites. He had received over 90 percent of the votes cast by blacks in the Democratic run-off and 98 percent in the general election, while getting nearly 40 percent of white votes.[50] Landrieu owed much of his mandate to the leaders of the black community. For this reason, it was possible to broker an acceptable shift in authority over the multi-million dollar food-stamp enterprise. The program's crisis brought together leaders from local government and the local business community who wanted to find solutions to this necessary program. One of the key brokers in transferring the program to City Hall was the Metropolitan Area Committee (MAC). The MAC leadership's involvement in this social welfare issue reflected a new reality in New Orleans politics. Instead of finding ways to ignore the interests of black residents, many of the city's civic and economic elite were working diligently to accommodate them.

Mayor Landrieu blended input from the MAC; the black community, and local social welfare bureaucracies in his attempt to fashion a solution to the Food Stamp dilemma. He orchestrated a meeting between Harry McCall, president of TCA and one of the most visible progressive members of the city's social elite; Daniel Vincent, director of TCA; Councilman Philip Ciaccio, a white representative of several large black neighborhoods; Jim Pezant, director of research for the city council; and Jim King, director of the recently formed City Demonstration Agency (Model Cities). One admiring leader of MAC depicted the meeting as a "vigorous," "efficient," and "impressive" coming together of the brightest leaders from City Hall, from the federal programs, and from progressive civic groups. He left the meeting "feeling good about what I had seen happen."[51]

The opinion of this MAC member may have ignored some of the tensions between the groups seeking a solution. Its ebullience, however, did show the willingness of local leaders to resolve problems and preserve control of the program. One proposed temporary solution involved funneling "flexible funds" from the Model Cities program into the Food Stamp program.[52] In July another controversial stopgap solution proposed to transfer $75,000 from an employee pay-raise fund to the mayor's office to support the Food Stamp program.[53] The permanent solution involved the City Demonstration Agency operating the program from October to December 1970 and the city government taking over permanently in December.[54] This solution did not involve a major shift of control and satisfied most parties. It brought New Orleans into line with the operation of Food Stamp programs in the rest of the state, since New Orleans's program had been the only one administered by a Community Action Program. The transfer also satisfied the OEO, which preferred that the CAP focus on innovation instead of traditional service delivery. The takeover also pleased the members of the local Social Welfare Planning Council, who believed that the arrangement would provide more accountability and create a more efficient program.[55]

The transfer of the Food Stamp program was part of a broader transformation in the local antipoverty movement and a maturation of the civil rights movement. Partly as a result of funding cuts and administrative changes for OEO, Total Community Action was losing prestige and power. By late 1969, the Model Cities program and the local Urban Renewal effort had become the focus of innovative efforts. The Nixon administration was moving away from supporting Community Action Agencies and shunting control over War on Poverty programs to various federal departments and agencies. Locally, TCA became a victim of its own success. Its community organization efforts had cultivated black leaders and organizations, and they were gaining their own influence. By 1970, TCA was merely one of several options for ambitious black leaders wanting to secure power bases. When Great Society liberals took over City Hall, they centralized the federal pipeline in the local governing structures. Street-level activists and neighborhood leaders still mattered, but their power had to flow through City Hall rather than the Great Society web of federal administrators and private social welfare organizations. Besides being important for the development of new biracial political arrangements, the Food Stamp program did help thousands of local people to feed their families. It was not, as some had hoped, part of a revolutionary redistribution of wealth and power. It was traditional American social welfare policy geared to relieve misery, reduce dissent, and reward its benefactors.[56] Farmers and grocers made millions. Savvy politicians stabilized their bases of power. Middle-class Americans felt less guilt about the vagaries of the marketplace. Hungry people ate better, as long as the food was domestically produced.

In its broadest outline, New Orleans's Food Stamp story shows how the politics of hunger mixed with the politics of race and the Sunbelt's politics of growth to produce a compromised, but permanent, antihunger program. The push for a local Food Stamp program intensified only after the disorder of the middle 1960s exacerbated white political paranoia and after many locals became increasingly unsettled by the idea of children not getting enough to eat. In a narrower sense, local Food Stamp history also shows how local policy entrepreneurs used the quiet Louisiana way of coalition-building to overcome resistance to programs benefiting black citizens and, in the process, to help low-income people make groceries.

CHAPTER NINE

Making a Model New Orleans

We meet this morning with an opportunity . . . to take
advantage of untold millions of dollars.
—Mayor Victor Schiro to the City Council, September 1968

In 1965 and 1966, several black neighborhood leaders complained that
their areas were ignored by a disinterested Mayor Victor Hugo Schiro.
By mid-April 1968, however, target-area residents had forced City Hall
to take notice. Victor Schiro finally targeted the "slums" as a serious problem. According to the mayor, target areas contained only 25 percent of
the city's homes and provided only 6 percent of its tax revenue, but they
took up 45 percent of city services and accounted for 50 percent of all
major crime, 50 percent of "all major diseases," and 35 percent of the
city's fires.[1] Schiro and his liberal successor Maurice E. "Moon" Landrieu
took advantage of the federal public housing, Urban Renewal, and Model
Cities programs, among others, to improve housing, infrastructure, and
economic development. Initially targeting the Lower Ninth Ward, Central City, and Desire, the rehabilitation efforts established some of the
most direct paths to power for local African Americans and white progressives. The blend of construction projects with antipoverty and civil
rights initiatives appealed to a wide range of interests and solidified the
role of quiet patronage in post-Jim Crow politics and race relations. In
keeping with the broader therapeutic trends of the War on Poverty, many
of the policies were designed to improve the city by improving the ghetto

dweller as well as the ghetto. One local television commentator reported that 89 percent of the people living in the city's "slums" were black, and those "slums" bred "an atmosphere of hopelessness and despair." Upgrading real estate there would mean "improving the quality of life for all citizens."[2]

From 1968 to the mid-1970s, the rehabilitation process produced a wide variety of education, housing development, and community participation programs and yielded some much-needed facility improvements in a few target areas. Federal programs also were used to underwrite massive projects in the downtown area. In 1972 when the federal government temporarily suspended all federal funds until the city stopped dumping raw sewage into the Mississippi River, then-mayor Moon Landrieu explained, "when federal funds are cut off in this city, it is like having your arteries stopped up."[3]

Federal funds sustained the growth of biracial liberalism. Combined with Total Community Action, which was largely led by African Americans after 1968, the institutions responsible for administering Urban Renewal and, especially, Model Cities were a formidable bureaucratic triumvirate. For example, in 1969 TCA controlled almost $10 million, employed well over 500 people, and funded a variety of neighborhood centers and influential programs.[4] Model Cities and Urban Renewal considerably increased the number of public sector jobs and private sector contracts available to minorities, especially after April 1970 when a racially liberal mayor took office. From 1968 to 1975, the Model Cities program generated over $20 million in federal funds and employed professional and subprofessional staffs for approximately 50 programs that included daycare, healthcare, education, credit unions, housing development, and bonding and capital pooling for minority contractors. The chief administrative entity was the City Demonstration Agency (CDA), which lasted from late 1969 until 1975. The Nixon administration's support of these programs wavered, and securing appropriations was an annual, dramatic congressional battle until 1974, when Gerald Ford signed the Housing and Community Development Act. This legislation effectively eliminated Model Cities and redefined Urban Renewal in favor of a block grant system.[5]

Housing

Before the federal Model Cities and Urban Renewal programs were established, local housing reformers had limited options. One place was City Hall. Partially to encourage landlords to take better care of their properties, the city council passed the Minimum Housing Ordinance in January 1967 that gave more authority to the Division of Housing Improvement. In November 1967, the council created the Citizen's Advisory Committee on Community Improvement to assist in deciding housing issues.[6] Much of the city government's housing improvement efforts, however, focused on encouraging tenants and landlords to have pride, to get along, and to conduct "voluntary maintenance." Housing inspectors tended to emphasize "tenant responsibility."[7] Another housing effort was the local Catholic archdiocese Christopher Homes project that provided homes to a few local citizens in need.[8] One housing development plan came from the Johnson administration's encouragement of major insurance companies to invest in the inner city. In New Orleans, the Metropolitan Life Company funded an $800,000 federally insured housing loan program for nurses working at the predominantly black Flint-Goodridge Hospital in Central City. The insurance company had twin goals: to improve real estate values and to help "the urban poor to live like human beings . . . with dignity and no holes in the roof." According to Edgar Bright Jr., head of Met Life in New Orleans, their efforts were part of their "debt to society" and a "matter of good will." The insurance company's representatives claimed they wanted to help the "working man"—although virtually all of the beneficiaries of the program were female nurses and would not be considered poor—and to "be part of the uplifting process."[9]

Since good will was in short supply in the private sector, other efforts relied on the federal government. The legislative basis for most of New Orleans's public housing policies began with the Housing Acts of 1937, 1949, and 1954, which provided for the creation of America's massive public housing program and Urban Renewal. After 1961, several other housing bills expanded federal involvement. The creation of the Department of Housing and Urban Development (HUD), the Rent Supplements Act, and the Demonstration Cities and Metropolitan Development Act (Model Cities) were all part of an often contradictory set of federal policies that also included massive funding for highways and home loans that encouraged the suburban exodus.[10]

In the fall of 1967, the Housing Authority of New Orleans (HANO) controlled 12,270 residences that were home to almost 17,000 adults and 31,000 minors, 25,000 of whom were under the age of fifteen. Most of New Orleans's housing developments were racially segregated New Deal and post-World War II projects that averaged of three thousand residents each. The exception was Desire, which contained over 11,000 official residents and many more unofficial ones. In 1966, HANO opened its last large-scale public housing project. The Fischer Homes in Algiers cost approximately $17 million to construct and provided homes for 4,400 residents in a high-rise apartment building and a series of low-rise units. After the middle 1960s, the public housing construction trend, called Scattered Site housing, was to scatter small developments throughout the city. In late summer of 1968, HANO projected that this program would inject 3,350 units into the local rental market, with 90 percent of them going to black renters. The project was estimated to cost $55 million, and most of the construction contracts apparently went to established white companies because of bonding difficulties that plagued black contractors. This prompted a local underground newspaper to remark that "once again it is the white man who is profiting from the needs of Black folks."[11]

Public housing offered shelter, but the bureaucracy overseeing it did not encourage black activism. Urban Renewal and Model Cities did. The fight to bring Urban Renewal to New Orleans was similar to the Food Stamp struggle because it brought together a diverse coalition whose members used intimidation, compassion, guilt, and growth advocacy to achieve their goals. The development of Urban Renewal, however, involved a much more clearly defined use of identity politics. A barometer of black power at the turn of the decade, Urban Renewal served as a cheaper way—politically and financially—to satisfy black demands for better infrastructure in their neighborhoods.

Urban Renewal

When Urban Renewal emerged in the 1950s, it promised an almost ideal response to the slums in America's cities. Its projects seemed to offer opportunities to bring about the creative destruction of the nation's most blighted areas. A product of legislation passed in 1949 and 1954, Urban Renewal allowed the federal government to pay two-thirds of construction costs for local slum clearance and rebuilding projects. But as the program progressed, critics began to complain that instead of helping low-income residents, it often simply pushed them out of their homes and neighborhoods. All over the United States, sports arenas, civic centers, highways, and skyscrapers began to sprout where poor people used to live. To many critics, Urban Renewal became synonymous with "Negro Removal." According to one source, only one unit of housing for the poor was built for every four that were destroyed. In 1961, a representative of the Chamber of Commerce of Greater New Orleans praised Urban Renewal in other cities, however, for preventing "the spread of blight into good areas of the community."[12]

New Orleans received neither many of the benefits nor the detriments of Urban Renewal. Of the nearly $5 billion in Urban Renewal grants doled out by the federal government by 1966, Louisiana received very little. The reason was historical. In 1954, a movement led by New Orleans Third Ward tax assessor James E. Comiskey and the newly formed Owners and Tenants Association convinced the Louisiana legislature to disallow public seizure of private property if that property were to be resold to private business interests. Partly as a result, the number of inadequate living structures in New Orleans rose from approximately 25,500 (14 percent of the total) in 1950 to approximately 50,000 (24 percent) in 1960.[13] Gaining momentum in the middle 1960s, Urban Renewal proponents in Louisiana's urban areas pursued a dual strategy. They worked to overturn the 1954 state legislation, and they looked for ways to subvert the spirit and intent of the act. "At stake," WDSU television explained in support of Urban Renewal enabling legislation in 1966, was "the lifeblood of our cities."[14]

Although Louisiana's Urban Renewal opponents had their way for over a decade, in 1968 the state legislature enacted enabling legislation. Partly because of the immense damage caused by Hurricane Betsy in 1965, a carefully developed political coalition that blended various white and black urban interest groups had already initiated efforts to bring in federal funding to improve drainage, sewerage, streets, and housing.[15]

The prospect of federal subsidy for infrastructural improvement, economic growth, and rising land values was seductive. By 1969, among the lobbyists for Urban Renewal were the Louisiana Municipal Association, the Chamber of Commerce of Greater New Orleans, the Social Welfare Planning Council, Total Community Action, the Urban League of Greater New Orleans, various target area councils (particularly the Lower Ninth Ward Neighborhood Council), the Human Relations Committee of New Orleans, and most important, the Council for a Better Louisiana (CABL), a group composed of some of the state's most influential businesspeople. The lobbying efforts of these groups benefited from a widespread change of public attitudes toward Urban Renewal. Almost three-fifths of Louisiana voters supported Urban Renewal; in New Orleans that number climbed to three-fourths.[16]

Before the city saw the flow of any substantial federal renewal money, the proponents of Urban Renewal had to counteract the entrenched opposition. That opposition is well characterized by the comments of Congressman Edward Hébert, who called Urban Renewal "one of the most vicious, damageable, and insidious pieces of legislation ever passed by Congress."[17] By the late 1960s, local and federal officials had learned from earlier mistakes and were giving local residents more influence over new projects. In 1968, however, Hébert continued to argue that Urban Renewal ignored "the right of an individual to keep his home."[18] He had plenty of company. One Irish Channel group of about one hundred residents called itself the "Office of AMERICANISM vs. COMMUNISM Committee" and demanded that Mayor Schiro prevent what they called "this communist slum clearance act." This group viewed Urban Renewal as "clearly a communist front organization" designed to "take away private property rights."[19] In another instance as late as August 1969, Irish Channel residents rebuffed plans by HANO, the Irish Channel Action Foundation (ICAF), and Tulane University architecture students to tear down homes in the Annunciation area and create about two hundred new scattered-site units. The opponents had the powerful support of tax assessor James Comiskey, councilman Eddie Sapir, and former state representative Stephen Daley. According to Reverend Delbert Fisher of the ICAF, the issue had "stirred them [Irish Channel residents] up."[20]

In 1968, objections to Urban Renewal like those of Congressman

Hébert and the residents of the Irish Channel were still quite prevalent in the state. Although a solid majority of Louisiana's urban dwellers—and their elected state representatives—favored Urban Renewal legislation, the state's large contingent of rural legislators coalesced with enough of their apprehensive urban colleagues to postpone the enabling legislation for four years after Betsy. The absence of enabling legislation did not stop some New Orleans leaders from seeking creative ways to fund projects. In the 1950s, federal transportation money helped build the Pontchartrain Expressway and a new Mississippi River bridge, while municipal funds financed much of the Union Railway Terminal and the downtown Civic Center complex.[21] In 1965 under the auspices of the Community Renewal Program, the city received an almost $400,000 grant to conduct an architectural survey and to develop a "master plan" for improving the city's physical environment. Conducted by Bernard Lemann, Tulane University professor of architecture, the study attempted to find blighted housing, to explore why it existed, and to examine its relationship to crime and social problems.[22] Surveys did not violate Louisiana's laws against Urban Renewal. Turning survey data into concrete and steel did. Several times between 1966 and 1969, city officials tried to find loopholes. In December 1966, officials applied for a HUD grant for the Lower Ninth Ward, but HUD representatives turned them down because Louisiana law prevented the city from carrying the project out.[23] Unwilling to give up, the Schiro administration re-applied. This second time, they proposed that the city pay for improvements and then get reimbursed by HUD, thereby bypassing restrictions against loans. Still unconvinced, HUD rejected their application once again.[24]

Despite those rejections by HUD, city officials continued to seek funding for improvement projects. In September, HUD did approve nearly $400,000 in grant money to determine the feasibility of renewal projects.[25] If construction funds could be found, city leadership would have priority areas established. In November, Stuart Brehm, director of the City Planning Commission, tried to gain the city council's approval for starting storm drainage work in the Lower Ninth Ward.[26] By July 1968, Richard Johnson, a Washington, D.C.-based aide to New Orleans's Chief Administrative Officer, claimed that New Orleans had begun a number of "vital projects" despite the state's legal barriers.[27]

While city leaders were trying to find ways around the lack of enabling legislation, other leaders across the state were working furiously to pass legislation that would open the Urban Renewal floodgates. Initially these efforts were spurned. The CABL-led coalition considered a statewide referendum, but abandoned the plan for fear that rural areas might defeat the proposal. Their final, successful solution involved bypassing rural areas all together by opting for local referenda. In New Orleans, the tenuous coalition of black activists, white businessmen, and civic progressives conducted a successful campaign that called upon the familiar goals of economic growth, civic compassion, and riot prevention.

Mayor Schiro's support for the final Urban Renewal bill revealed major changes in the city's politics. Schiro began repackaging himself as a vocal critic of slumlords and an advocate for the city's renters. He respected private property, he reassured his constituents, but the city's renters were not getting their money's worth from often exploitative slumlords. To the argument that stronger code enforcement was the answer, he retorted that it was not possible to bring many of the houses up to standard. One "can't paint a hole," he chided. Although certainly not in "favor of the total bulldozer approach," he believed in a comprehensive effort that included serious improvements to streets and drainage and aggressive housing rehabilitation. For the displaced, he advocated the construction of more low-cost housing.[28] His position was politically tactful. It gave him credit for having a more active civic presence on behalf of the dispossessed, but still provided room to dedicate most future funding toward infrastructural improvement. Perhaps most important, his position allowed him to take credit for upgrading services in black neighborhoods at little cost to the city.

Schiro's arguments were part of the deliberations over the Urban Renewal bill during the spring of 1968. In February 1968, CABL sought to solidify a coalition of leaders from urban and semi-urban areas. The group brought together the mayors from nine Louisiana cities. Other representatives at this planning session included members of New Orleans Community Advisory Committee on Housing Improvement (CACHI).[29] Baton Rouge mayor Woodrow W. "Woody" Dumas advised the state's six cities with over fifty thousand residents (Shreveport, New Orleans, Baton Rouge, Monroe, Lake Charles, and Lafayette) to develop a common legislative strategy for distributing Community Renewal Program funding.[30] The efforts in 1968 proved successful. By July, the legislature had approved legislation allowing for Urban Renewal referenda for Shreveport, Baton Rouge, and New Orleans.[31] In early June, City Hall began its public campaign for passage. Mayor Schiro encouraged the CACHI to begin a door-to-door rallying effort because his administration wanted "total community participation."[32] Associated Catholic Charities, the Catholic Church's major social work agency, augmented City Hall efforts by endorsing Urban Renewal as the only answer to the city's housing crisis. HANO and the Catholic Church's Christopher Homes were inadequate for the task. In July, the *New Orleans States-Item* tentatively endorsed the idea of a referendum, provided that the city avoided mistakes made in other cities.[33]

City officials apparently expected the referendum to pass. Schiro and the city council began developing the city's Community Improvement Agency (CIA), an entity centered at City Hall that would oversee future Urban Renewal grants and construction projects. City Planning director Stuart Brehm, the eventual director of the CIA, advocated that the new agency be a completely new organization that would represent a break from the city's past and with no ties to HANO. He wanted it to have no "preconceived ideas" and to be "an entirely fresh approach." For Urban Renewal to work, Brehm contended, it would "have to present to the public an entirely new image."[34]

By endorsing that approach, Mayor Schiro demonstrated his evolution into a more active civic leader. At 10:00 a.m. on September 4, 1968, the mayor asked the city council to approve the CIA, telling them that they had "an opportunity for positive action never before available to us." They had a chance "to take advantage of untold millions of dollars of financial assistance to rid this community of substandard living conditions." Schiro implored the council to "open our eyes and our hearts." In outlining the program, he emphasized that growth of federal influence need not worry council members. The CIA would use federal money for improvements, but its decision-making power rested largely with officials at City Hall. According to Schiro's outline to the council, Neighborhood Advisory Committees would advise each project, but all projects had to have approval from the City Planning Commission and the City Council. That approval would be followed by a public hearing in the project area, and then there would be a bond election for property owners to decide either to accept or reject the city's one-third share of the costs. One day after Schiro's plea, the City Council passed a resolution that officially created the CIA.[35] Almost a year later, the council put out a $3.58 million grant proposal.[36]

The CIA offered the mayor a remarkable political opportunity, despite warnings from the local press not to let the agency become "politically motivated."[37] For little financial and political cost, he could begin major improvements to infrastructure in black target areas that were becoming centers of political influence. City Hall could help drain the flood-prone Lower Ninth Ward while boosting the allegiance of its increasingly powerful neighborhood leadership to City Hall. Partly due to a growing national emphasis on returning power to the local sphere, the CIA offered a cheap way to implement a vision of physical progress and racial amity. Even better for the mayor's office, the CIA provided a means for controlling the contracts for construction and for feasibility consultation, and if things went wrong, the federal government stood as a ready scapegoat. This relationship between black power, civic rejuvenation, neighborhood revitalization, and participatory democracy helped to alter patterns of local political patronage.

The mayor had the authority to appoint the CIA's seven board members. Schiro stacked it with political insiders, rising black leaders, and businessmen with heavy investments in New Orleans real estate. All of them were men, and each of the appointees either was deeply involved in New Orleans's real estate ventures and construction or represented links to populous black areas. Schiro rewarded many of the people who played important roles in passing the enabling legislation. There were two at-large appointments. One was Walter M. Barnett, an attorney who had chaired the CACHI and headed the New Orleans Property Owners Association. The other was Thomas J. Heier Jr., the city's Chief Administrative Officer since 1961 and a crucial behind-the-scenes operator in the push for enabling legislation. Schiro's public relations director called Heier "the most knowledgeable and informed appointive government official in New Orleans." Two other appointments consisted of two local philanthropists. Edgar B. Stern Jr. was a wealthy beneficiary of the Sears, Roebuck & Company fortune and leader of CABL. Laurance Eustis Jr. was director of the New Orleans and Trust Company, the Royal St. Louis Hotel Corporation, and the Stratton-Baldwin Hardware Company. Eustis had also served twenty years as state senator and was former chair of the HANO board. Another white appointment was Mark Smith III, a thirty-two-year-old engineer, developer, and chairman of the board for New Orleans Federal Savings and Loan Association.

The final two appointments were up and coming black political leaders. Lawrence A. Wheeler was a politician and attorney nominated by Ernest "Dutch" Morial, the first black Louisiana legislator since the onset of Jim Crow. Wheeler was president of the Second Ward Voters League (Central City), founder of the Louisiana Advancement Association, and member of the Louisiana Civic and Voters League. Rounding out the appointments was Andrew Peter Sanchez Sr., an industrial arts teacher at Chalmette High School, the vice chair of the Lower Ninth Ward Neighborhood Council (LNWNC), and a major influence in the increasingly powerful cadre of Ninth Ward leaders who constituted the Southern Organization for Unified Leadership (SOUL).[38]

The formation of the CIA and the ensuing campaign for the local option referendum involved a complicated political balancing act. One local commentator viewed the referendum as a moment where the city had an "unprecedented chance to forge an alliance between the predominantly white 'preservationists' and the predominantly black poor."[39] The biracial, cross-class support that eventually passed the legislation and referendum was shaky at best. Urban Renewal meant different things to different people. For traditional businessmen with enormous sums of money tied into land value and the general growth of the local economy, it represented a way to improve their investments and secure their fortunes, while possibly quieting black demands and tempering black rage. For local white leaders, Urban Renewal offered money for almost nothing and peace at bargain rates. For black leaders, Urban Renewal represented the best available way to bring physical improvements to their neighborhoods and a fertile opportunity to establish their own positions as policy advocates.

Some of those black leaders, like their white counterparts, also saw a chance to improve their own financial situation.

The most obvious tension in the Urban Renewal coalition was between the black leaders of the Lower Ninth Ward and the established white business leadership. Bill Rushton, a New Orleans architect who contributed in-depth investigative newspaper reports on housing issues, forecast dissension between the "old-line" members of the CIA and the forces in the Lower Ninth Ward. To Rushton, the CIA head Walter Barnett characterized the "old-line." He embodied what Rushton labeled the "Noblesse Oblige Syndrome—which insists that 'You-all can't plan your neighborhoods and your lives nearly as well as we patronizing Bourbons can.' "[40] Rushton's evaluation was cynical, but pointed to fundamental divisions over the purpose of Urban Renewal.

Urban Renewal dramatically expanded the influence of the Southern Organization for Unified Leadership. SOUL's leaders forced the CIA to cast renewal projects in the Lower Ninth Ward in SOUL's image. Eight months prior to the November referendum, SOUL activists dictated the terms of their support. The federal renewal project proposed for the Lower Ninth Ward had to involve "community people" in all phases and respect the community's "culture and values." SOUL demanded control over most of the key functions of the grant. Federal contracts had to ensure employment for neighborhood residents and involve black-owned companies. SOUL's chief goal was to control housing initiatives and, especially, to encourage home ownership. According to them, "no one can truly feel that he is directing his own destiny" without owning a residence. Encouraging ownership helped a person transition "into a viable society while retaining his individuality." They refused to accept any program that would "destroy the roots of our people." Particularly, they were "unalterably opposed" to massive housing projects and would allow only scattered-site programs. SOUL could not accept their community being turned into a "public housing reservation." Without community control over Urban Renewal, they warned, New Orleans's leadership could expect "hostility and negativism" and "anxieties and frustration."[41]

SOUL's statement of black pride and black unity did not mean that everyone in the Lower Ninth Ward supported SOUL. Ruby C. Sumler, a respected community leader affiliated with Leontine Luke and the Ninth Ward Civic Improvement League and a community worker with TCA, led an attack against the SOUL-Lower Ninth Ward Neighborhood Council forces. Claiming that the Lower Ninth Ward was a "split community," she argued that the leaders of the Neighborhood Council did not represent the thirty thousand residents of the area, but only a dozen or so people. To her, Lower Ninth Ward political leaders such as Sam Bell and Theodore Marchand, a contractor, were fighting for Urban Renewal for personal gain. She claimed that Marchand had formed a corporation that had purchased land in the area and was using "the poor people and the black people" as an "excuse" to make money for himself. In an argument that revealed how important it was for Urban Renewal to reward the individuals who supported it, she explained that "the poor man is not interested in how much money Mr. Bell or Mr. Marchand or any already established contractor makes," but what they could make for themselves. She and other leaders like her wanted the poor to get jobs, learn skills, and "become professionals in that field." In her most pointed allegation, she stated that "many residents" in the area were "tired of the White man exploiting the poor and also of the Black man exploiting the poor and we intend to fight both!!!" Although her arguments did not curtail SOUL's influence, it did raise some serious questions about the role of self-interest in the rise of black power. Was Urban Renewal offering the community minimal improvements while showering a privileged few with disproportionate benefits?[42]

Opposition to the November referendum echoed Sumler's protests. Local radicals who lobbied for more grassroots involvement complained about the program serving the interests of a few in the name of the many. Writers for the *NOLA Express*, an underground newspaper, worried about the composition of the CIA board because members Stern, Eustis, Heier, and Smith were all set to benefit from their ventures in construction, real estate, and financing.[43] In more fiery rhetoric, Father William Miller of the Irish Channel referred to the backers of the enabling legislation effort as "shrewd, scheming self-interested men, bogus philanthropists, pretenders of promoting the interests of the poorer man." Those men were laying a "stepping stone to Communism!"[44]

The issue came to a vote on November 8, 1969. At stake was approval of a five-year-long project in the Lower Ninth Ward. The city expected $31 million to be spent there between 1970 and 1974, with the federal government providing two-thirds of the costs. The projects included improving street lighting, renovating a school, closing a drainage canal, rehabilitating 2,200 housing units, and demolishing 236 substandard structures. This plan was supported by all mayoral candidates in the 1969 primary and the mainstream media.[45] Commentators at WWL television expressed the consensus surrounding Urban Renewal: it was "a bargain you can't beat." They marveled that New Orleans could get $31 million worth of work for $10 million.[46] WDSU highlighted two of the chief selling points of Urban Renewal: it would help New Orleans compete with other southern cities, and "by arresting decay," the program would "protect property values for everyone."[47] The clearest evidence of the strange alliance behind the referendum was the endorsement by *The Plain Truth*, which was the leading voice of black radicalism in New Orleans. The editors believed that the referendum was more important than even the mayor's race "in terms of immediate relevancy to our community's existence." Although they had reservations about the intentions of City Hall, they were certain that local folk would "halt the bulldozers in the streets" if they were not involved in the process.[48]

In the end, the vote was a smashing victory, passing by a margin of almost three to one. A few months later, HUD finally made a $2.5 million grant to the city for the Lower Ninth Ward's Neighborhood Development Program. Later in the year, HUD added another $900,000 to raise the initial appropriation to $3.4 million. For 1971, it provided another $3.1 million. In all, this $7.4 million effort (approximately $35 million in 2003 dollars) covered a 695-acre area.[49] Minority contractors were expected to receive a major portion of the work. In the first two years, the project results were modest. The most noticeable improvements were for infrastructure. The CIA worked with Model Cities and the Sewerage and Water Board to cover the Tupelo Avenue Canal, to build subsurface drainage systems, and to pave numerous streets. Additionally, the CIA took control over approximately twenty parcels of land, including a junk yard, and made plans to buy up another forty in 1972. Housing rehabilitation was slow. A small staff of five counselors inspected 316 homes and offered advice to homeowners about how to pay for repairs. Approximately one hundred homeowners brought their dwellings up to code, and the CIA helped thirty-three of them with grants. The rest, however, had to seek private financing. A beautification campaign was led by community committees and landscaping contractors.[50]

Many additional Urban Renewal projects got underway. Housing Development Corporations in Central City and Desire-Florida took the lead in upgrading individual homes and acquiring land for development. The Gravier Improvement Project covered a five-block area adjacent to the site of the new Orleans Parish Prison. The most ambitious project was the Health Education Authority of Louisiana (HEAL), located just north of the French Quarter. Designed to expand the facilities of Charity Hospital, Tulane Medical School, and Louisiana State University Medical School, neighborhood activists opposed the early plan, but a revised plan with a smaller footprint met approval.[51] Just north of the French Quarter, one of the most controversial projects remade an area of Tremé that was once a famous cultural gathering place and is considered one of the mythical birthplaces of jazz. Louis Armstrong Park replaced the traditional architecture with landscaped lagoons, office buildings, the Municipal Auditorium, and a new performing arts center that was later named after Mahalia Jackson. The development ostensibly preserved Congo Square and served as a memorial. It opened in 1973 and housed the New Orleans Philharmonic Orchestra, but concerns about crime and parking caused many affluent patrons to avoid it. The park is now surrounded by a tall steel and concrete fence and is the site for many high-priced formal productions.[52]

Evaluating the benefits of Urban Renewal for New Orleans requires examining its role in long-term political development, in the alteration of the city's infrastructure, in the growth of black power, and in the lives of the poor. Clearly, Urban Renewal was better than nothing. The contracts that brought black jobs and black power into the Lower Ninth Ward resulted in improved lighting, drainage, and housing. Urban Renewal was a chip that empowered local black leaders to broker concessions from local and federal leaders. As with the Food Stamp program and the Concentrated Employment Program, black leaders used the emerging urban and racial crisis to negotiate control over the federal funding pipeline. Urban Renewal did not remarkably transform the lives of poor people in New Orleans, but it did drain water out of the Lower Ninth Ward and probably reduced mosquito populations. Urban Renewal offered some fixes to street surfacing and street lighting problems and contained sewerage more tightly. Construction ventures improved the value of some homes, handsomely rewarded real estate interests and construction companies, and created a framework for further renewal projects. Urban Renewal in New Orleans did avoid some of the major blunders of earlier projects in other cities. Planning reduced the problem of relocating people, and potential backlash was forestalled by getting the approval of local residents. Although Urban Renewal projects did very little to alleviate systemic inequality and the low-wage economy, they did further the careers of several new politicians and helped those leaders finesse a modicum of biracial accord. The political model set in motion by Urban Renewal created new channels for black power.

Public Accommodations

Almost simultaneously with New Orleans's Urban Renewal referendum, the City Council moved to close some of loopholes in the federal Civil Rights Act of 1964. Introduced by Councilmen Moon Landrieu and Henry Curtis, the Public Accommodations Ordinance of 1969 forbade businesses from refusing service based on race, religion, or ethnicity.[53] Ninth Ward Councilman Philip Ciaccio tried to limit the ordinance to downtown, but his motion failed. Like the Urban Renewal referendum of November 1969, the Public Accommodations Ordinance resulted from a confluence of black power, civic boosterism, and the desire for economic growth. It gained the support of all of the local newspapers, key civic groups, and dozens of other church and civic organizations.[54] Tourist and convention commerce was the argument for its passage. The city "suffers financially each time a visitor is rejected," argued New Orleans NAACP president Wallace Young Jr., summing up the general mood of civic leaders.[55]

Several highly publicized incidents of service being refused to African American visitors had sparked a worry that outsiders were beginning to see the city as closed and inhospitable.[56] In 1964, the Roosevelt Hotel, perhaps the finest accommodations in the city, did not allow a black colonel in the New York National Guard to stay in one of its rooms. In 1965, black football players boycotted the American Football League all-star game because of local discrimination. By 1969, local papers had reported countless incidents of visitors being refused service in restaurants and bars.[57] The problem was that local white business owners were exploiting gaps in the Civil Rights Act of 1964, tending to refuse service to blacks in bars, restaurants, and taxicabs that were not clearly associated with interstate travel. But the persistent racial bigotry was beginning to cost New Orleans too much money. Tourism had long been a mainstay of the city's economy. It became a visible cornerstone of economic growth in the 1960s, bringing in close to $64 million during the first nine months of 1969. Over 600 conventions had attracted almost 350,000 visitors, and Carnival and other events attracted thousands more.[58] However, the Human Relations Committee at City Hall saw the ordinance as bigger than tourism. They saw it as a critical measure for ensuring black residents full citizenship. The Committee predicted that the ordinance would be "a tremendous psychological and material boost for black residents of New Orleans." Encapsulating the need for an "open city," they argued that it was "time" for New Orleans to join "the major league cities in the human half of the Twentieth Century."[59]

The Public Accommodations Ordinance had the all-important support of white civic leaders and moderate black organizations, but it also received strong endorsements from the more radicalized young black groups. SOUL threw its weight behind the ordinance. Speaking for SOUL, Sam Bell argued that failure to pass the ordinance "would only serve to perpetuate the ante-bellum ideologies."[60] The Black City Council, a grassroots group of neighborhood-based leaders, made an impassioned appeal for the ordinance. "In a supposedly civilized society," they argued, "it should not be necessary to pass laws protecting the rights of certain citizens from the savagery of other members in the society." In New Orleans and the United States, however, they believed that too many people were "uncivilized and tend to engage in anti-social behavior whenever they are not socially pressured to do otherwise." If the ordinance was not passed soon, they predicted, "other recourse would be necessary."[61]

Throughout the rest of 1969, pressure built for the passage of the ordinance. Moon Landrieu's strong endorsement of it and his call to extend it to all areas of New Orleans helped him become the Democratic mayoral nominee. Soon after that December race, Moon Landrieu used his victory as evidence of support for the law, and the City Council passed it in December, unanimously. The local black newspaper the *Louisiana Weekly* cited the passage as evidence that some white citizens were "beginning to realize the full meaning of democracy."[62]

Model Cities

Whereas the push for Urban Renewal and the public accommodations ordinance relied heavily on local electoral politics, the local Model Cities program was more a product of bureaucratic entrepreneurism. The federal legislation originated in two task forces chaired by Robert Wood, a political scientist at MIT who later became undersecretary of HUD. The Task Force on Metropolitan and Urban Problems report in late November 1964 included proposals for experimental programs. The task force advocated a comprehensive strategy that could reform a broad range of interrelated phenomena—including the minds of poor urban dwellers. From October to December 1965, a second Model Cities task force headed by Wood developed plans for a comprehensive attack on the interconnected problems of housing, health, education, employment, community organization, and recreation. This task force proposed that local entities provide 20 percent of the total program funding and the federal government pick up the rest. Presented to Congress in January 1966, the Demonstration Cities legislation that resulted from the work of these two task forces received lukewarm liberal support and was denounced by many conservatives. Like the original Community Action Program of OEO, the original version of Model Cities was supposed to be an experimental program limited to a few areas. Model Cities was designed to put comprehensive, intensive programs into well-defined and well-studied target areas. Once opened to the policy process in Congress, however, the program became an exercise in pork barrel politics. When implemented, Model Cities provided something for every congressman who supported it. Model Cities eventually offered money at little local cost and spread it out to over 150 cities. In October, the Demonstration Cities bill passed both houses with a slim majority.[63]

President Johnson signed the Demonstration Cities and Metropolitan Development Act into law on November 3, quickly renaming it the "Model Cities program." Through HUD, the bill would hand out $1.2 billion over a three-year span. The final legislation had ten major components, or titles. The most important one for New Orleans was Title I, which created the Comprehensive City Demonstration Programs. This title funded local programs attempting to reform the "total environment" of carefully selected model neighborhoods. Another important provision was Title VII, which reduced the local share of Urban Renewal costs from one-third of a total project to one-fourth. Other titles were designed to improve metropolitan planning and coordination, to broaden eligibility for federally insured property loans, to facilitate federal loan insurance for "new towns," and to provide more technical assistance on urban issues. Unlike the original administration of the Community Action Program of the Economic Opportunity Act, control over Model Cities would rest clearly in the hands of local government. One prominent study argues that this was a throwback to the Ford Foundation's Gray Areas strategy of integrating city government and social reform into a broad attack on poverty.[64]

Several Louisiana political leaders lobbied for the Model Cities Act and worked hard to ensure that New Orleans would be one of the host cities. In February 1966, shortly after President Johnson's associates proposed the initial Model Cities bill, Senator Allen Ellender, according to his own description, made a "strong appeal" to HUD secretary Robert Weaver to make sure New Orleans made the cut. Ellender continued his lobbying efforts for New Orleans well into the summer months.[65] In July, state senator William J. Guste attempted to build political support for Model Cities among the state's congressional delegation by emphasizing New Orleans's deprivations. He declared that "the slow death of the city has begun." Deteriorating housing and "absentee ownership" was a "cancer" that was "likely to spread," he warned, "and as it spreads, more and more people run from the ghetto, and indeed run from the city to the suburbs."[66]

The program's overwhelming dependence on federal funding made building local support for Model Cities easier. Although public opinion data is incomplete, there is ample anecdotal evidence that a sizeable portion of the white local electorate perceived it as a program for African Americans and, therefore, something unworthy of their support. One local white resident warned Mayor Schiro that the "dastardly Cities Demonstration bill" was "masquerading as a 'slums rehabilitation' bill when it is, in fact, one of the slickest, slyest, and most diabolical pieces of civil rights legislation that was ever put before Congress." He was especially upset with Congressman Hale Boggs's support of the bill. The bill was evidence of Boggs's "usual disregard for the wishes of his constituents and the good of his own race. . . . What more can we expect from these traitorous scalawags?" he asked. "What do they care about subjecting white children to the fiendish attacks and molestation of disease-ridden youth." His sentiments seem extreme, but based on opinion polls they were likely entertained at some level by an overwhelming white majority.[67]

After the bill passed, New Orleans's City Hall scrambled to assemble grant applications. By 1968, New Orleans had put together its package for HUD and was on track to become one of the first cities to implement Model Cities. Much of the credit goes to local black groups and to state senator Guste, who provided crucial encouragement to Mayor Schiro to apply.[68] Guste's primary role was as chair of the mayor's Special Ad Hoc Committee on Model Cities. That 58-member committee decided to focus Model Cities resources on three areas: the Lower Ninth Ward, Desire-Florida, and Central City. The committee justified the selection of those areas based on the problems they presented for the rest of the city. While the three sections contained only 10.6 percent of the city's population, they harbored 17 percent of its citizens living below the federal poverty level, 14 percent of its unemployment, 18 percent of its crime, 13 percent of its bad housing, 15 percent of its tuberculosis, and 22 percent of its infant mortality. Central City alone accounted for less than 5 percent of the city's total population, but over 12 percent of its arrests. The Ad Hoc Committee found that the basis of those problems was "poverty," and the roots of that poverty were "discrimination in all forms, lack of education and skills, and lack of desire or motivation." On March 21, 1968, the City Council unanimously passed a resolution supporting the three proposed areas. On April 12, 1968, the City of New Orleans officially appealed to HUD, contending that the program would complement the city's Community Renewal Program, Youth Opportunity Program, and the Lower Ninth Ward Feasibility Survey.

The April application became the basis for the Model Cities program, and it brought together a wide range of public and private agencies. The chief administrative entity was the City Demonstration Agency. Put in place in 1969, it was headed by a well-paid director and associate director. Overseeing the CDA was an Executive Board composed of eighteen members, including the mayor, two councilmen-at-large, two councilmen who represented the model areas, an appointee from the governor's office, two representatives from each Model Neighborhood Area, and six people from the executive board of the Human Relations Committee of New Orleans. A local Model Cities advisory committee included representatives from fifty-eight institutions (see appendix 5).[69]

In July 1968, New Orleans's unofficial acceptance as one of the first experimental cities came with a five-year expectation of almost $100 million to remake the city. Programmers planned to eliminate the "subcultural web" of poverty in the model areas that prevented "the hope of escape" for neighborhood residents. One media source felt the Model Cities funding meant that the city no longer had any excuses.[70] In September 1968, however, New Orleans's effort to develop a Model Cities program encountered a snag. HUD officials threatened to rescind Model Cities funding because the HANO was not complying with Title VI of the 1964 Civil Rights Act. HANO's tenant selection procedure allowed residents to decide where they wanted to live regardless of the racial makeup of a particular project.

According to HUD, HANO's policy encouraged the continued segregation of public housing in the city. HUD recommended that all potential tenants be placed on a waiting list. When a "client" reached the top of the list, they could choose between three designated projects or go to the bottom of the waiting list. Disagreeing intensely, HANO officials explained that most potential tenants wanted to reside in the older, better-constructed projects or in the new Guste Homes for the elderly. The most frequent vacancies, however, occurred in the Desire, Algiers-Fischer, Florida, St. Bernard, and St. Thomas projects. Forcefully placing tenants into projects they did not choose would unnecessarily dislocate and probably drive apart families. Eventually this impediment was worked out, and the Model Cities application went through apparently unhindered. The issue of integrating housing soon became moot. HANO executive director Gilbert Scheib summed up the situation. "White people" refused to "live in Negro projects." In the next five years, those "white people" largely abandoned the public housing projects in Orleans Parish, in the process increasing the segregation of local public housing.[71] New Orleans had three historically white housing projects, St. Thomas, Iberville, and Florida. In early 1965, they were completely white. In April 1969, the white population in St. Thomas had dropped to 47 percent, in Iberville to 61 percent, and Florida to 24 percent. Over the next decade, they became essentially black-only.[72]

In November 1968, the mayor's office hired its first Model Cities director. Surprisingly, considering the pervasive search for patronage opportunities in New Orleans politics, the new director was a technocrat from the outside. At a salary of $19,500 per year (approximately $103,000 in 2003 spending), James R. King, previously a special assistant secretary at HUD, was selected.[73] He guided the program through its first two years before leaving for a better-paying job. In May 1969, New Orleans's City Demonstration Agency had twenty employees. The thirteen professionals and seven secretaries were gathering facts for their first-year plan and attempting to coordinate community efforts. Assistant Director Sherman Copelin, a rising African American leader and recent graduate of Dillard University, worked with city and local agencies, and Oliver St. Pee, a leader of the Irish Channel Action Foundation, was the liaison to federal and state bureaucracies.[74]

Despite a rhetorical commitment to the participation of neighborhood residents and leaders, the administrative leaders of Model Cities in 1969 left out many important voices. In response, black neighborhood leaders worked diligently to ensure their control over Model Cities. When the council presidents of the three model neighborhoods were passed over as delegates to the Model Cities Advisory Committee, a protest ensued. Winifred Edwards, vice president of the Central City Economic Opportunity Committee, proclaimed that the CCEOC would "make it our business, by whatever means possible, to have something to do with the shaping" of their community's future. Joining Edwards were the Human Relations Committee of New Orleans, the Urban League, the NAACP, and SOUL.[75] However, once the Model Cities program got underway in the Moon Landrieu administration, black concerns about lack of participation became muted.

The goals of local administrators were ambitious and built on other parts of the War on Poverty. They wanted to create full employment, reduce crime, improve health, modernize infrastructure, rehabilitate bad housing, expand recreational opportunities, upgrade transportation, and stimulate black economic development.[76] The three Model Neighborhood Areas (MNA) were already War on Poverty target areas. By adhering to the target-area model, the City Demonstration Agency also experienced many of the same problems associated with the Community Action Program. The officials directing Model Cities had to balance a supposedly colorblind federal bureaucratic structure and an inflamed local white electorate with a restless and growing black electorate and fragmented social welfare system. Like the creation of TCA, Model Cities depended on building a coalition of progressive white and black support and on at least neutralizing the opposition of businessmen and conservative politicians, if not getting their support. Similar to the local coalitions that supported other efforts, the support for Model Cities evolved at the root from white fear about black civil disorder and black demands for more services and public influence. African American leaders in the three model neighborhoods grasped at the chance to rehabilitate housing, encourage black capitalism, and stimulate optimism. A new group of black organizations came to life, and the housing committees of neighborhood councils in Central City, the Lower Ninth Ward, and Florida-Desire became housing development corporations capable of creating housing policy on their own.[77]

The City Demonstration Agency began full operation in 1970. In January, preliminary housing work began, and the Regional Planning Commission began meeting with participating agencies.[78] One month later, HUD announced that a $9,249,000 grant (almost $44 million in 2003 spending) had been reserved for New Orleans.[79] That money, which officially arrived in New Orleans in June, funded an ambitious effort. From 1970 to 1973, local Model Cities planners sought grants for over fifty projects and received funding for at least thirty-six of them.[80] A vast majority of the funds went to health services, health care, and facilities procurement and construction. The rest went to manpower training, economic development, a few education and citizenship programs, and housing code enforcement. Most of the local projects were renewed for the next two fiscal years (from September 1 to August 31). By July 1973, however, HUD, under the leadership of the Nixon administration, had excised funding for over half of them (see appendix 6).[81]

Because most of the Model Cities projects operated only briefly, assessing their impact is difficult. Perhaps the longest lasting legacies came from construction projects. Building community centers, recreation facilities, and health centers created much needed space and services for neighborhood residents. Under the Landrieu administration, Model Cities projects helped to improve black participation in the local construction industry and to secure more federal contracts. Two black-dominated organizations pushed Model Cities' black capitalism components. Taking Care of Business, Inc., a new nonprofit "economic development corporation," was a predominantly black organization that administered Model Cities loans and contracted out day-to-day administration to the Interracial Council for Black Opportunities (ICBO). This nationwide group strove "to make more Negroes a part of the mainstream of the free enterprise system," and hoped to establish a Model Neighborhood Area Economic Development fund that would evolve into a city-wide fund for minority economic development. Taking Care of Business operated five offices nationally that tried to stimulate grassroots economic development. Its New Orleans office was headed by Robert Tucker, a key Landrieu advisor who continued to be a major black political and business leader for the next thirty years. ICBO in New Orleans was headed by former Baton Rouge attorney and TCA employee Leonard Avery, and it had used a $50,000 grant from the Stern Fund to create the first ICBO program in the Deep South. As proposed, the ICBO-Taking Care of Business economic development fund would give residents a structure in which to "participate, without limit, in determining the economic destiny of their community."[82]

The most important black-oriented, nonprofit economic development corporation was Amalgamated Builders and Contractors of Louisiana (ABCOL). Some of the key shapers of ABCOL policy were some of the city's most influential African American leaders.[83] ABCOL was dedicated to training black workers for construction jobs and to creating more business for black contractors. Begun in January 1969, ABCOL was sponsored by the National Office of Minority Contractors Assistance Program and was given office space and technical assistance by ICBO. One of its original purposes was to secure employment for black workers who had construction experience but lacked journeymen status and union wages. ABCOL provided six hours of training per week, and contractors agreed to pay union wages to trainees. In November 1970, New Orleans's Model Cities office contracted with ABCOL to provide personnel costs (approximately $81,000) and a "revolving fund" of $75,000 for loans. In 1971, local Model Cities administrators negotiated to involve ABCOL in the construction of the massive Louisiana Superdome. During its operation from 1969 to 1973, ABCOL also was a clearinghouse for black contractors who wished to bid on construction projects. In many instances, ABCOL provided up to half of the capital for wide-ranging projects. This program provided $507,000 from the City Demonstration Agency and $2.7 million worth of construction bonding for 108 black contractors. By 1973, ABCOL had served over 442 minority contractors in New Orleans and generated over $5 million in business. It was a boon for many black workers and contractors; 71 percent of workers involved were Model Neighborhood residents.

The most promising Model Cities project provided health care to poor women and to Model Neighborhood residents. In 1966, Tulane University, under the direction of population control specialist Dr. Joseph Beasley, established a nonprofit organization to conduct family planning in Louisiana. With funding from the Ford, Rockefeller, and Lilly Foundations, Beasley established health clinics and a network of healthcare professionals to serve hard-to-reach populations. In an innovative patient outreach system, local people were hired to promote the program's health services. Over time, this entity morphed from the Louisiana Family Planning Program to the Family Health Foundation and oversaw operations from rural Lincoln Parish in northern Louisiana to neighborhoods in Brazil. By 1972, Beasley's enterprise had provided health care and reproductive services to over seventy thousand poor families in 170 facilities. His efforts received numerous accolades and the program was considered a model for healthcare delivery. According to a scholar who wrote the standard history of Beasley's program, he was rumored to be a candidate for the Nobel Peace Prize. In the late 1960s, the program's administrators began to target Total Community Action and Model Cities for an expansion of health services in poor New Orleans neighborhoods. Funneled through the new New Orleans Health Corporation, several million dollars in federal funding eventually reached Family Health. Much of that money went into an effort, in the words of TCA officials, to "bring the hospitals to the people." Parts of the funding paid for the construction of temporary "modular" buildings. In the Lower Ninth Ward, the contract went to a construction company owned by Theodore Marchand. Although they did not reach their goal of serving three hundred thousand patients, Family Health leaders in New Orleans were able to establish satellites in Central City, Desire, and the Lower Ninth Ward and to initiate an ambulance service.[84]

Those temporary clinics led to the collapse of Family Health. At the height of operation, the foundation had an annual budget of $18 million that was largely financed by grants and federal aid programs. Family Health employed over one thousand people, of whom 81 percent were women. Fifty-two percent were minorities, mostly from areas being served. Family Health operated clinics in over 125 places in Louisiana, a Parent-Child Development program, an academic program affiliated with Tulane University, and programs in Brazil, Colombia, and Mexico. This massive expansion of the Family Health Foundation came with some serious costs. Many white conservatives and black militants were critical of its close association with several members of the SOUL political organization, including Sherman Copelin, deputy director of the City Demonstration Agency; Nils Douglas, a prominent civil rights attorney and associate of Family Health; Don Hubbard, a close friend of Copelin; and Maxine Copelin, Sherman's wife.[85]

Family Health also came under fire from several militant black activists who accused the program of promoting genocide and providing involuntary sterilizations. A local writer borrowed from Tom Wolfe's 1970 book on San Francisco's War on Poverty, *Radical Chic and Mau-Mauing the Flak Catchers*, to describe these militants as "Mau-Maus" who were extorting the "Flak Catchers" at Family Health. From another front came a more serious problem. After an internal audit raised concerns, several investigators began looking into allegations of inappropriate use of appropriations. Several politicians were outraged that Family Health was flying around in airplanes and holding parties and engaging in political lobbying activities apparently with Title IV A funds from the Social Security Administration. In 1973, the Family Health Foundation became the target of inquiries by the state government, a federal grand jury, the local federal attorney, the Governmental Accounting Office, the U.S. Agency for International Development, HEW, and HUD.[86]

Beyond the allegedly lavish spending habits of administrators, the chief concern was the use of funds earmarked to purchase the modular health clinics. According to published reports, Joseph Beasley approved cash payments to Sherman Copelin to curry favor from Model Cities and, eventually, to facilitate the implementation of the health clinic plan. At least one of these payments involved a roll of $1,000 cash given to Copelin in the men's bathroom of the Saxony Restaurant on Canal Street. Payments to Copelin supposedly were part of a complicated money laundering scheme involving at least five institutions. Family Health overpaid for the modular clinics, and the overpayment was then funneled to Copelin and his associates. Martha Ward, the historian of the Family Health Foundation, contends that the payments were made to Copelin to buy his support and to quiet criticism of the program from black activists who had seized upon the genocide issue. Adding to the public relations problems of Family Health, six of the modular health buildings apparently were found in an overgrown lot behind a motel. In the late spring of 1974, Family Health was put in receivership, and U.S. Marshals seized its records. By September, Family Health had ceased to function as an independent agency and had become part of the state government under the Department of Health and Human Resources. The next year, Beasley was convicted on charges of malfeasance regarding the mobile clinics. His attorney was Jim Garrison, former district attorney for Orleans Parish and promulgator of a prominent John Kennedy assassination theory. In a bit of irony, Garrison proved unable to refute the conspiracy theory that had entangled Dr. Beasley, and the self-declared "baby doctor" joined a long line of Louisiana officials who ended up in prison, this time heading off for a seventeen month stint at a federal facility in Florida, the Sunshine State.[87]

Considering the politics that grew out of the War on Poverty in the late 1960s and early 1970s, the Family Health Foundation matter was but one complex episode in a complicated history. The negotiations ensuing from the development and implementation of the Food Stamp program, the Concentrated Employment Program, Urban Renewal, and Model Cities established a larger context for Louisiana's biracial politics. In many ways—as evidenced by the Family Health Foundation's rise and fall—the new biracial politics perpetuated tendencies of the old white-dominated political world. Power—or getting things done for the right people at the right time with the least amount of fanfare—required skill and guile and timing. In the new biracial world, the ability to get votes, contracts, favors for supporters, good tables at the right restaurants, and bills through the legislature still determined the level of one's influence. The federal government, however, had changed the means to that power.

Black power arose as much from technocracy as from democracy. Effectively, the Model Cities program constituted a city agency for black neighborhoods and represented the most sizable expansion of the Soft State. In New Orleans, Model Cities was clearly about building black power. The program helped Moon Landrieu solidify a base in the black community that sustained his eight years in office. Dozens of African American professionals obtained well-paying jobs and invaluable leadership experience through Model Cities and became part of a new generation of African American leaders. In the years following their involvement in Model Cities, Sherman Copelin became a state representative, Donald Hubbard an affluent bureaucrat and political power broker, Johnny Jackson a state representative and longtime city council member, James Singleton a longtime city council member, Terrence Duvernay a high-ranking local and federal official, and Charles Elloie a criminal court judge. Part bureaucrat, part technocrat, part politician, each of them had to be able to blend the bureaucratic parlance of the often white-dominated boardroom with the moral and rebellious vibrancy of the black ghetto. They had to shift between worlds without losing connections to any of them. Their power—and that of their organizations—depended on their ability to negotiate confusing boundaries between black and white, upper class and working class, individual progress and group solidarity. Those emerging liberal leaders benefited greatly from Model Cities because it forced contractors to give "preferential treatment" to neighborhood residents and to seek out black companies. Between 1968 and July 1971, Model Cities was responsible for creating 490 jobs, of which 89 percent were filled by residents from Model Neighborhoods.[88] By being able to influence contracts and jobs, numerous black and white liberal leaders built political organizations that dominated elections, appointments, and city contracts for over thirty years. This new politics was intensified by racial identity and white backlash. The Voting Rights Act of 1965 was an important part of the new political arrangement, but perhaps more important were the ways that black leaders used the power of those votes to grab power in quiet conversations in corridors long kept closed to them. Black leaders who lacked that access proved to be much more vocal.

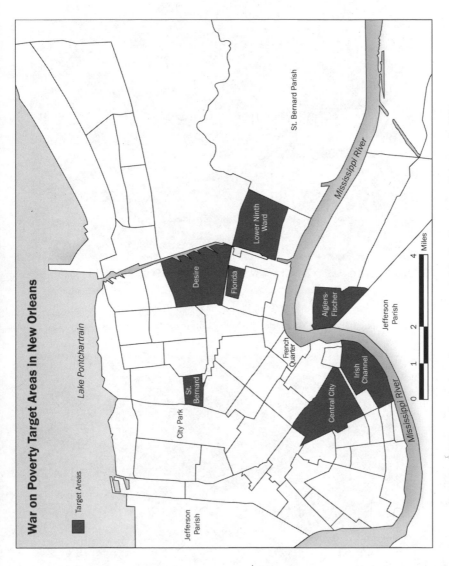

Cartography by David Wasserboehr based on a map created by Joy Bonoguro, February 3, 2004, http://www.gnocdc.org.

Looking northward at downtown New Orleans, circa 1960. The wide avenue on the right is Canal Street. The one on the left is Poydras Street, a corridor enveloped by skyscrapers by 1980. Photograph by J. R. St. Julien, courtesy of Louisiana Division, New Orleans Public Library.

Looking southeast at New Orleans's Central Business District, circa 1980. The Superdome sits on the western edge of Poydras Street. Courtesy of Louisiana Division, New Orleans Public Library.

Agriculture Secretary Orville Freeman, New Orleans Congressman
Hale Boggs, President Lyndon Johnson, and Louisiana Senator Russell
Long view the damage caused by Hurricane Betsy, September 10, 1965.
Courtesy of Yoichi R. Okamoto, LBJ Library.

Betsy flooding in the Lower Ninth Ward as seen from Air Force One on September 10, 1965.
Courtesy of Yoichi R. Okamoto, LBJ Library.

Mayor Victor Hugo Schiro (in the white suit, waving) and his wife, Mary Margaret "Sunny" Schiro, at festivities for his 1966 inauguration. Courtesy of Louisiana Division, New Orleans Public Library.

Mayor Maurice E. "Moon" Landrieu. Courtesy of Louisiana Division, New Orleans Public Library.

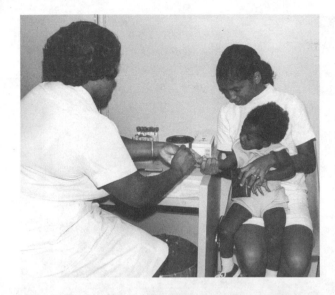

A young patient receives a blood test at the Great Society–funded Lower Ninth Ward Health Center, 1973. Courtesy of Louisiana Division, New Orleans Public Library.

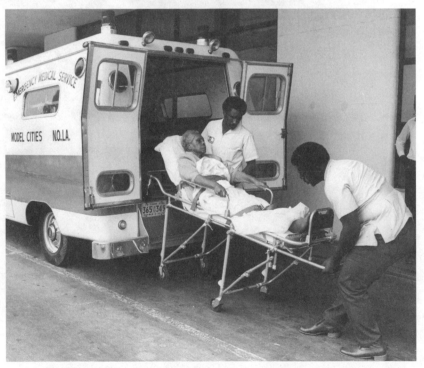

An elderly woman gets assistance from an ambulance service that is funded through the Model Cities program, 1973. Courtesy of Louisiana Division, New Orleans Public Library.

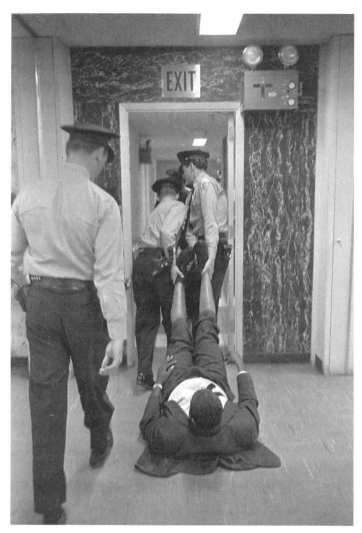

Officers remove the Reverend Avery Alexander from City Hall during an attempt to desegregate the building on Halloween 1963. Reproduced by permission of the Associated Press.

New Orleans Police Department officers used the tank nicknamed *Bertha* during a failed assault on the Black Panthers in the Desire Housing Development, November 20, 1970. Reproduced by permission of the Associated Press.

An event known as the Neighborhood City Hall, such as this gathering in 1973, represented a stark shift from the racial segregation of the 1960s.
Courtesy of Louisiana Division, New Orleans Public Library.

Three pioneering New Orleans Democrats appear together circa 1980: Ernest "Dutch" Morial, Mary Landrieu, and Maurice "Moon" Landrieu. Photograph by Harold Baquet, courtesy of Louisiana Division, New Orleans Public Library.

An aerial view of part of the St. Thomas Housing Development in 1954. Photograph by Hardy S. Williams Photography, courtesy of Louisiana Division, New Orleans Public Library.

Looking down the new Josephine Drive, a street in the new "River Garden" development that replaced the St. Thomas Housing Project, January 2005. A new Wal-Mart Supercenter is directly behind the camera. Photograph by Kent B. Germany.

PART TWO

BLACK POWER AND DIXIE'S DEMOCRATIC MOMENT, 1968–1974

A militant black activist stood in front of his house and handed a sack of beer to his friends. Two New Orleans police officers witnessed the exchange. Using the police department's "Stop and Frisk" policy, they rushed in to demand that the man, Lionel McIntyre, reveal the contents of his container. Someone in his group demanded a search warrant, to which one of the officers sneered, "What are you, a smart-ass nigger?" McIntyre dropped his beer and told the officer not to "push a man." The officer promptly pushed him. McIntyre told him to take off his gun and fight. The other officer then flipped McIntyre over, put a "Karate hold" on him, and hit him in the mouth and eye. According to McIntyre, "that's what started all the bleeding." The officer then threatened to "stomp" him "to death" and called in the riot squad, or as McIntyre referred to them, "the guys with the dogs." A crowd began to gather, and the patrolmen hustled their captive away from the intensifying scene at the corner of Dorgenois and Thalia near downtown. While immobilized, McIntyre heard a dozen or so officers discussing what they would do "if any of these niggers ever break my way like that." McIntyre believed this brutality was part of a movement to eliminate black radicals. One week earlier, another activist had been targeted by the police, and many other "Brothers" had been detained for "speaking out their minds." He was deeply troubled that local children would witness more victims "laying out there in the streets bleeding." He held out hope, though, that "the grassroots people in the community are beginning to get their eyes opened by this oppression of the pigs." Those neighborhood people had to "take major steps in the right way on settling this matter of power."[1]

Lionel McIntyre was correct in identifying a serious struggle for power underway, and it went beyond the police department. This one turned bloody, and the shots fired were not between segregationists and integrationists. The most startling showdowns were between liberals who had seized power and militants who wanted them to do more.

Some poor women fought white bureaucrats to protect their children and homes. Some middle-class white women acted on an almost hereditary impulse for democracy and civic reform to assist black inclusion. Some self-described thugs wanted to become men of value and respect and set out to rehabilitate their neighborhoods and themselves. With some surprise, Chamber of Commerce men got involved. Wanting to believe in biracial activism, they risked derision from their peers to join hands with black men to seek solutions. Other activists calling themselves Panthers tried to start a revolution for the poor. At the center of it all was a man named Moon who wanted to be mayor and turn his beloved city into a superstar. His election in 1970 signified a new era, and it signaled to many whites that it was time to leave.

CHAPTER TEN

The Thugs United and the Politics of Manhood

We must massively assert our dignity and our worth. . . . We can
no longer be ashamed of who we are or what we are. . . . The
Black man [must] rise up with an affirmation of his own
Olympian manhood. . . . Say Loud, Clear, Strong and with his
own voice, I am somebody. I am a Man.
—The Thugs United, Inc., *Street Scene Community Newspaper*,
February 1971

During the late 1960s, New Orleans experienced an intense political
transformation. It was the democratic moment that black leaders had
wanted for so long. The conditions for creating something new for the
South were finally set. Competition on the streets, in the bureaucracies,
and at the polls would determine what kind of city emerged from the
shadows of Jim Crow. Racial rules were in flux and ready to be redefined.
Black voter registration was rising, and organizations were springing up
to channel the power of those votes. The Great Society was providing
local people with unprecedented resources and was encouraging public
and private political mobilization. The urban crisis had created deep dis-
tress and the political incentive for action. Black unrest had become a
central issue in local and national politics, and the poverty of the nation's
cities could no longer be ignored. Equally important was white unrest,
as backlash to racial liberalism and black assertiveness was helping break
apart the bases of the Democratic Party. Hovering over all of this were

the dreams of southern capitalists who saw that there was money to be made—no matter what happened.

The concluding section of this book examines the expansion of black power and its role in the solidification of southern liberalism. A number of grassroots groups formed—including The Thugs United, Inc. and the National Committee to Combat Fascism, better known as the Black Panthers—and War on Poverty efforts (such as community action and Urban Renewal) cultivated other black organizations known by their acronyms (especially SOUL, COUP, and BOLD). These essentially private groups challenged notions of white power, but they often disagreed over strategies and goals. Some accepted gradualist reform, while others pushed for racial revolution. The most successful of them did whatever it took to seize influence. SOUL leader and black militant Sam Bell offered a pragmatic assessment of the situation when he told reporters, "We take our help anywhere we can get it."[1] Along the way, these organizations helped chart the political triumph of racial liberalism, but they also exposed some of its most serious flaws. They proved once again that democratic moments are rarely easy.

The Thugs United, Inc., was led by young black men. This militant community organization emerged from a gang summit at a housing project in 1966, flourished for a few years, and then disappeared. Under the leadership of Warren Carmouche—a nineteen-year-old, 240-pound former pimp, janitor, and War on Poverty organizer—the Thugs United garnered attention from local and national media for both scaring and inspiring people. From 1968 until 1971, Carmouche and his lieutenants used their ability to strike fear and admiration to attract funding from the Model Cities program and from private, predominantly white sources. They focused on mobilizing their peers and running an adult education program known as the People's College. They also operated an ex-convict training program, a high school dropout program, a Shell gas station, a recreation program, some small retail ventures, and several other smaller initiatives. At the height of its operations, the Thugs United had three offices and over a dozen subgroups. The total number of Thugs members is unknown. The Thugs United leadership claimed they had over six thousand members, but less biased sources give the range as several hundred. Their primary focus was local, especially Central City and other New Orleans target areas, but they did have an affiliation with the national Youth Organizations United (YOU). Carmouche served as a YOU vice president. Formed in May 1968 in East St. Louis, YOU eventually had affiliates in almost sixty cities and received a number of high-profile grants from the OEO and other federal entities. Among the over three hundred street organizations in YOU were the Conservative Vice Lords in Chicago, the Son of Watts in Los Angeles, the Real Great Society in New York, the Twelfth and Oxford Film Maker Corporation in Philadelphia, the Black Knights in Memphis, and the Mission Rebels in Action in San Francisco.[2]

Like many of those groups, the Thugs United did not last. By 1973, Carmouche had left New Orleans and was under indictment for murder in Florida, two of the Thugs United officers were in prison for heroin distribution, and the organization was effectively disbanded.[3] The group's rise in the late 1960s, however, offers a perspective on the limits of racial inclusion, psychological empowerment, and black capitalism. Established when the call for Black Power and the escalation of urban disorder were reshaping the meaning of the War on Poverty and the civil rights movement, the Thugs United brought together a strange coalition of white progressives, white conservatives, federal bureaucrats, and black militants. Their image and their tactics shocked many people into supporting them, but beneath the muscular style, their major activities focused on entrepreneurism and education—ways to improve the black individual's ability to fit into the marketplace. They were black capitalists, though less polished than counterparts at the Model Cities-affiliated ICBO, ABCOL, or Taking Care of Business, Inc. As expressions of their motto, "from these hands some good things will live," the Thugs's efforts offer a study in the use of anger and alienation to create opportunity, particularly through a deeply masculine search for self-worth.[4] One leader captured the goal that permeated the Thugs's thinking and activities: to make it possible for the "Black Man" to "rise up with an affirmation of his own Olympian manhood." To achieve that lofty status, the black man had to reach "down into the inner-depth of his own being" to create "psychological freedom" and a "firm sense of self-esteem." Men in the ghetto had to declare to the world: "I am somebody. I am a Man."[5]

The Thugs presented themselves as embodiments of the hope and the despair of the ghetto. Roosevelt Smith, a counselor in the Thugs's exconvict program for almost two years, had spent five years in jail. Alvin "Butte" Harris, director of the Thugs's exconvict program, claimed to have been "a pimp for about ten girls."[6] Donald "Monster" Sanders had spent seven years behind bars and sported "wounds on his arms, legs, face and torso where he had been shot, stabbed, bruised, and scarred."[7] Leroy "The Danger Zone" Malone had been a homeless drunk. Warren Carmouche, the Thugs's chief leader, had acted as a "pimp" for his mother at the age of seven. According to him, his childhood acquaintances had included "dope pushers, dope addicts, hustlers, ex-convicts, as well as other whores and pimps," in short, "outcasts of society." Carmouche took offense at criticism of informal, and often illegal, economic activity in the ghetto and told an academic investigator that in his early life "the dope pusher was supporting him, the whore fed, clothed him, and sent him to school, and the hustler disciplined him when he played 'hooky' from school." In his youth, they were the "only people who loved and cared" for him, and he "respected them as people." In 1971, a Thugs United newspaper described Carmouche as a "Phi Beta Kappa graduate of the University of the Streets, where he earned a bachelor's degree in niggerology and streetology" and a "a masters degree in common sinces [sic]."[8]

For members of Thugs United, confrontation—often violent—was essential to their lives. "Fighting can make you feel like a man," explained Carmouche. "If you are afraid of someone and you fight him," he continued, "you are not afraid anymore—even if you lose."[9] From 1968 through 1971, this group of exconvicts and self-proclaimed thugs engaged in a different kind of clash. Instead of picking fights among their counterparts in target areas, they took on the ghetto itself. Most important, the leaders attacked the sense of alienation that they believed was undermining the status and dignity of young black men.[10] A trouble-plagued youth who had engaged in countless brawls, Carmouche was transformed when his principal told him that "only dumb people fight with their fists" and that "smart people fight with their heads." Carmouche decided to "see what would happen if I didn't fight." He took a janitor position at the Algiers-Fischer housing project, and he claimed that job turned his life around because it enabled him to see his neighborhood from a different perspective. "I felt we had to change the image," he recounted later, "and show the community that even thugs have creativity and competence." [11]

In a Fischer hallway, he called a meeting with gang leaders and the residents with an influential presence on the streets to attempt to improve social conditions in the project. From this group of people between the ages of eleven and twenty-three, Carmouche developed committees that broke up fights, held social dances, encouraged better sanitation, helped get associates who had been arrested out of jail, and pressured drug dealers not to sell to high school students. In this early informal stage, the Thugs United was a harsh group run largely by teenagers. The organizational structure was quite loose, but its leaders dealt stiffly with rules violations. A special committee administered punishment. Carmouche chose sixteen-year-old Fluckie Theodore as "the judge" because he was "smart" and knew "how to use his fist." First time offenders were required to sit on their knees all night or write out the sentence "I will be good" over and over. [12]

Between the spring of 1966 and the summer of 1968, there is little evidence that the Thugs United had much of an organized presence in the city, except through Carmouche's new job as a community worker with the TCA-funded Algiers-Fischer Community Organization. Their story does show some of the devastating consequences of not having an adequate organizational structure. From 1968 to 1971, the three main years of the Thugs's existence, its leaders worked hard to establish a usable public image and a vision of reform; developed a base of program ideas and projects, some of which were actually put into operation; and labored to raise funds to implement their programmatic visions. They were remarkably successful at the first task, setting out an aggressive critique of segregation and alienation.

The Thugs's modest success at putting their plans into action and raising funds to support them evaporated after 1971. The Thugs United rarely had enough capital to pay employees and bills. Unable to secure a nonprofit tax status, the group relied on grants and gifts funneled through other nonprofit groups. With the exception of a Model Cities grant to operate an education program and an almost $30,000 grant funneled through the Urban League by the U.S. Department of Health, Education, and Welfare, almost all of the Thugs's operating funds came from private foundations, corporations, and concerned citizens. The local United Fund refused to take on the group as a constituent organization because the group's finances were in disarray and it had poorly defined long-term goals, unpredictable staffing, and overly ambitious expectations that included thirteen disparate programs.[13] In late 1971 when City Hall and the Urban League effectively cancelled the Thugs's Model Cities participation due to financial irregularities and some of the leaders became hard to track down, the fears of the United Fund and other established groups were confirmed. Like many other gang-linked antipoverty groups across the country, the Thugs United collapsed amid controversial charges of mismanagement and/or fraud. The failures of the organization were acute and reflect poorly on some of the decision-making of some of the leaders. Focusing only on the failures, though, obscures the significance of the Thugs and other groups like them. They were a unique product of the democratic flux created by the civil rights movement and the urban crisis.

Perhaps the Thugs's most significant legacy was forcing an influential segment of the local white business community to consider the problems of the ghetto in clear terms. The Thugs were important simply because they showed that a group of alienated black men could shake up a southern city if they persisted with a politically powerful message. Their efforts also demonstrated that the concern about personal identity was a widespread phenomenon and not simply a fetish of War on Poverty policymakers. The mission statement of the Thugs United summed up a central message. The "grass root youth of New Orleans" had once believed that their "only alternative" was to "destroy the society causing our hopelessness, oppression, exploitation, and denying us a voice in our destiny." The Thugs United provided "an alternative to revolution." The Thugs United claimed that they had "taken on the challenge to 'do it ourselves' and [for] our country," and that they had "dedicated our lives to making the American dream a reality and making the United States of America truly united."[14]

Fiercely independent and bitterly protective of their conception of manliness, the Thugs leadership struggled to reconcile their need for status and self-determination with their need for funding. In a compromise, they backed away from black separatism in order to cultivate white donors. They were willing to accept white money if it was primarily distributed by black organizers. In their public statements and in their fundraising appeals, Thugs leaders advocated an impassioned inclusion agenda. One of their major goals was to make ghetto residents more productive members of the community. Equating manliness with self-determination, they tried—like countless War on Poverty organizers before them—to make full citizens by rehabilitating black minds. Officers of Thugs United struggled to maintain legitimacy in the boardrooms of their white benefactors and the neighborhoods in which they operated. Edward "Sticks" Hall, president of the Thugs in 1969, explained, "We are thugs. We are real thugs. We are of the street. We have done it all." The Thugs claimed superiority in community organizing because "the guys on the street look up to three types of people. The athlete, the dope fiend, and the hustler." Confidently, Hall asserted, "We got all of them." Another Thugs United leader, Rudolph Muse, explained that the Thugs's programs helped the white community because it showed young black men "that they don't have to rob and break into places, that they can do something constructive." He explained that the Thugs "show them that when they get into fights they only confirm what white people think." The Thugs United wanted to show young people that they could get "desk jobs and white collar and tie jobs."[15]

In keeping with Great Society inclusion thinking, an essential goal was to develop "pride in themselves" and improve one's "potential to contribute to society."[16] As Carmouche explained in a speech to the New Orleans Travelers Aid Association, "A sense of self-esteem is the most powerful weapon against slavery."[17] Extending a pattern of the early War on Poverty, the Thugs used deprivation as a political tool. In a proposal seeking Model Cities funds for a dropout school, Warren Carmouche argued that Thugs United was "a part of that segment of the population that our society has failed the most." Ranging in age from sixteen to twenty-four, this alienated group, he claimed, had a dropout rate of 60 percent and an unemployment rate of over 30 percent. "Is it any wonder," he mused, "that the segment of society we come from also has the highest crime rate, and the greatest participation in the summer disturbances?" It was not, he stressed, because they were "dumb and lazy." In a warning to those who were listening, Carmouche cautioned that his group was walking "a tight rope between the pen[ned] up frustrations and hopes of the youth and the establishment."[18] Like many of their more affluent counterparts, the Thugs were most concerned with dropouts who spent "their time shooting dice, drinking wine, and taking part in gang fights."[19] Thugs leaders wanted to improve the uncertain terrain between childhood and adulthood. They warned that people who felt "unsatisfied, unsuccessful, and unworthy" often opted for the "destruction of themselves, their peers, and the 'society' they feel does not offer the means for self-fulfillment." When that happened, dropouts "create their own society and 'prove' themselves in raw combat with peers or testing themselves against symbols of authority." They survived by "stealing and burglarizing." The Thugs United planned to push "alienated Black youth back into an acceptable path, and to participate in a broad program of holsum [sic] self created self respect."[20]

Complementing the Thugs's politics of social deprivation was an astute invocation of the politics of individual investment. The Thugs United sought and secured Model Cities funding for a "street" school for about forty dropouts that would offer basic instruction in reading, writing, and arithmetic. The curriculum involved much remedial work and an emphasis on essay writing and leadership skills. Each student, they assured, would be taught to take personal responsibility and to work hard.[21] To lobby for an exconvict counseling program, Thugs leaders declared that the United States was ready to invest in ambitious former inmates.[22] The Thugs's public image and its social vision were essential for getting support from white businessmen. Gideon Stanton, a white Tulane University law student, served as the principal advisor to the Thugs United. David Hunter of the Stern Family Fund believed that Stanton "worked out just the right kind of relationship between a group of ghetto youth and a white middle class senior law student in a southern city."[23]

One of the most remarkable developments in New Orleans's urban crisis was the relationship it sparked between the Thugs United and the Greater New Orleans Chamber of Commerce. In the summer of 1964, the Chamber had resisted efforts in the city to create a local War on Poverty. Four years later, in November 1968, the Chamber still seemed to be disconnected. In a display of either deep ignorance or blatant dishonesty, one official told a middle school student from New Jersey that the city had experienced "no race riots and no demonstrations and there have not even been 'peaceful' marches." He described the vicious 1960 school desegregation crisis as a "slight controversy which was exaggerated in the Northern press." According to his neutered version, "some person stood on the street, made faces, and cat-called a little about the Negroes entering the white schools. There was no disorder, no violence and no arrests."[24] Notwithstanding that official's opinion, one month earlier in October 1968, the Chamber of Commerce agreed (in a nineteen to twelve vote) to help Thugs United raise $32,000 in the local business community, although they eventually raised only $15,000. The Chamber's motivation came from a concern for social order and economic growth. Proponents within the Chamber believed the Thugs offered a way to help "underprivileged blacks" live a "life of self-respect as contributors to our free society." In other words, the poor could become more like other people.[25]

The decision to help the Thugs raise money was difficult for the Chamber. Many members were "repulsed" by the Thugs's name and their public opposition to the Vietnam War. Others worried that involvement with ghetto groups would lead to the Chamber being blackmailed. Three arguments, however, outweighed the possible downside and enabled the Chamber to stake its reputation on a group of admitted thugs: the Chamber would be stimulating self-sufficiency in the ghetto, upholding civic duty, and preventing riots. Carmouche and his group offered a way for the Chamber to attempt to mollify the masses without actually interacting with them. Carmouche, they stated, had an "established record as a peacemaker and a steadying influence among his people." Nevertheless, Chamber proponents had reservations. Because of "the classes of people" being helped by the Thugs, the Chamber's committee on the Thugs United warned of possible shake-downs for money. The Chamber would be dealing with "bitter, doubtful and frustrated persons" who were likely not worth the Chamber's investments of time and money.[26]

In the final contract, the Chamber agreed to lend its name and its members to the fundraising effort. In return, the Thugs agreed to amend their black-only membership policy by allowing two Chamber representatives to sit on the Thugs's finance committee. The broader significance of this contract is that it created an unlikely bridge between two historically disconnected worlds. The Chamber made contact with black grassroots activists, a possible way to market more goods in the ghetto, and a way to stay aware of conditions that could lead to riots. The Thugs received a boost in funding and reputation, and they gained an institution that could funnel tax-deductible contributions to them since they lacked nonprofit status.[27] In seeking funds from the business community, the Thugs hoped to create new business relations in the white community. In return, the Thugs claimed that they offered the white community, particularly the Chamber and the Metropolitan Area Committee, an opportunity to know about the Thugs's lives and to realize that white leaders had to "desist in the colonialization of the Black community."[28] That relationship did not indicate any subservience by the Thugs to their benefactors. The Thugs wanted assistance with "no strings." "We want to use you," Thugs leaders explained. "We are looking for what we know you have and we can use—money, technical assistance and technical knowhow."[29]

In August 1969, the Metropolitan Area Committee's most influential members also used their reputations and contacts in the white community to solicit financial support. They endorsed the Thugs United as a "group of reformed, hard-core underprivileged young adults" who had "come to realize that they can render a service to their race and to their city."[30] They backed the Thugs's mission of constructive citizenship. They also hoped the Thugs could provide a cheap way to maintain peace. One local attorney and civic leader with deep roots in the families of old New Orleans, Eads Poitevent, was quite specific in the reason for his support. "The frankly one-time rough characters," Poitevent explained, had worked with "the Police and other bodies in 'hot spots' and have aided effectively in several tense situations." Speaking in early June 1969, he urged his colleagues to help find $2,600 to help the Thugs meet expenses "when the funds are most needed, namely the upcoming hot summer."[31] Murray Fincher, president of the Chamber of Commerce, praised the Thugs as "one of the better 'self help' groups" in America.[32] David Hunter, director of the Stern Family Fund, believed that the Thugs's relationship to the white leadership class was "unprecedented in the United States."[33]

By 1970, the Thugs were a growing institution in the city's poor areas. They had received almost $20,000 in funds from private sources that subsidized the work of a growing staff of ten.[34] From their headquarters in Central City, they oversaw thirteen subgroups citywide and several programs. Their People's College and their dropout program offered classes to a few dozen residents. A Legal Aid program helped the New Orleans Legal Assistance Corporation (NOLAC) encourage public defenders to try cases instead of opting for plea bargains. Their Ex-Convict Counseling Program, they claimed, had gotten parole for almost three hundred prisoners. Other programs included community beautification and summer recreation. Most important, they focused on improving communication with politicians, federal officials, and school representatives.[35] An original goal of Thugs United was to stimulate the development of small businesses for black residents. Lack of operating capital stymied this effort and they were successful in opening only one business, a Shell gasoline station in Central City.[36] In another effort, they created the New Orleans Youth Enterprises to facilitate small business development, but with little success. One experiment was Operation Shoe Shine, in which they attempted to establish a consistent client base by seeking year-long contracts worth $68. A candy-selling operation also lost money.[37] After these failures, existing programs and agencies became the focus of their plans for providing more jobs.

The most active period for the Thugs United came between 1970 and 1971. During the late spring of 1970, Warren Carmouche, "Sticks" Hall, and Jim Linn, a local white accountant, aggressively lobbied local industries and businesses for donations and for job pledges, with a goal of $60,000 for the year.[38] In May, a run-in with the New Orleans Police Department made their job more difficult. Incensed after witnessing the police beating a business owner near the Thugs United headquarters in Central City, several Thugs members placed signs in their storefront windows with the words, "The White Pig Police—Kill, Kill, Kill Them." The artwork superimposed a swastika and the letters "KKK" over a NOPD badge. In response, police superintendent Joseph Giarrusso asked the officers in question to attend a Thugs-led seminar. The chairman of the Police Association of New Orleans deemed the solution ridiculous, saying that officers did not need to learn from "convicted felons" and that the Thugs were merely a front to protect criminals. The Thugs stated that they posted the sign to show that they were "mad enough to even kill, yes, kill the two officers." Surprisingly, many in the local press sided with the Thugs in the matter, although others did not. A few days after the incident, a mysterious fire caused $2,000 worth of damage to the Thugs United main offices.[39] But as the local fundraising efforts became complicated, the Thugs United received news that they would be awarded a $55,000 Model Cities grant for a dropout program to begin in August. This infusion of money was the most substantial in the history of the organization and gave the Thugs United leadership a chance to build a more long-term, meaningful presence in New Orleans's target areas.

A few days after the Model Cities grant commenced, however, the Thugs received ominous news. The United Fund had once again refused to make the Thugs United part of its fundraising effort. The Fund endorsed the "philosophy and the necessity" of the Thugs, but did not believe that the Thugs's leadership could sustain the organization, citing "a great deal of tension, fragmentation, and disagreement" inside and outside the group. Perhaps most telling, the Fund believed that Carmouche needed "to be controlled or silenced."[40] Over the next year, the Thugs United continued to operate their programs and to administer the Model Cities dropout program, but Carmouche essentially abandoned the efforts to "Sticks" Hall and Leroy "The Danger Zone" Malone. Soon into 1971, an FBI investigation and financial audits showed inconsistencies, and in June, the Thugs United grant from Model Cities was suspended. By August, the Thugs United were largely finished as a functioning organization. Six months later, in March 1972, "Sticks" Hall was arrested for heroin distribution, and all remaining financial accounts were closed. Four months after that, in July, Leroy Malone was arrested for distributing heroin, and the New Orleans District Attorney pressed charges against "Sticks" Hall and an assistant for misuse of over $10,000 in federal money. In March 1973, according to the *New Orleans States-Item*, Warren Carmouche, who had departed two years earlier, was under indictment for the murder of a community organizer in Miami, Florida. The events left many of the opponents of the Thugs United congratulating themselves on their earlier predictions of doom. The failed experiment in biracial, cross-class cooperation narrowed the amount of goodwill left for the future.[41]

CHAPTER ELEVEN

Women, Welfare, and Political Mobilization

We got the governor scared. He wants to tell us we ought to
express ourselves through the vote, but I told him our children
are starving and they can't vote.
—Shirley Lampton, New Orleans Welfare Rights Organization,
August 1969

Generalizing about men and women is dangerous business. In the late
1960s, however, a few trends in local black activism do stand out. In particular, organizations and/or activities that focused on black capitalism or
political mobilization (e.g., negotiating construction contracts, running
for public office) were almost always led by men. As advocates of black
capitalism, they often saw political power and economic growth as insep-
arable, frequently using muscular tactics to attract support from white
business leaders and governmental bureaucrats. Women were certainly
interested in those issues and quite willing to be aggressive. Dorothy Mae
Taylor, Oretha Castle Haley, Lavada Jefferson, and others pioneered War
on Poverty organizing efforts. In 1971, Taylor was elected to the state
legislature and became a local political legend, and Haley pushed vigor-
ously to redraw voting districts in the city. Plenty of other women were
involved in political organizations and made key contributions.[1] Nevertheless, women antipoverty organizers tended to concentrate on matters of family and safety. Two local woman-led groups offer examples
of how women organized to help their families and men. Comprised

mostly of poor black women, the New Orleans Welfare Rights Organization (NOWRO)—and its sister organization, the New Orleans Tenants Organization (NOTO)—took on bureaucratic white men and their segregationist institutions. Driven by compassion and a sense of civic duty, the New Orleans League of Women Voters (comprised mostly of affluent white women) settled into a poor area of town and encouraged the political rise of neighborhood black men. To achieve any progress, these two disparate groups of women had to clash intensely with some men, while cultivating support from others.

The Welfare Rights Movement

The New Orleans Welfare Rights Organization was started in the late 1960s, and it likely had more direct impact on the lives of the poor than any other local group. A small group of black, female welfare recipients led NOWRO, and they were helped by attorneys from the New Orleans Legal Assistance Corporation (NOLAC), a few community organizers, and occasional representatives from the National Welfare Rights Organization. These women were not trained social theorists demanding entitlements. They were mothers trying to feed their children and pay the rent on their public housing apartments. They became social activists to prevent welfare benefits from declining, not to expand the welfare rolls and to redefine the social and economic rights of citizenship. Eartha St. Ann, Shirley Lampton, Audrey Delair, Clementine Brumfield, Monica Hunter, and others took on a massive state bureaucracy well-known for making brutal cuts in welfare relief. In the late 1960s and early 1970s, Louisiana's Department of Public Welfare created a series of welfare crises when it systematically reduced benefits in the Aid to Families with Dependent Children program (AFDC was known as Aid to Dependent Children or ADC until 1962 amendments). It was that action of Louisiana bureaucrats and segregationists, not the oft-blamed "outside agitators," that radicalized the local welfare rights movement. Although the coalition supporting NOWRO was small and much less powerful than its opponents, its members lobbied and litigated their way to modest successes in preserving AFDC benefits and in publicizing the plight of welfare recipients.

The fight over AFDC was critical in sorting out the role of race in the post–Jim Crow South. From the late 1960s until the end of the millennium, few words were as politically powerful or as racially coded as *welfare*. For many it represented things un-American—sloth, parasitism, unproductiveness, and self-limitation. The confrontations between the NOWRO and the Louisiana Department of Public Welfare tested the new political meanings of individualism, productivity, and civic contribution. Savvy white conservatives interpreted those concepts in ways that reinforced traditional racial stereotypes and preserved a politically potent psychology of exclusion; black activists and liberal leaders employed their own interpretations in their Great Society-linked search for inclusion and economic progress.

There were many War on Poverty programs implemented in New Orleans because a wide variety of political leaders and business people were quite willing to use federally funded programs as deterrents to disorder and investments in human capital. Welfare payments represented a direct line to poor African Americans and, therefore, seemingly supported these social goals, as well. Nevertheless, Louisiana welfare bureaucrats stifled aid because they feared the AFDC retarded the development of efficient workers and aggressive consumers. Historian Gareth Davies has argued persuasively that in the late 1960s American liberals shifted away from traditional notions of individualism. Davies suggests the welfare rights movement and the endorsement of the Family Assistance Plan are evidence that American liberalism had swung toward accepting the idea of entitlement and away from ideas about the sanctity of work.[2] An examination of the NOWRO indicates, however, that the use of entitlement arguments was merely one tactic among several desperate choices.

AFDC was arguably the most consistently reviled social program in American history from its inception at the end of World War II until the "end of welfare as we know it," as President Bill Clinton called the 1996 creation of the Temporary Assistance for Needy Families (TANF) program.[3] The origins of the program, however, belied the later vitriol. In the late nineteenth and early twentieth centuries, veterans programs and state-level aid programs for the aged, infirm, unemployed, widowed, and the blind were the initial, fragmented basis of the welfare state. For most of the twentieth century, local, state, and federal governments—often in partnership with private entities—administered a mix of decentralized, noncomprehensive, and often racially discriminatory programs involving housing, social insurance, health, and public assistance. The closest that American policymakers came to creating a coherent system for the delivery of social welfare was the Social Security Act of 1935. This act maintained the distinction in American social policy between social insurance and public assistance, which confirmed at a national psychological level a difference between the "deserving" and the "undeserving."

The welfare battles of the 1960s were predicated on the Act's Title IV-A, which established the Aid to Dependent Children (ADC) program. Intended as compassionate legislation to enable widowed mothers to stay home with their children, it provided cash transfer payments according to formulas worked out in each state.[4] Like much of the American welfare state, its implementation and operation depended on local variables. Motivated by a need to keep expenditures low and to preserve a low-wage labor supply, southern states consistently paid out the lowest amounts, and in Louisiana, welfare workers clearly used ADC and then AFDC to control personal behavior and ensure fiscal austerity.

In the late 1960s, AFDC became extraordinarily controversial. In the two decades after World War II, the program's initial purpose as relief for widowed mothers quickly faded. According to one study, almost 50 percent of the children receiving AFDC in 1949 had fathers who had died, but by 1963 that number had dropped to 6 percent. Between 1965 and 1974, the federal budget for AFDC grew from approximately $1 billion to over $4 billion in order to accommodate approximately 11 million new participants. The massive expansion of the program was due to a number of factors, including an increase in political awareness among the poor, an economic downturn, a legal assault on the rules governing the program, and a concerted effort by welfare rights organizers to overwhelm the welfare system with new enrollees.[5]

An underlying reason for AFDC unpopularity was that many Americans thought it threatened to undermine productivity by discouraging work and reducing individual incentive. By not adhering to the contributory principle inherent in the more popular New Deal social insurance programs, AFDC seemed to reward the "undeserving" or "able-bodied" poor at least as often as it softened the desperation of the "deserving" poor—those who were too infirm or young or old to provide for themselves. That distinction constituted one of the major reasons that white Americans often associated the program with citizens of color. Largely because southern congressmen prevented domestic workers and agricultural workers from being included in social insurance programs such as the Old Age, Survivors, Disability Insurance program (OASDI) created by the Economic Security Act of 1935, black workers in grave circumstances had to seek aid through the means-tested public assistance side of the welfare state.[6]

Louisiana's matching state contributions to its AFDC program ranked consistently near the bottom of the nation, and the federal government provided almost 80 percent of its funding. For much of the post–World War II era, however, Louisiana was a national leader in one category: trimming welfare rolls by using so-called suitable home laws, which stipulated that recipients could not live with men who were not relatives. Caseworkers were notorious for asking recipients intimate questions about their sexual lives and for subjecting recipients to sweeps of their homes—according to common legend often in the middle of the night. This implementation of this policy achieved worldwide notoriety in 1959 and 1960 as Louisiana's state legislature and singing governor Jimmie Davis ratcheted up their massive resistance to racial desegregation. In 1959, in addition to passing numerous new Jim Crow measures, the state legislature enacted a law that prohibited women from receiving ADC benefits if they had ever had an illegitimate child while receiving ADC payments. In effect, the mere presence of an illegitimate child made a home unsuitable and the recipients there were stripped of their enrollment in the program. The burden for restoring these homes to suitable status lay with the mother, as she had to prove to local welfare officials that she was not violating the law.

When implemented in the summer and fall of 1960, the new law purged over 22,000 children from the ADC program. Almost 95 percent of those children were African American, despite the fact that black children accounted for less than 70 percent of child-recipients. Mary Evelyn

Parker, the state's public welfare commissioner, claimed that racial discrimination played no part. A state senator called the bill "one of the best pieces of legislation we have passed." In response, the Urban League of Greater New Orleans, led by Harvey Kerns, began a public relations offensive called "Operation Feed the Babies." This offensive in turn sparked a group of concerned citizens in Britain to begin a campaign, labeled the "Shame Governor Davis Campaign," to airlift food to the affected children in New Orleans. The cuts also received wide notoriety in the national and international press. Only after HEW threatened to cut off all ADC funds to Louisiana did state officials alter their policy. Under the compromise, the state had to prove unsuitability instead of the parent having to prove suitability. In 1962, the suitable home law was rescinded.[7] The state's welfare officials continued to use a form of the man-in-the-home or substitute father rule until March 1968 when a federal court restrained the practice. In June, the U.S. Supreme Court prohibited the practice altogether in its ruling in an Alabama case, *King v. Smith*.[8] After that, Louisiana welfare officials began reducing expenditures by making across-the-board cuts instead of targeting mothers in nonapproved relationships.

Compounding AFDC problems in Louisiana in early 1968 were congressional amendments to the national Economic Security Act that mandated changes in the AFDC program. Signed reluctantly by President Johnson in January 1968, the legislation included a 13 percent across-the-board rise in Social Security (OASDI) payments, but included mandatory work or job training requirements for AFDC recipients who were healthy, out of school, and over the age of 16. Another part of the bill limited the number of a state's AFDC recipients to their percentage of the state's population in January 1968. Federally subsidized daycare centers were supposed to take care of the children of welfare recipients who were forced into the labor market. Wilbur Mills, an Arkansas congressman and chair of the House Ways and Means Committee, was one of the bill's chief proponents, and he hoped that the bill would eliminate four hundred thousand AFDC recipients by 1972. Another key shaper of the bill was Louisiana's junior senator, Russell Long, the son of former Louisiana governor and senator Huey Long. In 1967, Long was chairman of the powerful Senate Finance Committee and Democratic Whip. Through a series of legislative maneuvers, the bill shifted some of the emphasis of AFDC policy from its early 1960s focus on encouraging rehabilitation to forcing recipients into the labor market.[9]

Hearings on the AFDC amendments before Russell Long's Senate committee were the public highlight of a long battle. On September 19, 1967, several black women from the National Welfare Rights Organization engaged in a three-hour protest in the hearing room, with one declaring that "the only time you listen to us is when the cities are burning and the people are dying." The next day, Long reportedly referred to the women as "brood mares" who did not know how to use their time. "If they can take the time to march in the street and picket and sit in the hearing room all day," he complained, "it seems to me they have enough time to get jobs."[10] Mills employed similar imagery to encourage President Johnson not to veto the final bill. He argued that the provisions would keep black women recipients—like the woman who supposedly lived across the street from his mother and had given birth to eleven children—from having large numbers of children that the federal government supported. Some historians argue that Johnson suspected that most members of Congress felt the same way but were reluctant to declare it in public.[11]

Ostensibly in response to problems at the federal level, Louisiana welfare officials made serious cuts in payments between May 1968 and January 1971. Reaction to those cuts demonstrated how much the state's politics had changed since the "Feed the Babies" crisis of 1960. No longer politically impotent, black women activists, with crucial aid from OEO-funded attorneys, led an intense campaign against AFDC reductions and for relief from the housing pressures ensuing from them. Through sit-ins, protest marches, political lobbying, and judicial battles, NOWRO helped mobilize some public sympathy and with lobbying assistance from the National Association of Social Workers, helped restore some of the money cut from the AFDC program. Together with NOLAC attorneys, they put forward an important moral argument about the harsh nature of Louisiana's welfare system, but like much of the War on Poverty, they often settled for vague appeals that focused on deprivation and intimidation. Antipoverty lawyers, for their part, pursued a "southern strategy" by coalescing with groups like the NOWRO and the NOTO.[12] While impassioned legal-assistance lawyers tried to restructure rights through case law, the women of NOWRO and NOTO fought to stave off starvation, eviction, and marginalization. In the long term, however, their aggressive public image, the waning of the national concern about poverty, and an increasingly conservative judicial environment undermined the biracial, liberal coalition upon which their organization depended.

In Louisiana, welfare activists encountered open hostility. Senator Russell Long's comments about welfare mothers being "brood mares" were mainstream white lingo. For instance, one blue-collar worker in New Orleans claimed that white workers in his shop complained about having "to work all day while some sonofabitch gets paid for doing nothing." One of his coworkers asked him, "Why should they take money out of my pay check and give it to niggers to have bastard black babies?"[13] The New Orleans Citizen's Council, led by C. E. Vitter, wanted to stop "immoral women and their illegitimate children clamoring for more money to continue their immorality." Uttering a prevalent plea among white citizens, Vitter demanded the state "quit coddling this cancerous condition and force these people to be responsible for their act."[14]

In this unfriendly climate, the women of NOWRO and NOTO initiated a political attack on bureaucratic decision-making structures, a legal attack on welfare rules and regulations, and a psychological attack on attitudes and behaviors associated with segregation and alienation. Shirley Lampton explained that they were trying to "effectively deal with long standing problems, with policies which keep us trapped in the poverty-and-welfare cycle, with social conditions which doom so many of our children to frustrated and defeated lives, and with attitudes which deprive us of our dignity." The NOWRO wanted to attack the "vicious cycle" that "provides for dependency on welfare and undermines self-respect." They had six basic goals: (1) adequate income, (2) dignity, (3) justice, (4) democracy, (5) decent jobs with adequate pay for those who can work, and (6) to inform all recipients of their rights.[15]

NOWRO's origins are traceable to the summer of 1967 when a group of social activists helped to organize the City-Wide Welfare Rights Organization. Over the next year, the movement expanded as a result of a rent strike and the reaction to welfare cuts. NOWRO denounced a May 1968 reduction as "a criminal act" and organized a largely fruitless protest.[16] A more organized response to a 10 percent cut in November proved more successful. First, a lawsuit was filed by Shirley Lampton, a mother of eight, and Leuthel Williams, a mother of nine, in the court of Judge Fred Cassibry, a former labor attorney and New Orleans city councilman. Judge Cassibry issued a temporary injunction against the cut. Second, approximately thirty-five welfare mothers from the Algiers-Fischer housing project staged a protest march and sit-in at the state welfare office building in New Orleans.[17] The Social Welfare Planning Council responded supportively, issuing a public statement against the 10 percent cut because of "humanitarian considerations" and fear of racial disorder.[18]

NOWRO's actions fed white dread about black civil disorder. Louisiana Public Welfare Commissioner Garland Bonin worried that the NOWRO planned to escalate their sit-ins and "attacks" against the local office. He was so concerned that he instructed individual workers to stop visiting housing projects. "I am still of the opinion," he told Governor McKeithen, "that the welfare situation in New Orleans is explosive and dangerous and anything could happen." Echoing a common accusation against the War on Poverty, he charged that OEO community workers were behind the sit-in at welfare offices. He claimed that he had proof from a taxi driver and the New Orleans Police Department that Total Community Action organizers had paid for the transportation of protesters. According to Bonin, the OEO had "convinced these people that they do have grievances and the way to resolve them is through violence." An investigation of the matter by the Southwest Regional Office of the OEO found no evidence to suggest that TCA representatives did anything more than provide sympathy for NOWRO activists.[19]

In the spring of 1969 the state pushed through a 27 percent AFDC cut for the months of May and June in order to stay afloat fiscally. For a family of four, this meant a grant reduction from $116 to $85. As in November, welfare activists litigated, lobbied, and protested. The federal courts upheld the state's right to make the 27 percent cut.[20] Making the matter worse, the state legislature was out of session and could do very little to restore the funds. Scurrying to find an alternative, the Human Relations Committee of New Orleans implored the state's legislators to implement a special emergency maneuver known as a "legislative poll." By holding a vote through registered mail, the legislature could release the $500,000 needed to fund May and June payments at full levels. "The health, safety, and welfare of 130,000 Louisiana children rides in the balance," they pleaded.[21] Bill Rousselle, a young black civic leader with the Human Relations Committee, pleaded with Bonin to restore the cuts because social order depended on it. "Any ADC payment reduction," Rousselle warned, would "only further alienate a segment of this society that has already suffered oppression and indignity too long." Secretary Bonin, he argued, was wrong to "play politics with the helpless children."[22]

The NOWRO also lobbied the Housing Authority of New Orleans (HANO) to lower rents in response to the grant cuts (HANO's rent amounted to 23 percent of a family's income). NOWRO leaders refused to accept the HANO argument that federal regulations mandated a minimum of $16.75 per month. Hoping to pressure HANO officials into adjusting their rents, NOWRO leaders conducted their most aggressive protest to date. On April 25, 1969, for over an hour members of NOWRO invaded HANO's downtown headquarters, led by Shirley Lampton and Anthony R. Henry, director of the Quakers' tenants rights program. In the words of J. Gilbert Scheib, executive director of HANO, a "very large group of men, women, and children . . . in a vicious manner forced their way into our first floor Reception Hall, using vulgar and profane language." Scheib added that the protestors warned, "if we do not get what we want, someone will be killed." According to Scheib, about half of the protestors went to a third floor assembly room. Henry, Lampton, and the others charged into his office and interrupted a conversation he was having with Thomas Callaham in the Ft. Worth office of HUD about the rent issue. "The vulgar and profane remarks continued," claimed Scheib, "and I was held hostage as the disorderly mob filled every space."[23]

Protesters "hung over" his desk, "completely surrounding" him. According to Scheib, they responded with "jeering and hostile remarks" to explanations that HANO had no influence over the cuts and that the state legislature would probably restore the funding. Scheib refrained from calling the police because local television crews had followed the welfare protesters. Eventually, the group departed of their own volition. Scheib told Lampton and Henry that if they wanted meetings in the future, they would have to follow the "channels of authority" in HANO. Not long after the occupation of HANO offices, the state legislature transferred funds that prevented the proposed cuts from taking effect.[24]

In July officials and activists faced another welfare crisis. With a new fiscal year beginning July 1, the Louisiana Department of Public Welfare had to meet a Social Security mandate to bring its "standard of need" into line with the cost of living. To fund that mandate, the department requested over $17 million for the 1969–1970 fiscal year budget, but the state legislature approved only $9 million, which was $400,000 lower than the previous year's appropriation. This put the Welfare Department in a bind because cost of living had risen 20 percent and enrollment in the program was escalating. The department's solution to this problem was based on the U.S. Supreme Court's *King v. Smith* decision that each state had "considerable latitude" in setting benefit levels. Louisiana officials, therefore, raised the *standard* of need, but lowered the *level* by which they fulfilled that need. To address its funding shortfall, the department moved away from basing payments on "dollar maximums," which set a limit on amounts without regard to the standard of need, to a "ratable reduction" system based on a percentage of need. This shift allowed a 42 percent reduction in benefits. Welfare Commissioner Bonin argued that the cuts were necessary because the state's AFDC rolls had ballooned after *King v. Smith* prohibited the substitute father rule. In an attempt to stave off the cuts, attorneys Jeffrey Schwartz and Richard Buckley of NOLAC sought an injunction against the state. In a two to one vote, a three-judge panel denied their appeal, citing the state's authority to determine the amount to which they would fund the standard of need. Fred Cassibry, the judge who had stopped an earlier cut, was the dissenting vote in the case.[25]

The defeat in federal court forced action in other areas. Once again, the cuts stirred action from progressive political quarters and even sparked Governor McKeithen to ask for federal intervention. In one instance, two white progressives on the city council tried to find a solution. Eddie Sapir, representative of Central City, and Moon Landrieu, councilperson-at-large, pushed a resolution premised on cooperation between the city and private interests.[26] Eventually, their efforts resulted in the city adding $20,000 to the emergency welfare fund.[27] At the state house, Dutch Morial and Edward H. Booker of the Joint Legislative Study Committee proposed several solutions to the welfare crisis. First, they asked officials from HEW to intercede in Louisiana. Second, they wanted to force public housing officials to take AFDC cuts into consideration in setting rents and to encourage the state's Charity hospitals and private hospitals to give free pharmaceuticals to welfare families. Third, they pleaded for churches, agencies, and local charities to raise funds to offset the cuts.[28] Another group of New Orleans progressives considered other measures. Led by Catholic Archbishop Philip Hannan, they wanted to boost funding for the Food Stamp program by $750 million. Avery Alexander suggested ending the federal income tax exemption in Louisiana's state income tax code, a potential $55 million gain. Louisiana legislative leader Michael O'Keefe proposed raising taxes on alcohol and cigarettes to make up the cuts.[29] Governor McKeithen's solution involved centralizing the AFDC system. His proposal to the National Conference of Governors asked for the federal government to take over the costs of the welfare program.[30]

As in previous AFDC crises, NOWRO provided the most aggressive response. In late July, its leadership called for an ambitious protest march from New Orleans to Baton Rouge. NOWRO spokesperson Shirley Lampton announced that her group chose to march to the state capitol because welfare recipients were too poor to drive. She expected three thousand marchers to make the journey between August 5 and August 11, a time when temperatures usually hovered near 100 degrees with comparably high humidity.[31]

When the marchers left on August 5, the temperature was climbing to 92 degrees. Reports indicated that there was "no cheering or singing." August heat and humidity, combined with the demands of work and the inconvenience of a week-long march, made for a poor turnout. Escorted by six motorcycle policemen and led by Lampton, Rudolph Muse of Thugs United, Carlton Pecot, Avery Alexander, and Monica Hunter, a group of fewer than one hundred protesters (the *Times-Picayune* counted sixty) headed down Washington Avenue in New Orleans toward the capitol in Baton Rouge. According to reports there were ten children under the age of twelve and only one white marcher, a three-hundred-pound man carrying an Army pack. Disappointment was evident. Rudolph Muse expressed frustration that "people don't hurt enough to get up off their backsides and do something about it."[32]

As the march progressed down Claiborne Avenue and northward along Highway 90 and other roads along the Mississippi River, the ranks thinned out. At one point along the way, only nine marchers continued, and they spent a good deal of the trip in the back of a pickup truck. Despite their low numbers, the marchers demonstrated flashes of spirited protest. Speaking from the Mississippi River levee in front of the Destrehan plantation house, Shirley Lampton boasted: "We got the governor scared. He wants to tell us we ought to express ourselves through the vote, but I told him our children are starving and they can't vote." John Hampton of the Urban League explained that they had stopped in front of the decaying plantation, "to symbolize" that blacks now lived "in a new kind of slavery—a slavery of hunger, a slavery of poverty." Writers for *The Plain Truth* lauded the marchers for trying "to take their destinies out of the white man's hands and to control their own and their children's futures." Most observers saw the march as a " 'Mission Impossible,' " they reported. "But you couldn't tell the welfare mothers that. They were going to meet the man."[33] When the marchers reached the capitol, however, "the man" was not there. Governor McKeithen was out of town, and the 150 or so protestors who had made a final leg of the trip spent most of their time waiting outside. Despite a promise by Lampton that "if it takes two months, we'll be here," they apparently never made it in. One voice among the marchers asserted, "I bet they would let a honky through here."[34]

Back in New Orleans, on August 9, the food riot chronicled in Chapter Eight was occurring downtown.[35] The protests and civil disturbances apparently had little impact on HANO's rent policies and did not prevent more AFDC cuts in November and again in December 1970 and January 1971. The November 1969 cuts caused NOWRO-NOTO to expand their rent strike. Just prior to the cuts, several NOWRO members again attempted to use direct action protest at HANO, but HANO was better prepared. They simply had the women arrested, sending NOWRO president Clementine Brumfield, NOTO director Shirley Lampton, Monica Hunter, and three others to jail for disturbing the peace. HANO officials later sent eviction notices to one thousand families who had not paid their rent. In retaliation, the women filed suit against HANO for harassment, and Shirley Lampton called for an extension of the rent strike beyond "welfare mothers" to include all tenants, and she demanded more control over HANO.[36] NOTO wanted to stop evictions and to be recognized as the "bargaining agent" for tenants. NOTO leaders demanded regularly scheduled meetings between NOTO and HANO and to control the selection of five of the nine members of the HANO board of directors. They also called for more vigilance in repairs and in promoting tenants into managerial positions. They wanted to eliminate minimum rent and to adjust the rent formula to 15 percent of one's income instead of almost 25 percent. In a clear protest gesture, they wanted AFDC families to pay only $1 per month until they received benefits equal to 100 percent of need.[37] NOLAC attorneys helped NOTO by informing residents that HANO had to accept partial payments and by gaining a temporary federal injunction that prevented evictions.[38] The leadership of the welfare rights movement shifted slightly in 1970 with the formation of the Emergency Welfare Coalition, which brought together activists and representatives from local social welfare organizations. The women activists remained the heart of the movement.[39]

As 1970 approached, relations between HANO and the activists reached their nadir. Monica Hunter of NOTO blamed the welfare predicament on a lack of commitment from the nation's leaders. "If this country can send a man to the moon," she chastised the HANO leadership, "it can keep a roof over the head of a poor family this Christmas." The editors of *The Plain Truth* were less diplomatic, claiming that the federal government had spent at least $5 billion on the space program and $58 billion on the Vietnam War. "After being tricked by the syphillis-mouthed [*sic*] white state officials," they wrote, "the Black mothers were thrown back into the polluted sea of the projects and ghettoes in New Orleans where a nickle [*sic*] costs a dime and loan sharks and economic barracudas like the housing authority make them easy game."[40] Holding tightly to their policies amid severe pressure, HANO leaders argued that their mission was to provide housing, not social reform. Willard Robertson, chairperson of the HANO board, blamed the rent strike on the "unwise leadership" of NOTO who misunderstood what HANO could accomplish.[41] Chairman Robertson emphasized HANO's tradition of "compassion and understanding." For example, HANO had evicted no families when, in one past instance, 1,200 residents were cut from welfare rolls for "environmental immorality." He stressed that public housing was not a poverty program. Its "purpose" was "to provide decent, safe and sanitary housing for families of low income, at rental within their means." Their policy had "always been to regard project residents the same as other citizens, and we feel that we have an obligation to preserve their dignity." That dignity, according to the philosophy of HANO leadership, was based on the resident's capacity to pay. Under HANO, the average cost for housing and dignity was $35 per month, with over 2,500 paying $50 and several hundred spending over $75.[42]

Whether HANO and Department of Public Welfare officials realized it or not, they were participating in a major shift in the search for black power and the Great Society. The rhetoric of Sam Bell, a Lower Ninth Ward activist, illustrates this shift. Bell worried that the cuts in AFDC would further alienate the black poor. He hinted that the government was sowing the "seeds of a revolution" that would emerge from the "polarization of a disenchanted people." In 1969, " 'the great (white) fathers' " of Louisiana seemed "totally oblivious of the potential chaos that lie dormant at their feet." As he explained, "Tomorrow is another day, who knows?"[43] Bell's anger highlights the fact that the welfare crises, the welfare rights movement, and the tenant rights movement were not merely peripheral events in the city's history or its search for the Great Society. Political and bureaucratic leaders at the city and state levels were usually willing to consider the interests of poor blacks only when faced with the possibility of disorder or when the courts left them no other choice. The NOWRO-NOTO leaders demonstrated the efficacy of using conflict to gain concessions from white leaders and the difficulty of sustaining a social welfare movement at the grassroots.

The Carrollton Experiment

While the women of the NOWRO were fighting against welfare cuts, another group of women were organizing in an area of the city left out of the War on Poverty. From 1967 until 1971, the New Orleans League of Women Voters spearheaded a community action effort in the city's historic Carrollton area. Although this effort did not receive as much attention as the NOWRO activities, it offers another view of the ways that black activists and white liberals tried to work together after Jim Crow.

The Carrollton section of New Orleans seems to have been one of the most racially mixed, economically diverse urban areas in the South. Spreading out from a bend in the Mississippi River, it was home to approximately ten thousand residents, over one-third below the poverty line. Around 5,300 of them were white and 4,800 black. Occasionally, white and black residents lived side by side, particularly on working class blocks. More often though, the races remained divided, with black residents typically segregated into colloquially named pockets.[44] The focus of most attention of antipoverty reformers was a section called Gert Town. Located on the edge of Xavier University and the upper side of Central City, the area had only one small playground, one public school, and one mobile medical unit that came twice a week. Gert Town was described by a Tulane sociologist as a place of "decay and apathy" that was as isolated "as a rural village."[45] Beginning in 1967, several local organizations tried to address the problems of Gert Town and make-up for Carrollton's omission as a War on Poverty target area. In one effort, Tulane University's School of Social Work partnered with the New Orleans Community Relations Council, the Urban League, and Xavier University to conduct a short-term, privately funded community action project, while the local League of Women Voters added a more substantial organizing effort that focused on Gert Town but included all of Carrollton.

In the previous two decades, the League had changed from being an outpost for upper-income white women with political inclinations to a multiracial group with a solid core of middle-class activists who were tackling serious political and social issues.[46] Hoping to deal with the "absence of leadership" in Carrollton, the League started a Citizenship Education project similar to those they had conducted in the Irish Channel and Desire areas.[47] The initial focus was on small meetings with approximately twenty people. To expand their efforts, the League sought a grant from the Office of Economic Opportunity.[48] When federal War on Poverty officials denied their appeal, the women's group turned to the Ford Foundation, a philanthropic organization whose funding and vision had been essential for parts of the early War on Poverty. The League's petition was successful, and New Orleans was one of six cities to receive a Ford grant to operate an Inner-City Citizenship Education project. Also chipping in funds locally were the Stern Family Fund and the Urban League.[49]

In 1968, the League used that project to enter a partnership with black leaders, mostly male, in the Carrollton area. One result was the Carrollton Central Steering Committee (CCSC), a biracial organization composed of representatives from the League of Women Voters, the Urban League, and several neighborhood associations. The chairman and central figure was Robert McFarland, a resident of the Carrollton section referred to as "Nigger Town" (now known as the Black Pearl). The CCSC operated from 1968 until 1971. In those three years, it established an aggressive agenda and proposed an innovative vision for the area's recovery. In 1970, the management of the CCSC passed from League officials to neighborhood leaders. In the process, the CCSC became a leading voice for some of the area's militant activists. In 1971, however, the organization collapsed under the weight of bureaucratic pressures and black separatism. Integrationist moderates created another group—the Carrollton Community Council—to carry out antipoverty activities and to coordinate efforts with local, state, and federal governments. In its three year span, the CCSC used public and private funding to operate a community center and a daycare center in conjunction with the Urban League. Among many other modest initiatives, the committee also published a community newspaper called the *Carrollton Advocate*, lobbied the City Council, sought to create a community health center, and conducted voter education and voter registration projects.[50] Measured in dollars, programs, and personnel, the CCSC was a small operation, and it produced little long-term economic change. But it did represent a rare thing in the South—white women working intimately with black men in service to the interests of those black men.

At the height of the national Black Power phenomenon, Carrollton became an experiment in biracial cooperation. Several financially well-off white women, politically ambitious black leaders, deeply concerned neighborhood activists, socially impassioned young people, and ideologically driven academics flung themselves into a complicated, and often heated, coalition. Espousing the central theme of the War on Poverty, the women in the League asserted that the CCSC's main goal was "to help the poor become more effective citizens." The League's members wanted to educate residents about relevant institutions. If armed with that understanding, residents would be better able to "overcome fear and hostility that have been generated in the past."[51] The League's president, Felicia Kahn, thought that the League could break "through the walls of the ghetto." In a bit of a stretch, she mused that the League may have been "the first organization to reach out from the larger community and to go behind the walls." Like so many others, she warned that without a breakthrough, New Orleans and America might expect a "revolution."[52] As much as League officials worried about black exclusion, they recognized that racial inclusion was difficult. "'Self-help' for the poor is a myth," Kahn advised. "The poor cannot help themselves." The poor had to learn how to "relate appropriately to the community at large."[53]

League members tried to avoid being intrusive and condescending, realizing that the poor had been soured by previous encounters with other "do-gooders." One League official cautioned her colleagues not to see Carrollton's black residents as "an inferior group." Language and imagery were especially important. She told them to avoid explaining their work as getting their "hands dirty" or referring to black residents as "you people."[54] Another member instructed the League's volunteers to ensure that Carrollton participants saw the League as a "a *partner* rather than a *parent*."[55] Despite the League of Women Voters' effort to eliminate condescension, the sense that the poor could not help themselves permeated the CCSC. According to CCSC leaders, low-income African Americans had been so alienated that they had constructed an understanding of themselves void of connections to community. Poor black residents lacked "self-knowledge" and "a sense of basic identity." To this end, CCSC leaders made the creation of a community center a top priority. This center represented more than a meeting place. It was the key to psychological progress. The psychological lives of the poor, according to CCSC leaders, were so inadequate that the act of getting approved for a community center grant "would represent a victory to them out of all proportion to the money actually involved." At the centers, the League planned to teach civic skills and to train individuals to address "cultural problems." Continuing the battle for self-image, they also wanted a black male to head the center to serve as a role model.[56]

The CCSC Community Center opened in late June 1968.[57] Hamstrung by limited funds and space, its operators struggled to overcome what they called a tendency among local adults to complain, but at the same time avoid involvement.[58] Despite those issues, in 1968 and 1969 at least four community organizations began operating as a result of the CCSC, and the CCSC brought some limited programs to the community. One group held a somewhat successful voter registration drive, and one report claimed that residents were "emerging as neighborhood leaders for the first time in their lives." But, as with community action elsewhere, obstacles severely limited progress.[59] The skepticism of neighborhood residents was a major impediment, and when combined with the lack of bureaucratic framework, uncertain funding, and the increasing militancy of young activists, it stifled significant institutional growth. In 1969 and 1970, some black leaders grew tired of oversight by the League, and tension led the League of Women Voters to scale back their official involvement.[60]

The primary conflict was between the League and Carrollton activist Robert McFarland, a man who was one of the most effective leaders in the area. Initially, he impressed the League women, and Felicia Kahn credited him for most of their "success."[61] Between 1968 and 1970, he developed a program for teenagers and contributed to the formation of the CCSC Community Center. Politically ambitious, he represented the Carrollton area on City Hall's Human Relations Committee, ran an unsuccessful campaign for a seat in the Louisiana House of Representatives, and coordinated voter registration drives with the Southern Organization for Unified Leadership (SOUL), Black Youth for Progress (BYP), the local NAACP, and a militant political group known as Black PAC.[62] Two moments defined McFarland's tenure with the CCSC. One was a showdown in the spring of 1970 with the Catholic Church over community action.

Another came a year later when the CCSC split apart, and well-connected progressive integrationists formed the Carrollton Community Council.

The tangle with the Catholic Church involved Xavier University's control over several programs in Gert Town, some of which received federal funding. Sister Loyola, a white nun employed by Xavier, had established a recreation program, a free breakfast program, and the Xavier Teacher Corps, a Head Start-like entity that involved over forty mothers. Also, in conjunction with Robert McFarland, she supervised VISTA volunteers assigned to Carrollton. A serious fissure in this alliance erupted in March 1970 when Sister Loyola proposed adding ten white VISTA volunteers. Several existing VISTA volunteers and members of the Gert Town community balked and began a movement to wrest control away from her. When four VISTA volunteers complained to the nun that the addition of more white volunteers would undermine their carefully developed relationships with black residents in Gert Town, Sister Loyola terminated their terms of service. This action caused a dramatic protest in the neighborhood and led to a series of meetings in early April, one of which attracted over one hundred Gert Town residents. The key issue became community control over the Xavier-run programs, leading one Gert Town activist to declare, "The university's gonna understand that as long as they come in and say things over here, we gonna go in and say things over there." A few days after the largest community meeting, local people formed the Gert Town Community Council to serve as the focal point of community politics. Robert McFarland explained that the council was needed "to control our own selves and our destinies" and to develop "black political power."[63]

McFarland contended that "community control does not mean that a bunch of black people will move in on worthwhile programs and destroy or discontinue them." Community control, to McFarland, meant that African Americans would be the primary leaders in their communities and would determine the usefulness of programs. Others would serve only in technical roles. Gert Towners should "throw the paternalistic concept that they can't run things out the window."[64] Gert Town leaders' concern about community control led them to become more involved in the few antipoverty programs in the area. It also underlay a promising search for federal funds to create the Carrollton Health Center. The search began in earnest in the late summer of 1970 when a local Vista, Ned Ferguson, began working with a Carrollton doctor who was willing to volunteer his services. In September, Ferguson and the CCSC's Nathaniel Muse headed to Washington, D.C., to lobby New Orleans congressman Hale Boggs and officials at OEO and HEW. Boggs signed on to the project, and relations with the OEO and HEW seemed to hold potential. The effort stalled in early 1971, though, when Ferguson announced his plans to go to medical school, and CCSC leaders learned that they could not receive funds because their organization did not meet federal requirements for a community organization. To receive funding through TCA or City Hall for a medical center—with revenue raised through a $200,000 bond issue and $160,000 in Hill-Burton hospital funds—the CCSC would have to hold community elections according to federal guidelines.[65] In April, haggling over those elections and the makeup of the CCSC led to the group's split. McFarland became belligerent and, according to an aide to Mayor Moon Landrieu, refused to "work with white[s]" and when presiding over meetings, provided "no opportunity for real debate."[66]

By March 1970, the League had reluctantly severed their official ties to the CCSC. According to League official Betty Wisdom, League women realized that the CCSC would likely prefer not to have " 'outsiders' like us in its midst." Despite the shift in the relationship, several of the League women remained active and, one year later, formed the Carrollton Community Council, the main purpose of which was to establish the Carrollton Health Corporation and to obtain funding for medical facilities.[67] After TCA agreed to arbitrate the dispute over who would represent the Carrollton area, the Carrollton Health Corporation oversaw the process of developing the neighborhood health center. By the end of the year, the Carrollton Council had begun the process of site selection and design for a twenty-thousand square foot facility.

At the dawn of a new decade, the CCSC highlighted some of the difficulties in the fight against black inequality and showed the danger of developing institutions in the bureaucratic softness at the edges of the Great Society. Vibrant leaders with aggressive messages and a few contacts among powerful whites could shape structures that could facilitate participation in the labor market and provide better services. But activism was not enough. Without a serious governmental commitment of funds and institutional support, actions served more as social criticism than social reform. For the public/private arrangements of the Soft State to work, the public had to bear nearly the entire financial burden, but leave control to the quiet hands of essentially private political leaders.

New Orleans's political culture was changing, and with some help from middle-class women volunteers, militant voices pushed those changes much faster. They would not be in the vanguard, however. The new black brokers were typically young, well-educated, bureaucratically astute leaders able to coalesce with whites. The radical and usually disorganized voices rising from the streets were important for shaping the vocabulary and the boundaries of political discussion, but they proved less impressive at election time. Another set of organizations on the periphery, however, were more capable of plying the personal, semi-private world of Louisiana politics. A group of black political organizations that this study calls the Acronyms began on the outskirts of power, but, unlike the Thugs United, the Carrollton Central Steering Committee, and the New Orleans Welfare Rights Organization, they did not remain there for long.

CHAPTER TWELVE

Acronyms, Liberalism, and Electoral Politics, 1969–1971

And you'll find that a good many of these people that you take in there and give them a job for a couple of years wind up being the leaders in your state.

—President Lyndon B. Johnson explaining the War on Poverty to Georgia Governor Carl Sanders, July 1964

The election season of 1969–1970 was a test of racial liberalism. Black voters, primarily organized by neighborhood councils and political groups that this study refers to as the Acronyms, put the racially liberal Moon Landrieu in the mayor's office. Seven years after the New Orleans Police Department dragged civil rights activists out of City Hall by their feet, racial liberals walked in through the front door with keys in hand, ready to set the post-Jim Crow political agenda. The coalition that produced Moon Landrieu's triumph was fragile, however, and endured severe early testing. How would progressive electoral success affect the arrangements of the Soft State, the energy of the grassroots, and the dialogue about the black role in public life? Could racial liberals continue to answer the voices from the streets, or could they actually evolve into alienators and segregators themselves?

The August 1965 Voting Rights Act was only one reason for Moon Landrieu's success. Immediately after the Act passed, a well-coordinated campaign raised the number of black voters from about 35,000 to approximately 52,000. Those new voters did affect the mayoral campaign that year. Victor Schiro changed campaign strategies and carefully reached out to certain black leaders, enabling him to win the campaign by attracting almost 30 percent of black votes. Between 1966 and the mayoral primaries of 1969, another 12,000 black residents had registered, but black voters still only accounted for approximately 30 percent of the local electorate. The city's 65,000 black voters could determine a close election if they were unified around one candidate and if that candidate could also secure about 40 percent of white voters.[1] In 1969, that candidate was a young white liberal with a history of opposing segregation and supporting federal social policies.

A new era in southern politics had arrived. Moon Landrieu received less than half of the white votes but over 90 percent of African Americans supported him. In 1969 and 1970, the liberal political triumph showed that black votes, black political activism, biracial cooperation, and Great Society programs could remake electoral and bureaucratic power. Nationally, liberalism was waning, but locally, Landrieu's election—and similar ones throughout the South—was part of the first legitimate stand of southern racial liberalism. These new long-haired, biracial leaders grafted the growth-based progressivism of the immediate post–World War II era onto the racially charged, therapeutic politics of the 1960s. In doing so, those biracial liberals—and occasional radicals—demonstrated a shrewd grasp of the issues at play and the broader changes underway in American culture, though shifts in governmental funding and a serious decline in the oil economy in the 1980s undercut them.

Black Politics

The history of black politics in New Orleans is one of enduring black frustration. During Reconstruction, groups such as the Fourth Ward Republicans and black leaders such as P. B. S. Pinchback provided well-organized black involvement in New Orleans's civic affairs. After Reconstruction, power returned to white supremacists and black political participation was limited to bargaining with white leaders and the occasional chance to influence federal patronage during Republican presidencies. In 1892, the black Comité des Citoyens, or Citizens Committee, challenged racial segregation on a Louisiana railway. Their defeat in the landmark *Plessy v. Ferguson* (1896) decision, which enshrined the principle of "separate but equal" as U.S. law, set the course for the Jim Crow racial system. In the early twentieth century, neighborhood-influenced social clubs became the primary source of black political organizations. The Autocrat Club, led by A. P. Tureaud, and the San Jacinto Club held sway over the Seventh Ward Civic League, the Federation of Civic Leagues, and the New Orleans NAACP. Tureaud, a Creole Radical, mounted persistent legal challenges to segregation.[2]

World War II was the pivotal event in the black search for power. The war stimulated economic growth, put black citizens into leadership roles (albeit typically segregated ones) in the armed forces, and shaped a moral and economic agenda that energized black activism in the South. In 1946, A. P. Tureaud and J. A. Thornton won a verdict in *Hall v. Nagel* that allowed plaintiffs to bring voting cases to federal courts without first having to go through the states. As a result of the *Hall* case, the Supreme Court's *Smith v. Allwright* (1944), and the growth of civil rights organizing, the number of registered black voters in New Orleans rose from approximately 400 in 1940 to 28,000 by 1952. Registration also rose dramatically in other Louisiana parishes, particularly in heavily Catholic areas in southern Louisiana where local sheriffs benefited from black votes. Nevertheless, in 1950 there were still no registered black voters in almost half of the state's parishes. After World War II, the church and the labor movement were at the center of black politics in New Orleans. Labor representative Ernest Wright organized the People's Defense League, and in 1947, A. P. Tureaud, *The Louisiana Weekly* publisher C. C. Dejoie Jr., labor leader Clarence "Chink" Henry, and the Reverends Abraham Lincoln Davis, Avery Alexander, and Dave Dennis (also a representative of the International Longshoremen's Association) formed the Orleans Parish Progressive Voters League (OPPVL). That group split in 1954 when Chink Henry created the Crescent City Independent Voters League. Other important groups were the United Voters League and the Ninth Ward Civic Improvement League.[3]

Black voter registration was better in Louisiana than in most Deep South states. In 1956, approximately 160,000 blacks were on the voting rolls. White supremacists responded with a four-year campaign to purge them from the rolls. North Louisiana state senator Willie Rainach and White Citizens Councils attempted to engineer the elimination of all black votes. Although unsuccessful in that goal, they did reduce black registration by 20 percent statewide and over 30 percent in New Orleans. Despite a number of voter drives, the numbers of black voters did not increase much until 1965. The Orleans registrar of voters, A. P. Gallinghouse, was a segregationist notorious for prejudicial enforcement of literacy requirements and delaying black registration.[4]

In the 1950s and early 1960s black leaders pursued power cautiously, trying "not to bite too much of the apple, but to take each little pocket of our community and make it work," as SOUL leader Donald Hubbard explained. A sprinkling of black politicians took to the campaign trail, aware they were unlikely to win, but willing to lose in the effort to build political momentum and encourage voter registration. Attorney Earl Amedee twice ran unsuccessfully—in 1950 for an Orleans Parish School Board seat and again in 1954 for councilman-at-large. Rev. James A. Lewis ran fifth out of seven candidates in his unsuccessful 1952 bid to represent Algiers in the Louisiana House of Representatives. In 1958, A. P. Tureaud failed to unseat arch-segregationist Edward Hébert in the First U.S. Congressional district. In 1960, Lawrence Wheeler, a prominent community leader, and Revius Ortique, a top black attorney who later joined the Louisiana Supreme Court, added their names to the list of defeated black candidates. As the civil rights movement escalated after the middle 1950s, the pursuit of black power also began to change. In 1954, Avery Alexander left OPPVL to focus on civil rights activities, and by 1960 he had formed the Consumer's League to conduct direct-action protests against segregationist practices in Central City. The Ninth Ward Citizens' Voters League was also formed in 1960, and these groups complemented the intense efforts of the Congress of Racial Equality (CORE), the NAACP, and the Interdenominational Ministerial Alliance.[5]

A major test of black power came in the 1961–1962 mayoral election. Three candidates—socially prominent Adrian Duplantier, Third District assessor James Comiskey, and assessor Paul Burke—courted the approximately 35,000 black voters in the city. Victor Schiro opted to use a wedge issue. Moon Landrieu later explained that Schiro was not a "mean man by any stretch," but was influenced by friends who were "not progressive." On race, Schiro "wasn't looking for trouble," he was "just not comfortable."[6] In the runoff between Duplantier, who had the support of black voters and white elites, and Schiro, Schiro's easy victory showed the limits of black influence.[7]

In 1963, activism on the streets and at the registrar's office encouraged more black residents to qualify for elections. In 1963–1964, the Coordinating Council of Greater New Orleans, led by sociologist Daniel Thompson and activist Virginia Collins, tried valiantly to challenge registration procedures in New Orleans, but with only limited success. When the Voting Rights Act passed in August 1965, the League of Women Voters coordinated "Operation Registration" for dozens of organizations, and the NAACP, the IMA, Avery Alexander's Consumer's League, and Ellis Hull's United Voters' League petitioned the Justice Department to send in federal examiners to review the local process. The voter registration movement boosted black registration by one-third in only a few months. This growth encouraged twenty-eight African Americans to run for office. In the Democratic runoff to the 1965 mayoral race, most of the city's black voters supported James Fitzmorris, a moderate white city councilman. So incumbent Schiro promised to appoint a black official to the city attorney's office, and he also had gained the support of some black organizations, both of which helped him garner 30 percent of black votes and a return to City Hall.[8]

After 1965, black voter registration slowed, but black candidates and voters grew bolder. In February 1966, thirty-two-year-old Nils Douglas, a well-known black civil rights attorney, won the primary to represent the newly redrawn Ninth-Ward district in the Louisiana House. Although he received almost 35 percent of the votes in the primary, he lost the runoff by an almost 2-to-1 margin to a white candidate, Ernest J. Hessler Jr. In 1966, thirty-five African Americans qualified for races, and three of them won. Ernest "Dutch" Morial won his race for the Louisiana House of Representatives. Earl Amedee and Avery Alexander took seats on the Orleans Parish Democratic Committee. Mack Spears, a Harvard-educated university administrator, later became the first African American elected to the Orleans Parish School Board.[9]

By November 1969, New Orleans had approximately 151,000 registered white Democrats, 64,500 registered black Democrats, 4,000 registered white Republicans, and 745 registered black Republicans.[10] Black political power was still untested and unproven. Dozens of politicians and organizational leaders labored to gain their allegiance. In this struggle, Acronym political groups made the difference.

The Acronyms

Perhaps the most important long-term sources of black public power were groups that this study calls the Acronyms, the private, predominantly black neighborhood-based political groups such as SOUL, BOLD, and COUP that developed after 1967. Prior to 1964, the Congress of Racial Equality, by the New Orleans branch of the NAACP, a few locally organized groups, and black ministers led grassroots political organizing. From 1964 to 1968, Total Community Action created structures in the city's black target areas that expanded the efforts of those groups. The economic opportunity committees and neighborhood councils put in place by TCA provided bureaucratic bases for the Acronyms. According to TCA Director Winston Lill, the Acronyms "came out of our community organization [effort] without any question." The new black political organizations and the local community action groups were "the same thing" and the "principal success" of TCA.[11] Local civil rights attorney Robert Collins described the Acronyms as filling a "political vacuum." His organization, the Community Organization for Urban Politics (COUP), had tried to create a "responsive" system and "hierarchy" because "we just haven't had this in black politics."[12] The Acronyms tied community action to rising black voter registration, rising black consciousness, and a rising sense of crisis in the white community. The first and ultimately most influential political groups were BOLD, SOUL, and COUP. In spirit, they were products of the century-long search for black freedom. In structure and leadership, they sprang from the Great Society and exerted substantial control over the Soft State. Though less influential than BOLD, COUP, and SOUL, dozens of acronym-groups came into being over the next decade. Some of them were TIPS, DAWN, BlackPAC, BOBUAC, BUC, BLAC, BYP, GAVEL, BUENO, and PACT.[13]

BOLD was centered in Central City, COUP in Tremé (on the northwestern edge of the French Quarter) and the Seventh Ward (on the northeastern edge of the French Quarter), and SOUL in the Ninth Ward. Despite their differing constituencies and leadership, they shared several common elements. First, they were tightly organized entities led by college-educated professionals who knew how to operate in complex bureaucracies. Second, each of them grew out of traditions of civic activism in their neighborhoods. Central City and the Seventh Ward had long been centers of power in New Orleans's black community, and the Lower Ninth Ward had grown into a force after World War II. Third, their power depended on mobilizing voters, providing patronage, and manipulating public bureaucracies. They all clearly benefited from their associations with the federal government. However, instead of providing social services, they tended to be policy-centered advocates. In essence, power for SOUL, BOLD, or COUP meant power for their communities that could translate into beneficial programs. As semi-private institutional wedges into the public world, the organizations often traded the restrictions of segregation for the more accessible, yet frustrating, iron cage of bureaucracy.

SOUL was perhaps the most influential Acronym, an occasionally militant organization with the most impressive network in the city. Its membership included some of the city's most talented politicos, such as Nils Douglas, Sherman Copelin, Don Hubbard, and Johnny Jackson Jr. SOUL's support of Moon Landrieu for mayor (which garnered approximately $19,000 in campaign fees) and for white liberal Nat Kiefer's victorious campaign to represent the Ninth Ward established their reputation as kingmakers.[14] Their power lay in winning elections and accruing unofficial patronage. Some of them proved to be unabashed influence peddlers, in many cases outperforming their white predecessors.

SOUL's gestation began in 1963 with Nils Douglas's unsuccessful run for office. It grew alongside the War on Poverty's Lower Ninth Ward

Neighborhood Council and the 1965 Voter Education Project. In 1966, Douglas's second campaign for office brought the organization into clearer focus, and it came into existence officially in 1968. SOUL leaders defined their objectives as gaining "the political-economic power to make New Orleans government and institutions relevant to the Black Community." They saw their involvement broadly, not simply in "specialized 'Negro Problems.' " They followed a "policy of enlightened self-interest."[15] By the middle 1970s, SOUL leaders thought their best contributions had come through influencing social policy in favor of poor blacks, electing officials, and attracting money.[16] Reynard Rochon, a SOUL board member, believed that SOUL's power grew because of its focus on "Urban Renewal, Model Cities, protesting incidents of police brutality, and voter registration." Nils Douglas remarked that SOUL's major goal was to "bring blacks toward political sophistication." By 1973, the group was, according to Rochon, primarily a political group that typically dealt with issues only through the officials they helped elect or appoint.[17]

SOUL's roots were an intertwining of the black working class of the Ninth Ward and the upwardly mobile professionalism of its young leadership. Like other Acronyms, SOUL contained a college-educated nucleus with ample civil rights experience. Many of their leaders were intricately tied to the Great Society antipoverty and housing efforts. SOUL operated as a confederation of Ninth Ward community groups. Its board of directors contained twenty-five members, five each from the Lower Ninth Ward, Gentilly, Desire, Florida, and Pontchartrain Park. The decisions, however, were made mostly at the top, and Nils Douglas supposedly made final decisions regarding candidates and races. By 1973, two of its most influential members had left the organization. Johnny Jackson Jr., director of the Desire Community Center in the late 1960s and state representative in the early 1970s, soon formed his own group known as the Development Association of Wards and Neighborhoods (DAWN). Sam Bell, an aggressive black radical and major leader of SOUL, resigned in 1969 after making inflammatory black separatist, procommunist remarks to a local reporter. In the 1970–1971 gubernatorial race, SOUL initially endorsed Bell, but quickly dropped him in favor of white liberal Democrat Gillis Long.[18]

COUP's history is explicitly linked to political campaigning and to the Catholic Church. Begun in September 1969 and reflecting the radical protest traditions of its Seventh Ward home, COUP also was a trailblazer of a distinctly modern, professionalized political culture.[19] Well educated and often descended from influential black Creole families, its leaders were positioned to take advantage of the political opportunities of the 1960s and 1970s. Several were quite astute at bureaucratic maneuvering, and this combined with the twelve thousand votes they influenced made them an almost instantly powerful group. By the gubernatorial campaigns of late 1970, they were supposedly capable of putting two thousand campaign workers on the streets on voting day.[20] COUP originally gelled during a 1969 campaign to elect black attorney Charles Elloie to the Louisiana House of Representatives and its activity increased during the mayoral race of the same year. COUP's original organizers included gifted administrators and attorneys whose influence was felt far beyond their electoral muscle. Compared to SOUL, its was much smaller, and control was concentrated in an eight-person board of directors who met monthly. Its objectives were straightforward. COUP's leadership wanted to increase black voter registration, to push candidates for office, and to access more government agencies.[21]

Key members of COUP included Elloie, an antipoverty veteran and future staunch ally of and aide to Edwin Edwards; Robert F. Collins, who became the South's first black federal judge; Sidney Barthelemy, an antipoverty bureaucrat who became mayor in 1987; and Robert H. Tucker Jr., a minister's son and businessman who served as Moon Landrieu's executive assistant.[22]

The third prominent Acronym was BOLD. This Central City organization coalesced during neighborhood antipoverty leader James Singleton's 1969 bid for a city council seat and the 1969 Black Primary. BOLD was a direct product of the War on Poverty, and it was more influenced by female leaders than the other Acronyms. Three of its most important leaders were all integral to antipoverty efforts. Oretha Castle Haley was probably the most influential female activist in New Orleans and also the wife of TCA Neighborhood Development director Richard Haley. She had been active in the fight to create more recreation programs and, in the late 1960s, the effort to stop another Mississippi River Bridge from dissecting Central City. Dorothy Mae Taylor, who would become the most powerful black woman in the city, was an antipoverty activist hand-picked by Richard Haley. Her campaign for the Louisiana House of Representatives in 1971 also solidified BOLD, but she distanced herself soon afterward. The third major leader was Jim Singleton. He was a Southern University alumnus, a teacher, and president of the Central City Economic Opportunity Committee, and he joined the City Council in 1978 and served for well over two decades.[23] Eventually, Singleton became the major force in BOLD and capitalized on his ties to TCA. Several other key figures were highly educated professionals. Peter Dangerfield and Melvin Dangerfield held master's degrees in political science. Ellis Smith was a graduate of Columbia University with a master's in business administration, and Eric Johnson left Tulane University with an M.B.A. Unlike SOUL and COUP, BOLD did not become the clear power in Central City, partly because it had to compete for influence over the fifty thousand-plus residents. In competition were Singleton, Taylor, Reverend Avery Alexander, Reverend A. L. Davis, and Eddie Sapir, a flashy, up-and-coming white liberal.[24] James Lee, a future director of BOLD, credited BOLD's success with the fact that they did not "get fat and forget about other folks."[25]

One of BOLD's most notable early accomplishments occurred in the spring of 1970, on the heels of Moon Landrieu's mayoral victory, when its members helped lead a movement to stop the construction of a new Mississippi River bridge through a black neighborhood. The Mississippi River Authority had long wanted to construct a third local bridge across the river to relieve pressure on the two existing structures and to spur economic development. In early 1970, the authority, under pressure from affluent white interests, had shifted the path from the somewhat tony, largely white Napoleon Avenue to one along General Taylor Street. According to local reports, this new General Taylor plan would have displaced almost 3,500 people, 90 percent of whom were black. Protest from a number of groups ensued, and Oretha Castle Haley led the organizing efforts through a BOLD-infused organization known as BOBUAC. In March, approximately one thousand people participated in a march against the bridge, and another three thousand signed a petition. About a month later, the City Council voted six to one against the General Taylor route. Activists celebrated this flexing of black political muscle as a profound victory.[26]

With a few exceptions, the leaders of the Acronyms were the most powerful voices in New Orleans for three decades after the Acronyms' creation. The reasons for the Acronyms' power are hard to determine. Was their secret merely a combination of federal funding, patronage, and the ability to get out the vote and attract white political money? Did they possess a moral suasion or a civic ideology that resonated with the grassroots? Did they represent more than vehicles for access and opportunity? Contemporary journalistic accounts favor an interpretation that focuses on these groups' ability to dole out patronage and attract white money. Typical accounts portray them as venal and self-advancing opportunists, with one commentator suggesting that to expect anything less in modern America was "silly."[27] In many cases, the critical portrayal is probably not an unfair characterization. It is, nevertheless, inadequate. To emphasize the rascality seemingly inherent in the state's politics obscures some of the truly profound changes these people engendered.

Power lay in controlling votes, contracts, and jobs, not in philosophy. The Acronyms' story shows that the most successful voices were those amplified by organizational structure. The capacity to mobilize thousands of other voices and voters and the ability to attract federal money meant more to the state's political and economic leadership than did Pan-Africanism or denunciations of white racism. In a political culture increasingly dominated by color, green, as usual, provided a source of continuity. Taking power wherever one could get it provided a grip over public resources, but it also exposed broad reform intentions to the dictates of spoils politics.

The process of accumulating power did not always match the ideals of efficient government or equal opportunity, and Acronym leaders knew when to remain in the background. Former governor Earl Long once counseled an associate: "Don't write anything you can phone. Don't phone anything you can talk face to face. Don't talk anything you can smile. Don't smile anything you can wink. Don't wink anything you can nod."[28] From 1969 to 1974, the phone calls, meetings, smiles, winks, and nods of the leaders of SOUL, BOLD, COUP, and other organizations helped remake southern liberalism. Being essentially private institutions, they could limit inquiries into their business and benefit from the air of mystery. Their capacity to mold opportunities out of the urban crisis, Black Power, and the civil rights and antipoverty elements of the Great Society shaped the local template for black civic power. By mobilizing votes and distributing contracts and jobs, they regulated biracial liberalism. After 1968, dozens of black political groups arose, often gelling in time for elections and then disappearing. Only a few persisted, but those that did became the lions of local politics and masters of the War on Poverty–Soft State.

Disunity

At the beginning of the 1970s, black politicians were in a tough position because white voters proved extremely reluctant to vote for any black candidate, and black voters held majorities in only a few districts. There were a few efforts to counteract this and to create a system to produce black candidates that could unify black support. The Black Unity Caucus initiative followed the assassination of Martin Luther King Jr. Led by former TCA associate director Clarence Jupiter, it brought together some of the most powerful moderate black political leaders of the city. Its goal was to identify the most promising black candidates and electoral strategies. In the harsh political climate, they were willing to support progressive white candidates if no black candidate stood a chance of winning.[29]

The boldest encouragement of black unity was the Black Primary in late 1969. Organized by BOLD and James Singleton, the Black Primary was a mock election designed to winnow out black candidates who could oppose white candidates in Central City. The effort lacked the support of two Central City powers—Ellis Hull and Bennett Ross—but had the support of Revius Ortique of the Community Relations Council, Norman Francis of Xavier University, and Arthur Chapital Sr. of the NAACP. Instead of fashioning racial solidarity, however, it revealed that the "bloc vote" was, with a few exceptions, a myth of the white mind. Fewer than 15 percent of the voters participated, but they chose Singleton to run for City Council and Southern Christian Leadership Conference pioneer Reverend A. L. Davis to contest for tax assessor. James Singleton thought the Black Primary was a success because it showed that black voters "can and will work freely for a candidate without the necessity of being paid."[30] But disorder ensued. The candidates who lost to Singleton and Reverend Davis refused to drop out of the race. The Free Southern Theater's *The Plain Truth* responded that "Nigger politics has once again played havoc with sincere efforts of Black people to get themselves together." They worried that BOLD would be hurt by "small minded" leaders who were "only concerned with their personal advantage." *The Plain Truth*'s editorialists believed that black unity was "not a dead concept" but "tomorrow's dream."[31]

In August 1969, prominent COUP member Charles Elloie lost the runoff for a Sixth and Seventh Ward state representative's seat against Benjamin Bagert, an ambitious young white politician whose father was a local judge and, ironically, was the landlord for the Black Panthers' first office in New Orleans. Elloie received most of the black support, but Bagert also received endorsements from several black leaders.[32] In Central City, neither Jim Singleton nor A. L. Davis made the runoff.[33] Black candidates' best chances to win in the Democratic runoffs came in two races. One was the Louisiana House District 26 race in the Ninth Ward between Earl Amedee, an African American attorney and political veteran, and African American contractor Theodore Marchand. Amedee was supported by the more traditional political organizations such as the Crescent City Independent Voter's League, the OPPVL, and the *Louisiana Weekly*. Theodore Marchand, the candidate most closely linked to Urban Renewal and Model Cities, was endorsed by his SOUL organization.[34] Marchand won the showdown between old and new in the Democratic runoff, but could not attract enough white votes in the general election to defeat Republican James R. Sutterfield, a candidate who won along bitterly divided racial lines. *The Plain Truth* charged that "the white folks in the ninth ward got together and lynched Teddy Marchand" because they could not let "another nigger to set foot into their sacred legislature." Meanwhile, Marchand himself explained that his major problem was promising that he "definitely intended to aid the black people" in the Ninth Ward. He refused to "play the white man's game" and be the "white man's nigger." The second race pitted Dutch Morial against Joseph DiRosa, the formidable white populist, for councilman-at-large. Although Dutch Morial was supported by Moon Landrieu and received more white votes than Marchand, he still could not overcome the racial gap.[35] According to Morial's campaign manager Philip Baptiste, the Morial campaign lacked the organization of SOUL or COUP, could not muster enough volunteers, and had difficulties raising funds.[36]

Part of the difficulty of building black political unity was that the local black community was itself fragmented. The War on Poverty may have unintentionally contributed to the problem by creating "cells" (federally funded community organizations) throughout the city that were often in competition with each other. Without these organizations, there might have been greater need among black leaders citywide to cooperate and centralize their efforts. Oretha Castle Haley explained with regret, "the federal neighborhood programs set up artificial boundaries that worked against unification."[37] Of course, this fragmentation may have just as easily occurred without the Great Society. The proliferation of Acronym groups suggests that citywide unity was unlikely unless black interests were significantly threatened. Also, black support often was split between candidates and often went to a white candidate who had a chance for victory instead of a black one almost sure to lose. One historian has noted that the Great Society in Mississippi pitted a newly politicized low-income constituency against the older, more established black middle class.[38] In New Orleans, that distinction was important, but not dominant. With or without a Great Society, the older generation would likely have conceded to the rising generation of politically savvy young people.

A more important reason for black political disunity was the way that black leaders seized and then exercised power. The rewards system of local politics encouraged a decentralized and fragmented scramble for power. Benefits went to individuals and to tightly organized groups, and the market rewarded those people who possessed the wherewithal to manipulate it. In New Orleans, the climb to power was inherently disruptive and discouraged racial solidarity. The elections of 1969 and 1970 showed that black support of black candidates was not necessary for the growth of black power. Many black leaders pursued coalitions with whites as essential political stepping-stones. Others denounced these politicians for putting their own careers above the interests of the black community.[39] Oretha Castle Haley spoke for "black women" who were "fed up" with being second-class citizens. She demanded that the city's black male politicians "stop being puppets and tools of the white man," stop being "traitors," and "stop pimping for the man to the detrement [sic] of your women, children and community." Black leaders who coalesced with white leaders, she declared, were simply selling themselves. In a stirring call for men to "fulfill" their masculine roles, she offered them a thundering challenge: "We dare you to become men!" If they did not, then the black woman was going to stop "standing 100% behind her man" and assume "responsibility" for the salvation of the race.[40]

James Singleton offered similar though less impassioned advice. Drawing on past experience in the Orleans Parish school system with white residents not "willing" to coalesce with blacks, he encouraged African Americans to "learn to use our power as Black people without the support of others." By building electoral power, they could "let the power structure know that we cannot be bought for a few dollars every time there is an election." The community had a responsibility to "let the Black leadership know that we will not accept deals for our votes that benefit the individual and not the community."[41]

Whatever the reasons for the lack of black political unity, in 1971 there remained no black leaders among the seven City Council members, only one black representative among twenty-eight local legislators, two black jurists among forty judges, and one black member of the local school board. However, that record improved substantially over the next few years. In 1971, Dorothy Mae Taylor put together a broad coalition of black and white liberal support to win a first primary victory for Dutch Morial's vacated Central City legislative seat. Also that year, Israel Augustine Jr. won a twelve-year post on the Criminal District Court. The biggest race of 1971 was for governor, and it was notable because overt racists did poorly. Most of the major candidates ran as progressives, including the top three vote-getters—a stark contrast to the 1959 race in which the two top candidates were arch-segregationists. Although this book does not explore that election in detail, the campaign provided some of the most vigorous and innovative electioneering in modern southern history.

In New Orleans, an eclectic lineup of 1970–1971 gubernatorial candidates fought intensively to gain the favor of the city's black political organizations: the liberal former OEO assistant director and U.S. congressman Gillis Long, the progressive Acadian evangelist Edwin Edwards, the North Louisiana populist J. Bennett Johnston, the black radical and former SOUL leader Sam Bell, and, to a far lesser extent, supermarket owner John Schwegmann. SOUL initially supported its one-time leader Sam Bell but dumped him for Gillis Long. Gillis Long contracted out a reported $65,000 in campaign work to SOUL, $40,000 to COUP, and $35,000 to BOLD. When Long failed to make the runoff, the endorsements and the skills of those Acronyms came up for grabs. Johnston and Edwards made the runoff, with SOUL supporting Edwards and COUP and BOLD for Johnston. Reportedly, Edwards paid SOUL $60,000 for campaign work, while Johnston provided $33,000 to COUP. Most of the money went into sophisticated election day get-out-the-vote efforts. Edwards won that race and then defeated Republican Dave Treen in the general election. After winning, Edwards put his arms around SOUL leader Nils Douglas in public and credited him for the victory. In a remarkably prescient statement, Jason Berry, a local journalist, wrote that Governor Edwards "could conceivably become one of the most influential and popular politicians in the state's history, providing he keeps his hands clean."[42] Nationally syndicated columnist Joseph Kraft suggested that the Edwards-Johnston race was a signal of the "end of the hayride" in Louisiana politics.[43]

In the end, a coalition of white and black voters elected a white progressive to the governor's mansion, and in New Orleans, voters sent five black legislators to the state capitol, partly due to reapportionment. Across the state by 1972, there were eight black legislators, thirty black school board members, almost thirty black police jury members, sixteen black justices of the peace and constables, three black city council leaders, and a black appellate court judge.[44] A move in 1972 led by Oretha Castle Haley and others to expand the New Orleans City Council from seven members (two at-large) to eleven members (none at-large), however, proved unsuccessful.[45]

Moon Landrieu Rising

As important as the local and state races in late 1971 and early 1972 were for the birth of serious black political power, the defining election in New Orleans had occurred a year earlier during the mayoral races of 1969–1970. Like most elections of the era, the dominant issues of the campaign were race, crime, taxes, and growth. Since the Great Society and the Soft State surrounding it were attempting to address these issues, it made sense that the top three vote-getters in the first Democratic primary were major supporters of the Great Society. Moon Landrieu finished first. Finishing second was James "Jimmy" Fitzmorris, a racially moderate former City Council member-at-large who had finished a close second in the 1965 mayoral race. Third was William Guste Jr., a young liberal attorney and son of the owner of the famous Antoine's Restaurant. Guste was serving as a state senator and was soon elected as the state attorney general. In fourth place was Judge David Gertler, a liberal who relied on support from labor constituencies.[46]

Landrieu was not the favorite, but he secured significant support from emerging black political organizations to race ahead in the first primary. In an energetic Democratic runoff, he parlayed that support into a mild upset over Jimmy Fitzmorris. Perhaps better than any figure of his time, Fitzmorris symbolized the complications of the new biracial politics. This ward-heeling railroad attorney and civic reformer bridged the racial politics of old and new. During the 1969 campaign, he tried to push platitudes of racial and economic progress, but too often appeared complacent and too closely aligned to conservative whites. Landrieu defeated Fitzmorris because he was far superior in articulating the benefits of a racially progressive future. Fitzmorris refused to promise publicly that he would appoint black department heads, and he hedged on applying the public accommodations ordinance to all parts of the city.[47] Landrieu, on the other hand, was eloquent and exuded confidence, passion, and determination. A new breed of technocratic Democrat who could encapsulate the city's worries in stirring language, Landrieu saw politics as a science, and his tightly organized campaign used polling data and the latest technology. Fitzmorris was from an older generation who tended to rely on traditional ward politics at a time when the wards themselves were undergoing serious demographic transformation. According to Winston Lill, who later served as Landrieu's director of public relations, moderate candidates in black wards could not defeat candidates produced through the War on Poverty's community organization machinery.[48]

The intense runoff campaign between Landrieu and Fitzmorris created a high turnout, with 76 percent of all voters going to the polls on December 12, 1969. When the numbers rolled in, Landrieu received an estimated 90 percent of the black votes and 40 percent of the white votes. A contemporary study by Loyola University of New Orleans political scientists claimed that Landrieu achieved what progressive politicians had been trying to do since the late 1940s by cementing a coalition of black voters with wealthy, well-educated whites from Uptown and Algiers, thus demolishing the idea that white voters would not support candidates who openly sought black votes. In 1969, the major difference was the expansion of the black electorate and the campaigns conducted by SOUL and COUP to get those votes. Landrieu worked carefully to gain the support of those Acronyms, and his campaign funded the activities of many of them, allegedly contracting out almost $20,000 of campaign work to SOUL. Some sources claim that Landrieu ensured the support of SOUL by promising its leaders extensive control over the local Model Cities program and other federal programs—part of what this study calls the Soft State. SOUL argued that it supported Landrieu because they wanted a candidate "who would help the masses of Black people and one who could be elected."[49]

In the general election in 1970, the limits of the Great Society coalition were apparent. Although Landrieu won 59 percent of the vote, it was not a landslide. Landrieu carried the general election with 98 percent of black voters and 40 percent of white voters, but among the wealthiest whites, his support dropped from 19 percent to 5 percent.[50] Furthermore, Benjamin Toledano, a white Republican in a solidly Democratic city, received 41 percent of the vote. Toledano's subtle racial campaign

was almost successful, as he took in many Democratic supporters of Fitzmorris. Landrieu's victory sparked an enthusiastic response from most of
the local media. WWL-TV proclaimed that "all of a sudden, the future
looks bright." Moon Landrieu was "a young man with guts and imagination and intelligence and enormous measures of decency and integrity."
He was "a fighter, and a man who doesn't give up."[51] Bill Rushton of the
Vieux Carré Courier viewed Landrieu's election as a turning point in the
city's politics because it demonstrated the shifting away from the postwar
progressive generation toward the "insurgents" made up of young managers, radicals, and urban reformers.[52] Although pleased that the election
had served as a catalyst for the rise of a new generation of black leaders, *The Plain Truth* expressed concern that it would lead to an interlude
of "signifying and half-stepping when the Black community momentarily
came awake and growled but went back to sleep to the lullabyes [*sic*] of
the promise of a new city administration."[53]

The Great Society Mayor

Moon Landrieu was one of the South's first Great Society mayors. It was
a fitting role since he was a force in its local implementation and development. Prior to becoming mayor, he had a decade of experience as a state
legislator, a War on Poverty board member, and a liberal City Council
member. In those jobs, he learned the benefits of controlling federal influence and the need for biracial cooperation to do it. Not surprisingly, his
mayoral coalition derived from the same constituencies that guided the
local Great Society. Moon Landrieu made his way to the mayor's office
for a number of reasons, but perhaps more than any other, his search for
the Great Society, politically and intellectually and symbolically, pushed
him there.

Landrieu's election was a product of a growing professionalization in
southern and urban politics and an increasing racial polarization in national politics. Landrieu and Edwin Edwards, Landrieu's liberal counter-
part at the state level, rose to power by making self-definition an essential
political commodity. They were engaging in a process that had become a
part of American politics and had long been a staple of Louisiana's demo-

cratic dialogue. The culture-wide emphasis on self-analysis meant that political leadership served an explicit psychological function. To hold together biracial urban coalitions after Jim Crow, successful liberal politicians like Landrieu had to be part booster, part huckster, part philosopher, part psychiatrist, part geographer, part boss, and part Santa Claus.

In 1970, leaders of diverse urban coalitions still had to provide jobs, contracts, and favors for supporters, but they had to be ever mindful of the psychological consequences of their decisions. In a tourist-dependent city like New Orleans or one desperate to attract new corporate business, perceptions were as valuable as hard currency. In fact, it could be argued that cities themselves took on the qualities of America's hyper-individualism. Beginning in the decade after World War II, leaders throughout America commissioned study after study of what made their cities tick. The New Orleans that Landrieu governed in the 1970s required a leader who could balance the problems created by Black Power, black poverty, white racial prejudice, and white economic privilege.

Landrieu represented a new generation of leaders in the South. Polished and progressive, highly educated and morally driven, this inheritor of the Jesuit tradition of compassionate conversion was one of the most important figures in New Orleans's race relations during the Great Society era. From a modest working-class background, he went on to attend Loyola University, where he was a top student and a pitcher for the baseball team. He graduated second in his law school class behind Pascal Calogero, a man who was Landrieu's law partner and eventually served as a Louisiana Supreme Court Justice for almost thirty years. Shortly thereafter, Landrieu went on to represent New Orleans's twelfth ward in the Louisiana House of Representatives at the height of its massive resistance to desegregation. Throughout the New Orleans school crisis of 1960, he was often the lone white liberal voice against segregationist retrenchment. Despite severe opposition from segregationists who characterized him as a "communist dupe or, at best, a pinko," he had by 1964 built what he called "a very liberal record" for the time and won re-election as part of gubernatorial candidate Chep Morrison's ticket. His legislative career helped him secure a powerful post in 1966 as one of two at-large City Council members. After that victory, this man who was "mostly French with a dash of German" was considered one of the front-runners to re-place Victor Schiro at City Hall.[54]

Moon Landrieu's vision for the city was a product of prevalent liberal thinking, but unlike his challengers, he was adept at linking his vision to his personality. Landrieu's conception of the city and its future, how-ever, was not superficial. He was a deeply religious man with an almost radical vision of Christian responsibility. As a student at the Jesuit-run Loyola University, he had been inspired to pursue a career in politics and social activism by his student-activist girlfriend—who trained to become an Ursuline nun but dropped out to marry Landrieu—and future Xavier University president Norman Francis, Loyola's first black student. Lan-drieu's experiences at Loyola, he explained later, made a deep and lasting impact on his approach to politics. He reflected, "I was so religiously and morally committed to being a great mayor, not just a good mayor [or] a great mayor in the sense of publicity or public recognition, but of doing the right thing."[55]

As much as any southern leader, he borrowed from the Great Soci-ety's rich debates about individualism and community. By calling for unity, growth, and inclusion, this father of nine children transformed his can-didacy into a referendum on the persona of the city. Like former Mayor Morrison, he was attempting to articulate a new mood, pushing for a more open, more livable urban environment. During his campaign and his en-suing administration, he pursued preservation and innovation, progress and conservation, sometimes linking them together and sometimes alien-ating all sides. Landrieu promised in a 1969 statement prior to the first Democratic primary that "New Orleans can be a city of hope, proof for people everywhere that cities are places of community, education, cul-ture, enterprise and security." Invoking the city's past inadequacies, he pleaded that "ours has been a pathetic history of destroying our common bonds." Landrieu was troubled by a sense that local people had become "confused and divided, uncertain of the future, almost fatally paralyzed by the idea that New Orleans has no faith in the future."[56]

During his mayoral campaign, Landrieu articulated plans to attack or-ganized crime and the drug trade and to improve the police department. He called for fiscal reform and for tax redistribution. He promised to make City Hall more efficient, to rehabilitate "blighted areas," to secure more outside funding, and to "purify" Lake Pontchartrain.[57] Over the next few years as mayor, Landrieu's efforts seemed to work. Errol Laborde, a local publisher and commentator, remarked that the image of the city as a backward-looking, stagnant society dominated by elites was being proven false.[58] Landrieu's agenda was rooted in the idea that investing in individuals and building self-awareness were cornerstones of economic growth. "To live a life as a responsible citizen," he declared, "man must have hope" and must have proof that "the American economic system has failed no one." The poor, he asserted, "want to work, to achieve, to give meaning and substance to their lives, to become substantial and responsible citizens capable of bearing their fair load." The economic system had been wonderful in providing a high standard of living, but its failure for the poor meant it had failed everyone. He worried in particular about New Orleans's "unfortunate drive toward self-destruction." It was "a quarter to midnight." New Orleans could not "afford anything less than the truth about itself."[59]

In 1970, Landrieu delivered unprecedented appointments to black leaders and constituents. During the entirety of Victor Schiro's two terms, his most notable appointment of black officials followed the Martin Luther King Jr. assassination, when he hired neighborhood organizer Philip Baptiste as a low-level aide and Sherman Copelin to conduct an Urban Renewal feasibility study. In Landrieu's first year in office, he appointed sixteen black leaders to nine committees (although seven were to the Sports Advisory Committee), eleven African Americans to nine boards, and ten black bureaucrats to high-level positions (see appendix 7). Many of them were in their late twenties, and most of the rest were in their thirties. Landrieu hired political supporters, but he claimed his first priority was to recruit "talented, energetic, creative" people who were "on a mission."[60] During his eight-year reign, the black presence in city government doubled from near 20 percent to over 40 percent. Especially significant was the increase in black workers under the civil service system. In 1972, the highest percentage of black workers in civil service positions were in Model Cities (with 92 percent of positions filled by black workers), manpower programs (91 percent), the Welfare Department (80 percent), the Recreation Department (75 percent), the Health Department (59 percent), and the Parkways and Parks Commission (55 percent). The public jobs funded through the 1973 Comprehensive Employment Training Act were a boon to the Landrieu administration, helping to underwrite approximately two thousand positions.[61]

The power held by the Acronyms was part of the reason that Landrieu was able to set himself apart from previous mayors. SOUL claimed a major portion of the benefits of black progress at City Hall, and their influence created tension and resistance from other groups. In 1971, SOUL's leadership took credit for an enormous portion of the good things happening for African Americans in New Orleans. They contended that they were responsible for establishing the War on Poverty-funded $500,000 Desire Community Center and for securing its yearly budget of $100,000, as well as a number of other grants. They also claimed responsibility for dozens of black appointments in Landrieu's administration, for several judges and city attorneys, and for several victorious candidates for local office and for spots on the Human Relations Committee. SOUL leaders asserted that they had control over several positions on boards and commissions and had drastically improved the employment picture for black New Orleanians. The block of Model Cities jobs controlled by Sherman Copelin was a prime example of their power. Most of the positions were spread throughout the Model Neighborhood Areas, but forty of those jobs went to African Americans at City Hall, with twenty-eight of them considered "significant" positions.[62] COUP and BOLD also received benefits because several of Landrieu's top advisers were linked to COUP, and a few BOLD members held key positions in health and antipoverty positions. During his early administration, Moon Landrieu skillfully tapped into the emerging black leadership. Most of those leaders were men. A study conducted in 1975 by Daniel Thompson found local black leadership was 88 percent male. Thompson also found that 80 percent of New Orleans's black leaders grew up in homes of "common, blue collar parents," but that almost 90 percent of them had earned college degrees, with 26 percent holding advanced degrees.[63]

Landrieu recalled that he was frequently referred to as "Moon the Coon" and a "nigger-lover," to which he responded, "You right, I am. I flat am, without any shame or apologies.' "[64] For some, that was a good thing. For them, Landrieu symbolized a new era. Through the force of personality and ideas, he represented openness, professionalism, and progress instead of segregation and suppression. Some people saw him as an inspiring liberator. Norma Freiberg, a prominent Jewish woman who worked for the Human Relations Committee, described him as the "right man at the right time" who was so "inspirational" that "we would all just die for him."[65] James R. Bobo, an economist at the University of New Orleans, credited Landrieu for being a "primary catalyst" for the city's economic future and characterized Landrieu's civil rights efforts as a "principal social and economic achievement of the post World War II era."[66] Not all local liberals, however, were happy with Landrieu's handling of his administration, and many thought he relied too heavily on federal resources to improve conditions for black residents instead of shaping local solutions that could stand on their own.[67] In that regard, Daniel Thompson's 1975 study found that 85 percent of black leaders had their power "confined to the Black community" and had little "sustained, meaningful interaction with their counterparts in the white community." Ten percent were "influential" in interracial settings, while only 4 to 5 percent were influential in a "city-wide" capacity.[68]

For still others, Landrieu's liberalism was a dirty thing that suggested a soft spine and a willingness to sell out for political gain. A secret FBI recording revealed some of the white perspectives on Landrieu, even within his City Attorney's office. In 1970, Pershing Gervais, a local political fixer and informant, recorded a conversation with Charles Ray Ward, a man who headed the Criminal Division of the City Attorney's office and had campaigned for Landrieu. On the tape, Ward told Gervais, "The only thing [the city] is going to do is something for the niggers. The city, everybody knows, it's in bad shape." To that, Gervais added, "Oh, f—— yeah. It's Moon the Coon around here. That's all you hear. Moon the Coon, that silly bastard, he's letting his hair grow long." Later, Ward offered that Landrieu was "bright," but in a "peculiar way . . . in a very liberal way."[69]

Landrieu received severe criticism from racial militants. A writer for the *Carrollton Advocate*, the newspaper of the Carrollton Central Steering Committee (CCSC), argued that "The Black community" had been duped. Landrieu was not "the Chosen One, The Messiah," just the "lesser of two evils." He was "nothing but an ambitious, power-seeking racist."[70] Another black militant summarized the situation in stark terms. "Even if Mr. Landrieu is some sort of a messianic liberal," instructed a writer for *The Plain Truth* who went by Uhuru no Umoja, "black people must not lose sight of the fact that he is a white liberal, working in a white racist municipality, against a white racist city machine and an entangling system of racist state regulation and hampering outside pressures."[71] In line with *The Plain Truth's* lament, the Landrieu administration's most dramatic dilemmas did not involve showdowns with white supremacists— most them were either fleeing the city or insulating themselves from it— but developed from confrontations with black militants and with grass-roots progressives. The public fights over race shifted from questions about how liberalism could emerge from Jim Crow's shadows to ones about what that liberalism really was, and what it would become.

CHAPTER THIRTEEN

Panthers, Snipers, and the Limits of Liberalism

It is time that we have begun to prove that moving on us isn't
such an easy job. The cards are on the table 'the enemy has
tobring [*sic*] ass to get ass' . . . and we the oppressed ain't
giving up *nothing*.
—*Desire: Voice of the People*, 1970

In 1964, a half-decade before Moon Landrieu's election, New Orleans
Urban League director J. Harvey Kerns had hoped that racial liberalism could produce "something new for the South." At the dawn of the
new decade, New Orleans seemed poised to do that, or at least to end
the Dixie defined by Jim Crow.[1] As several moments of violence demonstrated, however, the worst aspects of Dixie kept coming back. Two more
episodes were added to a long history stretching back at least to the Absolute Massacre of 1866. First, in the fall of 1970, an effort to purge the
Black Panthers from New Orleans led to two shoot-outs between the Panthers and local police and to a standoff between residents of the Desire
housing project and the New Orleans Police Department (NOPD). Over
a two-and-a-half-month period, several people were seriously injured, a
teenage boy was killed, two black undercover officers were beaten after
a community-led trial, and national attention was focused on the incidents, including a visit from the infamous actress Jane Fonda. Shortly
thereafter, a controversial Thanksgiving week showdown between city

police and the Panthers highlighted the city leaders' concern about the alienation of poor black citizens. The second episode was the rampage of Mark Essex, an embittered Navy veteran. In January 1973, he left the Downtown Howard Johnson Hotel in flames, ten people dead from gunshot wounds—including five police officers and Essex himself—dozens injured, millions shocked, and law enforcement agencies dazed and confused.

Those violent episodes forced turning points in the local search for the Great Society. Debates had shifted from the high ground of inclusion appeals and community pride to the realities of Louisiana politics and post–Jim Crow confusion. The Panthers' confrontations and the Essex tragedy shattered any illusions that the city had achieved Great Society status, and they were sobering lessons in the limits of liberalism. Since 1964, the War on Poverty had been a means to manage inequality and most important to involve black leaders in that management. One major public institution for managing the citizenry, however, was immune to much of the Great Society's progressive racial influence. The largely white police force was the most direct governmental presence in black communities, and it was far more difficult to reform than other parts of the Jim-Crow state. Some black leaders were heartened by the attitude of Clarence Giarrusso, the police chief during the Desire episodes and the Essex incident. As one black leader explained, "We'd be just fine if Clarence were in every patrol car." For them, the solution required not just good leadership, but reforming officers on the street.[2] The historic tensions between that department and the black community threatened to undo the liberal triumph of 1970, and might have if not for so many white racial conservatives leaving the city.

The Desire Shootouts

By 1970, the Desire area seemed to be developing into one of the great successes of the War on Poverty. As a federal target area, Desire had received an infusion of several million dollars over the previous five years, and community action had produced a number of vibrant community groups and improvement associations. The New Orleans Legal Assistance Corporation (NOLAC) had a thriving office there, and the War on Poverty–funded attorneys for the poor were actively involved in welfare rights issues and housing issues. They would become the attorneys for members of the Black Panthers in the aftermath of the two shootouts. Designated as a Model Neighborhood Area under the Model Cities program, Desire was set to receive another significant federal boost. Politically, the area was becoming a key bailiwick of the SOUL organization. Two of the most prominent black leaders were Sam Bell, the controversial gubernatorial candidate who would lose SOUL's backing in 1971, and Johnny Jackson Jr., the community activist and director of the Desire Community Center who had grown up in the area. Theodore Marchand, another SOUL leader, had recently lost a race for the state legislature to a white Republican candidate because the apportionment of his district had diluted the strength of black votes.

In the mayoral race of 1969–1970, Moon Landrieu enjoyed nearly unanimous support from Desire. A few months after he took office, however, City Hall's entanglement with militant activists tested that backing. Moon Landrieu believed that militants associated with the Black Panther Party posed a physical threat to most of the people in Desire and to the NOPD, and he used intelligence gathered on the Panthers to support his tough stand towards them. Local militants, for their part, learned that New Orleans's new spirit of political inclusion did not extend to black revolutionaries who openly stockpiled guns, threatened to kill police officers, criticized capitalism, and used inflammatory, procommunist rhetoric.

The national Black Panther Party was founded in 1966 in Oakland, California, by Bobby Seale and Huey P. Newton (born in Monroe, Louisiana, Newton was named for Louisiana's legendary politician Huey P. Long). Militant, masculine, unrelentingly defiant, and dedicated to self-defense, the Panthers quickly became the most widely recognized black radical organization and created hysteria akin to a miniature Red Scare. By 1969, the organization had spread to dozens of cities and had begun their hallmark free breakfast programs, but in July of that year, longtime FBI director J. Edgar Hoover declared that the party "without question, represents the greatest threat to the internal security of the country."[3] Over the previous year they had become the targets of an intense offensive conducted by local, state, and national law enforcement officials. By 1969, twenty-eight Panthers had reportedly been killed by the police. The most famous killing was of Illinois party chairman Fred Hampton, a man with Louisiana roots who would be buried in the small town of Haynesville in the northern part of the state. Chicago officials claimed Hampton was a casualty of a major shootout, and a month after the shooting a jury labeled the shootings "justifiable." Panthers claimed that Chicago police murdered the twenty-one-year-old Hampton in his sleep. Their claims were somewhat justified five months after the incident when all charges against the Panthers were dropped. Tests revealed that the police had fired seventy-five shots, but the Panthers had fired only once. Later investigations revealed that the raid had been meticulously planned with the help of the FBI, who were cooperating with local officials through the COINTELPRO initiative. Another thirteen years of litigation produced no guilty verdicts for the officers or the state's attorney, but did end with an almost $2 million nuisance settlement.[4]

After 1969, the history of the Panther Party is a narrative of suppression, with frequent shootouts and confrontations with police organizations. New Orleans was the scene for one significant part of that story. Like most Black Panther organizations throughout the United States, the one in New Orleans had a relatively short life. Organized as the local affiliate of the Panthers' National Committee to Combat Fascism (NCCF), the New Orleans branch established its initial presence in the Irish Channel in early 1970. Although opponents continually complained about outside leaders in the local party, most members were local and came primarily from the Calliope and Magnolia housing projects.[5] Like other Black Panthers, they preached self-reliance and self-defense and operated free breakfast programs and uplift programs for children. Their first office was at 2353 St. Thomas Street in a house owned by the wife of Criminal Court Judge Bernhard Bagert. This same judge later set the bail for the militants involved in the September and November confrontations. From that Irish Channel location, members began establishing contacts in the nearby St. Thomas housing project and setting up plans for community organizing. By mid-June, however, the NOPD, in a confidential memorandum, had identified the Panthers as the "greatest concern" of the department and the "most dangerous" of all of the activist organizations in the city. The police superintendent, Joseph Giarrusso (who resigned in the summer of 1970), had received several complaints that Panther members were harassing shoppers on Canal Street and other places. One woman contended that she was told by Panthers not to enter a store because "the manager is a fascist pig, and we are going to cut his throat some night." In the meantime, Judge Bagert had issued an eviction notice to take effect on July 21 and told the NOPD that he "was afraid of these people." Giarrusso was encouraged by other reports, though, that the Panthers wanted to avoid confrontation.[6]

Meanwhile in July, a police response to a fight in Desire almost spiraled out of control. In the aftermath of that incident, Moon Landrieu held a meeting with several of his aides and three black advisors—the director of Total Community Action (TCA), the deputy director of Model Cities, and the deputy director of the Human Relations Committee (HRC). They decided to place a patrol car on permanent alert in the Desire area, but the added patrols did little to reduce community concern about police brutality. Bill Rouselle, the HRC deputy director and a young black leader with ties to the militant Free Southern Theater, reported that Elaine Young, a twenty-two-year-old woman who was arrested after the September 14 shootout, had met with him and reported serious concern about four separate incidents.[7]

Because of the pressure against them in the Irish Channel and the widespread poverty of the Desire area, the Panthers relocated their office to Desire on August 1. A local underground newspaper, the NOLA Express, noted that the Panthers were welcome in Desire, where they lived "among the people like fish in the sea."[8] After settling into the new headquarters at 3542 Piety Street—in the same building as Johnny Jackson's Sons of Desire group—the Panthers quickly began organizing. While in Desire, the 20 or so active Black Panthers attracted a following reported to range between 100 to 150 residents. Their free breakfast program became popular, serving 120 children every day at a local Catholic church and others elsewhere. According to a minister, the Panthers even fed about ten "little white children who were hungry." Malik Rahim, a twenty-two year old then known as Donald Guyton Sr., later claimed hyperbolically that they had "reduced crime to just about 0 percent."[9]

With the Panthers' move to Desire, police superintendent Giarrusso's concerns intensified. He worried that an "alarming number of people" were becoming indoctrinated in the "panther philosophy" that taught "hatred toward law enforcement specifically and the 'establishment' in general." Of most concern, he reported to Mayor Landrieu that a "very reliable source" had informed him that the Panthers had obtained a scope-mounted .22 caliber rifle, three pistols, four shotguns, and lots of buckshot slugs, a source of ammunition that Giarrusso told the mayor was "seldom used for sporting purposes." Additionally, they had barricaded their offices with sandbags.[10] The likely source of the NOPD's intelligence was two black officers who had infiltrated the local organization, twenty-year-old Melvin Howard and twenty-one-year-old Israel Fields.

By early September, the tension between the Panthers and the NOPD was almost at a breaking point. On the evening of September 14, it broke—ironic since Mayor Landrieu was set to tour the Desire area the next day. Around 8:00 p.m., with temperatures hovering around 85 degrees, the Panthers were holding a political education meeting. What unfolded at that meeting became a subject of intense controversy and uncertainty. The Panthers discovered that two of their members were actually undercover officers, and, according to police chief Clarence B. Giarrusso, who had recently taken over from his brother Joseph, they began a "systematic reign of terror." The Panthers claimed that they released the men to a group of fifty or so residents, who beat them. The NOPD charged that the beatings occurred during an impromptu trial that included pistols and nail-spiked boards and then intensified after the release of the officers. Moon Landrieu told the public that the undercover officers were "tortured beyond your imagination and mine." During the melee, shots were fired, bottles and rocks thrown, and a house set on fire. The officers' car was burned and dumped in a canal, and a white couple was dragged from a car and accosted. The white male was beaten severely, receiving a broken jaw. The woman claimed to have been taken inside and beaten with guns until unconscious, and she awoke nude from the waist down. Panther sources claimed that she actually was unharmed and was taken into the headquarters for protection. In the confusion, both under-cover officers were able to escape. Melvin Howard hopped a tall fence be-hind the building. Israel Fields headed to Nellie's Grocery Store. Fields' choice of refuge did not help matters. The owner of Nellie's, Clarence Broussard, had a reputation for charging exorbitant prices, raising prices after Hurricane Betsy, and threatening to shoot anyone trying to steal food during that crisis. Broussard also owned the building housing the Pan-thers' headquarters and had initiated eviction proceedings against them. When community members demanded that Fields come out, Broussard opened fire, and his targets fired back, apparently resulting in injuries to Broussard's son and another Desire resident. Later, police chief Gi-arrusso described Broussard as a "courageous man" who "refused to be intimidated."[11]

In the meantime, two black NOPD patrolmen were shot at while in-vestigating the burning car. One of the patrolmen was Raymond Reed. A recent Panther flyer described him as a "bootlicking coward-hearted nigger pig" who was one of the "tools and fools to be used to terrorize the black community." He was a "traitor," and according to the propagan-dists, "the penalty for treason is death." Moon Landrieu recounted that militants "certainly did their best to kill him," but only sent him to the hospital to extract broken glass from his eye. If one shot had been "a few inches" closer, Landrieu reported, Officer Reed would have taken "a bul-let in the head." A few hours after the Reed shooting, at about a quarter to midnight (eerily, that was how Landrieu had described New Orleans in late 1969 during his mayoral campaign), the Panthers sent word over "the network" that the "pigs" were "amassing around the office." Shortly after, gunfire broke out again and continued for several hours. In all, a reported thirteen people were injured, but apparently no Panthers. Co-inciding with these events, the NOPD advised all residents near the Piety office to evacuate and promised to "protect the innocent citizens of our community."[12] Not far away in the Gulf of Mexico, Tropical Storm Felice, the sixth of the season, was soaking up energy from the hot September waters and sending storm bands over the Ninth Ward.

While Felice threatened to make landfall along the Louisiana coast, the NOPD prepared to descend upon the Panthers' Piety Street headquarters. Starting around 8:30 a.m. on September 15, 100 to 150 officers unleashed a full-scale assault with a helicopter, an armored tank nicknamed "Bertha," protective vests, machine guns, and assault shotguns. The Panthers fought back. The NOPD charged that the Panthers fired first and then continued to fire with "high power rifles, automatic weapons and hand guns." Panther leader and community activist Malik Rahim remembered having only a few .357 caliber handguns and "about 9 shotguns." The intense shootout persisted for twenty-five minutes, with witnesses reporting that some of the shots came from the helicopter in the sky. One Panther, eighteen-year-old Tyrone Edwards, described the predicament later. "What can you do when somebody's firing 100 bullets to your one shot. Just to be dying you dying a man, we shot back." After a long barrage, fourteen Panthers surrendered. In total, four African Americans were wounded, one of them a Panther. Tyrone Edwards later recounted, "I don't know who put out that white flag, but I am so glad they did. I'll never forget that day because I was so happy to be going to jail. . . . If I died at 18, people wouldn't have understood what I died for."[13]

The most devastating events occurred that night, when four men reportedly returned to Nellie's Grocery to burn it down. Four police officers inside engaged them and others in a prolonged gun battle. Four men were shot, and twenty-one-year-old Kenneth Michael Borden died from a head wound after lying in the street for two hours. The NOPD explained that they could not attend to Borden because of sniper fire, while community residents charged that the police fired on them when they tried to help. Ironically, Borden's father had recently been appointed a special officer with the NOPD. Landrieu described the scene that night as one in which the Panthers and associates "barricaded the streets at all four intersections, lined up behind the barricades with every type weapon imagineable [sic] as if it were an armed garrison and they simply declared war." In the aftermath, the local underground press worried about what they called "the very real possibility of unchecked slaughter of black and white political activists." Moon Landrieu emphasized, to the great disbelief of many black leaders, that the evening's events were "not a civil rights uprising" and "not a racial incident."[14]

When the bullets finally stopped, fourteen Panthers were put in jail on charges of attempted murder, and their bonds set at $100,000 each by Judge Bagert, their former landlord. Of the fourteen, three were female (aged eighteen, nineteen, and twenty-two), and eleven were male (one fourteen year old, five others under the age of twenty, five between twenty-one and twenty-two, and two between twenty-six and twenty-seven). One of them was wanted by the FBI in Connecticut. Three other residents (aged sixteen, twenty-two, and twenty-four) were arrested for attempted murder and arson for their part in the incidents at Nellie's Grocery. Moon Landrieu characterized the arrestees as a "small band" who had "embarked on a reign of terror" and had "abused the neighborhood people." Pointing out that the "two to three hundred people" who supported the Panthers were small in comparison to the entire population of Desire, Landrieu and Chief Giarrusso praised the thousands of Desire residents who did not "want" or "accept" the Panthers. Explaining away the Panthers' free breakfasts as "subterfuges" and a "come-on" to spread insidious ideas, Giarrusso claimed that they had only fed "about 28 kids." He assured New Orleans residents that Desire residents would not "buy some of the militancy they were trying to sell." The police assault did not stop the Panthers' organizing efforts.[15] The remnants regrouped and moved their headquarters into the Desire housing project, occupying a vacant apartment. The *NOLA Express* predicted that more "trouble" would come in the coming months because the people of Desire were the real force behind the Panthers. For the next two months, the Panthers continued their organizing efforts, and officials continued to try to find ways to eliminate their presence, once again forming committees to study the problems of Desire to try to improve living conditions there.[16]

The shootouts had done more than test the responsiveness of the NOPD. They showed the wide variety of opinions toward both the Panthers and the police. The moderately conservative, white-controlled *New Orleans Times-Picayune* called for "responsible members of the black community" to prevent groups like the Panthers from having influence and for white leaders to keep trying to reach out. They saw the shootouts as "exceptional, exotic growth that can be pruned away, and not representative of New Orleans' citizens nor reflective of New Orleans' real conditions."[17] In response to the local white press's coverage of the shootouts, a group of influential black leaders with close ties to the War on Poverty and the New Orleans Human Relations Committee issued a statement to correct what they viewed as distortion of the events and to announce their own investigation. They demanded that Moon Landrieu investigate the incidents personally (Landrieu assigned the task to his chief assistant Robert Tucker), and they expressed deep disagreement with Landrieu's assertion that social conditions were not a factor in the confrontations. Bill Rousselle suggested that Landrieu and Giarrusso had created a "climate of hostility and repression" that made it difficult to ensure a fair trial. The local Urban League worried about more violence and pressed for more than a "veneer of social order."[18] The local NAACP reminded residents to remember that this was "not the first time that an over abundance of police power has been mobilized to regulate and control black political philosophies in our community." A more personal appeal came from a white Uptown woman who told Landrieu, "If we are honest with ourselves, most of us will admit we just don't know what it must be like to live there." She asked him to visit Desire to "help dissipate some of the alienation," adding that they could take her car.[19]

Controversy continued during the Panthers' criminal trial. The Panthers' lead counsel was Ernest Jones, a black attorney for the War on Poverty-funded New Orleans Legal Aid Corporation (NOLAC). Assisting him were Lolis Elie, Charles Cotton, George Strickler, NOLAC attorneys Robert Glass and Robert Portman, and Richard Sobol, a prominent young civil rights attorney affiliated with the Washington Research Project antipoverty legal group. After arraignment, Judge Ben Bagert recused himself. Taking over the case was Israel Augustine Jr., the prominent black New Orleans attorney who had represented the Southern Christian Leadership Conference and had recently become a pioneering criminal court judge.[20] The involvement of NOLAC attorneys became a major problem for the Office of Economic Opportunity and for the Louisiana State Department of Welfare. Ben Toledano, the defeated Republican mayoral candidate, filed a protest with the OEO about NOLAC attorneys taking criminal cases beyond the arraignment phase and for taking on clients without adequately determining their poverty status. Additionally, the NOLAC attorneys had caused controversy by becoming involved in a Panther campaign to encourage—some said demand—AFDC recipients to donate 10 percent of their checks to the NCCF. In return the Panthers promised to help free recipients from being "slaves to this fascist government."[21] Administrators at the now Republican-controlled Office of Economic Opportunity were not pleased with the NOLAC lawyers and called for an investigation into their relationship with the Black Panthers.[22] NOLAC attorneys refused to back down much and, instead, continued to represent the Panthers. As for the fourteen Panthers arrested in September, two were dropped from the case before the trial, which began eleven months later in early August 1971. That August, the so-called Panther Twelve helped make local judicial history as they sat before a black judge, a black jury foreman, a jury with ten blacks and two whites, and a black defense attorney whose arguments criticized a mostly white police department rife with the legacies of "400 years of white racism." After deliberating for a mere thirty minutes, the jury acquitted the Panther Twelve on all counts. The prosecution could not establish beyond a reasonable doubt that the Panthers had fired the first shot. The mostly black gallery "shouted for joy."[23]

Those shouts were partly in response to what had happened in September 1970, but also to another dramatic showdown that had occurred in November 1970. At the national level, the events surrounding Thanksgiving helped speed OEO director Donald Rumsfeld's firing of the OEO's top legal services administrators and also tightened the oversight of local legal services offices.[24] Locally, they helped shake the belief that Desire residents felt abused by the Panthers. In October, HANO and the Panthers tried to negotiate a lease for a vacant apartment in Desire, but could not agree to terms. Units could only be occupied by families unless the Department of Housing and Urban Development gave special permission, which it had not granted to the Panthers. The Panthers, nevertheless, continued to stay in the apartment. The New Orleans Human Relations Committee tried unsuccessfully to find a church willing to house the Panthers' operation, and the Panthers refused an offer from the Desire Area Community Council to pay their rent. HANO initiated eviction proceedings. Around Halloween, the Panthers received a temporary stay, but soon after were ordered to vacate. Political power, not money, was the issue, as the maximum fine for their trespassing would have been $50.[25]

During the first few weeks of November, rumors began to intensify that the NOPD was planning another raid against the Panthers. The NCCF circulated a flyer touting that the NOPD was "going to make an example of the NCCF members in order to prove to those Niggers everywhere that they will not permit any individual, committee, or group to organize and fight for what they call freedom."[26] The Tulane University Student Senate passed a resolution by the Ad Hoc Committee to Prevent Disaster that predicted a "gun battle is likely to spread throughout the city."[27] Panthers in Apartment A at 3315 Desire Parkway began sandbagging the building and boarding up windows. The NOPD stepped up patrols of the project. When negotiations failed to oust the Panthers from the apartment, the NOPD became the enforcers of the will of City Hall. On November 19, the NOPD amassed a force larger than the one of the morning of September 15 and, fearing that the Panthers possessed fragmentary grenades, prepared for a massive assault on the apartment. Officers seized the apartments of several women who lived near the Panthers' unit to use as tactical positions and began parading a white armored tank to send a message of force. Broadcasting warnings from the tank's loudspeaker was NOPD counsel Charles Foti, a young self-described protégé of University of New Orleans historian Stephen Ambrose. Foti later became TCA president, Orleans Parish Criminal Sheriff, and then Louisiana attorney general.[28]

Around noon on the nineteenth, approximately two hundred officers armed with M-16 rifles, shotguns, tear gas, and other accoutrements moved toward Desire Parkway. Officers fired tear gas, and Panther sympathizers reportedly returned with sniper fire. Then something peculiar occurred. For months, the Panthers had been preaching about giving all power to the people. As the police approached with full force, the people stood between the Panthers' apartment building and the police, denying the helmeted, bandoliered officers. Some radicals claimed that over one thousand young people offered themselves as a shield to protect black militancy. One Panther recalled a crowd of about five thousand. Journalists set the figure at three hundred, and identified most of them as young males. During the almost six-hour standoff, NOLAC attorney Ernest Jones, several other black leaders, and a group of clergy were allowed to meet with the approximately ten Panthers inside the apartment. Throughout the ordeal, Landrieu's assistant Robert Tucker, SOUL leader and antipoverty administrator Donald Hubbard, COUP leader and youth administrator Charles Elloie, COUP leader and Landrieu appointee Cecil Carter Jr., and Concerned Residents of Desire leader Donald Faggen served as a liaison between the Panthers and City Hall. Hubbard claimed that he was not "trying to be a hero," but struggling to "do the right thing." Tucker recollected that they were all "damn fools," but were "too young to know the difference." With twilight approaching, the parties negotiated a settlement. The NOPD agreed to back off for twenty-four hours to allow the Panthers to try their luck in court once again. The response from the defiant Desire residents was euphoric, with some reports that the crowd hoisted the Panthers on their shoulders.[29]

The next day, Friday, the Panthers' NOLAC attorneys met with federal district Judge Frederick Heebe, and then again on Monday. While the attorneys sought a federal injunction, activists, student protesters, and city administrators pushed ahead with their own agendas. On Friday, approximately one hundred people, including student government leaders from Tulane University and the University of New Orleans and leaders of the New Orleans Peace Action Center, protested at City Hall. Some of their signs read, "Landrieu, Blood Is on Your Hands," "Landrieu and His Fascist Pigs Are Committing Murder," "Landrieu Is No Longer One of the People and Probably Never Was," and "Oink Now Landrieu, It May Be Your Last."[30] Hoping to influence HANO and to send a message to Judge Heebe, another protest was planned at HANO headquarters on November 24. The star of the late afternoon affair proved to be Jane Fonda, who also traveled to the Desire area and met with residents at the Desire Community Center. While in town, she did more than make appearances. She reportedly donated money for Hertz rental cars to take twenty-five Panthers to a convention in Washington, D.C.[31]

Unswayed by the protests and by Fonda's celebrity, HANO refused to alter their policies, and Judge Heebe denied the Panthers' request for a stay, clearing the way for more activity from the NOPD. On November 25, while Fonda was traveling westward to Denver, the Panthers' caravan headed eastward toward D.C. Waiting for them on Interstate 10 was a contingent from the NOPD, and they arrested the militants on the spot and detained nineteen blacks and six whites, including eight juveniles. The six Panthers remaining in the apartment expected another massive assault from the police department the next day. A minister who visited with them believed that "they really thought they were going to die."[32]

A little after midnight, however, there was a knock at the door. An officer posing as a Catholic minister claimed to have alms for the breakfast program. When a female Panther cracked the door open, several undercover police officers dressed as cab drivers, mail carriers, and priests burst in, led by Sergeant Robert Frey. Claiming that the Panthers fired at them first, the officers let off almost ten shots. One of them struck Betty Powell in the shoulder (along with an eleven-year-old boy wounded by errant fire on November 19, she was one of only two reported casualties during the weeklong showdown). The officers reported finding several shotguns, a rifle, and two tear gas canisters. According to one underground newspaper report, the officers then attempted to use three Desire residents as shields while they made their way to their support vehicles.[33]

In the early hours of Thanksgiving Day, the protracted struggle with the Panthers ended. The fallout from the early morning raid, however, continued for weeks to come. Numerous leaders of the local clergy wrote official protests about the use of the clerical collar for political purposes. Response from mainstream black leaders was measured, but filled with a sense of resignation and perhaps relief. Response from militants was not necessarily one of defeat. Rumors circulated throughout HANO that Panther sympathizers were trying to set up in another apartment. For the most part, though, militants were left only with their voices. One flyer circulating in the Desire area held out hope that the "spirit of the people is greater than the pigs' technology."[34] Another one lamented, "Today we fully realize that you [city leaders] make and break the laws to your convenience," and declared that it was "time for you to stop playing with our lives."[35] In the week after the final showdown, another group called for a boycott and for an anti-Landrieu movement. "We must hurt the man economically, where his heart is," explained one of their flyers. "Keep our money in the black community." This anonymous group wanted to "let

MOON know that he can't just listen to the white money people who back him, and not listen to the Black Community who voted him in office." They suggested a slogan: "Black Mayor for '74, Landrieu got to go."[36] Another community newspaper charged that Landrieu and Giarrusso were trying to "destroy the new political force in the black community." Infuriated by the Desire incidents, the authors served notice that they had "begun to prove that moving on us isn't such an easy job. The cards are on the table 'The enemy has tobring [sic] ass to get ass", [sic] And we the oppressed ain't giving up *nothing*."[37]

One angry voice counted more than the others. Johnny Jackson Jr., a SOUL member elected to the state house in the coming year, had been at the center of the Panther controversy as director of the Desire Community Center and had been arrested during the late November episodes on charges of interfering with the police and resisting arrest. In his version he and a colleague had been "kidnapped" by the police from the community center. His rage at the decisions of City Hall went so deep that he offered to resign his position at the Desire Community Center.[38] He characterized the arrests of Panthers as a result of "trumped up charges" and referred to the two black undercover officers involved in the September "trial" as "two 'colored' Judas[es]." In an open letter to the Desire community, he provided his summary of events: "Over 50 Black people have been jailed; Black people's homes have been broken into; Black people have been used as hostages; Black people have been beaten; the Black community has been exposed to lies by the elected representatives, the news media, and people who represent the 'WHITE AMERICANS' point of view and are now talking about establishing communications with the Black community. *They must be out of their minds*." In a not-so-veiled message to Moon Landrieu, he asserted, "Our people needed you and still need you and you STILL cannot be found. I sincerely hope that you begin to take stock and stop doing the smart things but the right things. That is why we elected *you*."[39] A little over a year later, he was elected to the Louisiana House of Representatives, and sixteen years later, to the first of two terms representing the district on the New Orleans City Council.

During the most intense pressure of his first year in office, Moon

Landrieu had opted to follow a reading of the law that required the elimination of the threat posed by the Panthers. He did not feel malice toward the militants, however, and claimed that although he believed that they were "terribly wrong and terribly misguided," he respected them for being "willing to put something on the line."[40] In more colorful language, Robert Tucker remembers Landrieu telling him once in a French Quarter bar ironically named The Pig's Eye, "I admire the shit out of those kids."[41] One incident on Thanksgiving Day demonstrated this flexibility of attitude. While the enormous Landrieu family was enjoying the holiday at their Uptown home, a group of upset militants arrived and wanted to have a word with the mayor. Instead of barricading the house or evacuating his family or slipping out the back, the new mayor walked out to the sidewalk and explained himself. Sitting on the front steps were a number of children watching their father conduct politics in the new South. Among them was a young girl bearing a strong resemblance to Landrieu's fifteen-year-old daughter Mary.[42] Nine years later, Mary Landrieu became the youngest woman ever elected to the Louisiana House of Representatives. In 1996, with strong black support, she achieved another first, becoming the first woman ever elected to represent Louisiana in the U.S. Senate.

As the situation in Desire indicated, the tension between black residents and the police department could not be resolved simply by liberal politicians assuming power. Across the nation crime rates seemed to be on the rise, and getting tough on criminals began to be a platform for political careers. A major challenge for urban mayors was to create a sense of security and livability among middle-class residents to stem their out-migration. Almost exactly two years after the first Desire incident, Landrieu faced another controversial moment when the NOPD announced the creation of the Felony Action Squad, a biracial unit designed for street interdiction and infiltration in high-crime areas. Many activists in black areas expressed worry that the squad was created to target black residents, and their worries increased dramatically on September 19, 1972, when police superintendent Clarence Giarrusso declared publicly that officers were authorized to shoot to kill if seriously threatened. This decision irritated many black New Orleans residents, and particularly troubled a young sailor who had had a tough experience in the U.S. Navy. Another controversial issue involving the police also concerned that sailor. On November 16, 1972, almost two years after the second Desire confrontation, two black students in Baton Rouge were killed by buckshot fired by deputy sheriffs during a confrontation at the historically black Southern University. The deaths were the most tragic result of several months of protest by Southern students. They were similar to the deaths of three black students at South Carolina State University in Orangeburg in February 1968 and two black students at Jackson State University in Mississippi in May 1970. Governor Edwin Edwards closed the university early for Thanksgiving, and school officials cancelled the annual football game with rival Grambling State University.[43] The problem of white police officers shooting young black people had not gone away. Somewhere during the next month and a half, the troubled Navy veteran chose to press ahead with violent revenge.

The Hojo Sniper and the Winter of 1973

At the dawn of the twentieth century, in late July, a man named Robert Charles got a gun and began shooting white people. A forty-four-year-old black immigrant from rural Mississippi, Charles had become fed up with second-class treatment and had become especially enraged by a Georgia lynching of a black man in which pieces of the man's heart and liver were marketed as souvenirs. On July 23, after shooting a white New Orleans police officer around 11:00 p.m., he went on a nearly week-long rampage that left seven white people dead (four of them police officers), approximately twenty white people wounded, and numerous white mobs roaming the streets in search of retribution. With his Winchester rifle in hand, Robert Charles made his final stand in an apartment at 1208 Saratoga Street in the Central City neighborhood. Somehow, he withstood a continual barrage of an estimated five thousand bullets. Eventually, authorities forced him from the building by setting it ablaze. Once flushed, he was shot and killed and then shot at least thirty-three more times and his body dragged into the street where a mob continued the attack on his corpse. White mobs continued to lash out against the black community, destroying much property and torching a prominent black school funded by philanthropists.[44]

Almost seventy-two years later, a sailor named Mark Essex bought a .44 caliber rifle at the Montgomery Ward department store in Emporia, Kansas, and eventually migrated to New Orleans after being court-martialed and expelled from the Navy. On New Year's Eve of 1972, he began shooting police officers and white people. A twenty-three-year-old black man, Essex had become severely alienated during his military service and had become a devout—and perhaps deranged—follower of the fringes of the black liberation movement. He covered the walls of his Central City apartment with writing in red paint: "Kill. Hate White People. Beast of the Earth. Kill," "Revolution," and "Kill Pig Devil." When not scribbling on his tenement walls, he was taking classes with Total Community Action to learn to be a candy machine repairman. Around 11:00 p.m. on December 31—the same time of night as Robert Charles's initial 1900 eruption—he shot and killed a New Orleans police officer, beginning a week-long manhunt that ended at the high-rise Downtown Howard Johnson Hotel. By the end of the ordeal on January 7, Essex had killed nine people (five police officers, one of whom was black), injured over twenty more people either with the bullets he fired or the fires he set, and caused a nation of viewers to glue themselves to the television as the networks cut into regular programming to cover parts of the incident. In addition to wounds caused by Essex, over a dozen officers were injured during the confusion, typically from ricocheting bullets or misfires.[45] In contrast to the reaction to the Robert Charles shootings of 1900, the Essex incident did not lead to a white riot, but it did cause many locals to question the extent of racial progress and to wonder out loud about the price of racial liberalism.

Finding a place to begin the story of Mark Essex is a slippery enterprise. Journalists covering the episode went back to the traditional starting points of family, school, and employment and found that he had a stable home life and a relatively normal educational experience until he joined the U.S. Navy. While in the Navy, he was picked on and ridiculed by whites and, according to reports, developed an intense hatred fed by bitter black acquaintances. In New Orleans, he continued his exploration of radical liberationism and apparently concocted a murderous plot to assassinate NOPD officers. In a brazen move, he sent an ominous letter to the local WWL-TV that was not received until after New Year's Day 1973 and not opened until January 6. In the letter, he warned: "On Dec 31 1972 appt 11 the Downtown New Orleans Police Dept will be attacked . . . Reason-many. But the deaths of two innocent brothers [from Southern University in 1972] will be avenged. And many others. P.S. Tell Pig Garrasso [police superintendent Clarence Giarrusso] the felony action squad ain't shit."[46]

True to his word, Essex began firing shots at the NOPD's Central Lockup facility at 10:52 p.m. on December 31. His first shot missed its intended target, but one of the next six struck Alfred Harrell Jr. in the chest. At 11:09 p.m., Harrell, an unarmed nineteen-year-old black cadet, part-time chef, and father of a nine-month-old son, was pronounced dead. While emergency technicians were trying to save Harrell, Essex ran several blocks away and broke into a warehouse in Central City to hide, triggering a burglar alarm in the process. When K-9 officers arrived, he shot Sgt. Edwin Hosli Sr., mortally wounding the twenty-seven-year-old husband and father of four. He died two months later.[47] Afterward, the search for the police-killer intensified, with officers fanning out into adjoining neighborhoods. Soon, however, Superintendent Giarrusso called off the search in the nearby Gert Town neighborhood because of the tension created by aggressive tactics, including officers kicking in several doors. Some Gert Towners responded to the search by shooting out streetlights. In the meantime, Essex apparently took refuge in the First New St. Mark Baptist Church at 1208 South Lopez Street and other places. For the rest of the week, he tended to his own wounds, apparently bought a razor, and kept a low profile.[48]

The major events of the week involved funerals and another police shooting. One funeral was for Cadet Harrell. The other was a memorial service for Congressman Hale Boggs (D-Louisiana), the House Majority Leader whose plane disappeared in bad weather on October 16, 1972, while campaigning for Nicholas Begich, an Alaska Democrat and its only congressperson. After a massive effort involving the U.S. military, the search was called off, and Boggs and three others were presumed dead, perhaps having crashed into Prince William Sound. On January 4, a number of dignitaries assembled for Boggs's Mass in the French Quarter at St. Louis Cathedral, including several associates from Congress, Vice President Spiro Agnew, First Lady Patricia Nixon (President Nixon chose to remain in Washington), and Boggs family friends Lyndon and Lady Bird Johnson. Security was especially tight because of the New Year's Eve police killings and another police shooting in the Desire area, eventually deemed unrelated to Essex. The man in charge of that security was deputy police superintendent Louis Sirgo.[49]

Three days after the city began officially coping with the loss of its most powerful legislator, Mark Essex quickly forced attention away from what might have lain beneath the Alaskan sea back to one of the city's newer high-rise hotels. The day's tumult began shortly after 10:00 a.m., when Essex shot an Italian-American Central City grocer in the chest, allegedly for informing the police of his potential whereabouts. With a small stockpile of ammunition purchased from a local Schwegmann Brothers Giant Supermarket, Essex hijacked a car at Broad and Thalia streets and quickly covered the few blocks to the Downtown Howard Johnson Hotel garage, parking the stolen car on the fourth floor. Unable to enter the lower floors of the hotel, he found a way onto the eighteenth floor, where he saw two black maids and told them, "Don't worry, I'm not going to hurt you black people. I want the whites."[50] While on the eighteenth floor, he ran into Dr. Robert Steagall, a recent graduate of the University of Virginia medical school, on his honeymoon. After wrestling with Steagall, Essex shot him in the chest while the doctor's wife, Betty Day Steagall, pleaded with him not to shoot. After the shots, according to journalist Peter Hernon, she "knelt next to her husband," and as she was "cradling his head in her arms," Essex shot her "through the base of the skull" and then started a fire in Steagall's open room.[51]

A few minutes later, Essex made it to the eleventh floor and shot the hotel's office manager Frank Schneider in the head as he left an elevator, killing him. Shortly thereafter, he shot the hotel's general manager Walter Sherwood Collins in the back on the stairs. Collins died within two days. By 11:00 a.m., Essex was on the eighth floor pool patio, where he shot businessman Robert Bemish in the abdomen. For the next two hours, Bemish played dead, floating in the hotel pool. He ultimately was rescued and survived.[52] Essex proceeded to shoot several people from the pool deck before moving to the opposite side of the building where he shot three officers on the street, killing Philip Coleman, who was attempting to rescue the two other downed policemen. Essex then tried to make it back to his car, but when he found it surrounded, he ascended a now-familiar stairwell. At 12:18 a shot rang out from the sixteenth floor, hitting motorcycle officer Paul Persigo in the face and killing him. Sporadic firing continued for the next forty-nine minutes. In the meantime, Deputy Superintendent Louis Sirgo was leading a rescue team up a stairwell. At 1:07, he arrived at the sixteenth floor landing, and Essex shot him in the back, severing his spine. The forty-eight-year-old died shortly after. Essex soon found access to the roof and continued firing. At 2:01, Essex shot his last person, an officer who survived. In four hours, the disgraced former seaman had killed or mortally wounded seven people (four of them officers) and wounded twenty-two others (ten seriously).[53]

Beginning with that shot at 2:01, Essex had approximately six hours and fifty-one minutes to live. For the rest of the afternoon and early evening, he nestled into a sturdy cinderblock cube on the roof, yelled out taunts to officers, and reportedly fired occasionally. Essex stymied city officials until just after 6:00 p.m., when a Marine helicopter from the nearby Belle Chasse air base began making tactical passes at the hotel, with NOPD officers firing away at the roof box each time. Despite cold weather and bad winds, the Sea Knight troop helicopter, which had seen action in Vietnam, continued its sweeps for another two hours. Just before nine, the chopper swooped down again. This time, Essex left his urban pillbox, ran onto the roof firing away at the helicopter, and was struck by an estimated one hundred rounds of ammunition. Because of fears that more than one sniper was involved, police remained cautious the rest of the night and the next day. Essex's body lay on the roof for another seventeen hours. The danger was not over, however, as accidental shootings continued, and several officers were wounded by ricocheting bullets. The assault on the roof the next day was covered live on national television.[54] Events in the Big Easy became the topic of conversation across the nation. Syndicated columnists Rowland Evans and Robert Novak specu-

lated that the sniper attack might have driven a wedge between Mayor
Landrieu and some of his black supporters, but more likely just hastened
the "flight of the white" to "bedroom suburbs." They predicted that Landrieu's "present biracial partnership may merely be a way station between
white supremacy and black monopoly."[55]

The homicidal acts of Mark Essex attracted a reported six hundred
officers from Louisiana, Texas, and Mississippi, involved representatives
of twenty-six federal, state, and local agencies, and rallied rifle-toting civilians to downtown New Orleans to—in the words of one of them—"put
one right inside his brain pan. That's the only way you can stop a nigger.
Got to get him square in the head."[56] It was certainly not the city's finest
hour. Coordination of police activities was weakened by communication
problems and poor intelligence, and in several cases police actions en-
dangered other officers, guests of the hotel, and even the helicopter crew.
One unidentified observer stated that the story line should have read, "After thirty hours of fighting, six hundred police sharpshooters have killed a
single sniper."[57] A local black minister said that the police were "asses for
fighting a dead man with helicopters and machine guns and high-powered
rifles for almost a whole day in full view of the nation."[58] Mayor Landrieu
remarked later that the police's handling of the events was "outstanding,"
but "not pretty," attributing the problems to being unable to understand
what they were up against. On the day of the Hojo shootings, despite not
knowing who was shooting or how many people were involved, Landrieu
returned from a staff retreat thirty miles away, went to the office briefly,
then headed straight to the hotel to the operational command center.
While shots were still ringing out, Landrieu reported he "managed to get
into the building by kind of hugging the wall and running through the
side door on Gravier Street." The stairwell on Gravier Street was the one
used most frequently by Essex.[59]

One of the major unknowns was whether the shootings were the work
of one person, two people, or a well-organized conspiracy. The events
sparked worry that the much-feared "Black Revolution" was finally beginning after several years of tense but increasingly optimistic race relations.
The reaction of some local black youth seemed to confirm suspicions.
Peter Hernon of the *New Orleans States-Item* reported that some black

residents were sitting on cars, cheering "Right on" each time the sniper fired a shot. Near Canal Street, the major shopping district in downtown New Orleans, police officers were harassed by a crowd of about two hundred black youth who threw things and shouted, "Kill the pigs." "Hang on baby," one voice offered up to the shooter in the hotel. "When it gets dark, we gonna help you."[60] Another group of black youth near Tulane and Loyola Avenues openly cheered when a police bulletin about the death of an officer was broadcast. Bill Rousselle, a former administrator with the Human Relations Committee, surmised that "the cheering was born out of years of abuse by police." Others blamed the news reporters for blowing the reaction out of proportion. Almost all of the black leaders who commented on the situation were concerned for the loss of life, including Essex, and they placed part of the blame on the society that produced the conditions that enraged Essex.[61] One anonymous black politician, though, told two syndicated columnists, "I'm not going to condone or condemn what happened. There's a little of Mark Essex in all of us." The columnists, Evans and Novak, lamented that Essex was "a heroic figure to jobless young blacks."[62]

Larry Jones, a leader of the Black Youth for Progress (BYP) organization, a community organizer, and director of the Neighborhood Development Center in the St. Bernard target area, explained that Essex was not a "crazy nigger" or the "extremist" that many white residents believed. Jones contended, instead, that the housing project residents that he knew were "impressed" with Essex and saw him as a "hero," not because "he killed cops but because he attacked a repressive system."[63] The local reaction among African Americans was not atypical from reaction elsewhere. Essex became something of a cult figure. Reportedly, Stokeley Carmichael paid tribute to Essex for "carrying our struggle to the next quantitative level, the level of science."[64] Adrienne Kennedy, a writer in the Black Arts Movement, penned a play in 1973 called *An Evening with Dead Essex*.

White leaders were less charitable in their appraisal of Essex, expressing a mixture of shock, remorse, and sadness.[65] William J. Guste Jr., the attorney general for Louisiana in 1973, told a national reporter that he was "convinced that there is an underground, national suicidal group bent on creating terror in America." In other ways, the reaction followed the psychological lines that had guided the formation of the local Great Society. Governor Edwin Edwards speculated that the atrocities were "the work of a diseased mind."[66] Police superintendent Clarence Giarrusso offered that he had a "gut feeling" that caused him to "understand that as a result of years of degradation and deprivation, it might somehow be symbolic to some blacks." Nevertheless, his final take was that "Mark Essex's footnote in history should state clearly that he murdered and executed, without justifiable cause or purpose." Essex had "sacrificed fellow human beings to his god of revenge."[67]

If one wishes for history to be poetic, it can be easy to conclude that the search for the Great Society in New Orleans came to an end in January 1973, with smoke in the air, blood in the streets, and a double-rotor Marine helicopter blasting at a tourist hotel. If one can ignore the fact that the Great Society continued on in numerous programmatic forms, the events of January 1973 offer a tempting symbolic closing to its story in New Orleans. On January 8, the day that New Orleans officials removed Mark Essex's body from the Hojo Hotel, the United States resumed peace talks with North Vietnam in Paris. Twelve days later, Richard Nixon was inaugurated for a second term and despite setting a conciliatory tone in his address, set about to undo as much of the War on Poverty as possible. Two days after that, Lyndon Johnson felt a severe pain in his chest, called his Secret Service agents, and then died from a massive heart attack in his home at the LBJ Ranch. Three days later, his closest friends and family came "singing by the river" as he had long planned. They buried him among some live oaks along his beloved Pedernales River.[68] Two days after his interment, in a salient irony, the Paris Peace Accords were signed, effectively ending U.S. involvement in the Vietnam War.[69] Over the next year or so, President Nixon essentially finished off the Office of Economic Opportunity and Model Cities and set in place the core for the Housing and Community Development Act of 1974. Embodying Nixon's "New Federalism," that act restructured federal funding in local areas through the Community Development Block Grant system. In New Orleans, Moon Landrieu won reelection and secured his position at

City Hall. But he and other racial liberals were no longer facing the same world.

A constant theme of the search for the Great Society from the early 1960s until after 1973 was a deep concern about alienation. In New Orleans in 1973, some of that search ended with the expression of one man's alienation. Summarizing the issue was professor Daniel Thompson, one of the prominent black intellectuals who had helped chart the path of the local Great Society. "The problem for society to ponder out of all this is a fundamental one," Thompson conjectured. "How is it to deal with such supreme alienation? It doesn't matter whether the individual be black or white, although in Essex's case it's obvious that his blackness precipitated his action. The question is, what do you do with the man who is alone, cut off, willing to die?"[70]

After Jim Crow, after Mark Essex, and for the symbolic purposes of this book, after the Great Society, the most haunting metaphoric moment did not occur at the policy level or in the news or in the probing rhetoric of dedicated scholars, but in a place that had given birth to the very search itself—the voice of an enraged, alienated individual emboldened by a group of neighbors. Two weeks after the Essex rampage, near the Magnolia housing project in Central City, two NOPD officers chased a robbery suspect who had shot at them. All three were on foot when the assailant rounded a corner and met one of the patrolmen. With his gun drawn, he told the officer, "You're dead, pig," but his pistol failed to fire, giving the officer time to shoot the man in the chest. While the officers waited for the ambulance, several hundred residents of the Magnolia project— the sweet-scented magnolia had been the state flower of Louisiana since 1900—congregated and speculated on why another black man lay dying. The emergency technicians arrived soon, and according to the journalist Peter Hernon, as they rolled the young man into the ambulance, a woman yelled out, "Sniper comin' back. Sniper comin' back to get you all."[71]

CONCLUSION

Prelude to Katrina

Deep within the Southern heart there still beats the driving fear, the firm resistance, the attitude toward race and progress which, though slightly tempted, show the dilemma of the New South as a battle against time itself.
—Jason Berry, *Vieux Carré Courier*, 1972

In New Orleans, keeping faith in progress can be hard to do. Many people there have found it easier to put their confidence in things unseen and in life beyond life. In 1973, the Essex episode demonstrated that one man with a few dozen bullets could shut down a city at one of the most optimistic moments in its history. Thirty-two years later, Hurricane Katrina showed that an epic storm could do the same to a catastrophic degree. Unlike any others in New Orleans's modern history, those two events exposed the city's vulnerabilities. In both periods, the flaws were serious and anyone living there was aware of them unless they were partitioned by their own ignorance or arrogance or affluence. In the 1960s, the Great Society and the federal government were supposed to solve some of the problems. Tearing down Jim Crow and building up a War on Poverty—not to mention raising the levees—offered the chance to remake New Orleans into a city of "great destiny," as Urban League leader Harvey Kerns suggested in 1964.[1] In the 1970s, there was a growing optimism that the process was working, despite the Essex rampage. The city seemed to be in the early stages of a civic renaissance. By the early 1980s, that hope had collapsed, and the inclusive, expansive vision of the Great Society had become a historical relic. Lyndon Johnson had made his promises in 1964, but his successors rarely felt obliged to keep them. In hindsight, the decades that followed them became a prelude to Katrina.

During the 1970s, Moon Landrieu's administration helped to transform downtown, construct the Louisiana Superdome, improve infrastructure, and reshape race relations. In doing so, he proved to be one of the most effective and agile political leaders in recent U.S. history. He courted investors and tourists with impressive precision and attracted millions of federal dollars to help pay for much of it. Landrieu, who went on to serve as Secretary of the U.S. Department of Housing and Urban Development under Jimmy Carter, proved adept at capitalizing on the city's intriguing culture, its influence in Congress, and its historic role as a regional transportation and financial center. New Orleans's government had perennial fiscal crises, but money from the oil boom and the federal government were changing the city's skyline, roadways, and political culture. Glass towers beginning to rise downtown seemed to signal that the city was set to shake off the torpor of its traditional economy and join the success stories of the new Dixie. After so many troubling years, the Saints had come marching in—literally. Given a franchise by the National Football League, New Orleanians embraced their team, known as the Saints, with the strange boosterish glee produced by professional sports. They could finally claim that they belonged to the big leagues—only to be disappointed for two decades before the team had its first winning season. Many fans believed their losing ways came from constructing the team's home, the Superdome, on top of an old cemetery. The solution for some was to put paper grocery sacks over their heads and scream.

The football team notwithstanding, many of New Orleans's business leaders prized the city's image almost as much as oil and river traffic. It was too costly to be seen as a socially stuffy, racially bigoted town. In fact, after the 1970s, tolerance and cultural diversity became one of the city's strongest selling points, helping New Orleans seem to be a culturally authentic place in a crass age of materialism and homogeneity. Instead of leading the world in churning out high-tech components and computer parts, New Orleans became a center for manufacturing sensual liberation and enlightened relaxation, while comforting visitors with its colonial buildings, grand homes, narrow live-oak-lined streets, wrought iron, and quaint traditions. To market the city's continuity with the past, civic leaders labored to suppress the racial discomforts of that past.

This apparent transformation might be interpreted as a logical outcome of the search for the Great Society—once segregation was lifted and the South unbridled its best attributes, then the economy burst forth, unleashing southern entrepreneurism, ingenuity, and hospitality.[2] In some cases in Dixie that may have happened, as southern-based corporations reshaped the way people around the world got packages, bought things, flew places, refreshed themselves, and watched the news. Locally, the post–Jim Crow boom, if one can call it that, lasted all too briefly. In New Orleans, the oil bust of the 1980s accompanied federal austerity toward cities and left the metropolitan area in the throes of an economic crisis, exposing the problems of using growth as the chief engine for racial inclusion. After the mid-1970s, the new skyscrapers of the Central Business District had become symbols of New Orleans's place in the new Dixie. However, those mirrored buildings, like some aspects of the Great Society, offered little direct benefit to most low-income New Orleanians.[3]

This book is a study of aspirations, not a traditional political history about elections and critical turning points. If the story had been centrally about votes and vote-getters, the lens would have opened on Mayor DeLesseps S. "Chep" Morrison, the progressive white segregationist who helped modernize New Orleans's politics and economy after World War II, and it would have faded out on Mayor Ernest M. "Dutch" Morial, the unrelenting black Creole pioneer who struggled in the 1980s to cope with severe fiscal crises and the rapid out-migration of middle-class residents. He inherited the deepest problems of the white reaction to the civil rights movement. In between, the work would have focused on two "bridge" figures, Victor Hugo Schiro holding cautiously to the past and Moon Landrieu racing headlong into the future. Instead, this story started symbolically with the muted anxiety of a smiling child and closed with the death of a shattered man. When viewed in the perspective of decades or centuries, the progressive responses in New Orleans in between those two moments appear to have been the historical exception instead of the rule. They provided an interregnum of innovation that, regrettably, only narrowly tailored the arc of deprivation that has characterized the public history of poor southern blacks.

Uncertain Legacies

The scope of this study stops in the early 1970s. The legacies of the Great Society did not. Liberal policies from the 1960s continued to dominate domestic politics into the twenty-first century. Intense debates over their worth and their possible role in the rise and fall of the American republic have not relented, reflecting the unsettled visions for America that emerged from the 1960s. As a result, the Great Society remains something of a historical enigma. Detractors on the right have depicted it as a devolution into socialism that rewarded the poor—and by not-so-subtle implication, especially the black poor—for bad behavior. Leftist critics have often viewed the Great Society as a hopeless capitulation to corporate capitalism and bolstering the middle class. Arguing that the Great Society deterred self-responsibility, undermined the work ethic, and retarded entrepreneurism, political conservatives have used the racial, fiscal, and social antagonisms it arouses to append a strange coalition of southern whites, blue-collar whites, and religious conservatives to their traditional base of affluent whites. Liberals, on the other hand, have found themselves struggling to defend the agenda of tolerance, inclusion, and demand-stimulated economic growth. They have tended to be befuddled by the negative reactions to the overall Great Society, but have found solace in the significant popular support for components of it, particularly race-neutral things such as preschool education for the disadvantaged, healthcare for the elderly, environmental recovery, land conservation, consumer protection, workplace safety, aid to college students, and aid to local public schools.

In the 1970s, the federal commitment to cities waned, reflecting a major shift in the Great Society. A *New York Daily News* headline about the response of Gerald Ford's administration to New York City's fiscal problems in October 1974 captures this diminished concern starkly:

"Ford to City: Drop Dead." The most intense assault on the Great Society came after 1981. In 1985, the U.S. Conference of Mayors reported that the Reagan administration had cut grants to cities by 50 percent and trimmed support of other relevant federal programs by 80 percent. The president of the Conference of Mayors, New Orleans's Dutch Morial, called $20 billion worth of cuts to cities in the 1986 federal budget "the beginning of the end of the historical federal-city partnership." He predicted a disruption in "domestic tranquility in this nation." Out of desperation, Morial countered the New Federalism with his own call for a "new localism" defined by heavily courting business investment and the old standby hope that economic growth could address the problems of poverty and infrastructure.[4] Ronald Reagan's administration undid as much of the Great Society as it could—particularly in job training and antipoverty programs—but left a core imprint in place as it rewarded middle-class constituencies and powerful special-interest groups in housing, health, and education. Reflecting conclusions of conservative political scientists, however, Reagan did skillfully present the broader idea of Great Society liberalism as a menace.

In his final State of the Union Address, in 1988, the actor-turned-politician declared that in America's War on Poverty, "poverty won."[5] He was not alone. The question of who won the War on Poverty has dominated the examination of the Great Society's legacies. The one undeniable fact is that the official poverty rate did decline in the United States. It fell from 19 percent in 1964 to a low of 11.4 percent in 1978, rising to 13.1 by 1989. The rate was at 11.3 in the year 2000. In Louisiana, the rate fell from 26.3 percent in 1969 to 18.6 percent in 1979 before rising to 23.6 percent in 1989. By 2000, it was at 19.6 percent.[6] In New Orleans, the city's overall poverty rate was actually higher in 2000 (at 28 percent) than in 1960 (at 25 percent), attributable partly to demographic shifts. The local black poverty rate, however, fell dramatically from almost 50 percent in 1960 to near 30 percent in 2000, but the rate for local whites had gotten slightly worse, going from 14 percent to 16 percent. Liberal proponents have credited federal social policies for the national decline. They argue that federal programs and cash-transfer payments helped alleviate the economic pressure of baby boomers and increasing numbers of women entering the job market in the 1970s. They also accurately blame the Vietnam War for siphoning off money and political support for the Great Society. Opponents of the Great Society contend that federal policies were psychologically counterproductive, and they have credited economic expansion and free market impulses for the declines in poverty rates.[7]

Unfortunately, the modern-day perceptions of the Great Society are dangerously disengaged from the historical record. The Great Society that actually transpired in New Orleans indicates that the popular memory of 1960s era liberalism needs an overhaul. Great Society liberalism provided neither salvation nor damnation. It was neither a total sellout nor a total washout. It was the culmination of an impassioned but vague and decentralized search for a stable way to deal with the cultural, economic, and political diversity of the postwar American republic. During the post–Jim Crow era, Americans were having to come to grips, once again, with the role of the margins—including the psychological, racial, sexual, political, ethnic, and economic margins—in American life. Although the Great Society did not dramatically alter the foundations of poverty, it was a much better attempt to improve living conditions and public participation for marginalized people than had ever been attempted before, and, arguably, it contributed to the economic growth that many politicians and academics claim was responsible for the decline in poverty.

Locally, the longest lasting legacy of the Great Society was its impact on Louisiana's political culture. Most obviously, it helped eliminate outright legal segregation. Legitimate politicians could no longer openly appeal to the heritage and customs of Jim Crow. Although he had to couch his assault in coded language, even a politician with as vicious a racial past as David Duke, who was the Grand Wizard of the Ku Klux Klan and an open Nazi sympathizer, could win votes. When the margins gained more political power in the 1960s, they forced racial politics under the covers, or sheets if one considers the quip from legendary playboy Edwin Edwards that he and Duke were both "wizards under the sheets." They could not make race stay there, though. Racial retrenchment sold well to white Louisiana voters. In 1990, Duke attacked welfare and affirmative action to carry almost 60 percent of the white vote in the Senate race and close to 55 percent in the 1991 general election for governor.[8] To combat white supremacy in the 1960s, liberal leaders had settled on a subtle compromise that encouraged the rise of some black leaders but only by continuing a system that concentrated power in personalities and political machines. In this way another progressive moment became defined in large part by the resistance to it.

Bureaucratic arrangements within the Great Society sustained Louisiana's new racial liberalism, but they did not effectively reform the role of private influence over the public world. In the Bayou State, public policy had to reward private participants in local webs of power who wanted low wages, low taxes, and compliant workforces. Louisiana's political culture was rooted in the dispensation of favors, influence, and policy by local power brokers and influential interest groups. In the 1920s and 1930s, Huey Long initiated a political movement that broke the near-oligarchical domination of the state. That movement did not necessarily democratize the state. It merely shifted it away from oligarchy to a narrowly accessible pluralism. The emergence of new, lesser Huey Longs extended that trend. Tom Dent, the writer and civil rights activist and one-time War on Poverty organizer, explained the situation this way: "Politics in New Orleans has always been fascinating because the game is played with such cynicism. New Orleans politics is *trickster* politics; ideology means nothing."[9] Robert F. Collins, a prominent civil rights attorney, spoke for the Community Organization for Urban Politics (COUP) in 1972. "We have no permanent enemies," he declared. "We have no permanent friends. We have only permanent interests."[10] Six years later, in 1978, Collins became the South's first black federal judge.

In the 1960s, political activists talked about Jonah and Jesus and brotherhood and breakthroughs. In the 1970s, discussions centered more on bridges and expressways, Superdomes and Saints, contracts and conventions. Oddly, liberal electoral successes seemed to sap the intellectual vitality of the Great Society on the streets. Debates about systems, organizations, and individual leaders replaced debates about values, inclusion, and civic responsibility. Intricate policy considerations took over and the process of inclusion and empowerment became less about civic visions and more about budgets, procedures, and patronage. And, as the cycle in Louisiana has tended to be, the criminal investigations began, led by ambitious federal attorneys. In 1980, a former TCA food coordinator pled guilty to stealing $160,000 in meat that was supposed to feed poor children. That same year, two TCA attorneys pled guilty for misappropriating funds. In 1982, TCA director Daniel Vincent was convicted on conspiracy to embezzle federal funds and spent eight months in a federal prison in Fort Worth.[11] In 1991, Robert Collins's lack of permanent friends came back to haunt him, as he was convicted of accepting a bribe to reduce sentencing in a drug case. Two years later, while in prison, he was forced to finally resign from the bench.[12]

In Louisiana's extractive-based economy, success in the private market was frequently dependent on influence over government policy. Profit was often related to ability to influence taxation, labor laws, land-use rules, and government contracts. This made interest groups representing major landholders, farmers, contractors, manufacturers, and insurance companies the voices driving policy. Even the judicial system fell under their influence because in Louisiana, state judges are elected, and interest groups provided essential campaign contributions. Those arrangements meant that the new liberals and especially the leaders of New Orleans's Acronym groups had a choice: they could fight an altruistic but likely losing battle against the inequitable concentration of power, or they could promote their own political longevity—and effectiveness—by staking a claim in the existing process. Altruism was noble, but ineffectual against a budget ax threatening to cripple the Charity Hospital system, AFDC, or other programs vital to poor urban constituencies. As black politician Theodore Marchand explained, "You can't exercise pressure until you are in a position to hurt somebody."[13] Political power and personal power were often one and the same, and Louisiana history documents the alarming frequency with which personal interests overshadowed public duty. In Louisiana politics, power was concentrated, but it was not centralized. The introduction of black politicians in the late 1960s and early 1970s did little to stop it from being fragmented, factionalized, and personalized.

The most prominent of those black leaders was Dutch Morial. In 1978, he defeated the ethnic white populist Joseph DiRosa to become the city's first black mayor, carrying a historically unprecedented one-fifth of the white votes. Benefiting from Democratic control of Congress and the White House, as well as the boom of the oil economy, Morial had a productive first term. He achieved acclaim as a resourceful administrator with a stern managerial style. In his successful re-election bid, his personality became a major issue, and his opponents attached the race-coded label of "arrogant" (a stand-in term for "uppity") to him. In his second term, cuts from the Reagan administration and fiscal problems related to the oil bust exposed the fault lines of local politics. Black political disunity and internal wrangling weakened the power of black votes and of liberalism. According to Arnold Hirsch, one of the leading historians of the Morial administration, Morial deeply alienated several powerful black organizations by eschewing the patronage arrangements of the Landrieu administration. Hirsch explains that Morial wanted African Americans to be "respected rather than protected," and drawing on traditions of radical Creole protest, was unrelenting in his push for merit-based black gains. Most dramatic was his attack on COUP, the Seventh Ward Creole-dominated Acronym with a reputation for being more accommodating to white business leaders. As a consequence of black disunity, dwindling white minority often held the balance of power. White votes proved crucial in the defeat of Morial's bid to change the city charter to allow him to run for a third term, and they made the difference in the choice of Morial's successor, COUP leader and War on Poverty alumnus Sidney Barthelemy. In a majority-black city, Barthelemy coasted to victory with less than a third of votes cast by black voters but 85 percent cast by white voters.[14] Three political scientists argue that Landrieu and Morial moved the city away from a "Caretaker" regime of low taxes and small government to a "Progressive" regime with more services and some attempts at economic redistribution. Barthelemy's administration more resembled a "Corporate" regime that answered primarily to powerful private enterprises.[15]

Somewhere in the late 1970s and early 1980s, black residents of New Orleans came to outnumber white residents. Black voters had more influence in choosing elected officials than ever before, but that did not translate into as much power as proponents had hoped. The resulting counter-productive metropolitan turf battles gave state and federal leaders a reason to ignore New Orleans. After the innovative phase of the Great Society, who was left to care about the deep roots of poverty and racism in New Orleans? Leaders in the marketplace were largely unconcerned, and after 1974 a new federal funding system for local social programs discouraged the grassroots organizing that had enabled poor communities to participate in the local political process. Perhaps most important, as conservative whites disengaged from the city by moving to the suburbs, there were fewer incentives for white state and federal leaders to preserve funding for the city. Inside the city, the result was a return in the 1980s and 1990s to one-party politics, rife with factions and dominated by personalities.

The Great Society enabled black leaders to consolidate spheres of influence in public life and chiseled open more room in the private marketplace. But federal programs were not system-changers. There was no concomitant alteration of Louisiana's economy. The immediate political imperatives to reward established interests kept Louisiana's economy based on its natural resources, alluvium, petroleum, plants, animals, scenery, and mystique. Weak statewide commitment to investing in education kept Louisiana on a low trajectory. It insured an inviting atmosphere for talented athletes but not necessarily for software engineers or high-tech entrepreneurs—except perhaps while on vacation or at a convention. In retrospect, blaming local liberals for the lack of real social and economic change is akin to blaming farmers for the weather. Despite electoral victories in the early 1970s, liberals ended up with essentially three bargaining chips for civic control: Great Society-linked funding and patronage; control over a substantial but relatively small number of votes; and credit, at least temporarily, for implementing in the 1960s a marginally successful vision for economic growth. Those three things were important but could not compete with the economic control held by the corporations responsible for processing resources such as oil and gas and agricultural products. Through the Great Society, Louisiana's white racial conservatives were forced to alter their system of racial insularity in the interests of reshaping Louisiana's place in world capitalism, but deep, old roots remained.

There are many lingering questions about the search for black power that this book makes little attempt to answer. What ultimately happened to the Soft State? Did it really merge into the harder lines of traditional bureaucracies and new city trenches as it appeared to have, muting grassroots influence?[16] Did the decline in conservative electoral strength in New Orleans actually undermine the broader legitimacy of liberalism by reducing competition and isolating liberal power? After the innovative phase of the Great Society, which was driven by the antipoverty and civil rights movements, what options were available for energized activists? After the mid-1970s, what mechanisms existed to address the radicalized voices on the margins? Was a serious radical critique from the poor possible anymore? If it were, who would listen? From where would the post-civil rights generation of black and liberal leadership come? From the streets, the universities, the unions, the families of the civil rights generation? How could the voices of the post-1960s slow motion crisis be meaningfully integrated into public life? What would keep them connected, or in the words of Daniel Thompson, from being "cut off, willing to die"?

The End of Dixie?

In 1973 shortly after the Essex rampage, a black woman warned that a sniper was coming back.[17] Looking back thirty years later, snipers were not nearly as big a threat as the emergence of postindustrial, postmodern neighborhoods where a rootless market-driven nihilism seemed to have supplanted a drive to sustain a sense of community. Nostalgia for the "good old days" of neighborly old ladies who knew everything in the neighborhood and for community-preserving, black-owned, and black-controlled institutions caused some to look back at Jim Crow not so much in anger but in tears.

At the same time that the Great Society was integrating New Orleans citizens who had been segregated by law and alienated by circumstance, trends in the world economy and regional politics were already at work to isolate the city's black target-area neighborhoods. How could antipoverty and racial uplift programs have a lasting effect when entry-level jobs that had paid well and provided training were migrating out? How could they stabilize communities when highway funding, mortgage policies, and tax trends encouraged suburban flight, cultural segmentation, and privatization? How could they adequately fund vital local institutions such as schools and hospitals? By the late 1970s, according to one study, New Orleans's black leaders had experienced a "loss of faith in the integrity of the political process."[18] In the 1980s and 1990s, the extensive poverty and disorder in predominantly black inner-city neighborhoods made many people believe Ronald Reagan's declaration that poverty had won the War on Poverty. Criticism of governmental inadequacies became a way to relieve anxiety about the atomization of American life without having to address fundamental questions about the accumulation and distribution of political and economic power.

In this regard, the Great Society's great failing was ultimately what it could not do—or at least what Americans were not willing to allow it to do. No serious reform could occur in the 1960s era without first bowing to the gospel of economic growth. As the Great Society unfolded, activists and policy entrepreneurs attempted to encourage growth by expanding the human capital of the ghetto, primarily by enhancing institutions and improving individuals. The War on Poverty successfully built up human capital where the state could force changes in the market—or actually create a new market out of Great Society spending. Given the deplorable economic state of black residents in New Orleans, this Great Society marketplace did occasionally dramatically affect the people who could access it. But economic growth linked to the public sector was not enough. When federal funding became scarcer and presidential administrations fashioned rules to limit how much political benefit local liberals could gain from federal sources, the public marketplace suffered.

The shallow commitment to the promise of an "unconditional War on Poverty" was problematic in the 1960s era, but its real problems arrived in the 1980s. Severe economic and social problems in urban America became major national political issues. The War on Poverty had been replaced by a War on Drugs, and according to some scholars, a War on the Poor, which contributed to yet another generation of alienated and economically dispossessed citizens.[19] The Great Society, it seemed, had failed to provide a lasting buffer for the poor, and Americans were facing more threatening versions of old questions. Ironically, the relative prosperity of the 1980s for most Americans made it appear that the American system was working for everyone. For the poor, however, the slow motion crisis slouched onward.

In the 1970s and 1980s, as affluent Americans increasingly privatized their lives, hostility toward Great Society liberalism also forced community activism to become more privatized.[20] Several private nonprofit organizations such as the Association for Community Reform Now (ACORN) and the Industrial Areas Foundation (IAF) did serious work in the absence of a more centralized effort, but their reach and resources were limited. The range of possible influence also became quite narrow as activists confronted the challenges of urban economic decay and youthful violence often related to an informal, illicit economy. When the Great Society's community organizing functions were truncated in the 1970s, the state (in this sense referring to the general governing apparatus) helped diminish a complicated but potentially powerful democratic tool—that "direct line to the ghetto" celebrated by New Orleans civil rights activist Richard Haley.[21] By opting out of significant support for grassroots community action and by focusing social welfare policies primarily on the delivery of services and cash transfers to the poor, the state diluted the small bit of political capital that had been built up on the streets. In retrospect, the state's retrenchment stifled community activism at a time in American history when economically distressed communities needed community-building support the most. The broadly accepted, simple faith that market forces would solve economic problems was devastating to areas where market logic held that young blacks were dangerous and the safest economic choice was to avoid them. Throughout much of the twentieth century, a sustaining theme of liberalism was the belief that the market could be reshaped to help people otherwise deemed to have little market worth. In the final two decades of that century, one of the resounding defeats of that liberalism was the ascendance of market-centered policy innovation over explicitly people-centered policy innovation.

New Orleans's crisis after the 1970s was not exactly similar to the yellow fever and cholera epidemics of the previous century, the racial violence of Reconstruction and White Redemption, the influenza pandemic after the First World War, the ominous Mississippi flood of 1927, and the storms of almost every year. This time the crisis did not come from the Gulf or from the sky or from germs or from the violent defense of white supremacy. Those crises arrived, wreaked havoc, and then left, except for white supremacy itself. This one stayed. Part of the reason is that its origins and impact are deeply intertwined with the long story of racial and class privilege.

In the two decades before Hurricane Katrina, the urban crisis showed few signs of coming to an end. Worsening the situation was New Orleans's troubling tradition of violence that has for centuries resulted in bloody man-to-man combat. The local economic depression of the 1980s and 1990s and the mercilessly high rates of black male unemployment have reaffirmed the city's reputation as one of the most dangerous places in America. During the 1990s, approximately three thousand residents were murdered, most of them young and black. On the evening news, reports of young black men killing young black men were so commonplace that they became almost like macabre sports reporting, unless a toddler or a white person were caught in the crossfire. In an era when many young people looked increasingly to the informal economy for jobs and financial support, the ties of some of them to civil society became stretched as thinly as at any point in local history. The local response to this problem generally followed the trends of the 1960s. The prominent governmental reaction was to institute more law and order, often becoming the bureaucratic and judicial equivalent of shoot-to-kill: more police, more interdiction, more jails, more jail time, and less rehabilitation. Other responses reflected Great Society stand-bys: demands for more economic growth, more self-knowledge, and more investment in people and institutions, although without the commitment to community organization that had defined the Great Society. Politicians and community leaders frequently called for educational reform and job training, but they could not build the support to pay for substantial programs. Instead, reflecting Louisiana's political focus on personal interests and corporate economic growth strategies, capital investments tended to go into building hotels and casinos and, perhaps most revealing, widening the highways.

Recently, New Orleans has taken on a controversial experiment involving public housing and depending on extensive public and private collaboration. In the late 1990s, the HOPE VI program of the U.S. Department of Housing and Urban Development became the national catalyst for turning troubled public housing projects into mixed-income, mixed-use developments where some renters pay market prices and others pay subsidized rates. A growing criticism of the program, echoing Urban Renewal complaints, is that it displaces poor black families in favor of local developers and growth advocates. In New Orleans, one effort involved the Desire project, but the most incendiary initiative was the destruction of St. Thomas in the Irish Channel, the virtually all-black project that sat on top of valuable ground close to downtown. A consortium of developers, merchants, government officials, and public housing leaders replaced St. Thomas's repetitive, barracks-like apartment buildings with "River Garden," a planned neighborhood of gleaming white and pastel townhomes that imitate architectural styles from the neighboring Lower Garden District. Few of those homes went to the previous tenants. Those new homes, most of them with spacious porches, now rest on new streets with faux-brick intersections and imitation antique lamps, a conscious attempt to make the new feel old and to link historical imagination with economic development. Northward along the new Josephine Drive—named for Napoleon Bonaparte's wife—the skyline is dominated by two nineteenth century Catholic churches whose steeples send four giant crosses rising above a line of old oak trees. Southward toward the river the roads of River Garden run into a new Wal-Mart Supercenter a few hundred yards away, a product of the politics that made it all possible. Positioned between those two cultural axis points, River Garden sits as a symbol of powerful contradictions within modern New Orleans, a place where faith and race and commercialism and history intersect in a battle over hope.

The public decline in hope has been one unfortunate theme of the years between the Great Society and Hurricane Katrina. Idealism waned and public rituals of desperation became far too commonplace: attending funerals, creating memorials, putting more emphasis on the mystical, praying for passage to a better world. In 1960, the iconic image of New Orleans involved federal marshals escorting little black girls in defense of equality. In the 1990s, unfortunately, the image of a different procession dominated: mothers and fathers on their way to bury their children. In a city known for innovative ways to remember the dead, tee-shirt sellers at the turn of the century screened on pictures of the slain so that family and friends could literally wear their memories on their sleeves.[22] Other residents—like their ancestors from previous generations—were reduced to asking the simple questions of the downhearted: What is this world coming to? How did we get here? What can we do? In the absence of any real answers, they were mostly left to talk among themselves and escort the dead.

Hurricane Katrina came ashore early on August 29, 2005. Two days later, I received a phone call from my friend and colleague Timothy Naftali, a Canadian who was set to become a U.S. citizen the next day. He reached me as I was sitting down for a late lunch at a Latin restaurant at the base of Virginia's Blue Ridge Mountains. News about the suffering at New Orleans's Ernest M. Morial Convention Center was just breaking, and he asked me if I had seen it.[23] He followed with a question that I heard in almost every conversation I had about New Orleans for the next month: "Can this be happening in the United States of America?" As I stood on the back deck of this café that looked out over the same mountain range that Thomas Jefferson could once see from Monticello, I thought, "Absolutely, it's New Orleans." I knew it had been going on for decades. Katrina just made the situation less avoidable and the moral choices a little clearer. Over the next few days, the images were difficult to comprehend, and the stories of neglect and inefficiency and ignorance were unimaginable even for New Orleans. Rumors made the situation worse.[24] The events of August and September were shocking, even for a historian who used to call the place home. In researching this book, I had tried to review every document and piece of evidence dealing with responses to poverty and inequality in that city in the decade after Jim Crow. Yet I was unprepared for life after Katrina. In those days of late-summer 2005, I developed a feeling that only comes with the passing of a loved one, and I soon came to accept that yes, in fact, this *was* America.

President George W. Bush was excoriated for his response. He did not visit the city—a place that had voted overwhelmingly for his opponent ten months earlier—until four days after the storm. On the tarmac at Louis Armstrong International Airport on September 2, he gave a few words of encouragement about recovery and talked fondly about how much he had enjoyed himself in New Orleans as a younger man. Two weeks later, he gave his major speech on the recovery efforts. His advance team picked out a spot in Jackson Square a few feet from a statue of a horse-mounted Andrew Jackson, a man who had once ridden in to save the city from the British. Although electrical power was out for hundreds of miles along the Gulf Coast, the historic St. Louis Cathedral was illuminated in a glow befitting a Steven Speilberg movie. Striding out from the shadows, the president seized the podium. He was stern and solemn and wore a crisp blue shirt. Above his right shoulder was the church, above his left, a war hero. There was no tie and no sweat.

Being a politician in a crisis, he made promises. He committed his administration to helping people build their communities better than they had been before the storm. Federal funds would pay for the "great majority" of infrastructure repair, but the real engines for recovery would come from "armies of compassion," from "entrepreneurship," and from "ownership." The president made specific reference to the "deep, persistent poverty" in the area that had "roots in a history of racial discrimination, which cut off generations from the opportunity of America." In responding to Katrina, Americans had a "duty to confront this poverty with bold action" and "rise above the legacy of inequality." The last line was a stirring sentence crafted by a gifted speechwriter. It alluded to jazz funerals in which musicians play somber tunes on the way to the grave before ending in second-line celebrations once the body is laid down. Bush promised that the place was "still coming through the dirge" but we would "live to see the second-line."[25]

Like the promises of a previous president from Texas, Bush's pledges will test the bonds of community and of the idea of America. Catastrophes challenge the affections that keep communities and nations together, but usually reveal the internal character of those communities and those nations—and at least as important, the policies that govern them. Lyndon Johnson's promises were part of an attempt to create a Great Society, and they supported an agenda of inclusion and growth. In the aftermath of Katrina, George Bush's promises extended a vision of the ownership society, and they reflected an agenda of entrepreneurship and privatization. He pledged that when the "job is done, all Americans will have something to be very proud of."[26] No one knows what will really happen, but we are all now part of a new generation that will give meaning to a new set of commitments. And we wait again to see what happens to New Orleans after the promises.

APPENDIX 1

Members of the Leadership Group of the New Orleans Committee for the Economic Opportunity Program and Total Community Action, Inc., 1964

° Indicates African American
# Indicates participants in incorporation proceedings

Person	Affiliations
Darwin Fenner	Partner in Merrill, Lynch, Pierce, Fenner & Smith; key white negotiator in early 1960s desegregation discussions; prominent member of the Krewe of Rex
Matthew Sutherland	Orleans Parish School Board Member; counsel for Pan American Life Insurance; key moderate in the 1960–1961 school desegregation crisis
Lawrence Merrigan	President, Bank of New Orleans
Stephen Lemann#	Attorney
Harry McCall Jr.#	Businessman; key white negotiator in early 1960s desegregation discussions; prominent member of the Krewe of Rex
Winston Lill#	Advertising executive; former aide to former Mayor Chep Morrison (future TCA Director, Public Relations Director for Landrieu Administration)
Maurice "Moon" Landrieu#	State legislator (future City council member-at-large, Mayor, and HUD Secretary)
James Fitzmorris Jr.	City council member-at-large (future Lieutenant Governor)
Victor Schiro	Mayor of New Orleans (represented by aides Bernard Levy and Harold Katner)
Pat Stoddard#	President, Central Labor Council, AFL-CIO

Person	Affiliations
Albert Dent°	President of Dillard University (historically black)
Norman Francis°#	Assistant to the President (and future president) of Xavier University (historically black); ULGNO Board President
Herbert E. Longenecker#	President of Tulane University
Homer L. Hitt#	President of University of New Orleans
Rev. Andrew C. Smith	President of Loyola University
Rev. Homer R. Jolley#	Vice President, Loyola University
Rev. Henry C. Bezou	Superintendent, Archdiocesan Schools
O. Perry Walker	Superintendent, Orleans Parish School Board
J. Harvey Kerns°	Director, ULGNO
Dr. Leonard Burns°	ULGNO Board; Founder of United Clubs, a local civil rights protest organization
Helen Mervis	ULGNO Board; Southern Regional Council; National Council of Jewish Women; Save Our Schools; New Orleans Community Relations Council
Thomas Godchaux#	President of Godchaux's Department Store; prominent member of the local Jewish community
Margery Stich	Leader of the local National Council of Jewish Women; civic activist
Philip James	SWPC board member; businessman
Mrs. Henry Braden III°#	Wife of prominent black leader
Daniel Thompson°	Professor of Sociology, Dillard University
Reverend Abraham Lincoln Davis°#	Minister, New Zion Baptist Church; founding member of the Southern Christian Leadership Conference; SCLC founded in his church
Clarence "Chink" Henry°#	President, International Longshoremen's Association Local 1419 (the powerful black labor union)
C. C. DeJoie Jr.°#	Editor, the *Louisiana Weekly*
Emile Comar	Associate Editor, *Clarion Herald* (Catholic)
John Tims	Publisher of the *New Orleans Times-Picayune*
Ashton Phelps	Attorney; prominent member of the Krewe of Rex
Ellis Henican	Businessman with heavy interest in the oil industry; member of the Krewe of Rex

Person	Affiliations
Laurence M. Williams[#]	Businessman and financier
Morgan Whitney[#]	Executive, Whitney National Bank; member of the Krewe of Rex
James A. Comiskey[#]	Businessman
David M. Kleck[#]	Businessman
Daniel Ellis	Businessman
Clifford F. Favrot	Businessman and philanthropist; member of the Krewe of Rex
Louis M. Freeman	Local Coca-Cola bottler; member of the Krewe of Rex
Frank Friedler Jr.[#]	Businessman (and future city council member) ·
Mason Guillory	Executive, New Orleans Public Service Inc. (electricity provider)
Roy Schwarz[#]	Executive, Fitzgerald Advertising
Michael O'Keefe	State senator; attorney
Nash C. Roberts Jr.	Local television weatherman
Carolyn Gay "Blondie" Labouisse	Political and civic leader
Mrs. Robert Reisfeld	Civic volunteer
Mrs. George R. Montgomery[#]	Civic volunteer
Mrs. Harry Kelleher	Civic volunteer; wife of racially moderate attorney who headed the white Citizen's Committee in early 1960s desegregation discussions and prominent member of the Krewe of Rex
Mrs. Louis Abramson Jr.[#]	Civic volunteer
Moise Dennery	Attorney and member of the local Jewish community
Herman S. Kohlmeyer Jr.[#]	Businessman and investor; member of local Jewish community
Edith Stern	Daughter of Julius Rosenwald, one of the chief investors in the Sears, Roebuck, & Company; wife of Edgar Sterns of Lehman, Stern, & Company; controlled the Stern Family Fund; along with son, Edgar Jr., owned WDSU-TV, local NBC affiliate
Edgar B. Stern Jr.	Son of Edith and Edgar Stern; owner of WDSU-TV; prominent member of Jewish community

Person	*Affiliations*
David Hunter	Director, Stern Family Fund
T. Sterling Dunn	Executive, Sears, Roebuck, & Company
John Corporon	News Director, WDSU-TV

Godchaux to Schiro, 17 July 1964, Folder Economic Opportunity Program, Box 10, 1964, SC; "Roster," ibid; "Total Community Action, Inc." Folder TCA, Box 30, 1964, ibid.

APPENDIX 2
Local Institutions Involved with TCA, Delegate Agencies and Advisory

Public Institutions

Charity Hospital
City Planning Commission
Delgado Institute
Housing Authority of New Orleans
Louisiana Commission on Aging
Louisiana Division of Employment Security (LDES)
Louisiana State Board of Health
Louisiana State Department of Education
Louisiana State Department of Hospitals
Louisiana State Department of Public Welfare
LSU Medical School
Metropolitan Crime Commission
New Orleans City Department of Welfare
New Orleans City Health Department
New Orleans Department of Recreation
New Orleans Juvenile Court
New Orleans Police Department
New Orleans Public Library
Orleans Parish Department of Public Welfare
Orleans Parish School Board
Social Security Administration
United Fund
University of New Orleans
WYES-TV (PBS)
Youth Opportunity Center of the LDES

Private Institutions

Archdiocesan School Board
Associated Catholic Charities
Association for Retarded Children, Inc.
Boy Scouts of America
Children's Bureau of New Orleans
Citizens Housing Council of Greater New Orleans
Consumer Credit Counseling Service of New Orleans, Inc.
Family Service Society
Flint-Goodridge Hospital (black)
Girls Scouts of America
International Longshoremen's Association, Local No. 1419
Jewish Welfare Federation of New Orleans
Kingsley House (settlement)
Louisiana Association for Mental Health
Loyola University
National Council of Jewish Women
National Council of Negro Women
Neighborhood organizations (dozens were involved)
New Orleans Day Nursery
New Orleans Health Corporation
Orleans Neighborhood Centers
Peoples Methodist Community Center
Salvation Army
Several Protestant and Catholic Churches
Social Welfare Planning Council
Stern Family Fund
Travelers Aid Society
Tuberculosis Association of Greater New Orleans
Tulane University (and Medical School)
United Cerebral Palsy
Urban League
Xavier University
YMCA

New Orleans City Planning Commission, *Model Cities Application*; CDA, *Comprehensive Demonstration Plan*, 49; "Agencies Providing Services in Desire Area," Folder Desire 1963–1966, Box 23, CSC.

APPENDIX 3
Key Target-Area Organizing Groups, 1965–1968

Predominantly Black Organizations

Algiers-Fischer Community Organization
Central City Economic Opportunity Committee
Desire Area Community Council
Desire Economic Opportunity Committee
Florida Area Achievement Group
Lower Ninth Ward Neighborhood Council
Ninth Ward Civic Improvement League
St. Bernard Community Council

Predominantly White Organizations

Irish Channel Action Foundation
Kingsley House
National Council of Jewish Women (Florida Family Center)
St. Thomas Tenant's Council

Key Subgroups in the Desire Area

Better Citizens 5000
CEP Eighteen
Clouet and Peoples Improvement Group
Concerned Parents
Keystone Terrace Improvement Association
Liberty Terrace Improvement Association
Lockett Area Improvement Association
Metropolitan Street Improvement Association
Students for Human Advancement and Community
Welfare Rights Organization

Key Subgroups in the Irish Channel

Fourth Street Block Council
Rousseau Street Block Council
St. James Block Council
St. Thomas Neighborhood Council
Tchoupitoulas Neighborhood Council
Wednesday Morning Coffee Hour

APPENDIX 4

Total Community Action and Leadership Development: A Selective List

Person	*Position with TCA*	*Eventual Positions*
James Singleton	President, CCEOC; President TCA	President and member-at-large, New Orleans City Council
Maurice "Moon" Landrieu	NOCEOP Advisor; TCA Board Member	New Orleans mayor; secretary of HUD; appeals court judge
Ernest "Dutch" Morial	TCA Board Member; NOLAC	First black state legislator since nineteenth century; first black mayor of New Orleans
Sidney Barthelemy	New Careers administrative assistant	Second black mayor of New Orleans; first black state senator since Reconstruction; city council member-at-large; Director City Department of Welfare; Director of Family Health's Parent/Child Center
Johnny Ford	Recruitment and training	First black mayor of Tuskegee, Alabama; state legislator, Alabama
Dorothy Mae Taylor	CCEOC; TARC; Director of Central City Neighborhood Health Center	First black female legislator in Louisiana history; secretary of Louisiana Department of Urban and Community Affairs; first black woman on City Council
Terrence Duvernay	NYC assistant manager	First black chief administrative officer of New Orleans; assistant secretary of HUD

Person	Position with TCA	Eventual Positions
Sherman Copelin	On-the-Job Training Slot coordinator	Assessor; state legislator
Johnny Jackson Jr.	Community worker I	State legislator; city council member
Theodore Marchand	LNW Neighborhood Council	State legislator; prominent contractor
Henry Braden IV	On-the-Job Training coordinator	State legislator
Naomi White-Warren	Founder of SHAC	State legislator
William Rousselle	TCA clerical worker	Deputy Director of New Orleans HRC; national journalist; television reporter
Robert Tucker	New Careers slot developer	Assistant to the mayor
Rev. Avery Alexander	CCEOC	State legislator
Ed Lombard	President, Algiers-Fischer Community Organization	Clerk of criminal court
Irma Dixon	Head Start social worker	State legislator; Public Service Commissioner
Carolyn Green-Ford	Central City NDC director	President, Orleans Parish School Board
Donald Hubbard	Desire NDC director	Prominent businessman and political insider

Godchaux to Schiro, 17 July 1964, Folder Economic Opportunity Program, Box 10, 1964, SC; "Roster," ibid; "Total Community Action, Inc." Folder TCA, Box 30, 1964, ibid.; TCA, *A History of the Community Action Movement in New Orleans, 1964–2001*, 33–54.

APPENDIX 5

Local Institutions Involved with Model Cities Programs in New Orleans

Public Institutions

Board of Levee Commissioners of the Orleans Levee District
Charity Hospital
Housing Authority of New Orleans
Louisiana Commission on Aging
Louisiana Department of Education
Louisiana Department of Hospitals
Louisiana Department of Institutions
Louisiana Department of Public Welfare
Louisiana Division of Employment Security (LDES)
Louisiana State Board of Health
Orleans Parish School Board
Sewerage and Water Board of New Orleans
Youth Opportunity Center of the LDES

Private Institutions

Archdiocesan School Board
Associated Catholic Charities
Berean Community Center
Children's Bureau of New Orleans
Citizens Housing Council of Greater New Orleans
Family Service Society
Orleans Neighborhood Centers
Peoples Methodist Community Center
Salvation Army
Social Welfare Planning Council
TCA
10 Local Universities and School Systems
Travelers Aid Society
Tuberculosis Association of Greater New Orleans

United Cerebral Palsy
Urban League
YMCA

New Orleans City Planning Commission, *Model Cities Application*; CDA, *Comprehensive Demonstration Plan*, 49.

APPENDIX 6
Model Cities Projects in New Orleans

Programs Funded through 1973

Community schools
Success in Reading
Home Start
Environmental Health
Health services clinics
Day care centers for mentally retarded
Educational day care centers
Desire Community Center
Concentrated Code Enforcement
Relocation payments
Modern street improvement
Desire Citizen Participation
Lower Ninth Ward Citizen Participation
Central City Citizen Participation
Program administration

Programs with Funding Terminated in or before 1973

Bonding, Working Capital, and Technical Assistance for Minority Contractors
School for High School Dropouts (Thugs United)
Undergraduate Social Welfare
Comprehensive Health Planning
Home Health Services
Narcotics Addiction Treatment
Free Breakfast
Food Stamp Program Administration
Better Young Men's Boys Club
Model Neighborhood Area Resident Recruitment and Training
Para-Professional Health Worker Training and Education
Desire Credit Union

Central City Credit Union
Ninth Ward Credit Union
Press Park Homes
Central City Housing Development Corporation
Desire Housing Development Corporation
Lower Ninth Ward Housing Development Corporation
Central Relocation Agency
Metro-Link Community Design Center
Interim Assistance

Programs Proposed

Curriculum Change
Home Aids for Mentally Retarded
Social Services Outreach
Model Neighborhood Area Cultural Needs Study
Release on Recognizance of Bond
Council for Minority Economic Development
The Greater New Orleans Trust
Land Write Down
Neighborhood Assistance
Youth Study Center Program
Flint-Goodridge Hospital Services and Plans for the Future
Girl Scout Services
Dental and Eye Services for Central City Residents
Model Neighborhood Law Office
Central City Construction Training
Dashiki Project Theater

Programs Suspended or Closed out in 1973

Certified Area
Open-space land parks in cities
Comprehensive day care center construction
Swimming pool construction
Land acquisition and development
Taylor playground swimming pool and bath house construction
Development of agriculture playground
Improvement to Richard Lee playground
Zion City Improvement Phase I
Zion City Improvement Phase II

Central City Neighborhood Facility Complex
Neighborhood Facilities grant (Desire-Florida)

New Orleans City Planning Commission, *Model Cities Application*; CDA, *Comprehensive Demonstration Plan*, 49; CDA, *Comprehensive Demonstration Plan*, "Part II, Projects," 1–325.

APPENDIX 7

Selective List of African American Appointments and Contracting in the Landrieu Administration and Related Programs

Person	Position/Location	Other Affiliations
Robert Tucker	Executive Assistant to the mayor	COUP; Alumnus of Cohen High School, Clark University in Atlanta, previously with New Careers program and head of Interracial Council for Black Opportunities (ICBO)
Terrence Duvernay	Chief Administrative Officer for City Hall; Director of Operations for Model Cities, Director of Model Cities	Alumnus of Cohen High School and Dillard University, previously assistant director of TCA's Neighborhood Youth Corps, future deputy secretary of HUD
Sherman Copelin	Deputy Director of Model Cities, Director of Model Cities, head of Superdome Services, Inc.	SOUL, alumnus of St. Augustine High School and Dillard University, TCA Manpower programs, Lower Ninth Ward Feasibility Survey
James Singleton	Special Assistant on Health Matters	BOLD, TCA president, Central City Economic Opportunity Committee, Southern University Alumnus
Sidney Barthelemy	TCA; Director of City Department of Health	COUP, TCA Manpower programs, future mayor of New Orleans
Clyde T. J. McHenry	Director of ICBO, then Director of HANO	COUP

Person	Position/Location	Other Affiliations
William Rousselle	Deputy Director of the Human Relations Committee	BOLD, Free Southern Theater, TCA clerical worker
Daniel Vincent	Director of Total Community Action	SOUL, army veteran, Alumnus of Southern University, an engineer from NASA's Michoud facility
Nils Douglas	Counsel to Housing Authority of New Orleans (HANO), counsel to Family Health Foundation, contract for Superdome Services, Inc.	SOUL, president of Desire Community Development Corporation, civil rights attorney of the firm Collins, Douglas, and Elie
Donald Hubbard	Director of Youth Opportunities Program; Family Health Foundation; Superdome Services, Inc.; Cultural Resources Committee	SOUL, TCA, chair of Concerned Citizens on Police Matters Committee
Caston C. Elie	Public Relations Department	Brother of prominent civil rights attorney and informal Landrieu advisor Lolis E. Elie
Ed Lombard	Secretary, Utilities Department	Algiers-Fischer Community Organization (president)
Charles Elloie	Director of Federal Programs	COUP
Gerard Douglas	Director of Comprehensive Area Manpower Planning System (CAMPS)	COUP
George Cachere	Director of the New Careers Program	COUP
Andrew Peter Sanchez	Director of Property Management	SOUL, educator; CIA board member
King Wells Deputy	Director of Community Improvement Agency (CIA)	SOUL

Person	Position/Location	Other Affiliations
Emmet Moten	Director of Policy Planning	SOUL
Charles Brown	Director of Neighborhood Rehabilitation Program	SOUL
Arthur Simmons	Director of Youth Opportunities	SOUL, president of the Desire-Florida Educational Association; Southern University alumnus
Sidney Cates	Deputy Chief of Police; Federal Programs Officer	Xavier University alumnus
Henry Simmons	City financial officer, Federal Programs	
Eunice Carter	Executive secretary to mayor	
Michael Starks	City Attorney's office	
Alvin Jones	City Attorney's office	
James W. Lee Jr.	Community Improvement Agency	BOLD
Cecil Carter Jr.	Director, Human Relations Committee	COUP, Urban League, Loyola University Institute of Politics; accountant
Robert "Skip" Perkins	Architectural contracts	Prominent local architect
Clarence Barney	Delgado Community College Board of Trustees	Director, Urban League of Greater New Orleans
Reynard Rochon	Board member of HANO	SOUL
J.A. Blaine DeJoie Jr.	Upper Pontalba Commission	*Louisiana Weekly*; People's Life Insurance
Rev. Earl Hausey	Audubon Park Commission	In 1969, first black minister to open City Council meeting with a prayer
Millie Charles	City Board of Welfare	Faculty member of Southern University in New Orleans
Clementine Brumfield	City Board of Welfare	President of the New Orleans Welfare Rights Organization

Person	Position/Location	Other Affiliations
Edgar Poree	Parkway and Park Commission	Director of TCA's Neighborhood Youth Corps
Alton Glapion	Community Improvement Agency commissioner	Mortician
Rev. Edward Kennedy	Upper Pontalba Commission	
Andrew Douglas	Audubon Park Commission	
Wallace Young	New Orleans Public Library Board	
Rudolph McLeod	Railroad Terminal Board	
Irma Braden	Vieux Carré Commission	
Dr. Langston Reed	Regional Planning Commission	
Dr. Emile Riley Jr.	Board of Health	
Marcus Neustadter	Mardi Gras Advisory Committee	
Seven individuals	Sports Advisory Committee	

This table is not an exhaustive listing of African Americans involved in the Landrieu administration. Eunice Carter to Harvey Britton, 1970, Folder New Orleans Committee Memberships, Box 55, NAACP Field Office Records, ARC; Bill Rushton, "Presenting: The City Hall MOONSQUAD!" *VCC*, 8–14 December 1972; David Chandler, "Slicing Up the Cake," June 1974, 52–58; Bourg, "Involvement—Common Ground for Key Leaders," *NOSI*, 14 February 1973; Moon Landrieu, interview by Kent Germany, 4 June 2001; TCA, *A History of the Community Action Movement in New Orleans, 1964–2001*, 33–54.

NOTES

Abbreviations

ARC	Amistad Research Center
BC	Hale Boggs Collection, Tulane University Libraries
CDA	City Demonstration Agency Collection, New Orleans Public Library
CRC	Community Relations Council Collection, Amistad Research Center
CSC	Community Services Collection, University of New Orleans
FST	Free Southern Theater Collection, Amistad Research Center
HC	Edward Hébert Collection, Tulane University Libraries
Hill-LSU	Hill Memorial Library, Louisiana State University, Baton Rouge, Louisiana
HRC	Human Relations Committee Collection, New Orleans Public Library
LACOLL	Louisiana Collection, Tulane University Libraries
LAWK	*The Louisiana Weekly*
LBJL	Lyndon B. Johnson Library
LC	Winston Lill Collection, Tulane University Libraries
LU	Loyola University, Monroe Library, Department of Special Collections
LWV	League of Women Voters Collection, Tulane University Libraries
NACCD	National Advisory Commission on Civil Disorders
NARA	National Archives and Records Administration
NOPL	New Orleans Public Library, Louisiana Division, City Archives and Special Collections
NOSI	*New Orleans States-Item*
NOTP	*New Orleans Times-Picayune*
NYT	*New York Times*
PEC	Political Ephemera Collection, Tulane University Libraries
PRS	Public Relations Series, Schiro Collection, New Orleans Public Library

SC   Schiro Collection, New Orleans Public Library
TUL   Tulane University Libraries
UA   University Archives, Tulane University Libraries
UNO   University of New Orleans, Earl K. Long Memorial Library,
            Special Collections
VCC   . *Vieux Carré Courier*
WP   *Washington Post*

Introduction: Something New for the South?

1. Goodwin, *Remembering America*, 258.

2. Louis, Bowles, and Grace, *Study of Racial Attitudes*, 4–9; City Demonstration Agency [CDA], *Comprehensive Demonstration Plan*, 12–58; New Orleans City Planning Commission, *Model Cities Application*, 13 and 36–44; Report, Folder United Fund, Box 55, NAACP Field Office Records, Amistad Research Center [hereafter cited as ARC]; Bobo, *The New Orleans Economy*, 63–64.

3. *New York Times* [hereafter cited as *NYT*], 20, 21, and 22 September 1947.

4. Roy Reed, "Louisiana House for Tighter Definition," *NYT*, 4 June 1970; *The Louisiana Weekly* [hereafter cited as *LAWK*], 27 June 1970; *Washington Post* [hereafter cited as *WP*], 21 June 1970, 24 June 1970; Jo Ann Carrigan, *The Saffron Scourge*.

5. Campanella, *Time and Place in New Orleans*, 37–81; Spain, "Race Relations and Residential Segregation in New Orleans," 82–96.

6. Hirsch, "The Mayorality of Dutch Morial," 461–84.

7. *Public Papers of the Presidents of the United States, 1963–1964, Volume I*, Lyndon B. Johnson, "Annual Message to the Congress on the State of the Union," 8 January 1964, 113–14; "Remarks at the University of Michigan," 22 May 1964, ibid., 704–7.

8. *Public Papers of the Presidents, 1965, Volume I*, Lyndon B. Johnson, "Special Message to the Congress: The American Promise," 15 March 1965, 281–87; James Harvey Kerns, "Facing the Facts of the Racial Relations Dilemma in New Orleans, Louisiana, 1964," Folder Urban League of Greater New Orleans Serials, Box 64, Community Services Council Collection—Accession Number 34, Department of Special Collections, Earl K. Long Memorial Library [Community Services Council Collection, hereafter cited as CSC].

9. Sheldon Hackney, *Populism to Progressivism in Alabama*; C. Vann Woodward, *Origins of the New South, 1877–1913*, 369.

10. Civil rights pioneer and labor leader A. Philip Randolph called the passage of civil rights legislation a "crisis of victory." August Meier and John H. Bracey Jr., "The NAACP as a Reform Movement," 29.

11. Recently, statistical analyses of improvement, elaborate criticism of black leaders who "sold out," and penetrating expositions on the failures of urban regimes have given us a glimpse of the complications of inclusion. Reed, *Stirrings in the Jug*; Browning, Marshall, and Tabb, *Protest Is not Enough*; Stone, *Regime Politics*.

12. A search of the Proquest Historical Newspaper database reveals that the term *Great Society* appeared in over 2,500 articles in the *New York Times* and *Washington Post* between 1964 and 1966, in over 1,050 between 1967 and 1970, and in over 430 between 1971 and 1974. From 1950 to 1963, the combination had appeared only 58 times.

13. Anonymous black leader quoted in Clarence "Bombay" Smith, "The Common Man's Political Analysis," *Black PAC Epitath*, 11 August 1972, Political Ephemera Collection [hereafter cited as PEC], Department of Special Collections, Tulane University Libraries [hereafter cited as TUL].

14. John Egerton's *The Americanization of Dixie: The Southernization of America* was one of the first and most important identifiers of this regional/national dynamic. Other works are Applebome, *Dixie Rising*; Dan Carter, *The Politics of Rage*; Cochran, *Democracy Heading South*; Jacqueline Jones, *The Dispossessed*; Lemann, *The Promised Land*; Rae, *Southern Democrats*; Glaser, *Race, Campaign Politics, and the Realignment of the South*.

15. Bobo, *The New Orleans Economy*, 4–25.

16. There is some confusion over the origins of this statement about losing the South. Bill Moyers's account claims that the president made this statement to him following the signing of the Civil Rights Act. Lady Bird Johnson and Harry MacPherson trace the statement to the Voting Rights Act. Moyers, "Second Thoughts"; Jarboe, "Lady Bird Looks Back," 117; MacPherson and Valenti, "Achilles in the White House," 92.

17. President Lyndon B. Johnson to Hubert Humphrey and Walter Reuther, 2:31 p.m., 25 August 1964, Citation #5181, Tape WH6408.36, Recordings of Telephone Conversations—White House Series, Recordings and Transcripts of Conversations and Meetings, LBJL [hereafter cited as Recordings, LBJL].

18. Cash, *The Mind of the South*; Bartley, *The New South, 1945–1980*, 38–73 and 105–87; Sosna, *In Search of the Silent South*; Singal, *The War Within*; Hobson, *But Now I See* and *Tell About the South*; Goodwyn, *Democratic Promise*.

19. Odum, *Race and Rumors of Race*; Reed and Singal, eds., *Regionalism and the South*.

20. Schulman, *From Cotton Belt to Sunbelt*.

21. For an argument that American politics was dominated by a three-tiered Democratic regime after the New Deal, see Plotke, *Building a Democratic Political Order*.

22. Sullivan, *Days of Hope*; Carlton and Coclanis, "Another 'Great Migration,'" 37–62.

23. Some of these leaders included Frank Porter Graham of the University of North Carolina, Governor Jim Folsom of Alabama, Senator and then Supreme Court Justice Hugo Black of Alabama, Governor Earl K. Long of Louisiana, state senator and then Governor Terry Sanford of North Carolina, Senator Ralph Yarborough of Texas, and to some extent, Senator Lyndon Johnson of Texas.

24. See appendix 4, Total Community Action and Leadership Development, A Selective List.

25. Fairclough, *Race and Democracy*, 265–343; Rogers, *Righteous Lives*, 110–46.

26. The EOA created the framework for the Community Action Program, Volunteers in Service to America (VISTA), Head Start, Legal Services, the Job Corps, and the Neighborhood Youth Corps. Other key elements were the Neighborhood Development Centers, the college Work-Study program, Upward Bound, small business loan programs, remedial education projects, health care centers, and credit unions.

27. Readers are referred to the following web site to calculate equivalent dollar amounts for all those listed in this book: http://data.bls.gov/cgi-bin/cpicalc.pl. For amounts in excess of ten thousand dollars ($10,000), move the decimal point for the calculation, then reinsert the appropriate number of zeros (e.g., for $100,000 calculate $100, then add three zeros to the result to correctly place the decimal point).

28. This study recognizes that there was no single "African American interest" or "liberal interest" and that, instead, there were multiple competing interests and ideas. See Reed Jr., *Stirrings in the Jug*, 1–51, for criticism of African American leaders who he believed came to serve corporate interests over the interests of black working people.

29. Michael Brown and Steven Erie refer to a "social welfare economy" expanded by the Great Society, and the journalist Nicholas Lemann writes about the impressions of the role of the Great Society in girding the economy of Mississippi Delta communities. In this book's usage, the Great Society marketplace is a much broader enterprise that involves the political and economic exchanges involved in accumulation and distribution of Great Society funding. Brown and Erie, "Blacks and the Legacy of the Great Society," 299–330; Lemann, *The Promised Land*, 329–39.

30. This Soft State developed from the Community Action Program, Head Start, the Model Cities program, the Food Stamp Program, Volunteers in Service to America (VISTA), various job training programs, and Urban Renewal. Some

of the local bodies either created or expanded by this state-building were Total Community Action, Inc., the Social Welfare Planning Council, the New Orleans Legal Assistance Corporation, the New Orleans Human Relations Committee, the City Demonstration Agency (Model Cities), the Housing Authority of New Orleans (HANO), and the Community Improvement Agency (Urban Renewal). Besides the OEO, the U.S. Departments of Labor, Agriculture, Housing and Urban Development (HUD), and Health, Education, and Welfare (HEW) were the chief federal institutions involved. At varying times, civic, academic, religious, and other local organizations factored into the arrangements.

31. Moynihan, *Maximum Feasible Misunderstanding*.

32. Lemann, *The Promised Land*, 340–53.

33. Dewey, "The Ethics of Democracy."

34. See Herman, *The Romance of American Psychology*; Polsky, *The Rise of the Therapeutic State*; Alice O'Connor, *Poverty Knowledge*; Scott, *Contempt and Pity*; Morris, "Selling Service."

35. *Public Papers of the Presidents of the United States, 1963–1964, Volume 1*, Lyndon B. Johnson, 1964, "Remarks at the University of Michigan," 22 May 1964, 528.

Part One. A War on Poverty, Segregation, and Alienation, 1964–1974

1. John Steinbeck, *Travels with Charley*, 194–97.

2. Rockwell's painting appeared in *Look* magazine.

3. *NYT*, 17 November 1960.

Chapter One. A European-African-Caribbean-American-Southern City

1. Haas, *DeLesseps S. Morrison*, 42–65, 156–57.

2. New Orleans City Planning Commission, *Model Cities Application*; Bobo, *The New Orleans Economy*, 30–32; Haas, *DeLesseps S. Morrison*, 57.

3. Raabe, "Status and Its Impact"; Chai, "Who Rules New Orleans," 2–11.

4. *New Orleans Times-Picayune* [hereafter cited as *NOTP*], 11 March 1970 and 12 October 1969, as quoted in Raabe, "Status and Its Impact," 18–19.

5. Raabe, "Status and Its Impact," 112–16.

6. There is speculation that Long was also struck by the ricochet of a bullet from his bodyguards.

7. Haas, *DeLesseps S. Morrison*, 7, 124–39, 218.

8. Frederick Douglas Wright, "Black Political Participation in Louisiana," 43.

9. Bell, *The Afro-Creole Protest Tradition in Louisiana*.

10. Haas, *Political Leadership in a Southern City*; Haas, "Political Continuity in the Crescent City," 5–18; Joy Jackson, *New Orleans in the Gilded Age*.

11. On 30 May 1958, Federal District Judge J. Skelly Wright ordered the desegregation of public transportation in New Orleans. Golf courses, the public library, and recreation were also desegregated under Morrison. Haas, *DeLesseps S. Morrison*, 252–56.

12. Haas, *DeLesseps S. Morrison*, 98–282, 284–88; Haas, "The Expedient of Race," 5–29; Haas, "Victor H. Schiro, Hurricane Betsy and the 'Forgiveness Bill,'" 71–72; Folder CCDA and Folder CRDO, Box 23, Public Relations Series [hereafter cited as PRS], Mayor Victor H. Schiro Collection, City Archives, New Orleans Public Library [hereafter cited as SC]; Folder CCDA, Box 9, 1964, SC.

13. Raabe, "Status and Its Impact," 17, 191–99; Chai, "Who Rules New Orleans," 2–11. See also O'Brien, "The New Orleans Carnival Organizations"; Koolsbergen, "A Study in Popular Culture"; Jeffers, "Bank Asset Portfolios and Economic Activity."

14. See Malone, *Rabbi Max Heller*; Powell, *Troubled Memory*.

15. Louis, Bowles, and Grace, *Study of Racial Attitudes*, 4.

16. As quoted in Trillin, "The Zulus," 66.

17. Rohrer and Edmonson, *The Eighth Generation Grows Up*, 22–26, 59; Daniel Thompson, *The Negro Leadership Class*, 16–53.

18. James Harvey Kerns, "Facing the Facts of the Racial Relations Dilemma in New Orleans, Louisiana, 1964," Folder Urban League of Greater New Orleans Serials, Box 64, CSC, University of New Orleans. [Hereafter referred to as "Kerns, 'Facing the Facts.'"]

19. Hirsch, "The Mayorality of Dutch Morial," 468–69.

20. Kerns, "Facing the Facts"; SWPC, "School Dropout and Youth Employment Committee," December 1963, Unlabeled green folder, Unprocessed Box 39, CSC.

21. SWPC, "Report of Committee on Human Relations, June 1964," 30 July 1964, Folder Human Relations, 1962–1970, Box 77, CSC.

22. Kerns, "Facing the Facts."

23. SWPC, "School Dropout and Youth Employment Committee."

24. Norman Francis, in Urban League of Greater New Orleans, "28th Annual Report," 1965, Folder ULGNO Serials, Box 64, CSC.

25. Locally, 34,622 were "deteriorating" and 14,159 "dilapidated." Bobo, *Statistical Abstract of Louisiana*, 252; SWPC *Reports*, 1 December 1964, Folder 16, Box 3, Winston Lill Collection, TUL [hereafter referred to as LC]; *LAWK*, 4 April 1964.

26. Allen Dowling, HANO Tenant Relations Advisor, to Harry P. Gamble Jr., attorney, 4 March 1964, Folder Housing I, Box 64, SC; Haas, *DeLesseps S. Morrison*, 172–74.

27. Fairclough, *Race and Democracy*, 271–84; Rogers, *Righteous Lives*, 77–94.

28. *Dombrowski v. Pfister*, 380 U.S. 479 (1965); Frank T. Adams, *James A. Dombrowki*, 262–76.

29. Rogers, *Righteous Lives*, 74–79, 26–30; Tyler, *Silk Stockings and Ballot Boxes*, 203–37.

30. *WP*, 9 November 1960.

31. *WP*, 15 July 1971.

32. *LAWK*, 26 September 1964; 8 May 1965; 15 May 1965; 22 May 1965; 31 July 1965; 18 August 1964; 29 August 1964.

33. Senator Russell B. Long, *Washington Newsletter*, 1 May 1964, in Folder Civil Rights, Box 22, PRS, SC.

34. Public Relations Release, 1964, Folder Race Relations (#1), Box 32, PRS, SC.

35. Ibid.

36. *NYT*, 1 November 1963; Fairclough, *Race and Democracy*, 234–64; Rogers, *Righteous Lives*, 91–93, 101; Baker, *The Second Battle of New Orleans*, 394–436; Adams, *James A. Dombrowki*, 263.

Chapter Two. Establishing the Early War on Poverty

1. SWPC, "School Dropout and Youth Employment Committee," December 1963, Unlabeled green folder, Unprocessed Box 39, CSC.

2. TCA, "Information Item," Folder 15, Box 3, LC.

3. Bobo, *Statistical Abstract of Louisiana*, 36–37, 97, 98.

4. Katz, *In the Shadow of the Poorhouse* and *Poverty and Policy in American History*.

5. Dupont, "Regular Democrats and Reformers in New Orleans, 1896–1912"; Elna Green, "National Trends, Regional Differences, Local Circumstances: Social Welfare in New Orleans, 1870s–1920s," in *Before the New Deal*, Green ed., 81–99; Vandal, "The Nineteenth-Century Municipal Responses," 30–60; Wisner, *Public Welfare Administration in Louisiana* and *Social Welfare in the South*; Moran, "Public Relief in Louisiana, 369–70.

6. Carleton, *Politics and Punishment*.

7. Wisner, *Public Welfare Administration*, and *Social Welfare in the South*; Moran, "Public Relief in Louisiana," 371–85; Clement, "Children and Charity," 337–51; Gail S. Murray, "Poverty and Its Relief in the Antebellum South."

8. Guyol, "A Center of Brightness," 1–3; Jerrie Mary O'Connor, "A Study of 49 Unmarried Mothers"; Charles E. "Pie" Dufour, *The Years of the Women's Christian Exchange*.

9. Moran, "Public Relief," 369–85; Field, "The Politics of the New Deal in Louisiana"; MacLachlan, "Up From Paternalism"; Smith, *The New Deal in the Urban South*; Schulman, *From Cotton Belt to Sunbelt*; Quadagno, *The Transformation of Old Age Security*.

10. Galbraith, *The Affluent Society*; Harrington, *The Other America*; Caudill, *Night Comes to the Cumberlands*; Matusow, *The Unraveling of America*, 5–10, 119; Bernstein, *Guns or Butter*; Parris and Brooks, *Blacks in the City*, 410–21.

11. "Objects and Purposes of the Citizen's Housing Council of Greater New Orleans," Folder Citizen's Housing Council, Box 6, 1964, SC.

12. Transcript, Walter Heller Oral History Interview I, 20 February 1970, by David McComb, LBJL, 17–21; Gillette, *Launching the War on Poverty*, 1–25; Alice O'Connor, *Poverty Knowledge*, 127–32.

13. President Johnson and Sargent Shriver, 1 February 1964, Citation #1804, Tape WH 6402.01; Citation #1807, Tape WH6402.01; Citation #1809, Tape WH; Citation #1815, Tape WH, Recordings, LBJL.

14. *Public Papers of the Presidents of the United States, 1965*, Lyndon B. Johnson, 1965, 2, "Annual Message to the Congress on the State of the Union," 4 January 1965; Conkin, *Big Daddy from the Pedernales*; Kearns, *Lyndon Johnson and the American Dream*.

15. See Lasch, *The True and Only Heaven*.

16. *Public Papers of the Presidents, 1963–1964, Volume 2*, Lyndon B. Johnson, 648, "Remarks at a Fundraising Dinner in New Orleans," 9 October 1964; ibid., *Volume 1*, "Remarks at University of Michigan," 22 May 1964.

17. Goodwin, *Remembering America*, 272–92, quotes from 273, 277, and 291–92.

18. *Public Papers of the Presidents, 1965*, Lyndon B. Johnson, 2, "Annual Message to the Congress on the State of the Union," 4 January 1965; Davies, *From Opportunity to Entitlement*, 236 and 243.

19. *Public Papers of the Presidents, 1963–1964, Volume 1*, Lyndon B. Johnson, "Remarks at University of Michigan," 22 May 1964.

20. *Public Papers of the Presidents, 1963–1964, Volume 1*, Lyndon B. Johnson, 1964, 219, "Special Message to the Congress Proposing a Nationwide War on the Sources of Poverty," 16 March 1964.

21. President Lyndon Johnson and Walker Stone, 6 January 1964, in Germany and Johnson, *The Kennedy Assassination*, 179.

22. President Johnson and Robert Anderson, 7 January 1964, in Germany and Johnson, *The Kennedy Assassination*, 235–36.

23. President Johnson and Elliott Bell, 25 January 1965, in Germany and Johnson, *The Kennedy Assassination*, 870.

24. President Johnson and Richard Daley, 20 January 1964, in Germany and Johnson, *The Kennedy Assassination*, 651.

25. One of the quickest but most effective narratives of the bill's passage is *Congressional Quarterly Almanac*, vol. 20, 1964, 208–29. See also Matusow, *The Unraveling of America*, 97–130, 217–74; Bernstein, *Guns or Butter*, 93–113; Dallek, *Flawed Giant*, 60–80; Gillette, *Launching the War on Poverty*, 113–64.

26. Stern Grant Report, 1966, Folder Stern, Box 55, CSC.

27. Corliss, handwritten notes, n.d., after 29 July 1964, Folder TCA I, Box 55, CSC.

28. Ibid.; Notes, 14 May 1964, Folder TCA I, Box 55, CSC.

29. Daniel A. Ellis, coordinator Mayor's Youth Committee, to Shriver, 26 May 1964, Folder TCA I, Box 55, CSC; Shriver to Ellis, 10 June 1964, Folder Poverty Bill, Box 23, 1964, SC.

30. Corliss, handwritten notes, n.d., after 29 July 1964, Folder TCA I, Box 55, CSC.

31. Dufour, *Darwin Fenner: A Life of Service*.

32. Corliss, handwritten notes, n.d., after 29 July 1964, Folder TCA I, Box 55, CSC.

33. Corliss to Thomas Godchaux, 11 June 1964, Folder Stern, Box 55, CSC; "Minutes: Special Meeting of the Board of Directors," 19 June 1964, Folder Board of Director, 1964–1965. Box II C, CSC.

34. Corliss, handwritten notes, n.d., after 29 July 1964, Folder TCA I, Box 55, CSC.

35. "Procedural Recommendations," Folder TCA I, Box 55, CSC; Godchaux to Schiro, 17 July 1964, Folder Economic Opportunity Program, Box 10, 1964, SC.

36. Hale Boggs, in *Congressional Record*, 12 September 1969.

37. Godchaux to Members of Leadership Group Considering Economic Opportunity Act, "A Summary of Economic Opportunity Act of 1964," and "Summary of Title II Provisions," 14 July 1964, Folder Economic Opportunity Program, Box 10, 1964, SC.

38. In a bargain with southerners, Johnson dumped Adam Yarmolinsky, one of the chief architects of the War on Poverty who was expected to be the assistant director under Sargent Shriver and handle day-to-day operations of the OEO. Though apparently not related, Louisiana native Gillis Long became an assistant director shortly after the sacrificing of Yarmolinsky. Gillette, *Launching the War on Poverty*, 132–40.

39. President Johnson and Bill Moyers, 7 August 1964, Citation #4817, WH6408.12, Recordings, LBJL; President Johnson, Bill Moyers, and Walter Jenkins, 8 August 1964, Citations #4823 and #4824, WH6408.13, ibid.

40. O. C. W. Taylor, "President's Visit Hailed as 'Triumph,'" *LAWK*, 17 October 1964; Roman Heleniak, "Lyndon Johnson in New Orleans," 263–75; *Public Papers of the Presidents, 1963–1964, Volume 2*, "Remarks Upon Arrival of the

'Lady Bird Special'," 1278–79; "Remarks at a Fundraising Dinner in New Orleans," October 9, 1964, 1281–88.

41. Unlabeled Report, in Folder Poverty Bill, Box 23, 1964, SC; SWPC *Reports*, 1 December 1964, unprocessed Box 39, CSC.

42. "Schedule for Messrs. Lemann and Lill," Folder 14, Box 1, LC; Lill to Members NOCOEP, 16 September 1964, Folder Economic Opportunity Program, Box 10, 1964, SC; Iris Kelso, interview by Anne Ritchie, 17 February 1991, found in the National Press Club Foundation Library, Washington, D.C., p. 50.

43. "Preamble," Folder Total Community Action, Box 30, 1964, SC; Lee Stinnett, "War on Poverty Takes First Real Steps Here," *NOTP*, 9 December 1964.

44. For an explanation of the governor's authority, see Renwick, "The Governor"; Louisiana Legislature, *The Government of Louisiana*.

45. *NYT*, 13 May 1964.

46. Editorial, "How's That Again Governor?" *LAWK*, 12 June 1964.

47. Ibid.

48. William J. Dodd, Louisiana State Superintendent of Education, to Boggs, 17 December 1964, Folder Federal Agencies—OEO III, 1965 Subject Files, BC.

49. Louisiana State Economic Opportunity Office, *Handbook for Board Members*, 31–33.

50. Andrew, *Lyndon Johnson and the Great Society*, 79; Ashmore, "Carry It On."

51. Fairclough, *Race and Democracy*, 338; Baker, *The Second Battle of New Orleans*; Dodd, Louisiana Superintendent of Education, to Boggs, 17 December 1964, Federal Agencies—OEO III folder, 1965 Subject files, BC; "Joint Statement of Senator Russell B. Long and Congressman Hale Boggs," 1 April 1965, Folder Federal Agencies—OEO II, ibid.

52. James R. Oliver, President of the Louisiana Council on Human Relations, to Governor John McKeithen, 8 March 1965, Folder Louisiana Community Action Program, Box 31, Series E4, RG 381, NARA; Hubert H. Humphrey to James R. Oliver, 23 March 1965, ibid.

53. Willie W. Thompson, President of Seventh Ward Civic and Political Improvement League; Rev. Edward D. Hilliard; Rev. Zebadee Bridges, President Seventh Ward Ministry Alliance, to Boggs, 15 January 1965, Folder Federal Agencies—OEO II folder, 1965 Subject files, BC; Willie W. Thompson, Rev. Edward Hilliard, and Rev. Zebadee Bridges to Shriver, 15 January 1965, Folder Federal Agencies OEO III, 1965 Subject Files, BC; *LAWK*, 9 January 1965.

54. Ben A. Franklin, "Race Issue Snags Aid to Louisiana," *NYT*, 5 March 1965.

55. Baker to Boggs, 7 January 1965, Folder Federal Agencies OEO III, 1965 Subject Files, BC, TUL.

56. Baker to Hébert, 22 March 1965, Folder OEO, Box 10, Edward Hébert Collection, TUL [hereafter cited as HC] and Hébert to Shriver, 26 March 1965, ibid.

57. *LAWK*, 20 March 1965.

58. Baker to Ernest Morial, et al., 12 March 1965, Folder Louisiana Community Action Program, Box 31, Series E4, RG 381, NARA; *LAWK*, 27 March 1965; Ben A. Franklin, "Race Issue Snags Aid to Louisiana," *NYT*, 5 March 1965.

59. Tapp, "The Gubernatorial Election of 1964," 74–87; Dur and Kurtz, "North-South Changes in Louisiana Voting," 28–44; Kurtz and Peoples, *Earl K. Long*, 11–14.

60. Gillis Long to Hébert, 8 April 1965, Folder OEO, Box 10, HC; Ernest Morial, President New Orleans NAACP, to Hubert Humphrey, et al., 10 March 1965, Folder Louisiana Community Action Program, Box 31, Series E4, RG 381, NARA; Memorandum from Argyll C. to Boggs, 11 August 1966, Folder Poverty Louisiana, 1966 Subject files, BC.

61. Bill Bailey, "McKeithen Reports Clash with Shriver," Baton Rouge *Advocate*, 26 March 1965.

62. Baker to Shriver, 11 May 1965, Folder 1965 Louisiana, Box 4, Series 1030-CAP Office Records of the Director, State Files 1965–1968, RG 381, NARA; Bill Haddad to Ted Berry, 30 April 1965, ibid.; Lee Lendt to Theodore Berry, 6 August 1965, ibid.

63. *LAWK*, 29 May 1965; Samuel F. Yette, Special Assistant to the Director, to Arthur J. Chapital Sr., Executive Secretary New Orleans NAACP, 12 July 1965, Folder Louisiana Community Action Program, Box 31, Series E4, RG 381, NARA.

64. Baker to Jules Sugarman, Deputy Associate Director CAP, 26 July 1965, Folder Federal Agencies OEO I, 1965 Subject Files, BC, TUL.

65. *New Orleans States-Item* [hereafter cited as *NOSI*], 9 February 1965; *NOTP*, 10 February 1965.

66. Schiro to Shriver, 22 February 1965, Folder Economic Opportunity, Box 8, 1965, SC.

67. SWPC *Reports*, 15 January 1965; *NOTP*, 27 March 1965.

68. Corliss to Agency Executives, 4 April 1965, Folder TCA 2, Box 55, CSC; *LAWK*, 17 April 1965, 15 May 1965, 7 August 1965; Winston Lill, interview by Kent Germany, 29 April 1997, New Orleans, Louisiana, in possession of author.

69. *LAWK*, 22 August 1964.

70. Andrew Morris, "The Voluntary Sector's War on Poverty," 275–304.

71. "Work Program—Conduct and Administration," 30 September 1966, Folder Family Service Society Current 66–71, Box 25, CSC; "Project Enable," *Central City Areascope*, 23 January 1967, Folder SWPC Neighborhood Centers

1966–1968, Unprocessed Box 24, CSC; TCA, *History of the Community Action Movement*, 24.

72. Zigler and Styfco, *Head Start and Beyond*; Zigler and Valentine, *Project Head Start*; Mills, *Something Better for My Children*; Laumann, *Effects of Project Head Start, Summer 1965*; Levin, "A Decade of Policy Developments," 123–96; Jeffery, *Education for the Children of the Poor*; Graham, *The Uncertain Triumph*.

73. Martha McKay to William Haddad and Bob Clampitt, "CORE Complaints," 31 July 1965, Folder General, Box 101, Series E75, RG 381, NARA; "Project Head Start: Evaluation of Head Start Programs Sponsored by Southern Consumers' Education Foundation," ibid.; Law firm of Collins, Douglas, and Elie, to Sargent Shriver, 8 July 1966, Folder Bogalusa, Box 31, Series E4, RG 381, NARA.

74. Jack Gonzales to Ned Schnurman, "Field Inspection Report—New Orleans, Louisiana—HS#2105," 6 August 1965, Folder New Orleans, Box 102, Series 75, RG 381, NARA; Gonzalez to William F. Haddad, et al., 10 August 1965, ibid.; Carmen Donaldson, "Report," 26 April 1965, Folder Orleans Parish School Board, 1964–1966, Box 47, CSC; *LAWK*, 8 May 1965, 21 August 1965, 20 November 1965.

75. *News from the Louisiana Office of Economic Opportunity*, 19 August 1966, Folder Poverty Louisiana, 1966 Subject files, BC.

76. Allan Katz, "TCA Battles Age-Old Foe: Delay," New Orleans *State Item*, 29 May 65.

77. Hale Boggs in *Congressional Record*, 12 September 1969.

78. TCA, *History of the Community Action Movement*, 24.

79. *LAWK*, 10 April 1965, 21 August 1965.

80. *LAWK*, 10 April 1965.

81. TCA, *History of the Community Action Movement*, 22.

82. *LAWK*, 24 April 1965, 2 October 1965.

83. *LAWK*, 6 November 1965.

84. Stoddard to Public and Private Non-Profit Agencies, 8 November 1965, Folder TCA-Total Community Action (anti-poverty), Box 399, Greater New Orleans Chamber of Commerce Collection, Special Collections, Earl K. Long Memorial Library, University of New Orleans [hereafter cited as Chamber Collection, UNO].

Chapter Three. Building Community Action

1. William B. Cannon, in Gillette, *Launching the War on Poverty*, 80; Adam Yarmolinsky, ibid., 77; Jack T. Conway, ibid., 202.

2. President Johnson and Bill Moyers, 7 August 1964, Citation #4817,

WH6408.12, Recordings, LBJL; President Johnson and Dick West, 13 August 1964, Citation #4349, Tape WH6407.15, ibid.; "Speaking to You," *Central City Areascope*, April 1968.

3. Winston Lill, interview by Kent Germany, 27 April 1997; Newspaper clipping, "War on Poverty Funds and New Staff Member Florence Sytz Returns," 15 November 1965, Folder SWPC Reports and Notices of Meetings, Flyers, Invitations, etc., March, 1962–June, 1965, Unprocessed Box 39, CSC.

4. Iris Kelso, interview by Anne Ritchie, 17 February 1991, National Press Club Foundation Library, Washington, D.C., 50; NWCIL, "Meeting of the Executive Board," 10 November 1965, Folder Ninth Ward Civic and Improvement League, Box 47, CSC; TCA, *History of the Community Action Movement*, 20.

5. Rice, "In the Trenches of the War on Poverty"; Gillette, *Launching the War on Poverty*, 201–13; Matusow, *Unraveling of America*, 243–71; Ashmore, "Carry It On."

6. These numbers do not include children in Head Start, people who received social services, or residents in jobs programs. Rowena Courson, "Community Organization in Low-Income Neighborhoods in New Orleans," SWPC Project Report, December 1968, Folder Social Welfare Planning Council—Total Community Action ca. 1960s, Report Forms, Series II, Box L, CSC; Richard Haley, "Observations," 22 February 1968, Folder Board of Directors 1967–1968, Box II C, CSC.

7. Corliss to TCA Board of Directors, "Recommended Target Areas," 18 January 1965, Folder TCA 2, Box 55, CSC.

8. Maurice E. "Moon" Landrieu, interview by Kent Germany, 4 June 2001, in possession of the author.

9. Bill Rushton, TCA Urban Design Group, "Preliminary Report on Environmental Conditions in the Lower Ninth Ward Area of New Orleans: An Inventory of Physical Characteristics for Use as the Basis of Urban Design Decisions," 1 August 1968, Folder 15, Box 3, LC.

10. Levine, *Black Culture and Black Consciousness*; Gutman, *Work, Culture, and Society*; Bodnar, *The Transplanted*; Kelley, *Race Rebels*; Kusmer, *A Ghetto Stakes Shape*; Hirsch, *Making the Second Ghetto*; Clark, *Dark Ghetto*; Connolly, *A Ghetto Grows in Brooklyn*.

11. Aldon Morris, *Origins of the Civil Rights Movement*. On black ministers in New Orleans politics, see Haas, *DeLesseps S. Morrison*, 251, 258, and 282; Fairclough, *Race and Democracy*, 55–56, 211–13; Friedrichs, "The Role of the Negro Minister in Politics in New Orleans"; Hadley, "The Transformation of the Role of Black Ministers," 133–48; Wright, "Black Political Participation in Louisiana."

12. "Meeting of the Board of Directors of the Ninth Ward Civic and Im-

provement League and Representatives of the American Friends Service Committee," 16 November 1965, Folder NWCIL, Box 47, CSC; Jack Frazier, "Another Ninth Ward Project Set," *New Orleans Freedom Press*, May 1966, Folder 3, Box 48, Free Southern Theater Collection, ARC [hereafter cited as FST, ARC]; *Lower Ninth Ward Civic Center Chatter*, July 1967, SWPC Neighborhood Centers, Unprocessed Box 24, CSC.

13. Janet Moore, "Ghetto—An Exercise in Definition," *The Plain Truth*, 20 March 1970, Folder Plain Truth, PEC.

14. Arthur Cooper to Albert Rosenberg, 1 April 1966 to 19 August 1966, Folder SWPC Neighborhood Centers, 1966–1968, Unprocessed Box 24, CSC.

15. SWPC, "The Challenge We Face: Annual Report, 1964," Folder SWPC Reports and Notices of Meetings, Flyers, Invitations, etc., March 1962–June 1965, Unprocessed Box 39, CSC.

16. Clark Corliss, director of Social Welfare Planning Council, to Philip Ciaccio, city council member, 21 September 1967, Folder SWPC Neighborhood Centers, 1966–1968, Unprocessed Box 24, CSC.

17. On 1 January 1968, Haley transferred to TCA. SWPC Minutes, 17 November 1966, Folder Board of Directors 1967–1968, Box II C, CSC; Winston Lill, interview by Kent Germany, 27 April 1997; Courson, "Community Organization in Low-Income Neighborhoods in New Orleans."

18. VISTA Proposal by SWPC, July 1965, Folder Volunteers in Service to America (VISTA) 1964–1965, Box 66, CSC.

19. *LAWK*, 22 May 1965. TCA unveiled plans to add Florida, St. Bernard, the Johnson School area in Carrollton, and McDonogh 40.

20. Charles A Ferguson, "New Orleans' Central City, Life in a World Apart," *NOSI*, 5 June 1968.

21. Richard Haley, "Notes on Conference with Russell Jewert of VISTA," 29 August 1967, Folder VISTA 1966–1967, Box 66, CSC.

22. Ralph Wafer, "Crisis 1: Where Urban Renewal Is At," *VCC*, 7 October 1971.

23. Powell, "Average Income Less Than $2000," *NOSI*, 16 December 1964.

24. Bill Rushton, TCA Urban Design Group, "Preliminary Report on Environmental Conditions in the Lower Ninth Ward Area of New Orleans"; Rosemary Powell, "Average Income Less Than $2000; Worst Slums Mar Largest Ward," *NOSI*, 16 December 1964.

25. ULGNO, "A Community Organization Project—9th Ward," 20 October 1965, Folder ULGNO, 1960–71, Box 64, CSC.

26. ULGNO, "A Report on the Hurricane Betsy Disaster and the Urban League's Involvement," 30 September 1965, ULGNO Serials, Box 64, CSC.

27. "From Plantations to the Projects," *Southern Struggle* [Southern Con-

ference Education Fund], January 1977, in Oversize Box 7, FST, ARC; David Snyder, "Desire—Florida 'Target' Is Key to City Planning," *NOSI*, 3 June 1968; Corliss to TCA Board of Directors, "Recommended Target Areas," 18 January 1965, Folder TCA 2, Box 55, CSC.

28. Gilmore, "The Old New Orleans and the New," 386.

29. Corliss to TCA Board of Directors, "Proposed Role of SWPC in Community Action Program in Desire Area," 18 January 1965, Folder TCA 2, Box 55, CSC.

30. "Proposal Background," SWPC Proposal, n.d., [1965], Folder Desire, 1963–1966, Box 23, CSC.

31. Allen Dowling to Thomas C. Dent, 1 July 1966, Folder 21, Box 1, FST, ARC.

32. Ibid.

33. Mahoney, "The Changing Nature of Public Housing"; Louisiana Advisory Committee, *The Quest for Housing*; LaViolette and Taylor, *Negro Housing in New Orleans*.

34. For letters requesting placement in HANO apartments, see Folders for HANO, 1964–1968, SC.

35. Maurice d'Arlan Needham to Neighbor, 13 December 1964, Folder Federal Agencies OEO III, Subject Files, 1965, BC; Reverend John J. Vaughan, "Irish Channel Community Improvement Program," ibid.

36. "Minutes of the Meeting of the Board of Directors of Total Community Action, Inc." 21 January 1965, Folder TCA 2, Box 55, CSC.

37. T.H. Callaham, Fort Worth Director of Housing and Home Finance, to Lolis Elie, 25 March 1965, Folder Housing, Box 11, 1965, SC.

38. Rev. John J. Vaughan to Lill, 12 May 1965, Folder IC CDC, Box 28, CSC; Maurice d'Arlan Needham, Vice President ICAF, to Lill, 12 May 1965, ibid.

39. Ibid; Carolyn Kolb, "The Auld Sod on Adele Street," 9–16, 60.

40. Carolyn Kolb, "The Auld Sod on Adele Street," 9–16, 60.

41. *St. Thomas News*, August 1966, folder SWPC Neighborhood Centers 1966–1968, Unprocessed Box 24, CSC; Richard Haley, director Neighborhood development SWPC, to Ciaccio, 20 September 1967, folder SWPC Neighborhood Centers, 1966–1968, Unprocessed Box 24, CSC.

42. CCEOC Pamphlet, "Your Economic Opportunity Committee," Central City Economic Opportunity Committee Records, ARC. By 1968, the CCEOC had become a 501 c(3) nonprofit organization.

43. SWPC Minutes, 22 February 1968, Folder Board of Directors 1967–1968, Box II C, CSC; Richard Haley, "Observations," ibid.; Minutes, SWPC Board of Directors, 17 November 1966, Folder Board of Directors, 1966, Box II C, CSC.

44. Desire Area Council Meeting, 27 February 1965, Folder Desire, 1963–1966, Box 23, CSC.

45. *The Desire Digest*, May 1965, Folder Desire, 1963–1966, Box 23, CSC; *LAWK*, 1 May 1965.

46. Desire Area Community Council Flyer, 28 March 1965, Folder SWPC Reports and Notices of Meetings, Flyers, Invitations, etc., March, 1962–June, 1965, Unprocessed Box 39, CSC.

47. *LAWK*, 6 March 1965; Lydia Leblanc, Chair of DACC Health and Welfare Committee, to Joseph Giarusso, 4 April 1965, Folder Desire Area Community Council, Box 7, 1966, SC.

48. *The Desire Digest*, May 1965, Folder Desire, 1963–1966, Box 23, CSC.

49. Moweaner Mauldin to Joseph Giarrusso, 7 January 1966, Folder Desire Area Community Council, Box 7, 1966, SC; NWCIL, "Meeting of the Executive Board," 10 November 1965, Folder Ninth Ward Civic and Improvement League, Box 47, CSC.

50. Mauldin to Lill, 10 March 1966, Folder Desire Area Community Council, Box 7, 1966, SC.

51. Bivens, Chair Desire EOC, to Edmund F. Hughes, Sewerage and Water Board, 28 July 1967, Folder Economic Opportunity, Box 6, 1967, SC; Several letters in Folder NWCIL, Box 47, CSC; Don Hubbard to Schiro, 6 September 1966, Folder Central City Target Area, Box 4, 1966, SC; Duncan Waters to Ciaccio, 13 September 1966, Folder Board of Directors, 1966, Box II C, CSC; Corliss to Board, 15 September 1966, ibid.; Bivens to Edmund F. Hughes, Sewerage and Water Board, 28 July 1967, Folder Economic Opportunity, Box 6, 1967, SC; Leontine Luke to Lill, 22 November 1965, Folder NWCIL, Box 47, CSC.

52. Clouet and People's Improvement Group to Schiro, early 1967, Folder Clouet and People's Improvement Group, Box 4, 1967, SC; Minutes of Desire EOC, 21 February 1967, Folder Citizen Education Program, Box 68, League of Women Voters Collection, TUL [hereafter cited as LWV]; Pope to Haley, 9 June 1967, Folder Desire 67–68, Box 23, CSC.

53. Maurice d'Arlan Needham to Neighbor, 13 December 1964, Folder Federal Agencies OEO III, Subject Files, 1965, BC; Reverend John J. Vaughan, "Irish Channel Community Improvement Program," ibid.

54. Maurice d'Arlan Needham to Neighbor, 13 December 1964, Folder Federal Agencies OEO III, Subject Files, 1965, BC; and Reverend John J. Vaughan, "Irish Channel Community Improvement Program," ibid.

55. Arthur Cooper, "Daily Reports," 27 April 1966, Folder SWPC Neighborhood Centers, 1966–1968, Unprocessed Box 24, CSC.

56. SWPC Citizen Participation Committee, "Minutes," 6 July 1965, Folder IC CDC, Box 28, CSC; Douglas Freret et al. to Corliss, 30 November 1964, Folder Kingsley House, 1960–1964, Box 30, CSC.

57. John Wall and Elizabeth Lewis of Kingsley, Rev. Vaughan and Dr. Needham of ICAF, "Memorandum of Understanding of Cooperation in Community Organization Responsibilities for Irish Channel Economic Assistance Program, 1965–1966," 30 June 1965, Folder Kingsley House, 1960–1964, Box 30, CSC; Kingsley Board of Directors, "Minutes," 23 June 1965, Folder IC CDC, Box 28, CSC; Kingsley House report, 1969, Folder TCA Grants I-K, Box 56, CSC.

58. SWPC, "Meeting of the Civic League, Lower Ninth Ward Target Area," 18 January 1966, folder NWCIL, Box 47, CSC; other correspondence through April 1966, ibid.; *Lower Ninth Ward Civic Center Chatter*, July 1967, Folder SWPC Neighborhood Centers 1966–1968, Unprocessed Box 24, CSC.

59. George D. McCarthy, Assistant Director for Congressional Relations, OEO, to Boggs, 6 November 1967, Poverty-Louisiana-Correspondence II, Subject, 1967, BC.

60. "Summary Statement of Results of 7–1 Contract for Community Organization Program in Desire Area" 31 July 1966, folder TCA-SWPC Research Contract 1967, Unprocessed Box 35, CSC; Minutes, SWPC Board of Directors, 24 March 1966, Folder Board of Directors, 1965–1966, Box II C, CSC; Minutes, SWPC Board of Directors, 28 April 1966, Folder Board of Directors, 1965–1966, Box II C, CSC; Mauldin to Daniel Kelly, District E Council member, 18 March 1966, Folder Desire Area Community Council, Box 7, 1966, SC.

61. Betsy Flood Victims Open Letter to Schiro, 17 September 1966, Folder LNWNC, Box 15, 1966, SC; "Housing Meeting," 6 January 1966, Folder NWCIL, Box 47, CSC; William H. Forman Jr., "The Conflict Over Federal Urban Renewal," 254–57; Haas, "Victor H. Schiro, Hurricane Betsy and the 'Forgiveness Bill' "; J. R. Andre, "Urban Renewal and Housing in New Orleans, 1949–1962."

62. Dent and Aronson, report, 8 March 1966, Folder Ninth Ward Civic & Improvement League, Box 47, CSC. Press Clipping, "Poverty Funds Earmarked for Use by SWPC in Four Target Areas; Name Staff," 27 October 1965, Folder SWPC Reports and Notices of Meetings, Flyers, Invitations, etc., March, 1962–June, 1965, Unprocessed Box 39, CSC.

63. Irvin White, president Committee for Progressive Action in the Lower Ninth Ward, to Lill, 6 June 1966, folder NWCIL, Box 47, CSC; "Get the Answers" flyer, 7 June 1966, ibid.; *NOTP*, 24 January 1967; *NOTP*, 25 January 1967.

64. Daniel Patrick Moynihan, *Maximum Feasible Misunderstanding*.

65. "Proposal Background," SWPC Proposal, [1965], Folder Desire, 1963–1966, Box 23, CSC.

66. Courson, "Community Organization in Low-Income Neighborhoods in New Orleans."

67. Winifred Anderson, "An Open Letter to the Residents of the Central City Target Area," *Central City Areascope*, 23 January 1967, Folder SWPC Neighborhood Centers 1966–1968, Unprocessed Box 24, CSC.

68. "The 'War on Poverty in New Orleans'—What Do You Think?" *Central City Areascope*, October 1966, Folder SWPC Neighborhood Centers 1966–1968, Unprocessed Box 24, CSC.

69. Malcolm C. Barnes, "Editorial Comment," April 1967, Folder SWPC Neighborhood Centers 1966–1968, Unprocessed Box 24, CSC.

70. Capps, "Community Decision Making," 143–49; Minutes, SWPC Board of Directors, 24 March 1966, Folder Board of Directors, 1965–1966, Box II C, CSC; Minutes, SWPC Board of Directors, 28 April 1966, ibid.; Clark Corliss, director of Social Welfare Planning Council, to Philip Ciaccio, city council member, 21 September 1967, Folder SWPC Neighborhood Centers, 1966–1968, Unprocessed Box 24, CSC.

71. Community Relations Council, "Proposal Staffed Operation," June 1967, Folder Community Relations Council of Greater New Orleans, Box 21, CSC.

72. Dewey, "The Ethics of Democracy."

73. Boy Scout Report for Algiers-Fischer, n.d., prior to 1967, Folder Total Community Action, Inc., n.d. 1962–1964, Box 55, CSC.

74. James Gayle, "One Assessment of the Anti-Poverty Effort in Central City," *Central City Areascope*, 1 December 1966, Folder SWPC Neighborhood Centers 1966–1968, Unprocessed Box 24, CSC.

75. Louis King, TCA Board member and CCEOC member, "Did You Know? (But of Course)," 23 January 1967, Folder SWPC Neighborhood Centers 1966–1968, Unprocessed Box 24, CSC.

76. Mrs. N. Cunningham, "Religious Note: 'God and Poverty,'" *Algiers Sentinel*, September 1967, Folder SWPC Neighborhood Centers 1966–1968, Unprocessed Box 24, CSC.

77. Morris Jones, "Community Effort: Not Community Chaos," *Lower Ninth Ward Civic Center Chatter*, July 1967, Folder SWPC Neighborhood Centers 1966–1968, Unprocessed Box 24, CSC.

78. Ruby Sumler, "Ninth Ward Civic and Improvement League Emergency Aid Committee Aim and Objectives," 22 December 1965, Folder Proposal to Total Community Action, Leontine Luke Collection, UNO.

79. *Our Paper*, December 1966, Folder Desire Housing Project, Vertical File, Louisiana Collection, Tulane University Libraries [hereafter cited as LACOLL].

80. Reverend George Simon, "The God of Purpose," March 1967, *St. Thomas News*, SWPC Neighborhood Centers 1966–1968 folder, Unprocessed Box 24, CSC; *Public Papers of the Presidents, 1963–1964, Volume 1*, Lyndon B. Johnson, "Remarks at University of Michigan," 22 May 1964.

81. George Matthew Adams, "Team Work," *Our Paper*, December 1966, Folder Desire Housing Project, Vertical File, LACOLL; *Public Papers of the*

Presidents, 1963–1964, Volume 1, Lyndon B. Johnson, "Remarks at University of Michigan," 22 May 1964.

82. Sumler, "Ninth Ward Civic and Improvement League," 22 December 1965, Proposal to Total Community Action, Leontine Luke Collection, UNO.

83. One study argued that Irish Catholics were more likely to accept the church's dictates on integration than other Catholics in the area because Irish Catholics were reportedly more dedicated to their parishes and their church leaders. Leonard Reissman, K. H. Silvert, and Cliff W. Wing Jr., *The New Orleans Voter*.

84. Alex Benz, chair of St.Thomas Council, "St.Thomas Council," *St.Thomas News*, January 1968, Folder SWPC Neighborhood Centers 1966–1968, Unprocessed Box 24, CSC.

85. *St. Thomas News*, December 1967, Folder SWPC Neighborhood Centers 1966–1968, Unprocessed Box 24, CSC.

86. Martha McNair, "Meditation," *St. Thomas News*, July 1967, Folder SWPC Neighborhood Centers 1966–1968, Unprocessed Box 24, CSC.

87. Kolb, "The Auld Sod on Adele Street," 9–16, 60.

88. Richard Haley, proposal to VISTA, "Placement of VISTA Workers," 29 August 1967, Folder VISTA 1966–1967, Box 66, CSC.

89. Richard Haley, "Notes on Conference with Russell Jewert of VISTA," 29 August 1967, Folder VISTA 1966–1967, Box 66, CSC.

Chapter Four. Challenging the Establishment and the Color Line

1. Haas, *DeLesseps S. Morrison*, 51–52 and 67–81.

2. "SWPC LNW Target Area Teenage Club Meeting," 13 January and 20 January 1966, Folder NWCIL, Box 47, CSC; Moweaner Mauldin et al. to Schiro, 21 April 1967, Folder Desire Area Community Council, Box 5, 1967, SC.

3. Charlotte Hayes, "Guess Who's Running for Council, Mayor, Governor, None of the Above: Dorothy Mae Taylor," *VCC*, 27 April 1973.

4. Economic Opportunity Committee of the Desire Area Community Council to Mayor Schiro, 16 March 1966, Folder Economic Opportunity, Box 7, 1966, SC.

5. Notes on "TARC Meeting," 11 April 1966, Folder Ninth Ward Civic & Improvement League, Box 47, CSC; "TARC Areas Recreation Committee," ibid.

6. TARC meeting, 4 May 1966, Folder NWCIL, Box 47, CSC.

7. TARC to Schiro, 20 May 1966, ibid.

8. Later that year, Landrieu removed the flag himself. Aronson, "Report on Activities," 20 to 26 May 1966, Folder NWCIL, Box 47, CSC; NWCIL to Thomas

Godchaux, president of Total Community Action, 25 May 1966, ibid; Moon Landrieu, interview by Kent Germany, 4 June 2001.

9. Delores Davis, TARC, to TCA Board Members, 30 March 1967, Folder Central City Target Area, Box 3, 1967, SC.

10. TARC to TCA Board of Directors, 19 May 1967, Folder TCA 1966–1967, Box 55, CSC; Central City Target Area Recreation Committee, "Statement," 20 March 1967, Folder Central City Target Area, Box 3, 1967, SC; Jim Manning, "Citizens Push Opening," 13 June 1968, Folder 13, Box 393, Greater New Orleans Chamber Collection, UNO; TCA, "Program Account," 1969, Folder Project Proposals, Box 56, CSC.

11. Leontine Luke to Joseph Marchese, 10 February 1966, Folder Ninth Ward Civic & Improvement League, Box 47, CSC.

12. George D. McCarthy, assistant director for Congressional Relations OEO, to Hale Boggs, 6 November 1967, Folder Poverty Louisiana II, Subject Files, 1967, BC.

13. *Central City Areascope*, October 1966, in SWPC Neighborhood Centers 1966–1968, Unprocessed Box 24, CSC.

14. Virginia Y. Collins, Weekly Reports, 20 May 1966, Folder Central City— Reports Mrs. Virginia Y. Collins, Community Worker, 1965–1966, Unprocessed Box 41, CSC; Collins, report, 18 March 1966, ibid.

15. Collins Report, 29 April 1966, Folder Central City—Reports Mrs. Virginia Y. Collins, Unprocessed Box 41, CSC.

16. Editorial, "A War on Poverty???" *Central City Areascope*, October 1966, Folder SWPC Neighborhood Centers 1966–1968, Unprocessed Box 24, CSC; Winston Lill, interview by Kent Germany, 27 April 1997.

17. SWPC, VISTA Application, July 1965, Folder Volunteers in Service to America (VISTA) 1964–1965, Box 66, CSC; SWPC, "Sponsor Letter of Intent for Vista Volunteers," 16 June 1965, ibid.; Tom Laughlin, "Miscellaneous Notes," 30 June 1965, ibid.

18. Vincent J. Bonacci, VISTA volunteer in Algiers-Fischer, to President Lyndon B. Johnson, 29 August 1966, Folder VISTA, Box 66, CSC.

19. Charles Langley to Rosenberg, 19 April 1966, Folder Langley, Charles, 1966, Unprocessed Box 25, CSC; Markham Ball to Samuel Yette, 1 March 1966, Folder New Orleans, Box 31, Series E4, RG 381, NARA. The Team Chief in question was Leon J. Bickham.

20. Charles Langley to Rosenberg, 19 April 1966, Folder Langley, Charles, 1966, Unprocessed Box 25, CSC.

21. Warshawsky to Rosenberg, May 1966, Folder Warshawsky . . . VISTA, Unprocessed Box 25, CSC; Newspaper clipping, "Six VISTA Volunteers Now Assigned to SWPC," 15 November 1966, Folder SWPC Reports and Notices of

Meetings, Flyers, Invitations, etc., March, 1962–June, 1965, Unprocessed Box 39, CSC.

22. Warshawsky, reports, June and July 1966, Folder Warshawsky . . . VISTA, Unprocessed Box 25, CSC.

23. Minutes, TCA Board of Directors, 1967–1968, 25 January 1968, Box II C, CSC.

24. Warshawsky to Rosenberg, May 1966, Folder Warshawsky . . . VISTA, Unprocessed Box 25, CSC.

25. Warshawsky, reports, June and July 1966, ibid.

26. Warshawsky, reports, June and July 1966, ibid.; Rosenberg to James Johnson, Urban Project Division, VISTA, 2 May 1966, Folder VISTA, Unprocessed Box 25, CSC.

27. Warshawsky, SWPC Application for Employment, 19 June 1967, Folder Warshawsky . . . VISTA, Unprocessed Box 25, CSC; Mel Goldstein to Mal Mason, 19 January 1968, Folder New Orleans Community Action Program, Box 10, Series 1007, RG 381, NARA.

28. Minutes of the Executive Committee, SWPC, 11 August 1966, Folder Board of Directors, 1966, Box II C, CSC; Minutes of the Executive Committee, SWPC, 8 September 1966, ibid.

29. Peter Friedberg and Gary A. Sledge, "Central City Target Area," June 1966, Folder Friedberg, Peter (Central City) 1966, Unprocessed Box 25, CSC.

30. Friedberg and Sledge, "Central City Target Area"; Newspaper clipping, "Poverty Funds Earmarked for Use by SWPC in Four Target Areas," 27 October 1965, Folder SWPC Reports and Notices of Meetings, Flyers, Invitations, etc., March, 1962–June, 1965, Unprocessed Box 39, CSC; Allie Mae Williams to Rosenberg, 22 June 1966, Folder VISTA, 1966–1967, Box 66, CSC.

31. Corliss to Rosenberg, 26 July 1966, Folder Friedberg, Peter (Central City) 1966; Allie Mae Williams to Rosenberg, 3 August 1966, Folder VISTA, 1966–1967, Unprocessed Box 25, CSC.

32. Rogers, *Righteous Lives*, 106–7.

33. Kurtz and Peoples, *Earl K. Long*, xii.

34. Newspaper clipping, "TCA Staff Discusses New Developments," n.d. [January 1966], Folder SWPC Reports and Notices of Meetings, Flyers, Invitations, etc., March, 1962–June, 1965, Unprocessed Box 39, CSC; Minutes, SWPC Board of Directors, 27 October 1966, Folder Board of Directors, 1966, Box II C, CSC; Rogers, *Righteous Lives*, 101–3; The Joint Legislative Committee on Un-American Activities, *Aspects of the Poverty Program in South Louisiana* and *Students for a Democratic Society and the New Left*; Carolyn Thompson, "A Story of Hope."

35. *LAWK*, 5 December 1970; "Dismissal of Virginia Y. Collins, New Or-

leans, Louisiana," Ed Terrones to Edgar May, 2 September 1966, Folder Louisiana 1966 July–Sept., Box 30, Series 74, RG 381, NARA; Allie Mae Williams, "Evaluation of Virginia Y. Collins," ibid.; Clark Corliss to Viriginia Collins, 15 June 1966, Folder Louisiana 1966 April–June, ibid.; Peter Spruance to Edgar May, 10 March 1967, Folder Louisiana 1967 March, ibid.; *Lafayette Daily Advertiser*, 9 March 1967.

36. Virginia Y. Collins, weekly reports, 14 December 1965 to 20 May 1966, "Central City—Reports Mrs. Virginia Y. Collins, 1965–1966" Folder, Unprocessed Box 41, CSC; Untitled survey, 23 March 1966, Folder Citizen Education Project, Box 8, LWV.

37. Untitled survey, 23 March 1966, Citizen Education Project 1965–1968 folder, Box 8, LWV; Promotional literature in Folder CC-Collins, Unprocessed Box 41, CSC; Flyer, Folder Economic Opportunity, Box 7, 1966, SC; Lloyd Harris, CCEOC P.R. chair and Allie Mae Williams to Principals, Faculties, PTAs, . . . and Business executives in Central City area, 11 April 1966, Folder Central City Target Area, Box 4, 1966, SC, NOPL; Harris and Winifred Anderson, CCEOC President, to Schiro, 11 April 1966, Folder Economic Opportunity, Box 7, 1966, SC.

38. Virginia Y. Collins, Weekly Reports, 18 May 1966, Folder Central City—Reports Mrs. Virginia Y. Collins, Community Worker, 1965–1966, Unprocessed Box 41, CSC.

39. Clark Corliss, handwritten notes, Folder TCA 1966–1967, Box 55, CSC; Minutes, SWPC Board of Directors, 28 April 1966, Folder Board of Directors, 1965–1966, Box II C, CSC; John Daum to Ed May and Bob Clampitt, "New Orleans, CAP sign-off," 21 September 1965, Folder New Orleans, Box 31, Series 4, RG 381, NARA; TCA, "Up-to-date History of . . ." 1969, Folder TCA, Box 2, Series 1025, RG381, NARA; Mary K. Capps, "Community Decision Making," 138; Gillette, ed., *Launching the War on Poverty*, 65–88.

40. Corliss to Philip James, Maurice Anderson, and Mrs. Riesfeld, 23 October 1967, Folder Board of Directors, 1967–1968, Box II C, CSC; Minutes, SWPC Board of Directors, 25 May 1967, ibid.; Corliss to Lill, 19 September 1967, 2 October 1967, and 4 October 1967, Folder TCA 1966–1967, Box 55, CSC; "Work Program—Component 7–2A—For Calendar Year 1968," late 1967, Folder Board of Directors, 1967–1968, Box II C, CSC.

41. J. A. Blaine DeJoie Jr., committee chairman, to Special Committee, Community Organization Changeover, 4 June 1968, Folder TCA, Box 15, 1968, SC; Corliss to All SWPC Neighborhood Personnel, 9 November 1967, Folder TCA 66–67, Box 55, CSC.

42. Gary Lloyd, speech to Special Meeting of Board of Directors, SWPC, 20 January 1971, Folder Board of Directors, 1970–1971, Box II D, CSC.

43. Corliss to Lill, 4 January 1968, Folder TCA 68–71, Box 55, CSC.

44. Winston Lill, interview by Kent Germany, 27 April 1997.

45. SWPC Minutes, 22 February 1968, Folder Board of Directors 1967–1968, Box II C, CSC; Richard Haley, "Observations," ibid.

46. SWPC Minutes, 22 February 1968, Folder Board of Directors 1967–1968, Box II C, CSC; Richard Haley, "Observations," ibid.; Glen Jeansonne, *Leander Perez*; Bob Short, *Everything Is Pickrick*; Carter, *The Politics of Rage*.

47. SWPC Minutes, 22 February 1968, Folder Board of Directors 1967–1968, Box II C, CSC; Richard Haley, "Observations," ibid.

48. William J. Bryan to Long, Folder 8, Box 110, Senator Russell Long Collection, Hill Memorial Library, Louisiana State University, Baton Rouge, Louisiana [hereafter cited as Hill-LSU].

49. Helga Timothy to Boggs, 7 December 1968, Folder Federal Agencies OEO III, 1969, Subject Files, BC.

50. J. W. Kelly, Monroe, La., to Hébert, 25 May 1967, ibid., Folder Poverty, Box 10, HC.

51. Bettie Guidry of Welsh, La., to Edwin Edwards, 12 March 1968, Folder 8, Box 110, Russell Long Collection, Hill-LSU.

52. Russell Long to Mrs. E. M. Percy, 23 September 1968, ibid.

53. "Hebert Won't Vote Butter," newspaper clipping, Folder Poverty, Box 10, HC.

54. For an examination of Oregon Congresswoman Edith Green's OEO-saving amendment to the Economic Opportunity Act, see Matusow, *The Unraveling of America*, 113–14, 269–70; Donald M. Baker, interview with Stephen Goodell, 24 February 1969 and 5 March 1969, Gillette, *Launching the War on Poverty*, 202–5; Gillette, *Launching the War on Poverty*, 390; Robert A. Levine, interview with Stephen Goodell, 26 February 1969, Gillette, *Launching the War on Poverty*, 202–5; Gillette, *Launching the War on Poverty*, 210–11.

55. TCA, "Employment and Leadership: Alumni List," [1984], Folder 15, Box 3, LC; TCA, "Total Community Action: 20 Years of Community Service," Folder 15, Box 3, LC; Joan Treadway, "Poverty Agency Marks 20 Years," *NOTP*, 4 March 1985; TCA, *A History of the Community Action Movement in New Orleans, 1964–2001*, 20–23 and 33–54.

56. The social science and historical literature has built on those perceptions. Frances Fox Piven and Richard Cloward have written perhaps the most profoundly influential, and controversial, works on the War on Poverty, and they see the CAP as a clear attempt to mold black political development. Peter Marris and Martin Rein argue that CAP encouraged destructive competition between groups that could have worked together. Patrick Moynihan views it as a misdirected, overly ambitious mess. Allen Matusow describes it as a "war declared, not fought." August Meier, Elliott Rudwick, and Nicholas Lemann lament that it muted a more genuine, and more radical, activism. John Dittmer chronicles its

hijacking by racial moderates and powerful white conservatives. Thomas Jackson contends that CAP too often rewarded established interests and was a continuation of top-down policymaking. See Piven and Cloward, *Regulating the Poor* and *Poor People's Movements*; Moynihan, *Maximum Feasible Misunderstanding*; Peter Marris and Martin Rein, *Dilemmas of Social Reform*; Greenstone and Peterson, *Race and Authority in Urban Politics*; Kramer, *Participation of the Poor*; Sundquist, *On Fighting Poverty*; Levitan, *The Great Society's Poor Law*; Matusow, *The Unraveling of America*, 217–74; Lemann, *The Promised Land*; Dittmer, *Local People*, 363–88; Thomas Jackson, "The State, the Movement, and the Urban Poor."

57. President Lyndon Johnson with Charles Schultze, Elmer Staats, and Joseph Califano, 18 August 1965, Citation #8555, office conversation preceding conversation with Dwight Eisenhower, Tape WH6401.01, Recordings, LBJL.

58. Donald M. Baker, interview with Stephen Goodell, 24 February 1969 and 5 March 1969, in Gillette, *Launching the War on Poverty*, 202–5; Matusow, *Unraveling of America*, 270.

59. See the introduction to the Department of HHS's Office of Community Services website, http://www.acf.hhs.gov/programs/ocs/.

60. Meier and Rudwick, *CORE*; Rogers, *Righteous Lives*, 110–46, and Fairclough, *Race and Democracy*, 294–343.

61. Minutes, 18 November 1965, Folder Board of Directors, 1967–1968, Box II C, CSC; Winston Lill, interview by Kent Germany, 29 April 1997.

62. *Statistical Abstract of the United States, 1970*, 864.

Chapter Five. Making Better and Happier Citizens

1. A theme in the history of American responses to poverty has been that the poor pose a serious threat to community stability. Boyer, *Urban Masses and Moral Order*; Huggins, *Protestants Against Poverty*; Crocker, *Social Work and Social Order*; Bremner, *The Discovery of Poverty in the United States*.

2. Jean F. Craddock, acting director; John Wall Jr., executive designate; Frances K Burke, chairman of the board; and Maurice Stern, antipoverty committee chairman; to Corliss, 3 May 1965, Folder Kingsley House, 1960–1964, Box 30, CSC.

3. Hensgen, "Moving Toward Better Opportunities," *PAR Analysis* 141 (March 1967): 18.

4. Harrington, *The Other America*, 146; Office of Policy Planning and Research (Labor), *The Negro Family*, chapter 4.

5. Newell Schindler, "Poverty: The Problems the Promises," *Clarion Herald*, 13 May 1965.

6. SHAC's key leader, Naomi White, eventually became a state legislator. "Proposal of the Students for Human Advancement and Community," February 1966, Folder Desire 1963–1966, Box 23, CSC.

7. Martin Luther King Jr., "What Is Your Life's Blueprint," 27 October 1967, Philadelphia, Pennsylvania, transcript by the *Seattle Times*, http://seattletimes .nwsource.com/mlk/king/words/blueprint.html. In 1963, King had also used this concept of "somebodiness" in his "Letter from a Birmingham Jail."

8. TCA Research Department, "New Orleans," [1969], Folder 4, Box 55, NAACP Field Office Records, ARC.

9. SWPC, "Report of Findings and Action Recommendations: School Dropout and Youth Employment Committee," December 1963, Unlabeled Green Folder, Unprocessed Box 39, CSC.

10. Smith, *Civic Ideals*, 470–506. McClay, *The Masterless*, 277–83. Blake, in *Beloved Community*, 2–9 and 51, argues that Progressive-era intellectual Randolph Bourne's vision of a beloved community premised that the fulfillment of the self would solidify democratic culture.

11. See Rieff, *The Triumph of the Therapeutic*.

12. Myrdal, *An American Dilemma*; Katznelson, "Was the Great Society a Lost Opportunity?", 185–211.

13. The underclass theory borrowed themes from the culture of poverty. Although many critics have come to question its validity as a term, its practitioners contend that in post–World War II America, a permanent underclass developed in American cities because of racial and ethnic prejudices, welfare state inadequacy, family disorganization, and the dislocation of employment opportunities for residents. O'Connor, *Poverty Knowledge*, 86–106; Oscar Lewis, *The Children of Sanchez, Five Families*, and *La Vida*; Wilson, *The Truly Disadvantaged* and *When Work Disappears*; Mingione, *Urban Poverty and the Underclass*; Katz, *The Underclass Debate*; James Q. Wilson, "Culture, Inaction, and the Underclass."

14. Mittelstadt, "The Dilemmas of the Liberal Welfare State, 1945–1964," 3–5.

15. Mary Balthazar, "No Greater Need: An Early Assessment of Operation Upgrade," in Folder Guste Home, 1966, Box 26, CSC; Mary Balthazar to Irene C. Howard, chair Scholarship Committee at SUNO, 13 May 1966, ibid.

16. New Orleans Branch, National Association of College Women, "The Unmarried Mother: A Demonstration Project," April [1967], Folder Desire 63–66, Box 23, CSC.

17. Mildred Fossier, Proposal, Folder Welfare, Box 32, 1964, SC.

18. SWPC, "Social Welfare Planning Council's Desire Area Work Program" section 205 of Title II A of Economic Opportunity Act," n.d., [1965], Folder Desire, 1963–1966, Box 23, CSC; Rosenberg to Lill, 18 January 1965, Folder TCA

2, Box 55, CSC; Allen Dowling to Paul Sanzenbach, 16 January 1968, Folder Housing Authority of New Orleans, Unprocessed Box 22, CSC.

19. Gerald Bonnaffons, supervisor Kingsley House Community Organization, to Allen Dowling, September 1966, unlabeled HANO folder, Unprocessed Box 22, CSC.

20. Ibid.

21. VISTA Proposal by SWPC, July 1965, Folder Volunteers in Service to America (VISTA) 1964–1965, Box 66, CSC.

22. Arthur Cooper, Irish Channel Neighborhood Development Center Co-ordinator, "Statement of Community Workers Group RE: Role of the Community Organizer," [1966], Folder Irish Channel Community Development Center, Box 28, CSC.

23. Urban League of Greater New Orleans, "A Community Organization Project–9th Ward," 20 October 1965, Folder ULGNO, 1960–71, Box 64, CSC.

24. "Proposal Background," SWPC Proposal, [1965], Folder Desire, 1963–1966, Box 23, CSC.

25. Corliss to TCA Board of Directors, "Proposed Role of SWPC," 18 January 1965, Folder TCA 2, Box 55, CSC.

26. "Proposal Background," SWPC Proposal, [1965], Folder Desire, 1963–1966, Box 23, CSC.

27. Corliss to TCA Board of Directors, "Proposed Role of SWPC," 18 January 1965, Folder TCA 2, Box 55, CSC.

28. Gerald Bonnaffons, supervisor Kingsley House Community Organization, to Allen Dowling, September 1966, unlabeled HANO folder, Unprocessed Box 22, CSC.

29. New Orleans NACW, "The Unmarried Mother," April [1967], Folder Desire 63–66, Box 23, CSC.

30. Rosemary James, "Jobs Bring Dignity: Self-Respect Lost by Idleness, Want," NOSI, 6 June 1968.

31. Rosemary Powell, "Census Data Bares Blight: City and State Declared Poverty War Battlefield," NOSI, n.d., in Folder TCA-newspaper clippings, Box 55, CSC.

32. John J. Stretch, Ph.D., "What Makes a Man Poor," Folder Poverty Social Welfare Planning Commission, Box 80, CSC.

33. Edward J. Steimel, "Impact on Louisiana's Economy," PAR Analysis 141 (March 1967): 5.

34. Thomas Hale Boggs, "Speech for the Executive Club in N.O.," 30 April 1964, Box 5, Speaking Engagements, BC.

35. Mary Balthazar, "No Greater Need: An Early Assessment of Operation Upgrade," in Folder Guste Home, 1966, Box 26, CSC.

36. "PAR Conference—1967: The Impact of the Negro on Louisiana's Future," *PAR Analysis* 141 (March, 1967): 1–23.

37. Ramon S. Scruggs, "Our Common Economic Problems," *PAR Analysis* 141 (March 1967): 15–16.

38. Earl M. Lewis, "The Negro Today: The Improvement of Education for Negro Students," *PAR Analysis* 141 (March 1967), 12–15.

39. Reverend Eugene P. McManus, "Motivating Negro Youth," *PAR Analysis* 141 (March 1967): 1.

40. For a historical overview of this, see Weems, *Desegregating the Dollar*.

41. Bussie, "Opportunities in the Labor Union," *PAR Analysis* 141 (March 1967): 14; WDSU-TV, Editorial, "The Concentrated Employment Program," WDSU Television, 11 January 1968, Folder WDSU Editorials, Box 37, PRS, SC; Feldstein, *The CEA*; Norton, *The Council of Economic Advisers*, 50–70; Tobin and Weidenbaum, *Two Revolutions in Economic Policy*; Bower, "Investment in Human Capital and Economic Growth."

42. Boggs, "Speech for the Executive Club in N.O.," BC.

43. Bussie, "Opportunities in the Labor Union," 14.

44. Scruggs, "Our Common Economic Problems," 15–16.

45. *Our Paper*, September 1966, Folder Desire Housing Project, Vertical File, LACOLL.

46. Clark Corliss, "Some Major Community Challenges: Report of the Executive Director" to the Annual Meeting of the SWPC, 27 June 1966, Folder SWPC—Assembly of Members, 1970–71, Unprocessed Box 38, CSC.

47. McManus, "Motivating Negro Youth," 4.

48. Quote from Allen Johnson Jr., "The Aggressive Pacifist," *Gambit Weekly*, 31 December 2002.

49. Anonymous, "Where the Fault Lies," *Algiers Sentinel*, September 1967, Folder SWPC Neighborhood Centers 1966–1968, Unprocessed Box 24, CSC.

50. Emelda Washington, "Advantages for My Boy," 29 March 1968, Folder SWPC Neighborhood Centers 1966–1968, Unprocessed Box 24, CSC.

51. President Johnson and Robert Kennedy, 27 July 1964, Citation #4349, Tape WH6407.15, Recordings, LBJL.

52. A. P. "Pat" Stoddard, TCA Manpower Specialist, to Boggs, 10, 17, and 23 March 1967, Folder Poverty Community Action Program, Box 85, 1967 Subject files, BC.

53. Linda Adams, Behrman High School student, to Boggs, 2 June 1967, Folder Poverty NYC, Box 85, 1967 Subject Files, BC.

54. Karina Gracia to Boggs; Elaine Simoneaux to Boggs, 6 June 1967; Mary Ellen Laners to Boggs, 7 June 1967, Folder NYC, Box 85, 1967 Subject files, BC.

55. Karina Gracia to Boggs, 13 January 1967, Folder Poverty Louisiana Cor-

respondence I, Box 85, 1967 Subject files, BC; Betty Newsome to Boggs, 20 February 1967, Poverty Community Action Program folder, ibid.; miscellaneous correspondence in Folder Poverty NYC, ibid.

56. Loria C. Jordan, "Youth Interest and Lack of Interest in the Poverty Program," *Central City Areascope*, 23 January 1967, Folder SWPC Neighborhood Centers 1966–1968, Unprocessed Box 24, CSC.

57. Alma M. Cottles, New Orleans, to Boggs, 5 November 1966, Folder Federal Agencies OEO, 1966 Subject files, BC; Alma M. Cottles, "Idea for War on the Poverty Program," ibid.; Alma Cottles Collection, ARC.

58. Family Care Advisory Committee to Shriver, 10 January 1967, Folder Poverty Louisiana Correspondence I, 1967 Subject files, BC; Alma Chester to Boggs, 14 January 1967, ibid.

59. E. Gardner to Boggs, 13 January 1967, ibid.

60. Violet Johnson to Boggs, 13 January 1967, ibid.

61. Lavada Jefferson, Organizer of the Keystone Terrace Improvement Group, to Boggs, 26 February 1967, Folder Poverty Community Action Program, Box 85, 1967 Subject files, BC.

62. That funding was cut by 1967. Boy Scout Report for Algiers-Fischer, n.d. [prior to 1967], Folder Total Community Action, Inc., n.d. 1962–1964, Box 55, CSC.

63. Father Jerome Ledoux worked for Xavier University and later presided over the St. Augustine Church in New Orleans's Tremé area. Father Ledoux, "On Being Black," *The Plain Truth*, 23 December 1969, PEC.

64. Lower Ninth Ward Neighborhood Council, "Program Account Work Program," 1969, Folder TCA Grant Proposals A-C, Box 56, CSC.

65. St. Bernard Community Council, "Program Account Work Program," 1969, Folder Project Proposals, Box 56, CSC. The folders in Box 56 contain numerous other instances of this emphasis on the psyche.

66. Louis, Bowles, and Grace, *Study of Racial Attitudes*, 5.

67. William Van Deburg, in *New Day in Babylon*, 9–10 and 112, argues that "Black Power" was "essentially cultural" and "is best understood as a broad, adaptive, cultural term serving to connect and illuminate the differing ideological orientations of the movement's supporters." John T. McCartney, in *Black Power Ideologies*, argues that the Black Power phenomenon was an extension of a century-old debate among black leaders over the issue of Black Nationalism and integration, and the central theme of Black Power in the 1960s was group power over individualism because individuals were not strong enough on their own.

68. Mike Henderson and Danny Greene, "Militants Hold Varied Theories," *NOSI*, 5 August 1969; Lloyd E. Lazard to Brothers, Sisters, White Man, and Hunkies, [1969], Folder Racist [26], Box 55, NAACP Field Office Records, ARC;

Miscellaneous materials in Folder Black Power Conference, 1968 2 of 2, Box 52, Series 1031, CAP Subject Files, 1959–1969, RG381, NARA; "Where Have All The Radicals Gone?" (New Orleans) *Gambit*, 29 November 1999.

69. McCartney, *Black Power Ideologies*; Meier, *Negro Thought in America, 1880–1915*; Harlan, *Booker T. Washington, the Making of a Black Leader, 1856–1901* and *Booker T. Washington: The Wizard of Tuskegee, 1901–1915*; David Levering Lewis, *W.E.B. DuBois, Biography of a Race, 1868–1919*.

70. Kazin, *The Populist Persuasion*.

71. *The Plain Truth*, 20 August 1969, Oversize Box 7, FST, ARC.

72. Robert Richardson, "Every Black Man Is My Brother," *New Orleans* 2 (June 1968): 21+.

73. Ibid.

74. William J. Eads to McKeithen, 29 May 1968, Folder Race Relations 2, Box 32, PRS, SC.

75. Lee Green, "The Quintessential Power," *Methods and Money*, 28 February 1969, Folder TCA 68–69, Folder 15, Box 47, NAACP Field Office Records, ARC; and Roger Reverin, "Negro Business Pushed by ICBO," *NOSI*, 28 November 1967.

76. *NOSI*, 3 July 1968.

77. *The Plain Truth*, 21 October 1969, Oversize Box 7, FST, ARC; *The Plain Truth*, 23 December 1969, PEC.

78. Val Ferdinand [now Kalamu ya Salaam], "Message to the Brothers: nickle [*sic*] niggers killing each other for a dime," *The Plain Truth*, 20 September 1969, PEC.

79. Alvarrz Ferrouilet, "Student Column: Black Unity," *The Plain Truth*, 20 March 1970, PEC.

80. Ronald Watson, "A New Trick Bag—Black Capitalism," *The Plain Truth*, 23 December 1969, PEC. Numan Bartley, in *The New South, 1945–1980*, contends that one of the reasons for the civil rights crisis of victory was that racial progress occurred after the major period of southern economic modernization.

81. William U. Madden, "N.O. Negroes Show Progress But Goal Still Not Reached," *NOSI*, 11 June 1968.

82. Samuel Bell, "A New Day Has Dawned," *Lower Ninth Ward Civic Center Chatter*, July 1967, Folder SWPC Neighborhood Centers 1966–1968, Unprocessed Box 24, CSC.

83. Charles Carter, "Let Us Take What Belongs to Us," ibid.

Chapter Six. Defusing the Southern Powder Keg

1. This study generally accepts the definition of "riot" used by James Button, in which a riot is a form of "collective violence" and collective violence is

"an instance of group coercion which includes injury or destruction to persons or property." The National Advisory Commission favored using the term "disorder." Here, those terms are used interchangeably with disturbance, rebellion, protest, and revolt. The terms "riotous rebellion" or "riotous protest" are probably the most exact phrases to describe the incidents. Button, *Black Violence*, 3; The National Advisory Commission on Civil Disorders [referred to hereafter as NACCD], *Report*, 65.

2. Button, *Black Violence*, 10; Downes, "A Critical Reexamination," 349–60; Sitkoff, *The Struggle for Black Equality, 1954–1992*, 185; The NACCD, *Report*, 67.

3. Edward Hébert to Brad Baker, 23 January 1968, Folder Poverty, Box 10, HC. For an examination of the uses of anticommunism to fight against civil rights gains, see Woods, *Black Struggle, Red Scare*.

4. As quoted in Carter, *The Politics of Rage*, 305–6. For Chicago mayor Richard Daley's theories about a riot conspiracy, see President Lyndon Johnson and Richard Daley, 19 July 1966, Citation #10414, Tape WH6607.06, Recordings, LBJL.

5. Fred Panzer to President Lyndon Johnson, 16 September 1968, "Nixon's Campaign thrust on Domestic Issues," Folder PL/Name, Box 76, White House Central Files: Confidential File, LBJL.

6. NACCD, *Report*, 127–35.

7. Ibid., 95–112 and 64.

8. NACCD, *Report*, 112–15; Sugrue, *The Origins of the Urban Crisis*.

9. "A Slow Motion Riot: The Kerner Commission Revisited," *New Perspectives Quarterly* 4 (Winter 1987).

10. As quoted in Allen Dowling to Thomas C. Dent, 1 July 1966, Folder 21, Box 1, FST, ARC.

11. Hollandsworth, *An Absolute Massacre*; Gambino, *Vendetta*; Hair, *Carnival of Fury*.

12. This solution was quite similar to President Lyndon Johnson's decision to send advisers to investigate conditions in inner city neighborhoods in early 1967. David Carter, "Two Nations," 299–340; Larry Odom, Technical Assistance, to Ted Berry, CAP, "Proposed Action Plan to Combat Big City Civil Strife," 25 July 1967, Folder Subject Files 1965–1969, 1967, Mississippi—CDGM to Civil Rights—Newark-Riot 3 of 3, Box 36, Series 1031, RG381, NARA; Sidney M. Milkis, "Lyndon Johnson, the Great Society, and the 'Twighlight' of the Modern Presidency," 26–28.

13. NACCD, *Report*, 64; Editorial, "The Negro: Much Remains Undone," *NOSI*, 14 June 1968.

14. Daniel C. Thompson, "New Orleans and the Riot Report," *New Orleans* 2 (June 1968): 10.

15. Ibid., 10.

16. Dick Aronson, "Report on Police Problem," 11 April 1966, Folder NWCIL, Box 47, CSC.

17. Don C. Hubbard, chair of Concerned Citizen's on Police Matters, to Schiro, 1 May 1967, Folder Concerned Citizen's on Police Matters, Box 4, 1967, SC; "Stop and Frisk Revisited," *NOLA Express*, [June 1968], Folder NOLA Express, PEC.

18. Tom Knight, "To Protect . . . ," *NOLA Express*, September [1969], Folder NOLA Express, PEC. For other incident reports, see SC, particularly Allen Sims, "Complaint," 21 March 1969, Folder HRC, Box 24, PRS, SC, and the NAACP Collection, ARC.

19. Bettye Pope, "Special Report," 10 August 1965, Folder Executive Committee 1960 through 1967–1968, Unprocessed Box 17, CSC; Pope to Corliss, 3 September 1965, ibid.; SWPC Executive Committee Minutes, 17 September 1965, ibid.

20. Mrs. Moweaner Mauldin, president of DACC, to Joseph I. Giarrusso, chief of NOPD, 1 August 1967, Folder DACC, Box 5, 1967, SC.

21. Jean Spells, president of Concerned Parents of Desire, to Joseph Giarrusso, 8 December 1967, Folder Desire Project, Box 5, 1967, SC.

22. Frank J. Bivens, president of DACC, to Schiro, 25 August 1967, Folder DACC, Box 5, 1967, SC.

23. E. Bettye Pope to Philip C. Ciaccio, District E, 4 August 1967, Folder Desire Project, Box 5, 1967, SC.

24. Mauldin to Giarrusso, 1 August 1967, Folder DACC, Box 5, 1967, Schiro, NOPL.

25. Unnamed person to A. P. "Pat" Stoddard, 14 August 1967, Folder Federal Agencies OEO 2, 1967 Subject files, BC.

26. Harvey Ronald H. Britton, NAACP field director, to Giarrusso, 28 March 1968, Folder NAACP, Box 10, 1968, SC; Giarrusso to Horace C. Bynum, 27 July 1968, ibid.

27. *LAWK*, 23 March 1968 and 30 March 1968.

28. Richardson, "Every Black Man Is My Brother," 21+.

29. WDSU-TV, editorial, "On Rumors of Civil Disorders in New Orleans," 9 April 1968, Folder WDSU editorials, Box 37, PRS, SC.

30. *NOSI*, 6 April 1968; *NOTP*, 8 April 1968; Richardson, "Every Black Man Is My Brother," 21; David Snyder, "Police Ready—In Case: Militants Willing to Talk—Good Sign for Summer," *NOSI*, 14 June 1968.

31. "Tom Knight Interview," *NOLA Express*, April 1968, Folder NOLA Express, PEC; *NOSI*, 9 April 1968.

32. Snyder, "Police Ready—In Case"; Richardson, "Every Black Man Is My Brother."

33. *LAWK*, 13 April 1968. The *New Orleans States-Item* estimated the crowd at two hundred.

34. Eric L. Boyd to Schiro, 13 April 1968, Folder Employment, Box 4, 1968, SC; *LAWK*, 13 April 1968; *The Plain Truth*, 20 August 1969, Oversize Box 7, FST, ARC; *NOTP*, 7 April 1968; *NOTP*, 9 April 1968; *LAWK*, 20 April 1968.

35. WDSU-TV, editorial, "On Rumors of Civil Disorders in New Orleans," 9 April 1968, Folder WDSU editorials, Box 37, PRS, SC; Editorial, "Light Perpetual," *VCC*, 12 April 1968; Zebadee Bridges to Schiro, 13 April 1968, Folder Human Relations, Box 43, PRS, SC.

36. Snyder, "Police Ready—In Case," *NOSI*, 14 June 1968.

37. Winston Lill, interview by Kent Germany, 29 April 1997.

38. Gene Bourg, "Black Politics: 6," *NOSI*, 19 February 1973.

39. *NOTP*, 21 February 1968.

40. On Creole culture in New Orleans, see Anthony, "The Negro Creole Community in New Orleans, 1880–1920"; Bell, *Revolution, Romanticism, and the Afro-Creole Protest*; Dominquez, *White by Definition*; Rohrer and Edmonson, *The Eighth Generation Grows Up*; R. Bentley Anderson, *Black, White, and Catholic*; Frances J. Wood, *Marginality and Identity*.

41. Schiro to Vice President Humphrey, 26 July 1966, Folder Federal Government-1966, Box 23, PRS, SC; WDSU-TV, editorial, "The Police and the Community," 16 September 1966, Folder WDSU editorials, Box 27, ibid.; HANO Resolution, 28 September 1966, Folder HANO, Unprocessed Box 22, CSC.

42. *LAWK*, 6 April 1968; WDSU-TV, editorial, "Facing Up to the Urban Crisis," 26 March 1968, Folder WDSU editorials, Box 37, PRS, SC; Thompson, "New Orleans and the Riot Report," 10+.

43. Sidney Fine concludes that the Detroit police made the mistake of not following their riot plan and calling out overwhelming force to nip the disturbance in its early stage. Fine, *Violence in the Model City*, 172–73.

44. TCA Research Department, "New Orleans," 1969, Folder United Fund, Box 55, NAACP Field Office Records, ARC; Report, "Numbers of Persons Residing in Projects as of September 1, 1967," Folder HANO (2), Box 8, 1967, SC; WDSU-TV, editorial, "A Positive Step for Better Housing," 27 June 1966, Folder WDSU editorials, Box 37, PRS, SC; David Snyder, "Slum Dweller Loves Home, Resists City Urgings to Move," *NOSI*, 4 June 1968.

45. *NOSI*, 5 June 1967; "Notes of Meeting," Folder Fernandez, Lee, Box 42, PRS, SC; Ministers Group to Schiro, 23 May 1967, Folder TCA-1, Box 34, ibid.

46. Sargent Shriver, "Statement by Sargent Shriver, July 31, 1967," Folder Subject Files 1965–1969, 1967, Mississippi—CDGM to Civil Rights—Newark-Riot 2 of 3, Box 36, Series 1031, RG381, NARA.

47. Shriver to Boggs, 2 September 1967, Folder Federal Agencies OEO II, 1967 Subject files, BC.

48. Winston Lill, interview by Kent Germany, 29 April 1997.

49. OEO, "OEO and the Riots—A Summary," Folder Federal Agencies, Office of Economic Opportunity II, 1967 Subject Files, BC; Shriver to Boggs, 2 September 1967, ibid.; "Responses to Ted Berry's Southern Peace Keeping Activities," 28 July 1967, Folder Subject Files 1965–1969, 1967, Mississippi—CDGM to Civil Rights—Newark-Riot 3 of 3, Box 36, Series 1031, RG381, NARA; Robert W Saunders, civil rights coordinator, to Dr. M.A. Dawkins, assistant to the director, "Riot Conditions and OEO Action in Southern Communities," 27 July 1967, ibid.; Mrs. Charles F. Hunter to Russell Long, 13 September 1967, Folder LPW Poverty, Box 104, Russell Long Collection, Hill-LSU.

50. Harvey Ronald H. Britton, NAACP Field Director, to Giarrusso, 28 March 1968, Folder NAACP, Box 10, 1968, NOPL; Giarrusso to Horace C. Bynum, 27 July 1968, ibid.

51. Button, *Black Violence*.

52. Schiro to McKeithen, 14 August 1968, Folder McKeithen, Box 9, 1968, SC.

53. Ruth Dreyfous to Boggs, 15 January 1967, Folder Poverty-LA-Correspondence I, 1967 Subject Files, BC.

54. *NOTP*, 21 May 1968; Norma Frieberg, interview by Kent Germany, 17 April 1997, in possession of author.

55. *Metropolitan Area Committee Newsletter*, August–September 1968, Folder MAC, Box 40, CSC. The MAC members included: John G. Weinmann, Wallace L. Young Jr., Charles C. Teamer, Richard W. Freeman Jr., General Ellsworth I. Davis, and Charles Keller III.

56. Charles Keller Jr., "MAC Voices," *Metropolitan Area Committee Newsletter*, August–September 1968, Folder MAC, Box 40, CSC.

57. CRC, "Description, Aims, and History of the Community Relations Council," n.d. [1967], Folder CRC Proposal, Box 21, CSC; Board of Directors, June 1968, Folder 20, Box 3, CRCGNO Collection, ARC.

58. Baker to Boggs, 31 March 1966, Folder Poverty-Louisiana, 1966 Subject files, BC; *WP*, 25 August 1965; *LAWK*, 29 June 1968; Fairclough, *Race and Democracy*, 411.

59. Minutes, Mayor's Community Relations Committee Meeting, 14 August 1967, Folder CRCGNO, Box 41, PRS, SC. Attending were Darwin Fenner; Monsignor Screen; Harry Kelleher, a prominent businessman who had been a chief negotiator during the downtown desegregation in the early 1960s; Arthur Chapital, leader of the local NAACP; Revius Ortique, a well-regarded black attorney; Thomas Godchaux, a prominent merchant and president of TCA; Pat Stoddard, labor leader and TCA manpower specialist; Archbishop Philip Hannan; businessman Philip James; Father Eugene McManus; Rabbi Leo Bergman, Head of Rabbinical Council; Rev. Willie Early Hausey; Rev. George Wilson, president

of Greater New Orleans Federation of Churches; and Richard Montgomery of the Chamber of Commerce.

60. A. S. "Lee" Fernandez, "Progress Report: Community Relations Committee," 21 August [1967], Folder Community Relations Council—1967, Box 4, 1967, SC; HRC, "Modus Operandi for Selecting Minority Group Representatives to Commission," 22 August 1967, Folder CRCGNO, Box 41, Schiro Public Relations, NOPL; Edmond Walker Sr., president AFCO, to Schiro, 18 September 1967, Folder AFCO, Box 1, 1967, SC.

61. Planning Committee Meeting for Community Affairs Council, "Summary of Minutes," 17 August 1967, Folder CRCGNO, Box 41, PRS, SC.

62. Mayor's Office, "Fact Sheet City Human Relations Committee," 11 January 1968, Folder Human Relations, Box 43, Schiro Public Relations, NOPL.

63. Rt. Rev. Monsignor A. T. Screen to Jack McGuire, Director of Public Relations Office City Hall, 14 March 1968, Human Relations, Box 43, Schiro Public Relations, NOPL; Dennis J. Lacey Jr., Executive Assistant to Mayor, to All Councilmen, 2 April 1968, Human Relations, Box 43, Schiro Public Relations, NOPL.

64. Press release, Folder HR, SPR-43.

65. HRC, "Annual Report," April 1969, Folder Human Relations, Box 43, PRS, SC.

66. HRC, "Annual Report," April 1969, Folder Human Relations, Box 43, PRS, SC; HRC, "Human Relations Committee," April 1969, Folder HRC, Box 24, PRS, SC; Dorothy Ellis, HRC member and League of Women Voters of New Orleans, "Some Notes on the Human Relations Committee," [April 1969], Folder 7, Box 18, LWV; Norma Frieberg, interview by Kent Germany, 17 April 1997.

67. Editorial, "The Negro: Much Remains Undone," *NOSI*, 14 June 1968.

68. Sargent Shriver, "Statement by Sargent Shriver, July 31, 1967," Folder Subject Files 1965–1969, 1967, Mississippi—CDGM to Civil Rights—Newark-Riot 2 of 3, Box 36, Series 1031, RG381, NARA.

69. Ibid.

70. "Responses to Ted Berry's Southern Peace Keeping Activities," 28 July 1967, Folder Subject Files 1965–1969, 1967, Mississippi—CDGM to Civil Rights—Newark-Riot 3 of 3, Box 36, Series 1031, RG381; Robert W Saunders, Civil Rights Coordinator, to Dr. M.A. Dawkins, Assistant to the Director, "Riot Conditions and OEO Action in Southern Communities," 27 July 1967, ibid.

71. Ted Berry to Hubert Humphrey, "Comments on Recent Riots," 2 August 1967, Folder Subject Files 1965–1969, 1967, Mississippi—CDGM to Civil Rights—Newark-Riot 1 of 3, Box 36, Series 1031, RG381, NARA.

72. Larry Sylvester Odom, OEO Technical Assistance office, to Theodore Berry, Director of CAP, "The Riot Cities and CAP," 24 July 1967, Folder Subject

Files 1965–1969, 1967, Mississippi—CDGM to Civil Rights—Newark-Riot 3 of 3, Box 36, Series 1031, RG381, NARA.

73. Carter, "Two Nations," 342–414; Fred R. Harris, "The 1967 Riots and the Kerner Commission," in Harris and Wilkins, *Quiet Riots*, 9–13; John Herbers, "The Kerner Report: A Journalist's View," in ibid., 21–22; Gary Orfield, "Separate Societies: Have the Kerner Warnings Come True?" in ibid., 100–103.

74. Myrdal, *An American Dilemma*; Jackson, *Gunnar Myrdal and America's Conscience*.

75. NACCD, *Report*, v and 1; Fred R. Harris, "The 1967 Riots," 9–13; Herbers, "The Kerner Report," 21–22; Orfield, "Separate Societies," 100–103.

76. NACCD, *Report*, 1, 10–13, and 229–63.

77. There is some evidence that the Johnson White House viewed the first two-and-a-half years of the Johnson presidency as a distinct period of policy development. By August of 1966, the White House had compiled assessments by Cabinet Secretaries in a volume titled *The Great Advance: The First Phase of the Great Society*. See Folder Confidential File Oversize Attachments: 8/17/66, Book: The Great Advance: The First Phase of the Great Society; Box 169, Confidential Files, White House Central Files, LBJL.

78. O'Connor, *Poverty Knowledge*, 139–43.

79. Orville Freeman, Secretary of Agriculture to President Johnson, 29 August 1966, "The Food Stamp Program—A Progress Report," Folder AG 7 Surplus Products, 11/23/63–11/12/66, Box 10, Legislative Series, White House Central Files, LBJL.

80. Matusow, *The Unraveling of America*, 270.

Chapter Seven. Making Workers and Jobs

1. CDA, *Comprehensive Demonstration Plan*, 18–20.

2. Rowena Courson, "Community Organization in Low-Income Neighborhoods in New Orleans," SWPC Project Report, December 1968, Folder Social Welfare Planning Council—Total Community Action ca. 1960s Report Forms, Series II, Box L, CSC.

3. Labor-Manpower Branch to the Director, "Evaluation of the Concentrated Employment Program," 21 May 1968, Folder CEP General 1968, Box 51, 1968, CAP Subject Files, 1959–1969, Series 1031, RG 381, NARA; Baker to Boggs, 7 January 1965, Folder Federal Agencies OEO III, 1965 Subject Files, BC; Laurie J. Bassi and Orley Ashenfelter, "The Effect of Direct Job Creation and Training Programs on Low-Skilled Workers," 134–37; Henry M. Levin, "A Decade of Policy Developments in Improving Education and Training for Low-Income Populations," 138–39 and 143–47.

4. "An Outline Proposal for the New Orleans Concentrated Employment Program," 31 March 1967, Folder TCA, Box 25, 1967, SC; "Secretary Wirtz Announces," 3 July 1967, Folder Poverty Community Action Program, Box 85, 1967 Subject Files, BC.

5. The CEP operated in the following cities: Atlanta; Baltimore; Birmingham; Boston; Chicago; Cleveland; Detroit; Houston; Los Angeles; Newark; New Orleans; New York (South Bronx); Northern Michigan; Mississippi Delta; Oakland; Philadelphia; Phoenix; Pittsburgh; San Antonio; San Francisco; St. Louis; and Washington, D.C. In 1968, Congress appropriated $210 million for 76 programs, with an estimated $495 million for 146 CEPs to follow in 1969. "Secretary Wirtz Announces," 3 July 1967, Folder Poverty Community Action Program, Box 85, 1967 Subject Files, BC; Agenda, TCA Board of Directors, 28 June 1967, Folder TCA, Box 25, 1967, SC; "Summary Reports from CEP Projects," Maurice L. Hill to Donald K. Hess, 22 November 1967, Folder CEP General 1968, Box 51, 1968, CAP Subject Files, 1959–1969, Series 1031, RG 381, NARA.

6. "Summary Reports from CEP Projects," Maurice L. Hill to Donald K. Hess, 22 November 1967, Folder CEP General 1968, Box 51, 1968, CAP Subject Files, 1959–1969, Series 1031, RG 381, NARA.

7. "An Outline Proposal for the New Orleans Concentrated Employment Program," 31 March 1967, Folder TCA, Box 25, 1967, SC.

8. Ibid.

9. As quoted in Rosemary James, "In-Depth Training May End Plight of Area Jobless," NOSI, 5 August 1967.

10. Bill Voelker, "Possible Causes Cited by Slow Start of CEP," NOTP, 6 January 1968; Pat Stoddard to Joseph Simon, executive director GNOCC, 23 February 1967, Folder TCA-Total Community Action (anti-poverty), Box 399, Chamber Collection, UNO; James, "In-Depth Training May End Plight of Area Jobless."

11. Robert I. Pack, "Record of Job Training Unit Seems to Justify Criticism," 7 August 1969, NOTP; Pack, "Low Level of Heavy Industry at Root of Employment Jam," 8 August 1969, ibid.; TCA Manpower Programs report [evaluation of CEP II], 22 April 1969, Folder TCA 68–69, Box 47, NAACP Field Office Records, ARC.

12. James, "In-Depth Training May End Plight of Area Jobless."

13. Materials in Folder TCA-Total Community Action (anti-poverty), Box 399, Chamber Collection, UNO.

14. Editorial, "Unemployment Grant," NOSI, 6 June 1967; NOSI, 28 July 1967.

15. James, "In-Depth Training May End Plight of Area Jobless"; Bernstein, Guns or Butter, 261–62.

16. Labor-Manpower Branch to the Director, "Evaluation of the Concentrated Employment Program," 21 May 1968, Folder CEP General 1968, Box 51, 1968, CAP Subject Files, 1959–1969, Series 1031, RG 381, NARA; Voelker, "Possible Causes Cited by Slow Start of CEP."

17. Schiro and City Council to Shriver, Boggs, Ellender, Long, and Edward Hébert, 10 May 1967, Folder CRC GNO, Box 41, PRS, SC; David Snyder, "$4.6 Million Grant Sought by Poverty Unit," *NOSI*, 11 May 1967; Senator Russell Long to Schiro, 5 June 1967, Folder Long, Russell, Box 12, 1967, SC.

18. *NOTP*, 18 May 1967; Schiro to Lillian Lee Deslattes, A-1 Employment Service, 18 May 1967, Folder CRC GNO, Box 41, PRS, SC.

19. Rosemary James, "Will Train 5,000," *NOSI*, 3 August 1967.

20. *NOTP*, 15 November 1967 and 30 November 1967; Minutes, Community Relations Council of Greater New Orleans, 21 December 1967, Folder Community Relations Council, 1964–1971, Box 21, CSC; Voelker, "Possible Causes Cited by Slow Start of CEP."

21. Donald K. Hess, to Theodore Berry, director of CAP, OEO, 27 November 1967, Folder CEP General 1968, Box 51, 1968, CAP Subject Files, 1959–1969, Series 1031, RG 381, NARA; "Summary Reports from CEP Projects," Maurice L. Hill to Donald K. Hess, 22 November 1967, ibid.; Labor-Manpower Branch to the Director, "Evaluation of the Concentrated Employment Program," 21 May 1968, ibid.

22. Voelker, "Possible Causes Cited by Slow Start of CEP."

23. *NOTP*, 29 November 1967.

24. Soul Go Getters, Central City Neighborhood Development Center, to Richard B. Montgomery, 5 October 1967, Folder Soul Go-Getters—Negro, Box 398, Chamber Collection, UNO.

25. *NOTP*, 11 October 1967; *NOSI*, 10 October 1967; *NOTP*, 24 October 1967 and 13 October 1967.

26. John Cotter, "Loud Debate Erupts Over Program," *NOTP*, 20 October 1967; Memorandum, Rosemary to Millicent, 19 May 1967, CRC GNO, Box 41, PRS, SC.

27. Charles Keller Jr., to Boggs, 2 November 1967, Folder Poverty Community Action, Box 85, Subject Files, 1967, BC.

28. Robert I. Pack, "Record of Job Training Unit" and "Low Level of Heavy Industry."

29. Voelker, "Possible Causes Cited by Slow Start of CEP"; Lill to Department heads, 10 October 1968, TCA 1968–1971, Box 55, CSC. Diamond became CEP director on 7 October 1968.

30. *NOSI*, 28 July 1967; Editorial, "Training and Jobs for the Willing," *NOTP*, 29 July 1967; Labor-Manpower Branch to the Director, "Evaluation of the Con-

centrated Employment Program," 21 May 1968, Folder CEP General 1968, Box 51, 1968, CAP Subject Files, 1959–1969, Series 1031, RG 381, NARA.

31. *The Plain Truth*, 20 September 1969, PEC.

32. Labor-Manpower Branch to the Director, "Evaluation of the Concentrated Employment Program," 21 May 1968, Folder CEP General 1968, Box 51, CAP Subject Files, 1959–1969, Series 1031, RG 381, NARA.

33. James, "Will Train 5,000"; *The Plain Truth*, 20 September 1969, PEC.

34. Voelker, "Possible Causes Cited by Slow Start of CEP."

35. William T. Bailey, Regional Manpower Administrator U.S. Department of Labor, to Harry McCall, 31 January 1969, Folder TCA, Box 15, 1969, SC.

36. Donald K. Hess to Ben Zimmerman, 1 July 1968, Folder CEP General 1968, Box 51, 1968, CAP Subject Files, 1959–1969, Series 1031, RG 381, NARA; Labor-Manpower Branch to the Director, "Evaluation of the Concentrated Employment Program," 21 May 1968, ibid.

37. Labor-Manpower Branch to the Director, "Evaluation of the Concentrated Employment Program," 21 May 1968, Folder CEP General 1968, Box 51, 1968, CAP Subject Files, 1959–1969, Series 1031, RG 381, NARA.

38. "Inquiry into Concentrated Employment Program, Review of CEP I," Folder TCA 68–69, Box 47, NAACP Field Office Records, ARC; Target Area President's Council, to Schiro, 9 December 1968, Folder TCA, Box 15, 1968, SC.

39. Handwritten notes, in Folder TCA 68–69, Box 47, NAACP Field Office Records, ARC; Memorandum, Target Area President's Council, Gerald Williams, St. Bernard; James Singleton, Central City; Frank Bivens, Desire; Isaac Joshua, Lower Ninth Ward; and Edwin Lombard, Algiers-Fischer, 9 December 1968, Folder TCA, Box 15, 1968, SC.

40. William T. Bailey, Regional Manpower Administration, to Ray Diamond, 27 November 1968, Folder City Employment Program, Box 2, 1968, SC.

41. Marchese, to William T. Bailey, Regional Manpower Administrator, Department of Labor, 19 March 1969, Folder TCA, Box 15, 1969, SC.; Marchese and Dr. Fred Remero, US Department of Labor, to McCall and William T. Bailey, 28 March 1969, ibid.; "Agenda" and "Progress Report-Reorganization of CEP," 24 April 1969, ibid; Raymond Diamond to Neighborhood Council Presidents, 2 June 1969, Folder TCA 71, Box 3, Administrative Subject files, City Demonstration Agency [hereafter cited as CDA], NOPL.

42. Chief Administrative Officer, New Orleans, to Schiro, 29 July 1969, Folder TCA, Box 15, 1969, SC.

43. Criticism of federal involvement in manpower tended to focus on a cost/benefit analysis that indicated that more money was spent in training workers than was repaid in their contribution to the economy. One study that counteracts

those charges is John E. Schwarz's *America's Hidden Success*, 30–49 and 120–35, which contends that federal manpower programs, along with other Great Society and New Deal programs, contributed to a decline in poverty, provided solutions to a labor surplus caused by the entry of baby boomers and an increasing number of women into the labor pool, and actually helped to increase employment. Those programs demonstrated that government involvement could help the less fortunate better than simply relying on economic growth, which tended to offer uneven rewards. The growth of the federal government, he claimed, was actually small compared to the overall expansion of the American economy. See also Jencks, *Rethinking Social Policy*, 70–91.

Chapter Eight. Making Groceries

1. *NOSI*, 9 August 1969.

2. In New Orleans, locals often referred to grocery shopping as "making groceries," a usage supposedly derived from the French expressions *"faire la courses"* or *"faire son marché,"* which translate as "to do the shopping."

3. In the 1990s, the debates over defining hunger helped to reconceptualize the relationships between food and poverty. "Food security" and "food insecurity" were attempts to broaden definitions beyond nutritional criteria. Eisinger, *Toward an End to Hunger in America*, 2 and 11; Food and Consumer Service, *Household Food Security in the United States in 1995*.

4. On the clientage relationship between DeLesseps S. "Chep" Morrison, New Orleans' mayor from 1946 to 1961, and black political leaders before the 1960s, see Haas, *DeLesseps S. Morrison*, 250–60. For an argument that the nature of the "brokerage relationship" has continued after segregation, see Adolph Reed Jr., *Stirrings in the Jug*, 17.

5. Jeffrey M. Berry, *Feeding Hungry People*, 21–28; DeVault and Pitts, "Surplus and Scarcity," 545–56; Committee on Agriculture, U.S. Senate, *The Food Stamp Program*, 3–17.

6. Committee on Agriculture, U.S. Senate, *The Food Stamp Program*, 16–17; "Special Message to the Congress: Program for Economic Recovery and Growth," February 2, 1961, *Public Papers of the Presidents, John F. Kennedy, 1962*, p. 47; "Statement by the President on the Food Stamp Program," 2 August 1962, *Public Papers of the Presidents, John F. Kennedy, 1962*, p. 599; "Meeting on the Economy and Budget," 30 July 1962, in Naftali, *The Great Crises, Volume One*, 68–69.

7. Randall B. Ripley, "Legislative Bargaining and the Food Stamp Act, 1964," 279–310; Committee on Agriculture, U.S. Senate, *The Food Stamp Program*, 17–23; DeVault and Pitts, "Surplus and Scarcity," 545–56.

8. Gillette, *Launching the War on Poverty*, 308; John A. Baker, interview in Gillette, *Launching the War on Poverty*, 108; Finegold, "Agriculture and the Politics of U.S. Social Provision," 313–55; Lynn, "A Decade of Policy Developments in the Income-Maintenance System," 75–77. The Agriculture Department was given authority by Section 32 of the 1935 law known as PL 74–320 to use 30 percent of monies collected by the U.S. Customs Service to stimulate purchasing of agricultural goods. The 1964 Food Stamp bill was HR 10222. Congress continued the program through a series of extensions.

9. Berry, *Feeding Hungry People*, 40–42.

10. "Food Stamps Ribbon-Cutting Ceremony Programme," 4 February 1969, Folder Food Stamps, Box 42, PRS, SC; Susan Fels, Research Assistant for TCA, "The Food Stamp Program in Orleans Parish February–June 1969," June 1969, Folder Food Stamp Committee 1970, Unprocessed Box 21, CSC.

11. Orville Freeman, secretary of agriculture to President Johnson, 29 August 1966, "The Food Stamp Program—A Progress Report," Folder AG 7 Surplus Products, 11/23/63–11/12/66, Box 10, Legislative Series, White House Central Files, LBJL; Berry, *Feeding Hungry People*, 37 and 49; Committee on Agriculture, U.S. Senate, *The Food Stamp Program*, 46.

12. Schulman, *From Cotton Belt to Sunbelt*, 191–98.

13. Kotz, *Let Them Eat Promises*, 48–61.

14. Ramsey Clark, attorney general, to President Johnson, 18 June 1968, Folder AG 7 Surplus Products, 11/23/63–11/12/66, Box 10, Legislative Series, White House Central Files, LBJL; Berry, *Feeding Hungry People*, 25–55; Eisinger, *Toward an End to Hunger*, 37–56; King, *Budgeting Entitlements*, 40–62; DeVault and Pitts, "Surplus and Scarcity," 546–52; Kennedy, "Public Policy in Nutrition," 325–27. Two of the major influences on the late 1960s hunger debate were Nick Kotz, *Let Them Eat Promises* and the Citizen's Board of Inquiry, *Hunger U.S.A.*

15. Kotz, *Let Them Eat Promises*, 139–59.

16. Some other locales took much longer to develop Food Stamp programs; two New York counties were without programs until 1975. Lynn, "A Decade of Policy Developments," 77.

17. Pat Stoddard to Congressman Edward Hébert, 29 March 1965, Folder Hébert, Box 11, 1965, SC.

18. Stoddard to Garland Bonin, secretary Louisiana Department of Public Welfare, 17 April 1967, Folder TCA, Box 25, 1967, SC.

19. Bill Bailey, "McKeithen Reports Clash with Shriver," *Baton Rouge Advocate*, 26 March 1965.

20. Frank Meydrich, President Louisiana Supermarket Association, Inc., to T. Windle Dyer, TCA, 29 September 1967, Folder Poverty-Community Action, 1967 Subject Files, BC.

21. Rosemary Bresette to Schiro, 24 August 1967, ibid.; Stoddard to Schiro, confidential, 1 September 1967, ibid.; "The Food Stamp Program," September 1967, ibid.

22. "The Food Stamp Program," September 1967, ibid.

23. T. Windle Dyer, TCA administrative assistant, to Senator Allen J. Ellender, 5 October 1967, Folder Poverty-Community Action, 1967 Subject files, BC.

24. Frank Meydrich, President Louisiana Supermarket Association, Inc., to T. Windle Dyer, TCA, 29 September 1967, Folder Poverty-Community Action, 1967 Subject Files, BC.

25. Bonin to Schiro, 27 July 1967, Folder Louisiana Department of Welfare, Box 12, 1967, SC; Minutes, SWPC Board of Directors, 23 May 1968, Folder Board of Directors, 1967–1968, Box II C, CSC.

26. Audrey Delair to McKeithen, 11 December 1967, Folder NOWRO-1967, Box 15, 1967, SC.

27. Schiro to Bonin, 1967, Folder Louisiana Department of Welfare, Box 12, 1967, SC.

28. "Agenda for Special Meeting of the Council," 17 October 1967, Folder Food Stamp Program, Box 24, PRS, SC.

29. Delair to McKeithen, 11 December 1967, Folder NOWRO-1967, Box 15, 1967, SC.

30. Bonin to Delair, chair NOWRO, 12 December 1967, Folder Louisiana Department of Welfare, Box 12, 1967, NOPL.

31. WDSU-TV editorial, "Foot-Dragging on Food Stamps (I)," 12 July 1968, Folder WDSU editorials, Box 37, PRS, NOPL.

32. Jim Manning, "City Okays Cost Share," *NOSI*, 1 March 1968; Godchaux to TCA Board, 5 March 1968, Folder TCA, Box 15, 1968, SC; Frank McLaughlin, to City Council, 13 February 1968, Folder Food Stamps, Box 5, 1968, SC; Department of Public Welfare, Baton Rouge, La., "Food Stamp Program," August 1969, Folder New Orleans Food Stamp Office, Box 54, NAACP Field Office Records, ARC; "Food Stamp Guidelines of Greater New Orleans," Box 54, NAACP Field Office Records, ARC; Lill to TCA Board, 23 February 1968, Folder TCA, Box 15, 1968, SC.

33. Schiro to Bonin, 28 June 1968, Folder Food Stamps, Box 5, 1968, SC.

34. "Program Account Work Program," October 1968, Folder TCA Grant proposals d-f, Box 56, CSC.

35. Editorial, "Finally: Food Stamps for New Orleans," WDSU-TV, 13 December 1968, Folder WDSU editorials, Box 37, PRS, SC; City Council Resolution and Contract, 9 January 1969, Folder Food Stamps, Box 5, 1969, SC; James N. Pezant, director of Department of Council Research, to Schiro and All Councilmen, "Interim Report—Food Coupon Program—Personal-Confidential," 23 April 1969, Folder Food Stamps, Box 5, 1969, SC; Susan Fels, "The Food Stamp

Program in Orleans Parish February–June 1969," June 1969, Folder Food Stamp Committee 1970, Unprocessed Box 21, CSC.

36. Lynn, "Developments in Income-Maintenance Programs," 75–77.

37. Louisiana Department of Public Welfare, "Food Stamp Program," August 1969, Folder New Orleans Food Stamp Office, Box 54, NAACP Field Office Records, ARC; Folder Food Stamp Committee, 1970, Unprocessed Box 21, CSC; James Jurnak and Celeste Newbrough, TCA Department of Research and Planning, "The Food Stamp Program Analysis and Recommendations," April 1970, Folder Food Stamps Program, Box 3, Administrative Subject Files, CDA, NOPL.

38. "Food Stamp Summary," Folder TCA, Box 15, 1969, SC; "Food Stamp Guidelines of Greater New Orleans," August [?] 1969, Folder New Orleans Food Stamp Office, Box 54, NAACP Field Office Records, ARC.

39. Clark Corliss to Vincent, 13 August 1970, Folder TCA, 1968–1971, Box 55, CSC; "Report of Committee to Review Certain Aspects of the Food Stamp Program in Orleans Parish," August 1970, ibid.

40. Corliss to Dean Peter A. Firmin, Tulane University Graduate School of Business Administration, 18 June 1970, Food Stamp Committee, Unprocessed Box 21, CSC.

41. "Report of Committee to Review," August 1970, Folder TCA, 1968–1971, Box 55, CSC; Corliss to Vincent, 13 August 1970, ibid.

42. Ibid; "ICAF Advocacy Planning Program Status Report #3," Folder Irish Channel Community Development Center, Box 28, CSC.

43. James N. Pezant, "Interim Report—Food Coupon Program." Folder Food Stamps, Box 5, 1969, SC, NOPL.

44. Ibid.

45. Susan Fels, "The Food Stamp Program in Orleans Parish February–June 1969," June 1969, Folder Food Stamp Committee 1970, Unprocessed Box 21, CSC.

In 1970, Congressman W. R. Poage (D-Texas), chair of the House Agriculture Committee after 1967, fought diligently to have included in Food Stamp amendments a work requirement that forced recipients to accept offers of work. Berry, *Feeding Hungry People*, 71.

46. James Jurnak and Celeste Newbrough, "The Food Stamp Program Analysis and Recommendations," April 1970, Folder Food Stamps Program, Box 3, Administrative Subject Files, City Demonstration Agency Collection, NOPL.

47. *Carrollton Advocate*, Folder 48, Box 8, LWV; Ferdinand Grayson to Daniel Vincent, 24 April 1970, Food Stamp Committee 1970, Unprocessed Box 21, CSC.

Winston Lill had resigned from TCA's director's post in early 1969 "with great regret." At the time he said it was for a better career opportunity, but during a recent interview he stated that fatigue and the constant pressure placed on him by vocal critics in the neighborhoods speeded his resignation. During Moon Landrieu's administration, however, he returned as director of public relations. Lill to Harry McCall, 30 January 1969, Folder TCA, Box 15, 1969, SC; Winston Lill, interview by Kent Germany, 29 April 1997.

48. *NOTP*, 16 June 1970.

49. Betsy Halstead, "Problems of Food Stamp Program Stir Controversy," *NOTP*, 18 June 1970.

50. Chubbuck, Renwick, and Walker, "The Emergence of Coalition Politics in New Orleans," 17–23.

51. Carl M. Corbin, executive vice president of MAC, to Laurence Eustis, president of MAC, 8 May 1970, Folder MAC, Box 3, Administrative Subject Files, CDA.

52. Ibid.

53. *NOTP*, 24 July 1970.

54. Landrieu to Guy Seghers, H.U.D., 18 December 1970, Folder New Orleans Area H.U.D. Office, Box 2, Administrative Subject Files, CDA.

55. Corliss to Vincent, 13 August 1970, Folder TCA, 1968–1971, Box 55, CSC; "Report of Committee to Review," August 1970, ibid.

56. Michael B. Katz has identified four purposes of American social welfare policy: relieving misery, regulating the labor supply, preserving social order, and providing tools for political mobilization. Katz, *In the Shadow of the Poorhouse*.

Chapter Nine. Making a Model New Orleans

1. Victor Schiro to Marilyn Sublette Immualle, 17 April 1968, Folder Housing, Box 43, PRS, SC.

2. WDSU television, editorial, "City in Crisis," 16 September 1969, Folder WDSU editorials, Box 53, PRS, SC.

3. *WP*, 12 October 1972.

4. *NOSI*, 17 April 1969; "Staff Profile," 31 May 1969, Folder TCA, Box 7, Daniel Ellis Byrd Collection, ARC.

5. *Congressional Quarterly Almanac, 1974*, vol. 30, 345–63.

6. Christopher J. Bellone, Administrator Division of Housing Improvement in Department of Safety and Permits, to Committee Member, 31 March 1967, Folder HANO-1967, Box 24, PRS, SC; Minutes, Citizen's Advisory Committee on Community Improvement, Box 3, 1967, SC.

7. Rose Kahn, "Irish Channel Enjoys Full Beauty Treatment," *NOSI*, 8 August 1968; Editorial, "Irish Channel Plan Worth Copying," *NOSI*, 14 August

1968; WDSU television, editorial, "Irish Channel Attacks Blight," 14 August 1968, WDSU editorials, Box 37, PRS, SC.

8. WDSU-TV, editorial, "A Positive Step for Better Housing," 27 June 1966, Folder WDSU editorials, Box 37, PRS, SC.

9. Rosemary James, "Business: Toward Urban Renewal," *New Orleans* 4 (December, 1969): 66–69.

10. Wallace, "A Decade of Policy Developments," 349–59.

11. HANO Management Division, Occupancy Report, 22 September 1967, Folder HANO (2), Box 8, HANO Release, 20 August 1968, Folder Housing Authority of New Orleans, Unprocessed Box 22, CSC; *The Plain Truth*, 1 May 1970, PEC; Report, n.d., Folder Modernization File, Box 4, Administrative Subject Files, CDA.

12. Andrew, *Lyndon Johnson and the Great Society*, 133; Louis D. Brown, Manager Area Development Division of the Chamber of Commerce of the New Orleans Area, "The Case for Urban Renewal," 19 June 1961, Folder SWPC Board of Directors, 1967, Box II C, CSC.

13. Forman, "The Conflict over Federal Urban Renewal," 254–57; Doerries, "James E. Comiskey, the Irish Third Ward Boss"; Andre, "Urban Renewal and Housing in New Orleans, 1949–1962;" Haas, *DeLesseps S. Morrison*, 230.

14. WDSU-TV, Editorial, "Urban Renewal and the Legislature," 14 June 1966, Folder WDSU editorials, Box 37, PRS, SC.

15. Haas, "Victor H. Schiro, Hurricane Betsy, and the 'Forgiveness Bill,'" 67–90.

16. WDSU-TV, Editorial, "Slum Clearance in Louisiana," 14 June 1966, Folder WDSU Editorials, Box 37, PRS, SC.

17. Edward Hébert to John Dane, 30 August 1961, Folder Urban Renewal, Box 13, HC.

18. Hébert to Gretchen A. Amrhein, 28 March 1968, ibid.; Hébert to Schiro, 13 July 1966, Folder Hébert, Box 7, 1966, SC.

19. Irish Channel Americanism vs. Communism Committee, n.d., [1964], Folder Communism—1964, Box 7, 1964, SC.

20. *NOTP*, 3 August 1969; John Anderson, *Irish Channel*.

21. Ibid., 58–66.

22. Grant, 4 March 1965, Folder Urban Renewal, Box 34, 1965, SC; Schiro to E. L. Barthelemy, 11 June 1965, ibid.; Bernard Lemann to Schiro, 10 December 1965, Folder Lemann, Box 15, 1965, SC.

23. Schiro to unknown, 28 December 1966, Folder Urban Renewal, Box 30, 1966, SC.

24. Don Hummel, HUD Asst. Secretary, to Schiro, 9 February 1967, Folder Urban Renewal, Box 26, 1967, SC; Schiro to Hummel, 15 February 1967, ibid.

25. Ciaccio to Marchand, 16 June 1967, Folder LNWNC, Box 13, 1967, SC; Schiro to Laureal Engineering, 19 September 1967, Folder LNW Feasibility Study, Box 13, 1967, SC.

26. Stuart Brehm to City Council, 8 November 1967, Folder City Planning Commission, Box 4, 1967, SC.

27. Richard C. Johnson, Washington aide to CAO, to Don Hummel, 11 July 1968, Folder Urban Renewal Program, Box 16, 1968, SC; Don Hummel, HUD, to Schiro, 26 March 1968, Folder Community Renewal Program, Box 3, 1968, SC.

28. Schiro to Gretchen Amrhein, 8 April 1968, Folder Urban Renewal Program, Box 16, 1968, SC.

29. Schiro to Edward W. Stagg, executive director of CABL, 14 February 1968, Folder Urban Renewal Program, Box 16, 1968, SC.

30. Woodrow Dumas, mayor-president Baton Rouge, to Schiro, 21 February 1968, Folder Community Renewal Program, Box 3, 1968, SC; Draft of Urban Renewal Bill, March 1968, Folder CACHI, Box 2, 1968, SC; Walter Barnett, chair CACHI, to Schiro, 28 March 1968, Folder CACHI, Box 2, 1968, SC.

31. Forman, "The Conflict Over Federal Urban Renewal," 262.

32. Press Release, Mayor's Office, 11 June 1968, Folder Ninth Ward Rehab, Box 48, PRS, SC.

33. Editorial, "Initiative on Renewal," *NOSI*, 12 July 1968.

34. Stuart H. Brehm Jr., Director CPC, to Thomas H. Heier Jr., 23 July 1968, Folder Urban Renewal program, Box 16, 1968, SC.

35. "Notes for Mayor Victor H. Schiro," 4 September 1968, Folder CACCIA, Box 40, PRS, SC.

36. New Orleans City Council, Resolution, 11 September 1969, Folder CIA, Box 3, 1969, SC; Victor A. Firese, CIA executive director, to City Council, 29 August 1969, ibid.

37. WDSU-TV, "Keep Politics Out of Urban Renewal," 12 September 1968, Folder WDSU editorials, Box 37, Public Relations Series, SC.

38. News Release, Office of the Mayor, 27 September 1968, Folder CAC-CIA, Box 40, PRS, SC; Jack B. McGuire, Public Relations director, to City Council, 3 October 1968, ibid.

39. Bill Rushton, "Cityscape," *VCC*, 19 September 1969.

40. Ibid.

41. Lower Ninth Ward Citizens Advisory Committee, Resolution, 6 March 1969, Folder HANO (1), Box 5, 1969, SC; Willard Robertson, Director HANO, to Joseph Thomas, Director SOUL, April 1969, 7 April 1969, Folder HANO (1), Box 5, 1969, SC; Bernard Levy to Stuart Brehm, et al., 2 April 1969, Folder LNW Feasibility Study, Box 8, 1969, SC; "Summary of Total Objectives of the Lower

Ninth Ward Community Improvement Program," 10 September 1969, Folder CIA, Box 3, 1969, SC; Nils R. Douglas, Chair SOUL, to George Romney, Secretary HUD; 5 May 1969, Folder US-HUD, Box 15, 1969, SC.

42. Ruby C. Sumler to Walter Barnett, 14 April 1969, Folder Feasibility Study, Box 8, 1969, SC; Sumler to Colonel Ketchum, 23 April 1969, ibid; Sumler to Colonel Ketchum, 24 April 1969, ibid.

43. *NOLA Express*, September 1969, Folder NOLA Express, PEC.

44. Rev. William A. Miller, St. Alphonsus Parish, Redemptorist Fathers, prior to 9 November 1969, Folder Urban Renewal, Box 15, 1969, SC.

45. Citizens Housing Council of Greater New Orleans, "The Proposed Community Improvement Plan for the Lower Ninth Ward," Fall 1969, Folder New Orleans-City of—Urban Renewal (Approved for N.O., July 1968), Box 4, Chamber Collection, UNO.

46. WWL-TV, 6 November 1969, Folder WWL editorials, Box 53, PRS, SC; WDSU-TV, 15 October 1969, ibid.

47. WDSU-TV, editorial, "Urban Renewal Issue Wins," Folder WDSU-TV editorials, PRS, SC.

48. *The Plain Truth*, 1 October 1969, Oversize Box 7, FST, ARC.

49. The boundaries were Claiborne Avenue, Jourdan St., Florida Avenue, Dubreuil St., and Jackson Barracks.

50. Community Improvement Agency, *Annual Report 1970*, Records of the Community Improvement Agency, NOPL; Community Improvement Agency, *Annual Report 1971*, ibid.; Hébert letter, 1970, Folder Lower Ninth Ward-1970, Box 56, PRS, SC; *NOTP*, 10 January 1970.

51. Central City Urban Renewal Plan, 1971, Folder Community Improvement Agency, Box 3, Administrative Subject Files, CDA.

52. Ibid.; *NYT*, 16 November 1978.

53. *Codes of the City of New Orleans* No. 828 (January 1, 1970).

54. Close to thirty prominent civic, religious, and business organizations supported a Public Accommodations law that excluded barber shops and beauty shops. SOUL, the Central City Economic Opportunity Committee, the Algiers-Fischer Community Action Center, the Desire NDC, and the American Federation of Teachers preferred that no exceptions be made. Pamphlet, "Toward an Open City," 1969, Folder Public Accommodations Law, Box 395, Chamber Collection, UNO; Msgr. A. T. Screen to Landrieu, 5 December 1969, Folder Public Accommodations, Box 46, Landrieu Collection, Department of Special Collections, Monroe Library, Loyola University of New Orleans [hereafter cited as Landrieu Collection, LU].

55. Wallace M. Young Jr., New Orleans-NAACP president, to Dr. Kenneth O. Johnson, Executive Secretary American Speech and Hearing Association, 20 Oc-

tober 1969, Folder Race Relations, Box 395, Chamber Collection, UNO; Joseph Simon to Kenneth O. Johnson, 29 October 1969, ibid.; *NOTP*, 23 October 1969; Editorial, "Accommodations Law," *NOSI*, 24 October 1969; Editorial, "Eliminate Threat to Conventions," *New Orleans Times-Picayune*, 25 October 1969; WDSU television, editorial, "An Issue of Simple Justice," 18 December 1969, Folder WDSU editorials, Box 53, PRS, SC.

56. The term "Big Easy" was a product of the late 1960s and gained prominence as the title of James Conaway's novel.

57. *NOTP*, 25 July 1969; *NYT*, 12 January 1965.

58. Editorial, "Eliminate Threat to Conventions," *NOTP*, 25 October 1969.

59. Pamphlet, "Toward an Open City," 1969, Folder Public Accommodations Law (Urged for Orleans), Box 395, Chamber Collection, UNO; Msgr. A. T. Screen to Landrieu, 5 December 1969, Folder Public Accommodations, Box 46, Landrieu Collection, LU.

60. Sam Bell Jr., SOUL, to William Rousselle, 24 June 1969, Folder HRC, Box 24, PRS, SC.

61. Edward Hall, president of The Black City Council, to HRC, 24 June 1969, Folder HRC, Box 24, PRS, SC.

62. Editorial, "New Orleans Approaches Maturity," *LAWK*, 3 January 1970.

63. For a concise narrative of the passage of the Model Cities Act, see *Congressional Quarterly Almanac, 1966*, vol. 22, 210–30. See also Bernstein, *Guns or Butter*, 458–70; Andrew, *Lyndon Johnson and the Great Society*, 131–62; Dallek, *Flawed Giant*, 317–22; Frieden and Kaplan, *The Politics of Neglect*; Haar, *Between the Idea and the Reality*; Wood, "Model Cities: What Went Wrong."

64. *Congressional Quarterly Almanac, 1966*, vol. 22, 210–16; Marris and Rein, *Dilemmas of Social Reform*, 239.

65. Senator Ellender to Schiro, 18 February 1966, Folder Ellender, Box 7, 1966, SC; Guste to Schiro, 31 March 1966, Folder Guste, W.J. Jr., Box 7, 1966, SC.

66. William A. Guste Jr., to Hébert, 25 July 1966, Folder Urban Renewal, Box 13, HC.

67. Deane Settoon Mernaugh to Schiro, 23 October 1966, Folder Urban League, Box 30, 1966, SC; Donald A. Chase and Allen Rosenzweig, *Community Leaders Attitude Survey: A Summary*, 1–30; *Community Leaders Attitude Survey: Report*, 141–48.

68. WDSU editorial, "Model Neighborhood Grant," 16 February 1968, Folder WDSU editorials, Box 37, PRS, SC; U.S. Department of Housing and Urban Development, "The Model Cities Program Question and Answers," June 1968, Folder 13, Box 53, ARC.

69. New Orleans City Planning Commission, *Model Cities Application*, 44

and 41 for quotes; Stuart H. Brehm Jr., director CPC, to William W. Collins, regional administrator HUD, 9 April 1968, ibid.; "Resolution," City of New Orleans, 21 March 1968, ibid.; CDA, *Comprehensive Demonstration Plan*, 49.

70. City Planning Commission, *Model Cities Application*, 44; CDA, *Comprehensive Demonstration Plan*, 3; WDSU-TV editorial, "Unofficial O.K. for Model Cities Program," Folder WDSU editorials, Box 37, PRS, SC.

71. Willard Robertson, HANO Chair, to Don Hummel, Assistant Secretary of HUD, 5 September 1968, Folder US Department of HUD, Box 16, 1968, SC; *NOTP*, 7 September 1968; Compliance Report, 29 January 1969, Folder HANO (2), Box 5, 1969, SC.

72. George L. Bott to J. Gilbert Scheib, 1 August 1967, Folder HANO (1), Box 8, 1967, SC; Bott to Scheib, 2 January 1968, Folder HANO (3), Box 5, 1968, ibid.; Bott to Scheib, 1 April 1969, Folder HANO-2, Box 5, 1969, ibid.

73. Jim Manning, "Federal Official Selected as Model Cities Director," *NOSI*, 13 November 1968.

74. Paul Atkinson, "January Deadline Is Set for Model Cities," *NOTP*, 25 May 1969.

75. John A. Pecoul, executive director of NO-HRC, to Thomas Lupo, Regional Planning Commission, 17 July 1969, Folder Human Relations, Box 5, 1969, SC; Winifred Edwards to James King, 3 October 1969, Folder CCNDC, Box 2, 1969, SC.

76. CDA, *Comprehensive Demonstration Plan*, 58–80; Sherman Copelin to Staff Representatives, "The Model Cities Program in New Orleans (A Brief Overview)," 7 January 1970, Folder Model Cities Policy Advisory Board, Box 5, Administrative Subject Files, CDA; U.S. Department of HUD, "The Model Cities Program Question and Answers," June 1968, Folder 13, Box 53, NAACP Field Office Records, ARC.

77. *The Plain Truth*, 23 December 1969, PEC; Welcome Duncan, "Evaluation Report Desire Community HDC Project Number #30–029," 27 September 1971, Folder Desire-Florida Housing Deve. Corp., Box 1, Administrative Subject Files, CDA.

78. *NOTP*, 18 January 1970.

79. CDA, Press Release, 6 February 1970, Folder Model Cities, Box 57, PRS, SC; CDA, Press Release Telegram, 3 June 1970, Folder Telegrams, Box 3, Administrative Subject Files, CDA. For descriptions of staff positions, salaries, and duties for 1970 see related material in Folder TCA-71, Box 3, Administrative Subject Files, CDA.

80. CDA, *Comprehensive Demonstration Plan*, "Part II, Projects," 1–325; "Projects Status," [August 1973], Folder Management System, Box 4, Administrative Subject Files, CDA.

81. "Projects Status," [August 1973], Folder Management System, Box 4, Administrative Subject Files, CDA.

82. "Taking Care of Business, Inc.: An Outline for a Model Cities Economic Development Proposal," 1969, Folder Proposals, Box 5, Administrative Subject Files, CDA; Richard Haley to Jim King, 10 November 1969, Folder TCA, 1971, Box 3, Administrative Subject Files, CDA; Folder Stern, Box 55, CSC.

83. Among these leaders were Clarence Guillemet, business developer; Edwin Lombard, legal consultant; Andrew Sanchez, teacher and SOUL leader; James Singleton, Central City leader and founder of BOLD; and Frank Bivens, president of the Desire Area Community Council. "A Brief History and Background of the Technical Assistance and Services of ABCOL, Inc.," *ABCOL News*, February 1973, Folder Warren, Dane, Box 2, Administrative Subject files, CDA; "A Summary of the Second Action Evaluation Report on the Amalgamated Builders and Contractors of the Louisiana Project," [after April 1973], Folder Gautier, Adella, Box 1, ibid.; Claude J. Bean, "Interim Assistance Program Status Report for Month of August, 1971," August 1971, Folder Status Reports, Box 8, ibid.; "Newsletter," 12 November 1971, Folder ABCOL, Box 3, ibid.; Eddie Camese, executive director ABCOL, to Terrence Duvernay, deputy director CDA, 21 October 1971, Folder ABCOL, Box 3, ibid.; Proposals, Folder Proposals, Box 5, ibid.

84. Sherman Copelin to RICC, 21 August 1972, Box 7, CDA; the *CACTUS Newsletter*, November 1974, Folder 48, Box 1, FST, ARC; Mackintosh, "How Family Health Foundation Was Mau-Maued," 44–58; Martha Ward, *Poor Women, Powerful Men*, 73–85; TCA, *History of the Community Action Movement*, 26.

85. Mackintosh, "How Family Health Foundation Was Mau-Maued"; Ward, *Poor Women, Powerful Men*, 97–145.

86. Mackintosh, "How Family Health Foundation Was Mau-Maued"; Ward, *Poor Women, Powerful Men*, 97–145; Wolfe, *Radical Chic and Mau-Mauing the Flak Catchers*.

87. Mackintosh, "How Family Health Foundation Was Mau-Maued"; Ward, *Poor Women, Powerful Men*, 97–145.

88. CDA, *Second Action Year Comprehensive Demonstration Plan*, "Part II," 9–31; James R. King to Model Cities Project Sponsors on Employment of MNA Residents, 7 August 1970, Folder 16, Box 20, FST, ARC; James King to Francis Keevers, CIA, 6 July 1971, Folder CIA, Box 2, Administrative Subject files, CDA.

Part Two. Black Power and Dixie's Democratic Moment, 1968–1974

1. Lionel McIntyre, "Interview" by Ed Campbell, *NOLA Express*, no. 10, [August 1968].

Chapter Ten. The Thugs United and the Politics of Manhood

1. Mike Henderson and Danny Greene, "Militants Hold Varied Theories," *NOSI*, 5 August 1969. For examinations of Chicago's Vice Lords, the Blackstone Rangers, and the East Side Disciples and their involvement with the Southern Christian Leadership Conference and the Office of Economic Opportunity, see Fish, *Black Power/White Control*, 120–174. More personal accounts are Sale, *The Blackstone Rangers* and Fry, *Locked-Out Americans*.

2. Colman McCarthy, "The Impasse Between Bureaucrats and Streetcrats," *WP*, 23 March 1970; *NYT*, 10 June 1968; John Carmody, "Washington, D.C.: Fund City, U.S.A.," *WP*, 15 August 1971.

3. Jack Davis, "Ripping Off the Poverty Program," *Figaro*, 24 March 1973; *Star and Crescent* (New Orleans), August 1973.

4. *LAWK*, 22 August 1970.

5. The Black Eye, "Thugs United the Answer to Our Problems," *Street Scene Community Newspaper*, February 1971.

6. J. Lunsing et al., "Thugs United, Inc." [unpublished typescript report], n.d., 1970, Folder Thugs United, 1970, Stanton Collection, UA, TUL.

7. *The Plain Truth*, 21 October 1969, Oversize Box 7, FST, ARC.

8. Lunsing et al., "Thugs United, Inc."; *Street Scene Community Newspaper*, February 1971.

9. Thugs United, *Progress*, n.d., 1968[?], Folder Thugs United, Stanton Collection, UA, TUL.

10. Betsy Halstead, "Good-Guy Thugs," *Dixie Roto*, 15 June 1969.

11. Thugs United, *Progress*, 1969, Folder Thugs United, Stanton Collection, UA, TUL.

12. Thugs United, *Progress*, n.d., 1968[?], Folder Thugs United, Stanton Collection, UA, TUL; Betsy Halstead, "Good-Guy Thugs."

13. United Fund, "Preliminary Staff Report Thugs United," n.d., 1970?, Folder Thugs, Box 55, CSC.

14. Thugs United, *Progress*, n.d., 1968?, Folder Thugs United, Stanton Collection, UA, TUL.

15. Lucien Salvant, " 'We Are Thugs' . . . Who Help People," *Clarion Herald*, 8 May 1969.

16. Lunsing et al., "Thugs United, Inc."

17. *NOTP*, 21 April 1970.

18. Warren Carmouche to Sir, n.d., 1969[?], Folder Proposals, Box 5, CDA.

19. Thugs United, *Progress*, n.d., 1968[?], Folder Thugs United, Stanton Collection, UA, TUL.

20. Thugs United, proposal, "Job and Applicants Recruitment and Placement Program," Folder Program Proposals, Stanton Collection, UA, TUL.

21. Warren Carmouche to Sir, n.d., 1969?, Folder Proposals, Box 5, CDA.

22. "Thugs United Inc. Proposal for the Ex-Convict Job Placement Program," n.d., 1969?, Folder program proposals, Stanton Collection, UA, TUL; "T.U.I. Ex-Convict Job Placement Program," n.d., 1969?, Folder proposals, Box 5, CDA.

23. David R. Hunter to Gideon Stanton, 29 August 1968, Folder Thugs United 1968–1970, Stanton Collection, UA, TUL.

24. George B. Field, GNOCC assistant executive vice president, to Laurene Kennedy, 22 November 1968, Folder 13 Race Relations, Box 395, Chamber Collection, UNO.

25. Contract between GNOCC and Thugs, 20 November 1968, Folder Thugs, Box 476, Chamber Collection, UNO.

26. Committee to Investigate and Report on Thugs United, "Report to the Board of Directors Chamber of Commerce of the New Orleans Area," Folder Thugs United, Inc., Box 303, Chamber Collection, UNO; Minutes, GNOCC, 28 October 1968, ibid.

27. Thugs-Chamber Contract, 20 November 1968; Edward Hall to unknown, n.d., Folder Masterfile on fundraising, Stanton Collection, UA, TUL.

28. Edward Hall to unknown, n.d., Folder Masterfile on fundraising, Stanton Collection, UA, TUL. Proposed programs included People's College Pilot Program, Drop-out Program, Ex-Convict Job Placement and Counseling Program, Legal Counseling, Community Communication Program, Recreation Program, Community Services, Shell Service Station, Youth Employment Program (NOYES, New Orleans Youth Employment Service), and a Health Clinic.

29. Betsy Halstead, "Good-Guy Thugs."

30. Harry McCall, Sam Israel Jr., Harry Kelleher, Eads Poitevent, Richard Freeman, and Murray Fincher, to Friend, 22 August 1969, Folder Thugs United, Box 14, 1969, SC.

31. Eads Poitevent to Thomas B. Lemmann, 16 June 1969, Folder Thugs, Box 476, Chamber Collection, UNO.

32. Fincher to concerned (form letter), 17 December 1968, ibid.

33. David R. Hunter to Fincher, 22 December 1968, ibid.

34. "Grants Approved by the Stern Family Fund March 1968–March 1969," Folder Stern, Box 55, CSC; Earl Philips, associate director The Urban Coalition, to Carl Corbin, executive vice president MAC, 15 July 1969, Folder Thugs 1968–70, Stanton Collection, UA, TUL; David Hunter to Clarence Scheps, executive vice president Tulane University, 15 December 1969, Folder Thugs 68–70, ibid; "Thugs, United List of Contributions," 6 October 1969, Box 1, ibid.

35. Lunsing et al., "Thugs United, Inc."

36. James W. Newman Jr., Thugs finance board, to Michael J. Molony, 14 December 1968, Folder Thugs, Box 476, Chamber Collection, UNO; *The Plain Truth*, 22 November 1969, Oversize Box 7, FST, ARC.

37. "To the People a Profit with a Services Rendered," 2 April 1969, Folder Thugs, Box 476, Chamber Collection, UNO.

38. Various correspondence, Folder Financial reports, budgets, and Folder Thugs United 1968–1970, Stanton Collection, UA, TUL.

39. *NOTP*, 6 May 1970; *Star and Crescent* (New Orleans), August 1973; *LAWK*, 16 May 1970.

40. Eric V. Johnson and Henry Johnson Jr., to Jim Linn, 20 August 1970, Stanton Collection, UA, TUL.

41. Jack Davis, "Ripping Off the Poverty Program"; *NOTP*, 6 May 1970; *Star and Crescent* (New Orleans), August 1973.

Chapter Eleven. Women, Welfare, and Political Mobilization

1. Jeanne Nathan, "How New Orleans Women Play Politics," Parts 1, 2, and 3, *Figaro*, 17 March 1973, 24 March 1973, 7 April 1973.

2. Davies, *From Opportunity to Entitlement*, 236–43; Thomas F. Jackson, "The State, the Movement, and the Urban Poor," 403–9.

3. TANF was part of the Personal Responsibility and Work Opportunities Reconciliation Act signed on August 22, 1996.

4. Noble, *Welfare as We Knew It*, 71–73; Skocpol, *Protecting Soldiers and Mothers*; Mink, *The Wages of Motherhood*; Quadagno, *The Color of Welfare*.

5. Lynn, "Policy Developments in Income-Maintenance System," 60 and 73–74; Daniel Moynihan, "The Crisis in Welfare," *The Public Interest* 19 (Winter 1968): 13; Piven and Cloward, *Regulating the Poor* and *Poor People's Movements*; Kotz and Kotz, *A Passion for Equality*.

6. Quadagno, *The Transformation of Old Age Security*.

7. The law read: "No assistance shall be granted to a child living with its mother, if the mother has had an illegitimate child after receiving assistance from the Department of Public Welfare, unless and until proof satisfactory to the parish board of public welfare has been presented showing that the mother has ceased illicit relationships and is maintaining a suitable home for the children." *Lampton et al. v. Bonin et al.*, 299 F. Supp. 336, 15 April 1969; Levenstein, "From Innocent Children to Unwanted Migrants and Unwed Moms," 10–33; HANO, Press Release, 10 November 1969, Folder Housing Authority of New Orleans, Unprocessed Box 22, CSC; Isaac Reynolds to Clark Corliss, 7 May 1968, Folder Board of Directors Correspondence, 1967–1969, Box II C, CSC; *NYT*, 18 September 1960; *NYT*, 9 November 1960.

8. *King v. Smith*, 392 U.S. 309 (1968).

9. *Congressional Quarterly Almanac, 1967*, 892–916; Bernstein, *Guns or Butter*, 432–38; Davies, *From Opportunity to Entitlement*, 157–84; Lynn, "A Decade of Policy Development," 74–75.

10. *Congressional Quarterly Almanac, 1967*, 907.

11. Bernstein, *Guns or Butter*, 434 and 437.

12. The New Orleans Legal Assistance Corporation was approved by TCA in February 1967 and began operation in January 1968. Its advocates won out over a group representing the more conservative Legal Aid Society, which did not believe the law was the place to seek political reform. NOLAC received substantial support from Ernest "Dutch" Morial and John Nelson, a white civil rights attorney. Led by Richard Buckley, NOLAC had a core of attorneys who wanted to use the law to create social justice. John Nelson Collection, ARC; "Proposal for a Legal Assistance Program in New Orleans, Louisiana," 1 February 1967, Folder Leagal [*sic*] Assistance Program—1966, Box 14, 1966, Schiro, NOPL. For an introduction to Legal Services, see Davis, *Brutal Need*; Bussiere, *(Dis)Entitling the Poor*; Hollingsworth, "Ten Years of Legal Services for the Poor," 285–327; Sosin, "Legal Rights and Welfare Change, 1960–1980," 260–86; Melnick, *Between the Lines*.

13. *NOLA Express*, June 1968.

14. *NOTP*, 25 November 1968.

15. Lampton to Organization concerned about public housing tenants, 27 February 1970, Folder 13, Box 21, FST, ARC; Desire Welfare Rights Organization, "'To Gain These Rights,'" Folder Desire Area Community Council, Box 3, Administrative Subject Files, CDA.

16. Isaac Reynolds to Clark Corliss, 7 May 1968, Folder Board of Directors Correspondence, 1967–1969, Box II C, CSC; *NOTP*, 12 May 1968.

17. *Lampton et al. v. Bonin et al.*, 299 F. Supp. 336; 304. Supp. 1384; 397 U.S. 663, 90 S. Ct. 1408; Edward J. Lepoma, "Moms March in Welfare Slash Protest," *NOSI*, 14 November 1968; *NOTP*, 15 November 1968.

18. Maurice G. Anderson, president SWPC, 22 November 1968, Folder Board of Directors Correspondence, 1967–1969, Box II C, CSC.

19. Bonin to Boggs, 25 November 1968, Folder Federal Agencies—OEO III, 1969 Subject Files, BC; Bonin to McKeithen, 27 November 1968, ibid.; Walter Richter, Southwest OEO, to Boggs, 24 December 1968, ibid.

20. Report, 23 April 1969, Folder Board of Directors Correspondence 1967–1969, Box II C, CSC; HRCNO, "Welfare Fact Sheet," 23 April 1969, Folder HRC, Box 24, PRS, SC.

21. HRCNO, "Welfare Fact Sheet," 23 April 1969, Folder HRC, Box 24, PRS, SC.

22. William C. Rousselle to Bonin, 22 April 1969, ibid.

23. J. Gilbert Scheib to HANO Board, 19 May 1969, Folder HANO (2), Box 5, 1969, SC.

24. Ibid.

25. *Lampton et al. v. Bonin et al.*, 304 F. Supp. 1384, 16 July 1969. The U.S.

Supreme Court took up the *Lampton* case in April 1970, but remanded it to a lower court based on its April *Rosado v. Wyman* decision (397 U.S. 397), which affirmed that states could fund AFDC benefits at lower rates than the established standard of need.

26. *NOSI*, 15 July 1969.

27. Daniel Vincent to Schiro, 29 July 1969, Folder TCA, Box 15, 1969, SC.

28. *NOTP*, 30 July 1969.

29. *NOTP*, 5 August 1969 and 9 August 1969.

30. Ed Anderson, "Governor Backs Federal Welfare Costs Takeover," *NOTP*, 30 July 1969.

31. *NOTP*, 27 July 1969.

32. *NOSI*, 5 August 1969; Bill Niekirk, "Welfare March Halted at State Capitol Building," *NOTP*, 12 August 1969.

33. *The Plain Truth*, 20 August 1969, PEC.

34. Bill Niekirk, "Welfare March Halted at State Capitol Building."

35. *NOSI*, 9 August 1969.

36. *The Plain Truth*, 1 November 1969, PEC; Shirley Lampton letter, 18 December 1969, Folder HANO, Unprocessed Box 22, CSC; *LAWK*, 22 November 1969.

37. "New Orleans Tenants Organization Goals for Rent Strike," 11 December 1969, clipping in Folder 13, Box 21, FST, ARC.

38. Jeffrey B. Schwartz, NOLAC, "Legal Fact Sheet," December 1969, Folder HANO, Unprocessed Box 22, CSC.

39. Paul Sanzenbach to Steering Committee of the Emergency Welfare Coalition, 17 December 1970, Folder 7, Box 3, Community Relations Council of Greater New Orleans Collection, ARC; Sanzenbach to EWC members, 27 January 1970, Folder Emergency Welfare Coalition, Unprocessed Box 17, CSC.

40. Editorial, "Tenants Strike Is No Joke," *The Plain Truth*, 23 December 1969, PEC.

41. HANO, Press Release, 22 November 1969, Folder HANO, Unprocessed Box 22, CSC; Haas, "The Expedient of Race," 13.

42. HANO, Press Release, 10 November 1969, Folder HANO, Unprocessed Box 22, CSC.

43. Samuel Bell, president LNWNC, to Bonin, 15 December 1969, Folder LNWNC, Box 8, 1969, SC.

44. These pockets were called "Nigger Town," "Pension Town," "Mid-Carrollton," "Gert Town," "Zion City," "Upper Holly Grove," and "Lower Holly Grove." ULGNO, "Proposal for New Day Care Center, Carrollton Area," n.d., Folder 51, Box 8, LWV.

45. Gary A. Lloyd, project director, "Community Relations Council: Gert

Town Project," Folder Community Relations Council, 1964–1967, Box 21, CSC.

46. Tyler, *Silk Stockings and Ballot Boxes*.

47. "Background of the Carrollton Project," after July 1969, Folder 39, Box 8, LWV.

48. LWV Report, "Development of Human Resources," September 1966, Folder 53, Box 8, LWV.

49. "A Three Year Report," *ICCE Newsletter*, in Folder 65, Box 8, LWV; *Newsletter: Inner-City Project*, in Folder 66, Box 8, LWV; LWVNO, "Community Action Program Tips and Facts," November 1966, Folder 67, Box 8, ibid.

50. CCSC, Minutes, 15 January 1969, Folder 42, Box 8, LWV; McFarland to Richard Buckley, 12 December 1968, Folder 40, Box 8, LWV; Paul Sanzenbach to Professor Lloyd, 25 April 1969, Folder 40, Box 8, LWV; HRC, *Progress*, December 1969.

51. LWVNO, "Community Action Program Tips and Facts," November 1966, Folder 67, Box 8, LWV.

52. LWVNO President to Board, 25 May 1966, Folder 67, Box 8, LWV .

53. Ibid.

54. Lucille Soniat, Notes from Inner-City Education Conference, 1 March 1967, ibid.

55. LWV, report, "From Isolation to Cooperation and Coalition: Methods of Establishing Working Relationships Between Leagues and Inner-City and/or Black Organizations," January 1969, Folder 66, Box 8, LWV.

56. CCSC, "Carrollton Central Steering Committee Work Program," n.d., Folder 43, Box 8, LWV.

57. Unnamed list, 23 September 1968, Folder 44, Box 8, LWV.

58. *Newsletter: Inner-City Project*, 21 August 1968, Folder 66, Box 8, LWV.

59. CCSC, "Carrollton Central Steering Committee Work Program," n.d., around 1968?, Folder 43, Box 8, LWV; *Dawn: Danneel Area News*, 2 October 1968, Folder 49, Box 8, LWV.

60. Felicia Kahn, president LWVNO, to Joy, 8 February 1969, Folder 40, Box 8, LWV.

61. Felicia Kahn, president LWVNO, to Joy, 8 February 1969, Folder 40, Box 8, LWV.

62. "Background of the Carrollton Project," after July 1969, Folder 39, Box 8, LWV; *Carrollton Advocate*, 24 January 1970, Folder 48, Box 8, LWV.

63. *Carrollton Advocate*, 6 April 1970, Folder 48, Box 8, LWV.

64. Robert McFarland, "Gert Town Needs 'Community Control,'" *Carrollton Advocate*, 29 April 1970, Folder 48, Box 8, LWV.

65. "Agenda" for CCSC Meeting, 20 March 1971, Folder 43, Box 8, LWV.

66. Loose handwritten notes with "Bob Tucker" at top, April 1971, ibid; MONEY, "McFarland Has Repeatedly Violated His Own Bylaws," ibid.

67. Wisdom to LWVNO Board, March 1970, Folder 45, Box 8, LWV. Kahn and Wisdom continued their involvement on an individual basis.

Chapter Twelve. Acronyms, Liberalism, and Electoral Politics, 1969–1971

1. Voter Registration Statistics, 31 October 1969, Folder Election-1969, Box 41, PRS, SC; Kimball, *The Disconnected*, 251–54.

2. Fairclough, *Race and Democracy*, 104–5 and 111; Hirsch, "Simply a Matter of Black and White," 262–319; Bell, *The Afro-Creole Protest Tradition*.

3. Fairclough, *Race and Democracy*, 104–5 and 111; Hirsch, "Simply a Matter of Black and White," 272–75; Frederick Douglas Wright, "Black Political Participation in Louisiana." 89–90.

4. Kurtz and Peoples, *Earl K. Long*, 202–10; Kimball, *The Disconnected*, 251–54; Frederick Douglas Wright, "Black Political Participation in Louisiana," 89–90, 159–60.

5. Rogers, *Righteous Lives*, 307–20; Hirsch, "Simply a Matter of Black and White," 285–89.

6. Moon Landrieu, interview by Kent Germany, 4 June 2001.

7. Haas, "The Expedient of Race," 5–29; Gene Bourg, "Blacks Learn the White Man's Game of Politics," *NOSI*, 12 September 1973.

8. Penn, *The Disconnected*, 252–54; Furnell Chatman, "Black Politics," 29+; Rogers, *Righteous Lives*, 107; Bourg, "Black Politics 4: From the Pulpits and the Docks Came the Seeds of Activism," *NOSI*, 15 February 1973; Henry Dejoie and C. C. Dejoie, "Politics: From Slave to Freeman?" *New Orleans* 2 (June 1968): 38–43.

9. Furnell Chatman, "Black Politics," 29+; Bourg, "Black Politics 4"; Dejoie and Dejoie, "Politics," 38–43.

10. Voter Registration Statistics, 31 October 1969, Folder Election-1969, Box 41, PRS, SC.

11. Winston Lill, interview by Kent Germany, 29 April 1997.

12. Furnell Chatman, "Black Politics," 29+.

13. The full names were: TIPS—Tremé Improvement Political Society; DAWN—Development Association of Wards and Neighborhoods; BlackPAC—Black Political Action Committee; BOBUAC— Builders of a Better Uptown Area Committee; BUC—Black Unity Caucus; BLAC—Black Louisiana Action Caucus; BYP—Black Youth for Progress; GAVEL—Greater Algiers Voter Education League; BUENO—Black United Efforts of New Orleans; PACT—Provident Ad-

ministration of Community Theory, Inc. Bourg, "Black Politics 4"; Dejoie and Dejoie, "Politics," 38–43; Bourg, "Black Politics 11: The Neighborhoods: Grass Roots Go Deep," *NOSI*, 26 February 1973.

14. Bourg, "Black Politics—12: The Role of the Dollar," *NOSI*, 27 February 1973. A black candidate, C.C. Dejoie of *The Louisiana Weekly*, had dropped out of the race.

15. *NOSI*, 7 August 1969.

16. *EXTRA* [SOUL], 1971, in Oversized Folder, McGuire Collection, TUL.

17. Bourg, "Black Politics 7: Organizing for Political Clout," *NOSI*, 20 February 1973; Charlotte Hayes, "Black Power for Sale," *VCC*, 31 August 1972.

18. Bourg, "Black Politics 8: SOUL—The Pre-Eminent Political Organization," *NOSI*, 21 February 1973; *NOSI*, 7 August 1969.

19. Hirsch, "Race and Politics in Modern New Orleans," 461–84; Hirsch, "Simply a Matter of Black and White," 262–319; Bell, *The Afro-Creole Protest Tradition*; Daniel Thompson, *Negro Leadership Class*.

20. Bourg, "Black Politics 9: COUP—The Seventh Ward Power," 22 February 1973, *NOSI*.

21. *The Plain Truth*, 21 October 1969, Oversize Box 7, FST, ARC.

22. Other important members were Clyde T. J. McHenry, who became executive director of HANO in 1972; Henry Braden, IV, a major force in Democratic politics well into the 1980s; Albert Malveaux, a professor of computer technology at Xavier University; Gerard S. Douglas, eventually the director of the Cooperative Area Manpower Planning System (CAMPS) program; and George Cachere, director of the New Careers program. Elloie was a later defector. Another one was Louis Charbonnet, who formed the Tremé Improvement Political Society (TIPS).

23. Charlotte Hayes, "Black Power for Sale: The Slow Climb from Preacher to Patronage," *VCC*, 31 August 1972.

24. Bourg, "Black Politics 10: Organization, The Opening of Closed Doors," *NOSI*, 23 February 1973; *The Plain Truth*, 22 November 1969, Oversize Box 7, FST, ARC.

25. Hayes, "Black Power for Sale."

26. Oretha Haley, chairperson of BOBUAC, to New Orleans City Council, 19 March 1970, Folder Central City Housing Development Corporation, Box 3, Administrative Subject Files, CDA, NOPL; *The Plain Truth*, 22 January 1970, 20 March 1970, and 1 May 1970, PEC; *Carrollton Advocate*, 17 March 1970.

27. Bourg, "Organizing for Political Clout"; Hayes, "Black Power For Sale."

28. Kurtz and Peoples, *Earl K. Long*, 135.

29. "Pledges," 25 September 1968, Folder Politics, Box 55, NAACP Field Office Records, ARC; Minutes of Organizational Meeting, Black Unity Caucus,

Fall 1968, ibid.; "Minutes of Organizational Meeting, Black Unity Caucus, Fall 1968, ibid. Members included Revius Ortique, a longtime attorney and future Louisiana Supreme Court Justice; Cecil W. Carter Jr., future member of the Landrieu administration; Israel Augustine, elected as a judge in 1970; Ellis Hull, leader of Central City's United Voters League; Avery Alexander, veteran civil rights activist and soon-to-be state representative; Ernest "Dutch" Morial, the first black graduate of LSU Law School and, in 1978, New Orleans's first black mayor; Clarence Barney, head of the local Urban League; and Carlton Pecot, a leader of the Louisiana Advancement Association.

30. James Singleton, "Singleton Assesses Changes in District 'B' Council Race," *The Plain Truth*, 21 October 1969, Oversize Box 7, FST, ARC.

31. *The Plain Truth*, 21 October 1969, in Oversize Box 7, FST, ARC. Dr. Lawler P. Daniels would not concede to Singleton and Ellis Hull to Davis.

32. *The Plain Truth*, 20 August 1969, PEC.

33. Ibid.

34. Editorial, "Black Vs. Black in the Ninth Ward," *The Plain Truth*, 22 November 1969, PEC.

35. Moon Landrieu, interview by Kent Germany, 4 June 2001.

36. "Interview with Marchand: 'Only White Niggers Win,'" *The Plain Truth*, 1 May 1970 and 23 December 1969, PEC.

37. As quoted in Bourg, "Leaders Are Reluctant to Pool Power," *NOSI*, 28 February 1973.

38. Dittmer, *Local People*, 363–88; Lemann, *The Promised Land*, 303–39.

39. Alvarrz Ferrouilet, "Student Column: Black Unity," *The Plain Truth*, 20 March 1970, PEC.

40. Oretha Haley, "Black Women Are Fed Up!" *The Plain Truth*, 20 September 1969, ibid.

41. Jim Singleton, "Orleans Parish School System in Trouble," *The Plain Truth*, 20 August 1969, PEC; James Singleton, interview by Kent Germany, 23 July 2001, in possession of the author.

42. Bourg, "Black Politics 12"; Jason Berry, "Springtime in the New South: Elections Past and Future," *VCC*, 30 March 1972; Hayes, "Black Power for Sale."

43. Joseph Kraft, "End of the Hayride," *WP*, 14 December 1964.

44. Bourg, "Black Politics 5: Landrieu Marked Turning Point," *NOSI*, 16 February 1973.

45. Coalition for a Fair Redistricting, Position Paper, 16 February 1972, Folder 14 Urban League, Box 47, NAACP Field Office Records, ARC.

46. Chubbuck, Renwick, and Walker, "The Emergence of Coalition Politics," 17. Of the total vote in the first primary Fitzmorris received 34 percent; Landrieu, 19 percent; Guste, 17 percent; Councilman John Petre, 13 percent; Judge David

Gertler, 11 percent; and School Board Member Lloyd Rittiner in the single digits. Breaking down the vote in terms of race, Landrieu picked up 39 percent of black voters, but less than 15 percent of white voters. Guste attracted 30 percent of black voters, while David Gertler got 22 percent. Landrieu and Guste split the Uptown wealthy white vote. Fitzmorris's support was overwhelmingly white, contrasted to 1965 when he got 65 percent of black voters against Schiro.

47. Fitzmorris press release, 6 November 1969, Public Accommodations 1969 Folder, Box 46, Landrieu Collection, LU; Fitzmorris and Myers, *Frankly Fitz.*

48. Winston Lill, interview by Kent Germany, 29 April 1997; Haas, *De-Lesseps S. Morrison*, 284–88; Folder CCDA, Box 23, PRS, SC; Folder CRDO, ibid.; Folder CCDA, Box 9, 1964, SC.

49. Dent, "New Orleans Versus Atlanta," 66–68; David Chandler, "Slicing Up the Cake," *New Orleans* (June 1974): 52–58; Jack Davis, "Faust Revisited: Is SOUL for Sale?" *New Orleans* (November 1973): 40, 49, and 92–97; "Don't Bite the Hand That Feeds You," *EXTRA* [SOUL], 1971, in Oversized Folder, McGuire Collection, TUL.

50. Chubbuck, Renwick, and Walker, "The Emergence of Coalition Politics," 18–25.

51. WWL-TV editorial, 15 December 1969, Folder WWL-TV Editorials, Box 53, PRS, SC.

52. Bill Rushton, "Cityscape," *VCC*, 26 December 1969.

53. *The Plain Truth*, 23 December 1969, PEC.

54. Moon Landrieu, interview by Kent Germany, 4 June 2001; *New Orleans* 1 (December 1966): 58–59.

55. Moon Landrieu, interview by Kent Germany, 4 June 2001; Anderson, *Black, White, and Catholic*, 102–7.

56. Maurice "Moon" Landrieu, Statement for Mayoral Campaign, [1969], Folder Candidate for Mayor, Box 123, Maurice E. "Moon" Landrieu Collection, LU; "If We Courageously Face Up to Our Problems Then There Is Nothing We Cannot Do," *New Orleans* 3 (March, 1969): 9+; *VCC*, 21 November 1969.

57. Ibid.

58. Errol Laborde, "Politics: The Ways New Orleans Is Changing," *VCC*, 15 June 1972.

59. Maurice "Moon" Landrieu, Statement for Mayoral Campaign, [1969], Folder Candidate for Mayor, Box 123, Landrieu Collection, LU.

60. Moon Landrieu, interview by Kent Germany, 4 June 2001.

61. Bourg, "Black Politics 15: Landrieu a Popular Champion or a Product of Percentages?" *NOSI*, 2 March 1973; Philip Shabecoff, "Thousands on Public Payrolls Face Layoff," *NYT*, 1 October 1979; Banks et al., "Transformative

Leadership in the Post–Civil Rights Era," 173–87; Brown and Erie, "Blacks and the Legacy of the Great Society," 299–330; Eisinger, *Black Employment in City Government, 1973–1980*; Stein and Hamm, "Federal Aid and Mobilization," 97–115.

62. "SOUL: For the Record," *EXTRA* [SOUL], 1971, in Oversized Folder, McGuire Collection, TUL; Nils Douglas, Chair Desire CDC, to Everett Aultman, United Fund, 28 May 1970, Folder Desire CDC 1965–1970, Box 23, CSC.

63. Daniel C. Thompson, "Black Leadership in New Orleans," 1977, 6–9, Folder Black Leadership in New Orleans, Box 123, Landrieu Collection, LU.

64. Quote from Rogers, *Righteous Lives*, 109; Moon Landrieu, interview by Kent Germany, 4 June 2001.

65. Norma Frieberg, interview by Kent Germany, 17 April 1997.

66. Bobo, *The New Orleans Economy*, ii.

67. Rosemary James and Charlotte Hays, "Moon Landrieu: Did He Tell the Truth?" *New Orleans*, October 1973, 70; Bourg, "Black Politics 15: Landrieu a Popular Champion or a Product of Percentages?" *NOSI*, 2 March 1973.

68. Daniel Thompson, "Black Leadership in New Orleans," 1977, 10, LU.

69. As quoted in Tom Bethell, "Politics as an Investment: A Candid Conversation Between Pershing Gervais and Charles Ward," *VCC*, 17 August 1972.

70. Kurt J. Williams, "The Black Messiah," *Carrollton Advocate*, 3 November 1970, Folder 48, Box 8, LWV.

71. Uhuru No Umoja, "Moon Landrieu Ain't Santa Claus," *The Plain Truth*, 1 May 1970, PEC.

Chapter Thirteen. Panthers, Snipers, and the Limits of Liberalism

1. James Harvey Kerns, "Facing the Facts of the Racial Relations Dilemma in New Orleans, Louisiana, 1964," Folder Urban League of Greater New Orleans Serials, Box 64, CSC.

2. As quoted in Rosemary James, "White Opinion on Racial Tension," *New Orleans*, April 1973, 56

3. *WP*, 16 July 1969.

4. State Attorney Edward Hanrahan was acquitted of obstruction in 1972. Five years later, a $47 million civil suit against the officers ended with no verdict. In 1982, victims finally received a $1.8 million settlement from federal and local governments. Peter Osnos, "Black Panthers vs. the Police: The Rising Toll," *WP*, 7 December 1969; John Kifner, "Police in Chicago Slay 2 Panthers," *NYT*, 5 December 1969; *Chicago Tribune*, 22 January 1970, 8 February 1970, 9 March 1970; Jonathan Koziol and John O'Brien, "US Jury Panther Report," *Chicago Tribune*,

16 May 1970; Nathaniel Sheppard Jr., "Panther Plaintiffs," *NYT*, 14 November 1982.

5. Transcript, WTUL Interview with Malik Rahim and Ahmad Rahman, 13 March 2000.

6. Joseph I. Giarrusso, police superintendent, to Moon Landrieu, confidential memorandum, 17 July 1970, Black Panther File, Addenda, Human Relations Committee Collection, NOPL [hereafter HRC].

7. *NOTP*, 17 September 1970

8. *NOLA Express*, September 1970, Panthers Louisiana File, PEC; "We Have Never Used Our Guns to Go into the White Community to Shoot Up White People. We Only Defend Ourselves," *NOLA Express*, November 1970, ibid.

9. Reverend Joseph Putnam to Congregation of St. Francis De Sales Catholic Church, 20 September 1970, Folder Black Panthers, Vertical File, LACOLL; Transcript, WTUL Interview with Malik Rahim and Ahmad Rahman, 13 March 2000.

10. Joseph I. Giarrusso to Moon Landrieu, confidential memorandum, 5 August 1970, Black Panther File, Addenda, HRC.

11. Transcript, 15 September 1970, Black Panther File, Addenda, HRC; Transcript, Moon Landrieu and Joseph Giarrusso Press Conference, 15 September 1970, ibid.; "We Have Never Used Our Guns," *NOLA Express*, November 1970; *NOTP*, 25 September 1970.

12. Transcript, 15 September 1970, Black Panther File, Addenda, HRC; Transcript, Moon Landrieu and Joseph Giarrusso Press Conference, 15 September 1970, ibid.; "Exposure of Raymond Reed, Bootlicker, Puppet and Nigger-Pig," in ibid.; "We Have Never Used Our Guns," *NOLA Express*, November 1970.

13. Leslie Williams, "Ex-Panther Thankful He Survived," *NOTP*, 15 September 1995; Transcript, WTUL Interview with Malik Rahim and Ahmad Rahman, 13 March 2000; "We Have Never Used Our Guns," *NOLA Express*, November 1970; Roy Reed, "Panther Witness Describes Shots," *NYT*, 6 August 1971.

14. Transcript, Moon Landrieu Press Conference, 16 November 1970, Black Panthers File, Addenda, HRC; Transcript, Moon Landrieu and Joseph Giarrusso Press Conference, 15 September 1970, ibid.

15. Ibid.

16. Archbishop Philip Hannan and Rev. George H. Wilson, "Leaders Call for Adequate Planning," *The Cable*, 22 September 1970, in CSC, Box 23, Desire CDC, 1965–1970; Dr. Ernest Cherrie, B. Capers, and W. Wessel, Report, "CRC Sub-Committee on Desire Area," Folder 4, Box 3, CRC; "Chief Giarrusso Reports," *NOLA Express*, September 1970, Panthers Louisiana File, PEC.

17. Editorial, "Desire Project Terror Wrong-Way Tactic," *NOTP*, 16 September 1970.

18. Press Release, Black Panthers File, Addenda, HRC; *NOTP*, 22 September 1970.

19. Don Hughes and Bob Ussery, "Protest Grows in Panther Case," *NOTP*, 26 September 1970; Mrs. Jean Fischer, Octavia Street, to Landrieu, 23 September 1970, Black Panthers File, Addenda, HRC.

20. In 1997, the building housing the Orleans Criminal Court was renamed in honor of Judge Augustine.

21. "Power to the People" leaflet, around September 1970, Boggs, 1970, Subject files, Federal Agencies-OEO; Garland Bonin, Louisiana Commissioner of Public Welfare, to Hale Boggs, 30 September 1970, ibid.

22. Office of Economic Opportunity, "Statement on New Orleans Legal Assistance Corporation," 28 October 1970, Folder Statement on New Orleans Legal Assistance Corporation (10/28/70), Box 3, Entry 15A, RG 381, NARA.

23. Barry Portman, to Members of the NOLAC Board of Directors, 1 December 1970, Folder 15, Box 2, John Nelson Collection, ARC; Philip D. Carter, "OEO Firings," *WP*, 23 November 1970; Roy Reed, "Panthers Freed in New Orleans," *NYT*, 7 August 1971.

24. Barry Portman, to Members of the NOLAC Board of Directors, 1 December 1970, Folder 15, Box 2, John Nelson Collection, ARC.

25. Handwritten Notes on Back of Tulane University Flyer, November 1970, Panthers Louisiana File, PEC; *LAWK*, 31 October 1970.

26. "Do Not Be Alarmed But Do Be Informed" flyer, around November 1970, Panthers Louisiana File, PEC.

27. Prevent Disaster Resolution, November 1970, Tulane Ad Hoc Committee to Prevent Disaster File, PEC.

28. Roy Reed, "A Police-Panther Confrontation Ends Peacefully in New Orleans," *NYT*, 20 November 1970; David Snyder, "La. Police, Militants Clash," *WP*, 20 November 1970.

29. Moon Landrieu, interview by Kent Germany, 4 June 2001; Barry Portman, to Members of the NOLAC Board of Directors, 1 December 1970, Folder 15, Box 2, John Nelson Collection, ARC; Jerry Carfagno, "More Than a Foothold," *NOLA Express*, 1 December 1970, LACOLL; WTUL Interview with Malik Rahim and Ahmad Rahman, 13 March 2000; Roy Reed, "A Police-Panther Confrontation Ends Peacefully in New Orleans," *NYT*, 20 November 1970; David Snyder, "La. Police, Militants Clash," *WP*, 20 November 1970; *NOSI*, 28 February 1973; Orissa Arend, "Trio Ignited Controlled Revolution in the '70s," *LAWK*, 26 May 2003.

30. Barry Portman, to Members of the NOLAC Board of Directors, 1 De-

cember 1970, Folder 15, Box 2, John Nelson Collection, ARC; Don Lewis, "Pick-eters Back Panther Stand," *NOTP*, 20 November 1970.

31. George L. Bott to Scheib, 23 November 1970, Black Panthers File, Addenda, HRC; *NOSI*, 24 January 1964; "Stay in the Streets, Demonstrate with Jane Fond [*sic*]," 22 November 1970, Panthers Oakland File, PEC.

32. Orissa Arend, "Aftermath of the Panthers in Desire," *LAWK*, 16 June 2003.

33. Arrested Subjects on November 25, 1970, Black Panthers File, Addenda, HRC; *WP*, 27 November 1970; Jerry Carfagno, "More Than a Foothold," *NOLA Express*, 1 December 1970, LACOLL; *NYT*, 27 November 1970.

34. NCCF Flyer, 27 November 1970, Black Panthers File, HRC.

35. "Mourning" pamphlet, January 1970, oversize Box 7, FST, ARC.

36. "The People," 3 December 1970, Folder 55, Box 14, Politics Series, NAACP Field Office Records, ARC.

37. *Desire: Voice of the People*, [November] 1970, Oversize Box 7, FST, ARC.

38. Minutes of Desire Community Development Corporation Board Meeting, 1 December 1970, Folder 20, Box 22, FST, ARC.

39. Johnny Jackson Jr., "An Open Letter to All Black and Concerned People (No. 2 in a Series)," around November 1970, Panthers—Louisiana File, PEC.

40. Moon Landrieu, interview by Kent Germany, 4 June 2001.

41. Orissa Arend, "Aftermath of the Panthers in Desire," *LAWK*, 16 June 2003.

42. Jerry Carfagno, "More Than a Foothold," *NOLA Express*, 1 December 1970, LACOLL.

43. Nicholas C. Chriss, "La. Governor Says Deputies Shot Students," *WP*, 19 November 1972.

44. Hair, *Carnival of Fury*, 107, 119–20, and 156–82.

45. Austin Scott and George Lardner Jr., "Death on a Rooftop—Why?" *WP*, 11 January 1973; Dave Walker, "Secret Hojo Massacre Report," *Figaro*, 9 June 1973.

46. *WP*, 31 January 1973.

47. Dave Walker, "Secret Hojo Massacre Report," *Figaro*, 9 June 1973; Peter Hernon, *A Terrible Thunder: The Story of the New Orleans Sniper* (Garden City, N.Y.: Doubleday, 1978), 13–14, 19–22.

48. Hernon, *A Terrible Thunder*, 68, 70.

49. *NYT*, 5 January 1973; Hernon, *A Terrible Thunder*, 164.

50. Hernon, *A Terrible Thunder*, 109–14, Essex quote from p. 114.

51. Hernon, *A Terrible Thunder*, 113–15; Clarence Giarrusso letter, reprinted in Hernon, *A Terrible Thunder*, 277.

52. *WP*, 10 January 1973.

53. Walker, "Secret Hojo Massacre Report"; Hernon, *A Terrible Thunder*, 140–43.

54. Walker, "Secret Hojo Massacre Report"; "How to Preempt TV Time," *NYT*, 14 January 1973.

55. Rowland Evans and Robert Novak, "New Orleans: City in Transition," *WP*, 7 February 1973.

56. As quoted in Hernon, *A Terrible Thunder*, 154.

57. As quoted in Bob Krieger, "Chief Giarrusso's HoJo Strategy: Did It Pass or Fail?" *VCC*, 19–25 January 1973.

58. As quoted in Rosemary James, "Listen! Please Listen!" *New Orleans*, March 1973.

59. Landrieu quoted in Dennis Persica, "A City Under Siege," *NOTP*, 7 January 1998; for a timeline of Landrieu activities during the night, see Tom Bethell, "What Happened at Howard Johnson's?" *VCC*, 12–18 January 1973.

60. Hernon, *A Terrible Thunder*, 138 and 156.

61. *VCC*, 12–18 January 1973.

62. Evans and Novak, "New Orleans: City in Transition," *Washington Post*, 7 February 1973.

63. As quoted in Hernon, *A Terrible Thunder*, 277.

64. As quoted in Dennis Persica, "A City Under Siege," *NOTP*, 7 January 1998.

65. For reactions of prominent white and black leaders, see Rosemary James, "Listen! Please Listen!" 45–73; Rosemary James, "White Opinion on Racial Tension," 53–72.

66. *WP*, 9 January 1973.

67. Giarrusso quote from Rosemary James, "White Opinion on Racial Tension," 56; Giarrusso letter reprinted in Hernon, *A Terrible Thunder*, 278–79.

68. President Lyndon Johnson and Senator Ralph Yarborough, 4 February 1964, Citation #1883, Tape WH6402.05, Recordings, LBJL.

69. Later in 1973, another catastrophe struck New Orleans. On Sunday, June 24, the Upstairs lounge, a gay bar and club at Chartres and Iberville in the French Quarter, was set on fire, killing over thirty patrons. Roy Reed, "Arson Suspected in Deaths," *NYT*, 26 June 1973.

70. As quoted in Hernon, *A Terrible Thunder*, 216.

71. Story and quote from Hernon, *A Terrible Thunder*, 238.

Conclusion. Prelude to Katrina

1. James Harvey Kerns, "Facing the Facts of the Racial Relations Dilemma in New Orleans, Louisiana, 1964," Folder Urban League of Greater New Orleans Serials, Box 64, CSC.

2. David Goldfield, *Black, White, and Southern*, 21–23.

3. Berry, "Springtime in the New South."

4. As quoted in Milton Coleman, "Cities Feel Stranded, Mayor Reports," *WP*, 8 February 1985; John Herbers, "Mayors Stress 'New Localism,'" *NYT*, 18 June 1985.

5. *Public Papers of the Presidents of the United States, 1988*, Ronald W. Reagan, "Address Before a Joint Session of Congress on the State of the Union," 25 January 1988, p. 87.

6. U.S. Census Bureau, Census Historical Poverty Tables, "CPH-L-162. Persons By Poverty Status in 1969, 1979, and 1989, by State."

7. Murray, *Losing Ground;* Schwarz, *America's Hidden Success*. One leading study contends that economic growth certainly contributed to the decline in poverty, but equally important were the income transfer policies of the Great Society. Danziger, Haveman, and Plotnick, "Antipoverty Policy," 50–77.

8. Rickey, "The Nazi and the Republican," 64–74; Fairclough, *Race and Democracy*, 462–65.

9. Dent, "New Orleans Versus Atlanta," 64.

10. As quoted in Bourg, "Blacks Learn the White Man's Game of Politics," *NOSI*, 12 September 1973.

11. Joan Treadway, "Poverty Agency Marks 20 Years," *NOTP*, 4 March 1985; for a list of TCA's operational programs as of 2001, see TCA, *History of the Community Action Movement*, 44–45.

12. Honorable Jack Brooks, "Impeachment Resolution of Judge Robert F. Collins," 24 June 1993, U.S. House of Representatives.

13. As quoted in Bourg, "Black Politics 2," *NOSI*, 13 February 1973.

14. Hirsch, "Race and Politics in Modern New Orleans," 461–84; quote from Hirsch, "Simply a Matter of Black and White," 305.

15. Whelan, Young, and Lauria, "Urban Regimes and Racial Politics," 1–21.

16. On this process in Atlanta, see Reed, *Stirrings in the Jug*, 1–18.

17. Hernon, *A Terrible Thunder*, 238.

18. Daniel C. Thompson, "Black Leadership in New Orleans," 1977, p. 12, in Folder Black Leadership in New Orleans, Box 123, Landrieu Collection, LU.

19. Gans, *The War against the Poor*; Katz, *The Undeserving Poor*.

20. Schulman, "The Privatization of Everyday Life."

21. Richard Haley, "Observations," 22 February 1968, Folder Board of Directors 1967–1968, Box II C, CSC.

22. Drew Jubera, "In New Orleans, T-Shirt Tributes to Dead Do Brisk Business," *Atlanta Journal-Constitution*, 28 March 2004.

23. For Naftali's response, see "Department of Homeland Screw-Up" *Slate.com*, 1 September 2005.

24. For instance, see James Rainey, "Doubts Now Surround Account of Snipers Amid New Orleans Chaos," *Los Angeles Times*, 24 November 2005.

25. "Address to the Nation on Hurricane Relief," 15 September 2005, Public Papers of the President, transcript by the American Presidency Project, www.presidency.ucsb.edu.

26. Ibid.

BIBLIOGRAPHY

Manuscript Collections

Amistad Research Center. Tilton Hall. Tulane University. Byrd, Daniel Ellis Papers. Central City Economic Opportunity Committee Records. Community Relations Council of Greater New Orleans, Records. Cottles, Alma Papers. Douglas, Nils Papers. Dryades Street YMCA (New Orleans, La.), Records. Free Southern Theater, Records. National Association for the Advancement of Colored People, Office of Field Director of Louisiana, Records. Nelson, John Petit Papers. Urban League of Greater New Orleans, Records.

City Archives and Louisiana Division Special Collections. New Orleans Public Library. Davis, A. L. Collection. City Demonstration Agency Records [Model Cities]. Community Improvement Agency Records [Urban Renewal]. Human Relations Committee of New Orleans Records. Schiro, Mayor Victor Hugo Papers.

Department of Special Collections. Earl K. Long Memorial Library. University of New Orleans. Community Services Council Collection. National Association for the Advancement of Colored People, New Orleans Branch. Goals Foundation Council Collection. Luke, Leontine Collection. Greater New Orleans Chamber of Commerce.

Department of Special Collections. Hill Memorial Library. Louisiana State University Libraries. Louisiana State University. Long, Russell B. Collection.

Department of Special Collections. Tulane University Libraries. Jones Hall. Tulane University. Boggs, Congressman Hale Collection (Manuscripts Division). Hébert, Congressman Edward Collection (Manuscripts Division). Lemann, Bernard Collection (Manuscripts Division). League of Women Voters Collection (Manuscripts Division). Lill, Winston Collection (Manuscripts Division). McGuire, Jack B. Papers (Manuscripts Division). Political Ephemera Collection. Schiro, Mayor Victor H. (Manuscripts Division). Stanton, Gideon (University Archives). Vertical File (Louisiana Collection).

Lyndon B. Johnson Library, Austin, Texas. Collections of Organizational and Personal Papers. Recordings and Transcripts of Conversations and Meetings. White House Central Files.

National Archives at College Park. National Archives and Records Administration, College Park, Maryland. Records of the Community Services Administration [Office of Economic Opportunity]. Record Group 381. Records of the Department of Housing and Urban Development. Record Group 207.

Special Collections and Archives. J. Edgar and Louise S. Monroe Library at Loyola University New Orleans. Landrieu, Mayor Maurice E. "Moon" Collection.

Court Cases

Dombrowski v. Pfister, 380 U.S. 479 (1965).

King v. Smith, 392 U.S. 309 (1968).

Lampton, et al. v. Bonin, et al., 299 F. Supp. 336 (U.S. Dist. 1969).

Lampton, et al. v. Bonin, et al., 304. Supp. 1384 (U.S. Dist. 1969).

Lampton, et al. v. Bonin, et al., 397 U.S. 663, 90 S. Ct. 1408 (U.S. 1970).

Rosado v. Wyman, 397 U.S. 397 (1969).

Oral Histories

Chisom, Ronald. Interview by Kent Germany. 10 March 1998. In possession of the author.

Frieberg, Norma. Interview by Kent Germany. 17 April 1997. In possession of the author.

Gillette, Michael L., ed. *Launching the War on Poverty: An Oral History*. New York: Twayne, 1996.

Haley, Richard. Interview by Kim Lacy Rogers. 9 May 1979. In the Kim Lacy Rogers–Glenda B. Stevens Oral History Collection. Amistad Research Center. New Orleans, La.

Jackson, Johnny, and Abraham Sturges. Interview by Jesse Morrell. 6 May 1973 and 15 May 1973. WNNR Radio Recording. In Amistad Research Center. New Orleans, La.

Landrieu, Maurice E. "Moon." Interview by Kent Germany.

Lyndon B. Johnson Library, Oral History Collection: Donald M. Baker, Theodore Berry, Hale Boggs, Joseph Califano, William B. Cannon, Jack T. Conway, Allen J. Ellender, James C. Gaither, Charles M. Haar, F. Edward Hébert, Walter Heller, Nicholas DeB. Katzenbach, Robert A. Levine, Russell Long, Lawrence O'Brien, Harry MacPherson; Fred Panzer; Otis Singletary, Jules M. Sugarman, James L. Sundquist, Adam Yarmolinsky.

Singleton, James. Interview by Kent Germany. 23 July 2001. In possession of the author.

Stich, Margery. Interview by Kent Germany. 3 December 1997. In possession of the author.

Suarez, Matteo. Interview by Kim Lacy Rogers. 20 June 1988. In the Kim Lacy Rogers–Glenda B. Stevens Oral History Collection. Amistad Research Center. New Orleans, La.

Winston Lill. Interview by Kent Germany. 29 April 1997. In possession of the author.

Government Documents

The Annual Report of the Council of Economic Advisers. From U.S. President, *Economic Report of the President to the Congress*. Washington, D.C.: U. S. Government Printing Office, 1964.

Carter and Burgess, Inc. *Interim Assistance Application: Desire–Florida*. Fort Worth, Tex.: Carter and Burgess for Community Improvement Agency in and for the City of New Orleans, La., April 1970.

City Demonstration Agency. *Comprehensive Demonstration Plan*. New Orleans: City Demonstration Agency, 1970.

————. *Second Action Year Comprehensive Demonstration Plan*. New Orleans: City Demonstration Agency, June 1971.

Committee on Agriculture, Nutrition, and Forestry, U.S. Senate. *The Food Stamp Program: History, Description, Issues, and Options*. Washington, D.C.: US-GPO, 1985.

Community Improvement Agency for City of New Orleans. *Comprehensive Planning and Urban Design Study of the Lower Ninth Ward Community Improvement Area*. New Orleans: Environment Seven, 1973.

————. *Interim Assistance Application: Central City*. Fort Worth, Tex: n.p., 1970.

Food and Consumer Service. *Household Food Security in the United States in 1995: Summary Report of the Food Security Measurement Project*. Washington, D.C.: United States Department of Agriculture, 1997.

The Joint Legislative Committee on Un-American Activities, State of Louisiana. Report No. 8. *Aspects of the Poverty Program in South Louisiana*. Baton Rouge: n.p., 14 April 1967.

The Joint Legislative Committee on Un-American Activities, State of Louisiana. *Students for a Democratic Society and the New Left: Their Danger to the Educational Institutions of the State of Louisiana*. Baton Rouge: State of Louisiana, 1969.

Louisiana Advisory Committee to the United States Commission on Civil Rights. *The Quest for Housing: A Study of Housing Conditions in New Orleans, A Report*. Washington, D.C.: U.S. Commission on Civil Rights, 1974.

Louisiana Legislature, Legislative Council. *The Government of Louisiana*. Baton Rouge: n.p., 1959.

Bibliography 403

Louisiana State Economic Opportunity Office. Community Action Agencies. *Handbook for Board Members in Community Action Agencies.* Baton Rouge: Louisiana State Economic Opportunity Office, 1969.

————. *Handbook for Board Members in Community Action Agencies.* Baton Rouge: Office of Economic Opportunity, [1970].

————. *Report of the Louisiana Office of Economic Opportunity.* Baton Rouge: Louisiana Office of Economic Opportunity, 1 May 1965.

New Orleans City Planning Commission. *Model Cities Application: Application to the Department of Housing and Urban Development for a Grant to Plan a Comprehensive Model Cities Program.* New Orleans: City Planning Commission, April 1970.

New Orleans Data Analysis Unit. *Neighborhood Characteristics Summary.* New Orleans: The Office of City Planning, 1980.

New Orleans Office of Policy Planning. *Neighborhood Profiles.* Vols. 1–20. New Orleans: The Office, 1978–1981.

Office of the Mayor, New Orleans. *Blacks in City Government, 1981.* New Orleans: n.p., 1981.

Office of Policy Planning, Analysis Unit, City of New Orleans. *Citizen Attitude Survey.* Vols. 1–5. New Orleans: n.p., 1979.

Office of Policy Planning and Research of the United States Department of Labor, *The Negro Family: The Case for National Action.* Washington, D.C.: U.S. Government Printing Office, March 1965.

Ryscavage, Paul. *The Poor in 1970: A Chartbook.* Washington: Office of Economic Opportunity. Office of Planning, Research, and Evaluation, 1972.

U.S. Bureau of the Census, *Statistical Abstract of the United States, 1970,* 91st ed. Washington, D.C.: 1970.

U. S. President, *Public Papers of the Presidents of the United States.* Washington, D.C.: Office of the *Federal Register,* National Archives and Records Service, John F. Kennedy, 1963; Lyndon B. Johnson, 1964; Lyndon B. Johnson, 1965; Ronald W. Reagan, 1988.

Walk, Darlene M. and Carolyn Kuehling. *An Analysis of Blight in the City of New Orleans: Blight Index 1976.* New Orleans: New Orleans Office of Planning and Analysis, 1978.

Secondary Sources

Aaron, Henry. *Politics and the Professors: The Great Society in Perspective.* Washington, D.C.: Brookings Institution, 1978.

Abramovitz, Mimi. *Regulating the Lives of Women: Social Welfare Policy from Colonial Times to the Present.* Boston: South End, 1988.

Adams, Frank T. *James A. Dombrowski: An American Heretic, 1897–1983.* Knoxville: University of Tennessee Press, 1992.

Allswang, John. *The New Deal and American Politics: A Study in Political Change.* New York: John Wiley and Sons, 1978.

Anderson, John. *Irish Channel: A Study of Existing Conditions and Problems with Design Proposals.* n.p.: 1970.

Anderson, Kristi. *The Creation of a Democratic Majority, 1928–1936.* Chicago: University of Chicago Press, 1979.

Anderson, Martin. *The Federal Bulldozer: A Critical Analysis of Urban Renewal, 1949–1962.* Cambridge, Mass.: Massachusetts Institute of Technology Press, 1964.

Anderson, R. Bentley. *Black, White, and Catholic: New Orleans Interracialism, 1947–1956.* Nashville, Tenn.: Vanderbilt University Press, 2005.

Andre, J. R. "Urban Renewal and Housing in New Orleans, 1949–1962." M.A. thesis, Louisiana State University, 1963.

Andrew, John III. *Lyndon Johnson and the Great Society.* Chicago: Ivan R. Dee, 1998.

Anthony, Arthé Agnes. "The Negro Creole Community in New Orleans, 1880–1920: An Oral History." PhD diss., University of California at Irvine, 1978.

Applebome, Peter. *Dixie Rising: How the South Is Shaping American Values, Politics, and Culture.* New York: Times Books, 1996.

Ashmore, Susan Youngblood. "Carry It On: The War on Poverty and the Civil Rights Movement in Alabama, 1964–1970." PhD diss., Auburn University, 1999.

Ayers, H. Brandt and Thomas H. Naylor, eds. *You Can't Eat Magnolias.* New York: McGraw-Hill, 1972.

Baker, Liva. *The Second Battle of New Orleans: The Hundred-Year Struggle to Integrate the Schools.* New York: HarperCollins, 1996.

Banks, Manley Elliot, II, Nelson Wikstrom, Michon Moon, and Joseph E. Andrews. "Transformative Leadership in the Post–Civil Rights Era: The 'War on Poverty' and the Emergence of African-American Municipal Political Leadership." *The Western Journal of Black Studies* 20, no. 4 (1996): 173–87.

Bartley, Numan. *A History of the South.* Vol. 11, *The New South, 1945–1980.* Baton Rouge: Louisiana State University Press and the Littlefield Fund for Southern History of the University of Texas, 1995.

Bassi, Laurie J., and Orley Ashenfelter. "The Effect of Direct Job Creation and Training Programs on Low-Skilled Workers." In *Fighting Poverty: What Works and What Doesn't.* Edited by Sheldon H. Danziger and Daniel H. Weinberg. Cambridge, Mass.: Harvard University Press, 1986.

Baumbach, Richard O., Jr., and William E. Borah. *The Second Battle of New Orleans: A History of the Vieux Carré Riverfront-Controversy*. University, Ala.: University of Alabama Press, 1981.

Beardsley, Edward H. *A History of Neglect: Health Care for Blacks and Mill Workers in the Twentieth Century South*. Knoxville: University of Tennessee Press, 1987.

Bell, Karyn Cossè. *Revolution, Romanticism, and the Afro-Creole Protest Tradition in Louisiana, 1718–1868*. Baton Rouge: Louisiana State University Press, 1997.

Bellah, Robert N., R. Madsen, William Sullivan, A. Swindler, and S. M. Tipton. *Habits of the Heart: Individualism and Commitment in Public Life*. Berkeley: University of California Press, 1985.

Bellows, Barbara L. *Benevolence Among Slaveholders: Assisting the Poor in Charleston, 1670–1860*. Baton Rouge: Louisiana State University Press, 1993.

Bembry, Evelyn L. "A Study of Membership Status in Organization and Related Factors to Selected Families in Ten Poverty Areas of Orleans Parish." M.S.W. thesis, Tulane University, 1967.

Bernstein, Irving. *Guns or Butter: The Presidency of Lyndon Baines Johnson*. New York: Oxford University Press, 1996.

Berry, Jeffrey M. *Feeding Hungry People: Rulemaking in the Food Stamp Program*. New Brunswick, N.J.: Rutgers University Press, 1986.

Betz, Michael. "Riots and Welfare: Are They Related?" *Social Problems* 21 (1974): 345–55.

Blake, Casey Nelson. *Beloved Community: The Cultural Criticism of Randolph Bourne, Van Wyck Brooks, Waldo Frank, and Lewis Mumford*. Chapel Hill: University of North Carolina Press, 1990.

Bobo, James R. *The New Orleans Economy: Pro Bono Publico?* New Orleans: Division of Business and Economic Research, College of Business Administration, University of New Orleans, 1975.

Bobo, James R., compiler. *Statistical Abstract of Louisiana*. New Orleans: Division of Business and Economic Research, College of Business Administration, Louisiana State University New Orleans, 1965.

Bodnar, John E. *The Transplanted: A History of Immigrants in Urban America*. Bloomington, Ind.: Indiana University Press, 1985.

Bounds, Elizabeth M., Pamela K. Brubaker, and Mary E. Hobgood, eds. *Welfare Policy: Feminist Critiques*. Cleveland: Pilgrim Press, 1999.

Bower, William G. "Investment in Human Capital and Economic Growth." In *Perspectives on Economic Growth*. Edited by Walter W. Heller, 163–86. New York: Random House, 1968.

Boyer, Paul. *Urban Masses and Moral Order in America, 1820–1920*. Cambridge, Mass.: Harvard University Press, 1978.

Braeman, John. "The Making of the Roosevelt Coalition: Some Reconsiderations." *The Canadian Review of American Studies* 11 (Fall 1980): 233–53.

Bremner, Robert. *The Discovery of Poverty in the United States*. New Brunswick, N.J.: Transaction, 1992.

Brinkley, Allan. *End of Reform: New Deal Liberalism in Recession and War*. New York: Knopf, 1995.

Brock, William R. *Investigation and Responsibility: Public Responsibility in the United States, 1865–1900*. Cambridge: Cambridge University Press, 1984.

Brown, Michael K. and Steven P. Erie. "Blacks and the Legacy of the Great Society: The Economic and Political Impact of Federal Social Policy," *Public Policy* 29 (Summer 1981): 299–330.

Browning, Rufus P., Dale Rogers Marshall, and David H. Tabb. *Protest Is not Enough: The Struggle of Blacks and Hispanics for Equality in Urban Politics*. Berkeley: University of California Press, 1986.

Bullard, Robert D., ed. *In Search of the New South: The Black Urban Experience of the 1970s and 1980s*. Tuscaloosa: University of Alabama Press, 1989.

Bussiere, Elizabeth. *(Dis)Entitling the Poor: The Warren Court, Welfare Rights, and the American Political Tradition*. University Park, Penn.: Pennsylvania State University Press, 1997.

Button, James. *Blacks and Social Change: Impact of the Civil Rights Movement in Southern Communities*. Princeton: Princeton University Press, 1989.

———. *Black Violence: Political Impact of the 1960s Riots*. Princeton: Princeton University Press, 1978.

Califano, Joseph A. *The Triumph and Tragedy of Lyndon Johnson: The White House Years*. New York: Simon and Schuster, 1991.

Campanella, Richard. *Time and Place in New Orleans: Past Geographies in the Present Day*. Gretna, La.: Pelican, 2002.

Campbell, Ballard C. *The Growth of American Government: Governance from the Cleveland Era to the Present*. Bloomington: University of Indiana Press, 1995.

Capps, Mary K. "Community Decision Making: A Study of the Board of Directors of Total Community Action." PhD diss., Tulane University, 1970

Carlton, David L. and Peter A Coclanis. "Another 'Great Migration': From Region to Race in Southern Liberalism, 1938–1945." *Southern Culture* 3 (Winter 1997): 37–62.

Carleton, Mark. *Politics and Punishment: The History of the Louisiana State Penal System*. Baton Rouge, La.: Louisiana State University Press, 1971.

Carrigan, Jo Ann. *The Saffron Scourge: A History of Yellow Fever in Louisiana,*

1796–1905. Lafayette, La.: Center for Louisiana Studies, University of Southwestern Louisiana, 1994.

Carter, Dan. *The Politics of Rage: George Wallace, the Origins of the New Conservatism, and the Transformation of American Politics*. New York: Simon and Schuster, 1996.

Carter, David. "Two Nations: Social Insurgency and National Civil Rights Policymaking in the Johnson Administration, 1965–1968." PhD diss., Duke University, 2001.

Cash, Wilbur J. *The Mind of the South*. New York: Knopf, 1941.

Caudill, Harry. *Night Comes to the Cumberlands: A Biography of a Depressed Area*. Boston: Little, Brown, 1962.

Chai, Charles Y. W. "Who Rules New Orleans: A Study of Community Power Structure." *Louisiana Business Survey* 16, no. 5 (1972): 2–11.

Chamberlain, Charles. *Victory at Home: Manpower and Race in the American South During World War Two*. Athens: University of Georgia Press, 2003.

Chase, Donald A., and Allen Rosenzweig. *Community Leaders Attitude Survey: A Summary*. New Orleans: Rader and Associates for the Regional Planning Commission, 1969.

———. *Community Leaders Attitude Survey: Report*. New Orleans: Rader and Associates for the Regional Planning Commission, 1970.

Chubbuck, James, Edwin Renwick, and Joe E. Walker. "The Emergence of Coalition Politics in New Orleans." *New South* 26 (Winter 1971): 17–23

Citizen's Board of Inquiry into Hunger and Malnutrition in the United States. *Hunger U.S.A.* Boston: Beacon, 1969.

Clark, Kenneth B. *Dark Ghetto: Dilemmas of Social Power*. New York: Harper and Row, 1965.

Clement, Priscilla. "Children and Charity: Orphanages in New Orleans, 1817–1914." *Louisiana History* 27 (Fall 1986): 337–51.

Cloward, Richard A., and Lloyd E. Ohlin. *Delinquency and Opportunity: A Theory of Delinquent Gangs*. Glencoe, Ill.: Free Press, 1960.

Cochran, Augustus B. III. *Democracy Heading South: National Politics in the Shadow of Dixie*. Lawrence: University Press of Kansas, 2001.

Collins, Robert M. "Growth Liberalism in the Sixties: Great Societies at Home and Grand Designs Abroad." In *The Sixties: From Memory to History*. Edited by David Farber, 11–44. Chapel Hill: University of North Carolina Press, 1994.

Conaway, James. *The Big Easy*. Boston: Houghton-Mifflin, 1970.

Congressional Quarterly Almanac, 1964–1967, Vols. 20–23. Washington, D.C.: Congressional Quarterly Service, 1965–1968.

Conkin, Paul. *Big Daddy from the Pedernales: Lyndon Baines Johnson*. Boston: Twayne, 1986.

Connolly, Harold X. *A Ghetto Grows in Brooklyn*. New York: New York University Press, 1977.

Crapuchet, Simonne. *The Negro Population's Participation in the Community: A Statistical Analysis in the 9th Ward of New Orleans. A Study for the Urban League of Greater New Orleans and School of Social Work, Tulane University*. New Orleans: s.n., 1959.

Crocker, Ruth. *Social Work and Social Order: The Settlement Movement in Two Industrial Cities, 1889–1930*. Urbana: University of Illinois Press, 1992.

Cronon, Edmund David. *Black Moses: The Story of Marcus Garvey and the Universal Negro Improvement Association*. Madison: University of Wisconsin Press, 1955.

Cruthirds, Chalmers Thomas. "The Community Action Program Agency and Voluntary Delegate Organizations: Issues in Interorganizational Contracting." PhD diss., Tulane University, 1972.

Dallek, Robert. *Flawed Giant: Lyndon Johnson and His Times, 1961–1973*. New York: Oxford University Press, 1998.

———. *Lone Star Rising: Lyndon Johnson and His Times, 1908–1960*. New York: Oxford University Press, 1991.

Daniel, Pete. *Breaking the Land: The Transformation of Cotton, Tobacco, and Rice Cultures since 1880*. Urbana: University of Illinois Press, 1985.

Danziger, Sheldon H., and Daniel H. Weinberg, eds. *Fighting Poverty: What Works and What Doesn't*. Cambridge, Mass.: Harvard University Press, 1986.

Danziger, Sheldon, Robert H. Haveman, and Robert D. Plotnick. "Antipoverty Policy: Effects on the Poor and the Nonpoor." In *Fighting Poverty: What Works and What Doesn't*, Sheldon Danziger and Daniel Weinberg, eds., 50–77. Cambridge, Mass.: Harvard University Press, 1986.

Davies, Gareth. *From Opportunity to Entitlement: The Transformation and Decline of Great Society Liberalism*. Lawrence: University Press of Kansas, 1996.

Davis, Martha F. *Brutal Need: Lawyers and the Welfare Rights Movement*. New Haven, Conn.: Yale University Press, 1993.

Dawley, Alan. *Struggles for Justice: Social Responsibility and the Liberal State*. Cambridge, Mass.: Belknap Press, 1991.

Dent, Tom. "New Orleans Versus Atlanta," *Southern Exposure* 7 (Spring 1979): pp. 66–68.

DeVault, Marjorie, and James P. Pitts. "Surplus and Scarcity: Hunger and the Origins of the Food Stamp Program," *Social Problems* 31 (June 1984): 545–56.

Devore, Donald, and Joseph Logsdon. *Crescent City Schools: Public Education in New Orleans, 1841–1991*. Lafayette, La.: Center for Louisiana Studies, University of Southwestern Louisiana, 1991.

Dewey, John. "The Ethics of Democracy." In *University of Michigan Philosophical Papers, Second Series, No. 1*. Ann Arbor, Mich., 1888.

Dietrich, Christine E. "Francis Keppel, Lyndon Johnson, and the Elementary and Secondary Education Act, 1965." PhD diss., Lehigh University, 1994.

Dionne, E. J. *Why Americans Hate Politics*. New York: Simon and Schuster, 1991.

Dittmer, John. *Local People: The Struggle for Civil Rights in Mississippi*. Urbana: University of Illinois Press, 1994.

Doerries, Eric Wayne. "James E. Comiskey, the Irish Third Ward Boss: A Study of a Unique and Dying Brand of Politics." B.A. honors thesis, Tulane University, 1973.

Doherty, Mark Jonathan. "Hale Boggs and Civil Rights: A Case Study of a Southern Moderate." B.A. honors thesis, Tulane University, 1983.

Dominquez, Virginia R. *White by Definition: Social Classification in Creole Louisiana*. New Brunswick, N.J.: Rutgers University Press, 1986.

Downes, Brian T. "A Critical Reexamination of the Social and Political Characteristics of Riot Cities." *Social Science Quarterly* 51 (September 1970), 349–60.

Dufour, Charles E. "Pie." *Women Who Cared: The Years of the Women's Christian Exchange*. New Orleans: Christian Women's Exchange, 1980.

Dufour, Charles L. *Darwin Fenner: A Life of Service*. New Orleans: Friends of Darwin Fenner, 1984.

Dugas, Carroll Joseph. "The Dismantling of De Jure Segregation in Louisiana, 1954–1974." PhD diss., Louisiana State University, 1989.

Dupont, Robert. "Regular Democrats and Reformers in New Orleans, 1896–1912." PhD diss., Louisiana State University, 1999.

Dur, Philip F., and Don M. Kurtz, III. "North-South Changes in Louisiana Voting." *Louisiana Studies* 10 (1971): 28–44.

Durr, Virginia Foster. *Freedom Writer: Virginia Foster Durr, Letters from the Civil Rights Years*. Edited by Patricia Sullivan. Athens: University of Georgia Press, 2006 [reprint].

Eagles, Charles W. *Jonathan Daniels and Race Relations: The Evolution of a Southern Liberal*. Knoxville: University of Tennessee Press, 1982.

Edsall, Thomas Byrne, with Mary D. Edsall. *Chain Reaction: The Impact of Race, Rights, and Taxes on American Politics*. New York: W. W. Norton, 1991.

Egerton, John. *The Americanization of Dixie: The Southernization of America*. New York: Harper's Magazine Press, 1974.

Ehrenreich, John. *The Altruistic Imagination: A History of Social Work and Social Policy in the United States*. Ithaca, N.Y.: Cornell University Press, 1985.

Eisinger, Peter K. *Black Employment in City Government, 1973–1980*. Washington, D.C.: Joint Center for Political Studies, 1983.

————. "The Community Action Program and the Development of Black Political Leadership." In *Urban Policy Making*. Edited by Dale Rogers Marshall, 127–44. Beverly Hills: Sage, 1979.

————. *Toward an End to Hunger in America*. Washington, D.C.: The Brookings Institution, 1998.

Engstrom, Richard. "The Hale Boggs Gerrymander: Congressional Redistricting, 1969." *Louisiana History* 21 (Winter 1980): 59–66.

Evans, Sara. *Personal Politics: The Roots of Women's Liberation in the Civil Rights Movement and the New Left*. New York: Vintage, 1979.

Fairclough, Adam. *Race and Democracy: The Civil Rights Struggle in Louisiana, 1915–1972*. Athens: University of Georgia Press, 1995.

Feldstein, Martin S. *The CEA: From Stabilization to Resource Allocation*. Cambridge, Mass.: National Bureau of Economic Research, 1997.

Field, Betty. "The Politics of the New Deal in Louisiana," PhD diss., Tulane University, 1973.

Fine, Sidney. *Violence in the Model City: The Cavanagh Administration, Race Relations, and the Detroit Riot of 1967*. Ann Arbor: University of Michigan Press, 1989.

Finegold, Kenneth. "Agriculture and the Politics of U.S. Social Provision: Social Insurance and Food Stamps." In *The Politics of Social Policy in the United States*. Edited by Margaret Weir, Ana Orloff, and Theda Skocpol, 313–55. Princeton: Princeton University Press, 1988.

Fish, John Hall. *Black Power/White Control: The Struggle of the Woodlawn Organization in Chicago*. Princeton, N.J.: Princeton University Press, 1973.

Fite, Gilbert. *Cotton Fields No More: Southern Agriculture, 1865–1980*. Lexington: University of Kentucky Press, 1984.

————. *Richard B. Russell, Jr., Senator from Georgia*. Chapel Hill: University of North Carolina Press, 1991.

Fitzmorris, James and Kenneth D. Myers. *Frankly Fitz*. Gretna, La.: Pelican, 1992.

Flynt, J. Wayne. *Dixie's Forgotten People: The South's Poor Whites*. Bloomington: Indiana University Press, 1979.

————. *Poor But Proud: Alabama's Poor Whites*. Tuscaloosa: University of Alabama Press, 1989.

Foner, Eric. *Free Soil, Free Labor: The Ideology of the Republican Party Before the Civil War*. New York: Oxford University Press, 1995.

Forman, William H., Jr. "The Conflict Over Federal Urban Renewal Enabling Legislation in Louisiana." *Louisiana Studies* 8 (Fall 1969): 254–57.

Frieden, Bernard, and Marshall Kaplan. *The Politics of Neglect: Urban Aid from*

Model Cities to Revenue Sharing. Cambridge, Mass.: Massachusetts Institute of Technology Press, 1977.

Friedrichs, David William. "The Role of the Negro Minister in Politics in New Orleans." PhD diss., Tulane University, 1967.

Fry, John R. *Locked-Out Americans: A Memoir.* New York: Harper and Row, 1973.

Galbraith, John Kenneth. *The Affluent Society.* Boston: Houghton Mifflin, 1958.

Gambino, Richard. *Vendetta: A True Story of the Worst Lynching in America.* Garden City, N.Y.: Doubleday, 1977.

Gans, Herbert S. *The War against the Poor: The Underclass and Antipoverty Policy.* New York: Basic, 1995.

Germany, Kent. "Rise of the Dixiecrats: Louisiana's Conservative Defection from the National Democratic Party, 1944–1948." M.A. Thesis, Louisiana Tech University, 1994.

Germany, Kent B., and Robert D. Johnson, eds. *The Kennedy Assassination and the Transfer of Power: The Presidential Recordings of Lyndon B. Johnson, January 1964*, Vol. 3. New York: Norton, 2005.

Gettleman, Marvin E. and David Mermelstein, eds. *The Great Society Reader: The Failure of American Liberalism.* New York: Random House, 1967.

Gillette, Michael L., ed. *Launching the War on Poverty: An Oral History.* New York: Twayne, 1996.

Gilmore, Harmon. "The Old New Orleans and the New: A Case for Ecology," *American Sociological Review* 9 (August 1944): 386.

Ginzberg, Eli and Robert M. Solow, eds. *The Great Society: Lessons for the Future.* New York: Basic, 1974.

Glaser, James M. *Race, Campaign Politics, and the Realignment of the South.* New Haven, Conn.: Yale University Press, 1996.

Glassman, James K. "New Orleans: I Have Seen the Future and It's Houston." *Atlantic* 242 (July 1978): 10 ff.

Goals Foundation Council, New Orleans. *Framework for the Future*, vols. 1–3. New Orleans: Goals Foundation Council, 1973.

Goldfield, David R. *Black, White, and Southern: Race Relations and Southern Culture, the 1940s to the Present.* Baton Rouge, La.: Louisiana State University Press, 1990.

————. *Cotton Fields and Skyscrapers: Southern City and Region, 1607–1980.* Baton Rouge: Louisiana State University Press, 1982.

Goldsmith, John A. *Colleagues: Richard B. Russell and His Apprentice, Lyndon B. Johnson.* Macon, Ga.: Mercer University Press, 1998.

Goodwin, Richard. *Remembering America: A Voice from the Sixties.* Boston: Little, Brown, 1988.

Goodwyn, Lawrence. *Democratic Promise: The Populist Moment in America*. New York: Oxford University Press, 1976.

Gordon, Linda, ed. *Women, the State, and Welfare*. Madison: University of Wisconsin Press, 1990.

Gorrell, Donald K. *The Age of Social Responsibility: The Social Gospel in the Progressive Era, 1900–1920*. Macon, Ga.: Mercer University Press, 1988.

Grafton, Carl, and Anne Permaloff. *Big Mules and Branchheads: James E. Folsom and Political Power in Alabama*. Athens: University of Georgia Press, 1985.

Graham, Hugh Davis. *The Uncertain Triumph: Federal Education Policy in the Kennedy and Johnson Years*. Chapel Hill: University of North Carolina Press, 1984.

Grantham, Dewey. *Southern Progressivism: The Reconciliation of Progress and Tradition*. Knoxville: University of Tennessee Press, 1983.

Green, Elna, ed. *Before the New Deal: Social Welfare in the South Before 1930*. Athens: University of Georgia Press, 1999.

Greenstone, David J. and Paul E. Peterson. *Race and Authority in Urban Politics: Community Participation and the War on Poverty*. New York: Russell Sage, 1973.

Grinspan, Mel G., ed. *The Great Society Revisited: Success, Failure, or Remorse?* Memphis, Tenn.: Rhodes College, 1993.

Grossman, James R. *Land of Hope: Chicago, Black Southerners, and the Great Migration*. Chicago: University of Chicago Press, 1989.

Gutman, Herbert. *Work, Culture, and Society in Industrializing America: Essays in Working-Class and Social History*. New York: Knopf, 1976.

Guyol, Louise Hubert. *A Center of Brightness: History of the Pioneer Days of Kingsley House of New Orleans, 1896–1925*. New Orleans: Kingsley House, New Orleans Day Nursery Association, 1961.

Haar, Charles. *Between the Idea and the Reality: A Study in the Origin, Fate, and Legacy of the Model Cities Program*. Boston: Little, Brown, 1975.

Haas, Edward F. *DeLesseps S. Morrison and the Image of Reform: New Orleans Politics, 1946–1961*. Baton Rouge: Louisiana State University Press, 1974.

———. "The Expedient of Race: Victor H. Schiro, Scott Wilson and the New Orleans Mayoralty Campaign of 1962." *Louisiana History* 42 (Winter 2001): 5–29.

———. "Victor H. Schiro, Hurricane Betsy and the 'Forgiveness Bill.'" *Gulf Coast Historical Review* 6 (Fall 1990): 67–90.

Hackney, Sheldon. *Populism to Progressivism in Alabama*. Princeton, N.J.: Princeton University Press, 1969.

Hadley, Charles D. "The Transformation of the Role of Black Ministers and Black Political Organizations in Louisiana Politics." In *Blacks in Southern Politics*. Edited by Laurence W. Moreland, Robert P. Steed, and Tod A. Baker, 133–48. New York: Praeger, 1987.

Hair, William Ivy. *Carnival of Fury: Robert Charles and the New Orleans Race Riot of 1900*. Baton Rouge, La.: Louisiana State University Press, 1976.

Hale, Grace Elizabeth. *Making Whiteness: The Culture of Segregation in the South, 1890–1940*. New York: Pantheon, 1998.

Hamilton, Dona, and Charles Hamilton. *Dual Agenda: Race and Social Policies of Civil Rights Organizations*. New York: Columbia University Press, 1997.

Harlan, Louis R. *Booker T. Washington, the Making of a Black Leader, 1856–1901*. New York: Oxford University Press, 1972.

———. *Booker T. Washington: The Wizard of Tuskegee, 1901–1915*. New York: Oxford University Press, 1983.

Harrington, Michael. *The Other America: Poverty in the United States*. New York: Macmillan, 1962.

Harris, Fred R., and Roger W. Wilkins, eds. *Quiet Riots: Race and Poverty in the United States, the Kerner Report Twenty Years Later*. New York: Pantheon, 1988.

Harrison, Alferdteen. *Black Exodus: The Great Migration from the American South*. Jackson, Miss.: University Press of Mississippi, 1991.

Hartz, Louis. *The Liberal Tradition in America: An Interpretation of American Political Thought since the Revolution*. San Diego: Harcourt, Brace, Jovanovich, 1991 [1955].

Haveman, Robert H., ed. *A Decade of Federal Antipoverty Programs: Achievements, Failures, and Lessons*. New York: Academic Press, 1979.

———. *Poverty Policy and Poverty Research: The Great Society and the Social Sciences*. Madison: University of Wisconsin Press, 1987.

Hawley, Ellis. *The Great War and the Search for a Modern Order: A History of the American People and Their Institutions, 1917–1937*. New York: St. Martin's, 1979.

———. "Social Policy and the Liberal State in Twentieth-Century America." In *Federal Social Policy: The Historical Dimension*. Edited by Donald T. Critchlow and Ellis Hawley, 117–39. University Park, Penn.: Pennsylvania State University Press, 1988.

Heleniak, Roman. "Lyndon Johnson in New Orleans." *Louisiana History* 21 (Summer 1980): 263–75.

Herman, Ellen. *The Romance of American Psychology: Political Culture in the Age of Experts*. Berkeley: University of California Press, 1995.

Hernon, Peter. *A Terrible Thunder: The Story of the New Orleans Sniper.* Garden City, N.Y.: Doubleday, 1978.

Hirsch, Arnold R. *Making the Second Ghetto: Race and Housing in Chicago, 1940–1960.* Cambridge: Cambridge University Press, 1983.

———. "New Orleans: Sunbelt in the Swamp." In *Sunbelt Cities: Politics and Growth since World War II.* Edited by Richard M. Bernard and Bradley R. Rice, 100–37. Austin: University of Texas Press, 1983.

———. "Race and Politics in Modern New Orleans: The Mayorality of Dutch Morial." 35 *Amerikastudien* (April 1990): 461–84.

———. "Simply a Matter of Black and White: The Transformation of Race and Politics in Twentieth-Century New Orleans." In *Creole New Orleans: Race and Americanization.* Edited by Joseph Logsdon and Arnold Hirsch, 262–319. Baton Rouge: Louisiana State University Press, 1992.

Hirsch, Arnold R., and Joseph Logsdon, eds. *Creole New Orleans: Race and Americanization.* Baton Rouge: LSU Press, 1992.

Hobson, Fred. *But Now I See: The White Southern Racial Conversion Narrative.* Baton Rouge: Louisiana State University Press, 1999.

———. *Tell About the South: The Southern Rage to Explain.* Baton Rouge: Louisiana State University Press, 1998.

Hodgson, Godfrey. *America in Our Time: From World War II to Nixon—What Happened and Why.* New York: Vintage Books, 1976.

Hollandsworth, James G., Jr. *An Absolute Massacre: The New Orleans Race Riot of July 30, 1866.* Baton Rouge, La.: Louisiana State University Press, 2003.

Hollingsworth, Ellen Jane. "Ten Years of Legal Services for the Poor." In *A Decade of Federal Antipoverty Programs: Achievements, Failures, and Lessons.* Edited by Robert H. Haveman, 285–327. New York: Academic Press, 1979.

Horton, Myles. *The Long Haul: An Autobiography.* New York: Teachers College Press, 1998.

Huggins, Nathan. *Protestants against Poverty: Boston's Charities, 1870–1900.* Westport, Conn.: Greenwood, 1971.

Jackson, Joy. *New Orleans in the Gilded Age: Politics and Urban Progress, 1880–1896.* Baton Rouge, La: Louisiana State University Press, 1969.

Jackson, Thomas F. "The State, the Movement, and the Urban Poor: The War on Poverty and Political Mobilization in the 1960s." In *The "Underclass" Debate: Views from History.* Edited by Michael B. Katz, 403–9. Princeton: Princeton University Press, 1993.

Jackson, Walter A. *Gunnar Myrdal and America's Conscience: Social Engineering and Racial Liberalism, 1938–1987.* Chapel Hill: University of North Carolina Press, 1990.

Jacoway, Elizabeth and David R. Colburn, eds. *Southern Businessmen and De-segregation*. Baton Rouge: Louisiana State University Press, 1982.

James, Rosemary. "In-Depth Training May End Plight of Area Jobless," *New Orleans States-Item*, 5 August 1967.

Jarboe, Jan. "Lady Bird Looks Back: In Her Own Words, A Texas Icon Reflects on the Lessons of a Lifetime," *Texas Monthly* (December 1994): 117ff.

Jeansonne, Glen. *Leander Perez: Boss of the Delta*. Baton Rouge: Louisiana State University Press, 1977.

Jeffers, James Randall. "Bank Asset Portfolios and Economic Activity, New Orleans, Atlanta, and Houston, 1932–1962." PhD diss., Louisiana State University, 1966.

Jeffrey, Julie Roy. *Education for the Children of the Poor: A Study of the Origins and Implementation of the Elementary and Secondary Education Act of 1965*. Columbus, Ohio: Ohio State University Press, 1978.

Jencks, Christopher. *Rethinking Social Policy: Race, Poverty, and the Underclass*. Cambridge, Mass.: Harvard University Press, 1992.

Jencks, Christopher, and Paul E. Peterson, eds. *The Urban Underclass*. Washington, D.C.: Brookings Institution, 1991.

Jones, Jacqueline. *The Dispossessed: America's Underclass from the Civil War to the Present*. New York: Basic, 1992.

Jordan, Barbara, and Elspeth D. Rostow, eds. *The Great Society: A Twenty Year Critique*. Austin, Tex.: Lyndon Baines Johnson Library and the Lyndon Baines Johnson School of Public Affairs, 1986.

Kaplan, Marshall and Peggy L. Cucciti, eds. *The Great Society and Its Legacy: Twenty Years of U.S. Social Policy*. Durham: Duke University Press, 1986.

Kasson, John F. *Amusing the Million: Coney Island at the Turn of the Century*. New York: Hill and Wang, 1978.

Katz, Michael B. *In the Shadow of the Poorhouse: A Social History of Welfare in America*. New York: Basic, 1986.

———. *Poverty and Policy in American History*. New York: Academic, 1983.

———, ed. *The Underclass Debate: Views from History*. Princeton: Princeton University Press, 1993.

———. *The Undeserving Poor: From the War on Poverty to the War on Welfare*. New York: Pantheon, 1989.

Katznelson, Ira. "Was the Great Society a Lost Opportunity?" In *The Rise and Fall of the New Deal Order*. Edited by Steve Fraser and Gary Gestle, 185–211. Princeton: Princeton University Press, 1989.

Kazin, Michael. *The Populist Persuasion: An American History*. New York: Basic, 1995.

Kearns, Doris. *Lyndon Johnson and the American Dream*. New York: Signet, 1976.

Kelley, Robin D. G. *Race Rebels: Culture, Politics, and the Black Working Class*. New York: Free Press, 1994.

Kelso, Iris. *City in Crisis*. New Orleans: WDSU-TV, 1969.

Kelso, William. *Poverty and the Underclass: Changing Perceptions of the Poor in America*. New York: New York University Press, 1994.

Kennedy, Eileen. "Public Policy in Nutrition: The US Nutrition Safety Net— Past, Present, and Future." *Food Policy* 24 (1999): 325–27.

Kerns, J. Harvey. *The Negro in New Orleans: A Statistical Analysis of Population Trends and Characteristics, Their Effect on the Economic, Social and Civil Life of the Community*. New Orleans: Urban League of Greater New Orleans, 1959.

Kiffmeyer, Thomas J. "From Self-Help to Sedition: The Appalachian Volunteers in Eastern Kentucky, 1964–1970." *Journal of Southern History* 64 (February 1998): 65–95.

Kimball, Penn. *The Disconnected*. New York: Columbia University Press, 1972.

King, Richard H. *Civil Rights and the Idea of Freedom*. New York: Oxford University Press, 1992.

King, Ronald F. *Budgeting Entitlements: The Politics of Food Stamps*. Washington, D.C.: Georgetown University Press, 2000.

Kirby, Jack Temple. *Rural Worlds Lost: The American South, 1920–1960*. Baton Rouge, La.: Louisiana State University Press, 1987.

Kolb, Carolyn. "The Auld Sod on Adele Street," *New Orleans* 1 (December 1966): 9–16, 60.

Koolsbergen, William John. "A Study in Popular Culture: The New Orleans Mardi Gras; Formation of the Mystick Krewe of Comus and Krewe of Rex." PhD diss., City University of New York, 1989.

Kotz, Nick. *Let Them Eat Promises: The Politics of Hunger in America*. Garden City, N.Y.: Anchor, 1971.

Kotz, Nick and Mary Lynn Kotz. *A Passion for Equality: George Wiley and the Movement*. New York: W.W. Norton, 1977.

Kramer, Ralph. *Participation of the Poor: Comparative Community Studies in the War on Poverty*. Englewood Cliffs, N.J.: Prentice-Hall, 1969.

Kuklinski, Michael D. Cobb, and Martin Gilens. "Racial Attitudes and the 'New South.'" *Journal of Politics* 59 (May 1997): 323–49.

Kurtz, Michael L., and Morgan D. Peoples. *Earl K. Long: The Saga of Uncle Earl and Louisiana Politics*. Baton Rouge: Louisiana State University Press, 1990.

Kusmer, Kenneth. *A Ghetto Stakes Shape: Black Cleveland, 1870–1930*. Urbana: University of Illinois Press, 1976.

Landphair, Juliette Lee. "'For the Good of the Community': Reform Activism and Public Schools in New Orleans, 1920–1960." PhD diss., University of Virginia, 1999.

Lasch, Christopher. *Culture of Narcissism: American Life in an Age of Diminishing Expectations*. New York: Norton, 1991.

——. *True and Only Heaven: Progress and Its Critics*. New York: Norton, 1991.

Laumann, Lydia Fischer. *Effects of Project Head Start, Summer 1965: A Second Look at the Equality of Economic Opportunity Study*. Madison, Wisc.: University of Wisconsin Press, 1969.

LaViolette, Forrest Emmanuel, and Joseph T. Taylor. *Negro Housing in New Orleans*. New Orleans: Commission on Race and Housing, 1957.

Lawson, Steven F. *Black Ballots: Voting Rights in the South, 1944–1969*. New York: Columbia University Press, 1976.

——. *In Pursuit of Power: Southern Blacks and Electoral Politics, 1965–1982*. New York: Columbia University Press, 1985.

Leiby, James. *A History of Social Welfare and Social Work in the United States*. New York: Columbia University Press, 1978.

Leloudis, James L. *Schooling the New South: Pedagogy, Self, and Society in North Carolina, 1880–1920*. Chapel Hill: University of North Carolina Press, 1996.

Leloudis, James L., and Robert R. Korstad. "Citizen Soldiers: The North Carolina Volunteers and the War on Poverty." *Law and Contemporary Problems* 62 (Autumn 1999): 177–98.

Lemann, Nicholas. *The Promised Land: The Great Black Migration and How It Changed America*. New York: Alfred A. Knopf, 1991.

Levenstein, Lisa. "From Innocent Children to Unwanted Migrants and Unwed Moms: Two Chapters in the Public Discourse on Welfare in the United States, 1960–1961." *Journal of Women's History* 11 (Winter 2000): 10–33.

Levin, Henry M. "A Decade of Policy Developments in Improving Education and Training for Low-Income Populations." In *A Decade of Federal Antipoverty Programs: Achievements, Failures, and Lessons*. Edited by Robert H. Haveman, 123–96. New York: Regents of the University of Wisconsin Institute for Research on Poverty, 1979.

Levine, Lawrence. *Black Culture and Black Consciousness: Afro-American Folk Thought from Slavery to Freedom*. New York: Oxford University Press, 1977.

Levitan, Sar. *The Great Society's Poor Law: A New Approach to Poverty*. Baltimore: The Johns Hopkins Press, 1969.

Lewis, David Levering. *W.E.B. DuBois, Biography of a Race, 1868–1919*. New York: Holt, 1993.

Lewis, Oscar. *The Children of Sanchez: Autobiography of a Mexican Family*. New York: Random House, 1961.

——. *Five Families: Mexican Case Studies in the Culture of Poverty*. New York: Basic, 1959.

———. *La Vida: A Puerto Rican Family in the Culture of Poverty—San Juan and New York*. New York: Random House, 1966.

Link, William S. *The Paradox of Southern Progressivism, 1880–1930*. Chapel Hill: University of North Carolina Press, 1992.

Litwack, Leon. *Trouble in Mind: Black Southerners in the Age of Jim Crow*. New York: Knopf, 1998.

Long, Norton. *Public Policy, Private Enterprise and the Reduction of Poverty*. National Association of Manufacturers, 1964.

Louis, Alex, Walter Bowles, and Raymond Grace. *Study of Racial Attitudes in Louisiana Fall of 1966*. Vol. 1, *Principal Findings: Summary and Interpretation of Results of Three Sample Surveys of Public Opinion*. Dallas: Louis, Bowles, and Grace, 1967.

Lubove, Roy. *The Professional Altruist: The Emergence of Social Work as a Career, 1880–1930*. Cambridge, Mass.: Harvard University Press, 1965.

Lynn, Laurence E., Jr. "A Decade of Policy Developments in the Income-Maintenance System." In *A Decade of Federal Antipoverty Programs: Achievements, Failures, and Lessons*. Edited by Robert H. Haveman, 75–7. New York: Academic Press, 1979.

MacDonald, Dwight. "Our Invisible Poor." *The New Yorker*, 19 January 1963.

Mackintosh, Douglas. "How Family Health Foundation Was Mau-Maued." *New Orleans* (May 1975), 44–58.

MacLachlan, Alan Stuart. "Up From Paternalism: The New Deal and Race Relations in New Orleans." PhD diss., University of New Orleans, 1998.

MacPherson, Harry, and Jack Valenti. "Achilles in the White House: A Discussion with Harry McPherson and Jack Valenti." *Wilson Quarterly* 24 (Spring 2000): 92.

Magnuson, Norris. *Salvation in the Slums: Evangelical Social Work, 1865–1920*. Metuchen, N.J.: Scarecrow Press and the American Theological Library Association, 1977.

Mahoney, Martha Ruth "Marnie." "The Changing Nature of Public Housing in New Orleans, 1930–1974." M.A. thesis, Tulane University, 1985.

Malone, Bobbie. *Rabbi Max Heller: Reformer, Zionist, and Southerner, 1860–1929*. Tuscaloosa, Ala.: University of Alabama Press, 1997.

Mandle, Jay R. *The Roots of Black Poverty: The Southern Plantation Economy after the Civil War*. Durham, N.C.: Duke University Press, 1978.

Maney, Patrick J. "Hale Boggs, Organized Labor, and the Politics of Race in South Louisiana, 1940–1972." In *Southern Labor in Transition, 1940–1995*. Edited by Robert Zieger, 230–50. Knoxville: University of Tennessee Press, 1997.

———. "Hale Boggs: The Southerner as National Democrat." In *Masters of the*

House. Edited by Raymond Smock, Susan Hammond, and Roger Davidson, 223–58. Boulder, Co.: Westview Press, 1998.

Marcus, Isabel. *Dollars for Reform: The OEO Neighborhood Health Care Centers*. Lexington, Mass.: Lexington Books, 1981.

Margavio, Anthony V. "Population Change in New Orleans from 1940–1960." *Louisiana Studies* 9 (1970): 228–42.

———. *Residential Segregation in New Orleans: A Statistical Analysis of Census Data*. Baton Rouge: n.p., 1968.

Marris, Peter, and Martin Rein. *Dilemmas of Social Reform: Poverty and Community Action in the United States*. Chicago: University of Chicago Press, 1982.

Matusow, Allen J. *The Unraveling of America: A History of Liberalism in the 1960s*. New York: Harper Torchbooks, 1984.

McCarthy, Kathleen D. *Noblesse Oblige: Charity and Cultural Philanthropy in Chicago, 1849–1929*. Chicago: University of Chicago Press, 1982.

McCartney, John T. *Black Power Ideologies: An Essay in African-American Political Thought*. Philadelphia: Temple University Press, 1992.

McClay, Wilfred. *The Masterless: Self and Society in Modern America*. Chapel Hill: University of North Carolina Press, 1994.

McKee, Guian. "The Hidden History of Faith-Based Social Policy Initiatives: The War on Poverty and the Opportunities Industrialization Centers Movement." Paper presented at the Policy History Conference, Clayton, Mo., 2 June 2002.

McMillen, Neil R. *Dark Journey: Mississippi in the Age of Jim Crow*. Champaign: University of Illinois Press, 1989.

McMillen, Neil R., ed. *Remaking Dixie: The Impact of World War II on the American South*. Jackson, Miss.: University Press of Mississippi, 1997.

Meier, August. *Negro Thought in America, 1880–1915: Racial Ideologies in the Age of Booker T. Washington*. Ann Arbor: University of Michigan Press, 1988 [1963].

Meier, August, and John H. Bracey Jr. "The NAACP as a Reform Movement, 1909–1965: 'To Reach the Conscience of America.'" *Journal of Southern History* 59 (February 1993): 3–30.

Meier, August, and Elliot Rudwick. *CORE: A Study in the Civil Rights Movement, 1942–1968*. New York: Oxford University Press, 1973.

———. *From Plantation to Ghetto*. New York: Hill and Wang, 1970.

Melnick, R. Shep. *Between the Lines: Interpreting Welfare Rights*. Washington, D.C.: Brookings Institution, 1994.

Mertz, Paul E. *New Deal Policy and Southern Rural Poverty*. Baton Rouge: Louisiana State University Press, 1978.

Milkis, Sidney M. "Lyndon Johnson, the Great Society, and the 'Twighlight' of the Modern Presidency." In *The Great Society and the High Tide of Liberalism*. Edited by Sidney M. Milkis and Jerome M. Mileur, 1–49. Boston: University of Massachusetts Press, 2005.

Mills, Kay. *Something Better for My Children: The History and People of Head Start*. New York: Dutton, 1998.

Mingione, Enzo, ed. *Urban Poverty and the Underclass: A Reader*. Oxford: Blackwell, 1996.

Mink, Gwendolyn. *The Wages of Motherhood: Inequality in the Welfare State*. Ithaca, N.Y.: Cornell University Press, 1995.

Mittelstadt, Jennifer Leigh. "The Dilemmas of the Liberal Welfare State, 1945–1964: Gender, Race, and Aid to Dependent Children," PhD diss., University of Michigan, 2000.

Moran, Robert E., Sr. "Public Relief in Louisiana from 1928–1960." *Louisiana History* 14 (Winter 1973): 369–85.

Morris, Aldon. *Origins of the Civil Rights Movement: Black Communities Organizing for Change*. New York: Free Press, 1984.

Morris, Andrew. "Selling Service: Charity, Therapy, and Welfare in the Late 1940s," paper delivered to the Organization of American Historians, 27 April 2001, in possession of the author.

———. "The Voluntary Sector's War on Poverty." *Journal of Policy History* (Fall 2004): 275–304.

Moyers, Bill. "Second Thoughts: Reflections on the Great Society." *New Perspectives Quarterly* 4 (Winter 1987).

Moynihan, Daniel. "The Crisis in Welfare." *The Public Interest* 19 (Winter 1968): 13ff.

———. *Maximum Feasible Misunderstanding: Community Action in the War on Poverty*. New York: Free Press, 1970.

Murphy, James T. *New Orleans: A Statistical Profile of Economic and Other Characteristics*. n.p.: [1969].

Murray, Charles. *Losing Ground: American Social Policy, 1950–1980*. New York: Basic Books, 1984.

Murray, Gail S. "Poverty and Its Relief in the Antebellum South: Perception and Reality in 3 Selected Southern Cities." PhD diss., Memphis State University, 1991.

Myrdal, Gunnar, with the assistance of Richard Sterner and Arnold Rose. *An American Dilemma: The Negro Problem and Modern Democracy*. New York: Harper, 1944.

Naftali, Timothy, ed. *The Presidential Recordings, John F. Kennedy: The Great Crises, Volume One*. New York: W. W. Norton, 2001.

Needham, Maurice D'Arlan. *Negro Orleanian: Status and Stake in a City's Economy and Housing*. New Orleans: Tulane University Publishing, 1962.

Noble, Charles. *Welfare as We Knew It: A Political History of the American Welfare State*. New York: Oxford University Press, 1997.

Norrell, Robert Jefferson, III. *Reaping the Whirlwind: The Civil Rights Movement in Tuskegee*. New York: Alfred A. Knopf, 1985.

Norton, Hugh Stanton. *The Council of Economic Advisers: Three Periods of Influence*. Columbia, S.C.: Bureau of Business and Economic Research, University of South Carolina, 1973.

O'Brien, Rosary Hartel. "The New Orleans Carnival Organizations: Theater of Prestige." PhD diss., University of California at Los Angeles, 1973.

O'Connor, Alice. "Community Action, Urban Reform, and the Fight against Poverty: The Ford Foundation's Gray Areas Program." *Journal of Urban History* 22 (July 1996): 586–625.

———. *Poverty Knowledge: Social Science, Social Policy, and the Poor in Twentieth-Century U.S. History*. Princeton: Princeton University Press, 2001.

O'Connor, Jerrie Mary. "A Study of 49 Unmarried Mothers Known to the Associated Catholic Charities in New Orleans." M.A. thesis, Tulane University, 1945.

Odum, Howard W. *Race and Rumors of Race: The American South in the Early Forties*. Introduction by Bryant Simon. Baltimore: Johns Hopkins University Press, 1997 [original 1947].

Orfield, Gary. "Race and the Liberal Agenda: The Loss of the Integrationist Dream, 1965–1974." In *The Politics of Social Policy in the United States*. Edited by Margaret Weir, Ana Orloff, and Theda Skocpol, 313–55. Princeton: Princeton University Press, 1988.

Painter, Nell Irvin. *Exodusters: Black Migration to Kansas after Reconstruction*. New York: Knopf, 1977.

"PAR Conference—1967: The Impact of the Negro on Louisiana's Future." *PAR Analysis* 141 (March 1967): 1–23.

Parker, Joseph B. *The Morrison Era: Reform Politics in New Orleans*. Gretna, La.: Pelican, 1974.

Parris, Guichard, and Lester Brooks. *Blacks in the City: A History of the National Urban League*. Boston: Little, Brown, 1971.

Patterson, James T. *America's Struggle Against Poverty, 1900–1994*. Cambridge, Mass.: Harvard University Press, 1994.

Perlstein, Rick. "Who Owns the Sixties? The Opening of a Scholarly Generation Gap." *Lingua Franca* (May–June 1996): 30–37.

Phillips, Paul T. *A Kingdom on Earth: Anglo-American Social Christianity, 1880–1940*. University Park, Pa.: Pennsylvania State University Press, 1996.

Piven, Frances Fox, and Richard A. Cloward. *Poor People's Movements: Why They Succeed, How They Fail*. New York: Vintage, 1977.

———. *Regulating the Poor: The Functions of Public Welfare*. New York: Vintage, 1971.

Plotke, David. *Building a Democratic Political Order: Reshaping American Liberalism in the 1930s and 1940s*. New York: Cambridge University Press, 1996.

Pole, J. R. *American Individualism and the Promise of Progress*. New York: Oxford University Press, 1980.

Polsky, Andrew. *The Rise of the Therapeutic State*. Princeton: Princeton University Press, 1991.

Powell, Lawrence. *Troubled Memory: Anne Levy, the Holocaust, and David Duke's Louisiana*. Chapel Hill, N.C.: University of North Carolina Press, 2000.

Quadagno, Jill. *The Color of Welfare: How Racism Undermined the War on Poverty*. New York: Oxford University Press, 1994.

———. *The Transformation of Old Age Security: Class and Politics in the American Welfare State*. Chicago: University of Chicago Press, 1988.

Raabe, Phyllis Hutton. "Status and Its Impact: New Orleans' Carnival, the Social Upper Class and Upper Class Power." PhD diss., Pennsylvania State University, 1973.

Rae, Nicol. *Southern Democrats*. New York: Oxford University Press, 1994.

Reed, Adolph, Jr. *Stirrings in the Jug: Black Politics in the Post-Segregation Era*. Minneapolis: University of Minnesota Press, 1999.

Reed, John Shelton, and Daniel Singal, eds. *Regionalism and the South: Selected Papers of Rupert Vance*. Chapel Hill: University of North Carolina Press, 1982.

Reed, Linda. *Simple Decency and Common Sense: The Southern Conference Movement, 1938–1963*. Bloomington: Indiana University Press, 1991.

Reeves, T. Zane. *The Politics of the Peace Corps and VISTA*. Tuscaloosa: University of Alabama Press, 1988.

Reinecke, John A., and Caroline Fisher. "The Economic Impact of the Port of New Orleans." *Louisiana Business Survey* 12 (January 1981): 4–7.

Reissman, Leonard. *Attitudes Toward the Environment, New Orleans*. New Orleans: Department of Sociology, Tulane University, 1967.

———. *Housing Discrimination in New Orleans*. New Orleans: Urban Studies Center, Tulane University, 1970.

———. *Sociological Aspects of Community Renewal in New Orleans, Louisiana*. New Orleans: Department of Sociology, Tulane University, 1967.

———. *Trends in Residential Stability and Segregation in New Orleans*. New Orleans: Department of Sociology, Tulane University, 1967.

Reissman, Leonard, K. H. Silvert, and Cliff W. Wing, Jr. *The New Orleans Voter: A Handbook of Political Description*. New Orleans: Tulane University, Urban Life Research Institute, 1955.

Renwick, Ed. "The Governor." In *Louisiana Politics: Festival in a Labyrinth*. Edited by James Bolner, 75–88. Baton Rouge: Louisiana State University Press, 1982.

Reuben, Julie A. "Beyond Politics: Community Civics and the Redefinition of Citizenship in the Progressive Era." *History of Education Quarterly* 37 (Winter 1997): 399–420.

Rice, Leila Meier. "In the Trenches of the War on Poverty: The Local Implementation of the Community Action Program, 1964–1969." PhD diss., Vanderbilt University, 1997.

Richardson, Robert. "Every Black Man Is My Brother," *New Orleans* 2 (June, 1968): 21+.

Rickey, Elizabeth A. "The Nazi and the Republican: An Insider View of the Response of the Louisiana Republican Party to David Duke." In *The Emergence of David Duke and the Politics of Race*. Edited by Douglas D. Rose, 64–74. Chapel Hill: University of North Carolina Press, 1992.

Rieff, Philip. *The Triumph of the Therapeutic: Uses of Faith After Freud*. Chicago: University of Chicago Press, 1987 [originally 1966].

Ripley, Randall B. "Legislative Bargaining and the Food Stamp Act, 1964." In *Congress and Urban Problems*, Frederic N. Cleveland and associates. Washington, D.C.: The Brookings Institution, 1969, 279–310.

Rogers, Kim Lacy. "Humanity and Desire: Civil Rights Leaders and the Desegregation of New Orleans, 1954–1966." PhD diss., University of Minnesota, 1983.

————. *Righteous Lives: Narratives of the New Orleans Civil Rights Movement*. New York: New York University Press, 1993.

Rohrer, John H., and Munro S. Edmonson, eds. Co-authored with Harold Lief, Daniel Thompson, and William Thompson. *The Eighth Generation Grows Up: Cultures and Personalities of New Orleans Negroes*. New York: Harper, 1960.

Rosenweig, Allen. "The Influence of Class and Race on Political Behavior in New Orleans, 1960–1967." M.A. thesis, University of Oklahoma, 1967.

Rossinow, Doug. *The Politics of Authenticity: Liberalism, Christianity, and the New Left in America*. New York: Columbia University Press, 1998.

Rothman, Gerald C. *Philanthropists, Therapists and Activists: A Century of Ideological Conflict in Social Work*. Cambridge, Mass.: Schenckman, 1985.

Sale, Richard. *The Blackstone Rangers: A Reporter's Account of Time Spent with the Street Gang on Chicago's South Side*. New York: Random House, 1971.

Salvaggio, John. *New Orleans' Charity Hospital: A Story of Physicians, Politics, and Poverty*. Baton Rouge: Louisiana State University Press, 1992.

Schulman, Bruce J. *From Cotton Belt to Sunbelt: Federal Policy, Economic Development, and the Transformation of the South, 1938–1980*. New York: Oxford University Press, 1991.

———. "The Privatization of Everyday Life: Public Policy, Public Services and Public Space in the 1970s and 1980s," presented at the Twentieth Century U.S. Workshop of the Corcoran Department of History, 16 November 2001, University of Virginia, Charlottesville, Virginia.

Schwarz, John E. *America's Hidden Success: A Reassessment of Public Policy from Kennedy to Reagan*. New York: Norton, 1988.

Scott, Daryl. *Contempt and Pity: Social Policy and the Image of the Damaged Black Psyche, 1880–1996*. Chapel Hill: University of North Carolina Press, 1997.

Sernett, Milton C. *Bound for the Promised Land: African-American Religion and the Great Migration*. Durham, N.C.: Duke University Press, 1997.

Shiflett, Crandall A. *Patronage and Poverty in the Tobacco South: Louisa County, Virginia, 1860–1900*. Knoxville: University of Tennessee Press, 1982.

Short, Bob. *Everything Is Pickrick: The Life of Lester Maddox*. Macon, Ga: Mercer University Press, 1999.

Singal, Daniel. *The War Within: From Victorian to Modernist Thought, 1919–1945*. Chapel Hill: University of North Carolina Press, 1982.

Sitkoff, Harvard. *The Struggle for Black Equality, 1954–1992*. New York: Hill and Wang, 1993.

Sklar, Judith N. *American Citizenship: The Quest for Inclusion*. Cambridge, Mass.: Harvard University Press, 1991.

Skocpol, Theda. *Protecting Soldiers and Mothers: The Political Origins of Social Policy in America*. Cambridge, Mass.: Belknap Press, 1992.

Smith, Douglas. *The New Deal in the Urban South*. Baton Rouge: Louisiana State University Press, 1988.

Smith, Larry, and Company [for the New Orleans City Planning Commission]. *Economic Conditions and Influences*. San Francisco: Larry Smith, 1966.

———. *Economic Needs and Policies: Summary of Conclusions and Recommendations*. San Francisco: Larry Smith, 1968.

Smith, Rogers M. *Civic Ideals: Conflicting Visions of Citizenship in U.S. History*. New Haven, Conn.: Yale University Press, 1997.

Sosin, Michael R. "Legal Rights and Welfare Change, 1960–1980." In *Fighting Poverty: What Works and What Doesn't*. Edited by Sheldon H. Danziger and Daniel H. Weinberg, 260–86. Cambridge, Mass.: Harvard University Press, 1986.

Sosna, Morton. *In Search of the Silent South: Southern Liberals and the Race Issue*. New York: Columbia University Press, 1977.

———. "More Important Than the Civil War?: The Impact of World War II on the South." In *Perspectives on the American South: An Annual Review of Society, Politics and Culture*. Edited by James C. Cobb and Charles R. Wilson, 145–61. New York: Gordon and Breach Science, 1987.

Spain, Daphne. "Race Relations and Residential Segregation in New Orleans: Two Centuries of Paradox." *Annals of the American Academy of Political and Social Science* 82 (January 1979): 82–96.

Stein, Robert M., and Keith E. Hamm. "Federal Aid and Mobilization of Black Political Influence." *Research in Urban Policy* 2 (1986): 97–115.

Steinbeck, John. *Travels with Charley: In Search of America*. New York: Penguin, 2002 [reprint].

Steinmetz, George. *Regulating the Social: The Welfare State and Local Politics in Imperial Germany*. Princeton, N.J.: Princeton University Press, 1993.

Stone, Clarence. *Regime Politics: Governing Atlanta, 1946–1988*. Lawrence, Kan.: University Press of Kansas, 1989.

Stretch, John J. *Progress and Challenge: New Orleans Moves Ahead in Racial Justice, Results of a 1963 Before-Passage of the Civil Rights Act, and 1968 After-Passage of the Civil Rights Act Study of Progressive Movement in Racial Equality by Health and Welfare Agencies in the Metropolitan New Orleans Area*. New Orleans: Social Welfare Planning Council Research Department, July 1969.

Sturdivant, Frederick D., ed. *The Ghetto Marketplace*. New York: Free Press, 1969.

Sugrue, Thomas. *The Origins of the Urban Crisis: Race and Inequality in Postwar Detroit*. Princeton, N.J.: Princeton University Press, 1996.

Sullivan, Patricia. *Days of Hope: Race and Democracy in the New Deal Era*. Chapel Hill: University of North Carolina Press, 1996.

"A Sunbelt City Plays Catch-Up." *Business Week* 6 March 1978, 69–70.

Sundquist, James L. *Politics and Poverty: The Eisenhower, Kennedy, and Johnson Years*. Washington, D.C.: Brookings Institution, 1968.

Sundquist, James L., ed. *On Fighting Poverty: Perspectives from Experience*. New York: Basic Books, 1969.

Tapp, Charles W. "The Gubernatorial Election of 1964: An Affirmation of Political Trends." *Proceedings Louisiana Academy of Sciences* 27 (1964): 74–87.

Teaford, Jon C. *The Rough Road to Renaissance: Urban Revitalization in America, 1940–1985*. Baltimore: Johns Hopkins University Press, 1990.

Thernstrom, Stephan. *Poverty, Planning, and Politics in the New Boston: The Origins of ABCD*. New York: Basic, 1969.

Thomas, Susan L. *Gender and Poverty*. New York: Garland, 1994.

Thompson, Carolyn. "A Story of Hope: Southern Consumers Cooperative and the Origins of the War on Poverty in Southwest Louisiana." M.A. thesis, Tulane University, 2000.

Thompson, Daniel C. *A Black Elite: A Profile of Graduates of UNCF Colleges*. New York: Greenwood, 1986.

———. *The Negro Family in a Selected Ghetto*. New Orleans: Dillard University, Tulane University, and Orleans Parish School Board, 1968.

———. *The Negro Leadership Class*. Englewood Cliffs, N.J.: Prentice-Hall, 1963.

———. *Private Black Colleges at the Crossroads*. Westport, Conn.: Greenwood, 1973.

———. *Sociology of the Black Experience*. Westport, Conn.: Greenwood, 1974.

Tobin, James, and Murray Weidenbaum, eds. *Two Revolutions in Economic Policy: The First Economic Reports of Presidents Kennedy and Reagan*. Cambridge, Mass.: Massachusetts Institute of Technology Press, 1988.

Total Community Action. Department of Program Development. *A History of the Community Action Movement in New Orleans*. New Orleans: Total Community Action, 2001.

———. *Profile of Poverty in New Orleans*. New Orleans: Total Community Action, 1973.

Trillin, Calvin. "A Reporter at Large: The Zulus." *New Yorker* 20 June 1964, 66.

Tyler, Pam. *Silk Stockings and Ballot Boxes: Women and Politics in New Orleans, 1920–1963*. Athens: University of Georgia Press, 1996.

Urban League of Greater New Orleans. *A Study of the Social and Recreation Conditions of the Negro Population in Guste Homes and Adjoining Areas, November–December, 1963*. New Orleans: Urban League of Greater New Orleans, 1963.

Van Deburg, William. *New Day in Babylon: The Black Power Movement and American Culture*. Chicago: University of Chicago Press, 1992.

Van Deburg, William L., ed. *Modern Black Nationalism: From Marcus Garvey to Louis Farrakhan*. New York: New York University Press, 1997.

Vandal, Gilles. "The Nineteenth-Century Municipal Responses to the Problem of Poverty." *Journal of Urban History* 19 (November 1992): 30–60.

Voelker, Bill. "Possible Causes Cited by Slow Start of CEP," 6 January 1968, *New Orleans Times-Picayune*.

Wallace, Phyllis A. "A Decade of Policy Developments in Equal Opportunities in Employment and Housing." In *A Decade of Federal Antipoverty Programs: Achievements, Failures, and Lessons*. Edited by Robert H. Haveman, 349–59. New York: Academic Press, 1978.

Ward, David. *Poverty, Ethnicity, and the American City, 1840–1925: Changing Conceptions of the Slum and Ghetto*. Cambridge: Cambridge University Press, 1989.

Ward, Martha C. *Poor Women, Powerful Men: America's Great Experiment in Family Planning*. Boulder, Colo.: Westview Press, 1986.

Weems, Robert E., Jr. *Desegregating the Dollar: African-American Consumerism in the Twentieth Century*. New York: New York University Press, 1998.

Weiss, Nancy J. *Whitney M. Young, Jr., and the Struggle for Civil Rights*. Princeton, N.J.: Princeton University Press, 1989.

Whelan, Robert K., Alma H. Young, and Mickey Lauria. "Urban Regimes and Racial Politics in New Orleans." *Journal of Urban Affairs* 16, no. 1 (1994): 1–21.

Whisnant, David E. *Modernizing the Mountaineer: People, Power, and Planning in Appalachia*. Knoxville: University of Tennessee Press, 1994.

White, Ronald C. *Liberty and Justice for All: Racial Reform and the Social Gospel, 1877–1925*. San Francisco: Harper and Row, 1990.

White, Ronald C., Jr., and C. Howard Hopkins. *The Social Gospel: Religion and Reform in Changing America*. Philadelphia: Temple University Press, 1976.

Wiebe, Robert. *The Search for Order, 1877–1920*. New York: Hill and Wang, 1967.

———. *Self-Rule: A Cultural History of American Democracy*. Chicago: University of Chicago, 1995.

Wilson, James Q. "Culture, Inaction, and the Underclass." In *Values and Public Policy*, edited by Henry Aaron, Thomas E. Mann, and Timothy Taylor. Washington, D.C.: Brookings Institution, 1994.

Wilson, William Julius. *The Truly Disadvantaged: The Inner City, the Underclass, and Public Policy*. Chicago: University of Chicago Press, 1987.

———. *When Work Disappears: The World of the New Urban Poor*. New York: Knopf, 1997.

Wisner, Elizabeth. *Public Welfare Administration in Louisiana*. Chicago: University of Chicago Press, 1930.

———. *Social Welfare in the South from Colonial Times to World War I*. Baton Rouge: Louisiana State University Press, 1970.

Wolfe, Thomas. *Radical Chic and Mau-Mauing the Flak Catchers*. New York: Farrar, Straus, and Giroux, 1970.

Wood, Frances J. *Marginality and Identity: A Colored Creole Family through Ten Generations*. Baton Rouge: Louisiana State University Press, 1972.

Wood, Robert. "Model Cities: What Went Wrong—the Program or Its Critics?" In *Neighbourhood Policy and Programmes: Past and Present*. Edited by Naomi Carmon, 61–73. New York: St. Martin's, 1990.

Woodard, Komozi. *A Nation Within a Nation: Amiri Baraka (LeRoi Jones) and Black Power Politics*. Chapel Hill: University of North Carolina Press, 1999.

Woods, Jeff. *Black Struggle, Red Scare: Segregation and Anticommunism in the South, 1948–1968*. Baton Rouge: Louisiana State University Press, 2003.

Woodward, C. Vann *Origins of the New South, 1877–1913*. Baton Rouge, La.: Louisiana State University Press, 1971.

Wright, Beverly Hendrix. "New Orleans: A City That Care Forgot." In *In Search of the New South: The Black Urban Experience in the 1970s and 1980s*. Edited by Robert Bullard, 45–74. Tuscaloosa: University of Alabama Press, 1989.

Wright, Frederick Douglas. "Black Political Participation in Louisiana: The Cultural and Structural Determinants." PhD diss., Princeton University, 1982.

Zarefsky, David. *President Johnson's War on Poverty: Rhetoric and History*. University: University of Alabama Press, 1986.

Zigler, Edward, and Sally J. Styfco, eds. *Head Start and Beyond: A National Plan for Extended Childhood Intervention*. New Haven, Conn.: Yale University Press, 1993.

Zigler, Edward, and Jeannette Valentine, eds. *Project Head Start: A Legacy of the War on Poverty*. New York: Free Press, 1979.

INDEX

Ambrose, Stephen, 282

Amedee, Earl, 249, 250, 258

American Dilemma, An (Myrdal), 147

American Football League all-star game, 195

American Friends Service Committee, 65

Americanization of the South, 9

"American Promise, The," 5

American Way, 83

Anderson, Winifred, 77

Antoine's restaurant, 166, 262

Arnaud's restaurant, 166

Aronson, Richard, 76

Associated Catholic Charities, 40, 188

Association for Community Reform Now (ACORN), 208

AT&T, 112–13

Atlanta, 5, 370n5; "City Too Busy to Hate," 22; compared to New Orleans, 22–25, 39

Atlanta University, 131

Audubon Park Golf Club, 32

Audubon Park swimming pool, 142–43

Augustine, Israel, Jr., 260, 280, 392n29

Autocrat Club, 248

Avery, Leonard, 203

baby boomers, 2, 300, 373n43

Bagert, Benjamin, 258

Bagert, Bernhard "Ben," 274–75, 279, 280

Baker, Champ: Shelby Jackson controversy, 51–53; Virginia Collins controversy, 92–93

Balthazar, Mary, 108

Baptiste, Philip M., 135, 158, 259, 267

Barnes, Malcolm, 77

Barnett, Walter M., 53, 189, 191

Barney, Clarence, 392n29

Barthelemy, Sidney, 254, 304

Baton Rouge, Louisiana, 123, 203, 235, 236, 287; Urban Renewal, 187–88

Battle for Liberty Place, 129

Bayou St. John, 134

Beasley, Joseph, 204–7

Begich, Nicholas, 289

Behrman, Martin, 28

Bell, Elliot, 43

Bell, Sam: and AFDC, 238; on black power, 119–20, 125, 192, 212; public accommodations ordinance, 196; SOUL and campaigns, 253, 261, 272

Bemish, Robert, 290

Benson, Ezra Taft, 168

Berrigan, Philip, 114

Berry, Jason, 261

Berry, Theodore "Ted," 147

Bertha (tank), 278

Betsy, Hurricane, 4–5; clean-up jobs, 58; community action, 65; damage and recovery, 69, 75–76, 184–86, 277

Betsy Flood Victims, 75

Bivens, Frank, 132, 383n83

Black Arts Movement, 293

Black City Council, 196

Black Knights, Memphis, 213

Black Organization for Leadership Development (BOLD), 16, 212; Landrieu administration, 268; 1970–71 gubernatorial campaign, 261; origins and history, 251–52, 254–58

Black PAC, 242

Black Panthers, 210, 258, 271–86; alienation, 272; black political development, 212; breakfast

Children's Bureau, 141

Choctaws, 28

Christian ideas, impact of, 17, 60, 79–81, 266

Christopher Homes, 182, 188

churches: and black politics, 248; divisions, 27–28; George W. Bush, 312; local Irish population and loyalty to, 353n83; in Lower Ninth Ward, 68; poverty relief, 39, 41, 60; public accommodations, 195; "River Garden," 310; role of, 22–23, 65, 139; War on Poverty, 76, 94, 144, 235. *See also* Catholic Church

Ciaccio, Philip, 132, 178; and Urban Renewal, 195

Citizen's Advisory Committee on Community Improvement, 182

Citizen's Board of Inquiry into Malnutrition and Hunger, 170

Citizens Committee, 34–35, 37

citizenship, rationale for inclusion, 104–15

Citizenship Education project, of League of Women Voters, 240

Citizens League, 28

City Council of New Orleans, 85, 131; and Carrollton area, 240; Food Stamp program, 173–74; housing, 182; Human Relations Committee, 144; lack of black representation on, 260–61; Mississippi River Bridge, 256; Public Accommodations Ordinance, 195–96; Urban Renewal, 186, 188–89, 200; welfare rights, 234

City Demonstration Agency (CDA), 178, 181, 200, 203; ABCOL, 204; compared to the Community Action Program, 202; employees in 1969, 201; Family Health Foundation scandal, 206; Food Stamp program, 178. *See also* Model Cities

City Planning Commission, New Orleans, 23, 186, 188–89

City That Care Forgot, 20, 22

City-Wide Welfare Rights Organization, 231. *See also* New Orleans Welfare Rights Organization (NOWRO)

civil disorder, 62, 63, 141; community action, 85, 86; defined, 127–28, 364n1; history of, 127–28; Model Cities, 202; in New Orleans, 136–39, 143, 172; police, 131–34; welfare rights, 232. *See also* New Orleans Welfare Rights Organization (NOWRO); Thugs United, Inc.; violence

Civilian Conservation Corps (CCC), 152, 153

Civil Rights Act of 1964, 4, 10, 14–17, 62, 159; LBJ despondence after signing, 337n16; local violence after, 129; loopholes in, 195–96; Russell Long on, 36; Title VI, 200

civil rights movement: civil disorder, 126; Great Society speech, 42; impact of War on Poverty, 8, 47, 60, 83, 92, 99–103, 107, 178, 213, 306; Jewish participation, 30; jobs program, 163; local white reactions to, 5, 19–20, 35–37, 129, 199, 246, 298; in New Orleans, 3, 13–15, 32–37, 133, 144, 247–51, 269, 278; political challenge, 8, 26, 68, 107, 121, 216, 253, 257,

254, 258; campaigns, 259, 261, 263; "no permanent enemies," 302; as political structure, 251, 257; relationship with Dutch Morial, 304; relationship with Moon Landrieu, 268, 283

community organizing, 14, 59–82, 83–96, 99, 103, 305, 308; Black Panthers, 274–75, 279; civil disorder, 139; in early War on Poverty, 41, 46; as segregated phenomenon, 81, 95–96; tactics, 67–68; therapeutic influence of, 110; Thugs United, 217; transfer from SWPC to TCA, 95–97; "walking and talking" strategy, 60; women and, 224–45, 255. *See also* Carrollton Central Steering Committee (CCSC); Community Action Program (CAP); New Orleans Welfare Rights Organization (NOWRO); Social Welfare Planning Council (SCPC); Total Community Action (TCA); Volunteers in Service to America (VISTA)

Community Relations Council of Greater New Orleans, 35, 144; Black Primary, 257; Carrollton area, 239; on impact of community action, 78

Community Renewal Program, 188, 200

Comprehensive Employment and Training Act (CETA), 164

Comus, Krewe of, 29

Concentrated Employment Program (CEP): agencies involved in, 153; appropriation, 58, 154–55; assessment, 157–

64; changes in, 163–64; civil disorder, 156; described, 58–59, 153–64; mentioned, 152; Metropolitan Area Committee, 155; neighborhood criticism of, 157–58; orientation program, 155; perception as program for African Americans, 159; placements, 156–57; racial discrimination, 160; and reluctance of local businesses, 154

Concerned Parents of Desire, 132

Confederate flag, 85, 353n8

Congo Square, 194

Congress of Racial Equality (CORE), 13, 34, 68, 96; in New Orleans, 14, 34, 37, 52, 101, 249, 251; and War on Poverty, 101

Conservative Vice Lords, of Chicago, 213

Consumer's League, 34, 249, 250

Conway, Jack T., 59

Cooper, Arthur, 67

Coordinating Committee of Greater New Orleans, 34

Copelin, Sherman: Family Health Foundation scandal, 206; after Martin Luther King Jr. assassination, 135, 267; Model Cities, 201, 206, 208, 268; SOUL, 252, 268

Corliss, Clark: community action, 73, 94–95; dealing with alienation, 110, 113; origins of War on Poverty, 45–46

corruption, Louisiana, 26–27, 303. *See also* Family Health Foundation scandal

Cottles, Alma, 116–17, 124

Cotton, Charles, 280

Cottrell, Leonard, 41

Desire Digest, 73

Desire Economic Opportunity
    Council, 72

Desire Parkway, 282

Development Association of Wards
    and Neighborhoods (DAWN),
    252, 253

Dewey, John, 17–18, 78, 106

Diamond, Raymond, 158, 162

Dillard University, 34, 54, 76, 135,
    201; student activism, 121, 134

DiRosa, Joseph, 259, 303

discrimination: and George W. Bush,
    312; in hiring, 32, 37, 58; and
    hope, 114; jobs programs, 160,
    161; and origins of Model Cities,
    200; in private marketplace, 16;
    in public welfare, 229; as reason
    for Public Accommodations
    Ordinance, 196; in recreation, 85;
    in unions, 105. *See also* Jim Crow

Dixie, 7, 9, 20, 297–98; end of, 20,
    271, 306; urban crisis in, 128;
    writing about, 337n14

Dixiecrat movement, 127

Dock Board, 26, 39. *See also* Port of
    New Orleans

Dodd, William J., 49–50, 152

Dolce, Carl, 140

Dombrowski, James, 13

Dorgenois Street, 209

Douglas, Nils, 34, 36; campaigns, 250,
    252; Family Health Foundation
    scandal, 206; SOUL, 252–53;
    SOUL and Edwin Edwards, 261

Douglass, Emmitt, 133

Dryades Street, 34

Duke, David, 27, 301

Dumas, Woodrow W. "Woody," 187

Duplantier, Adrian, 29, 249–50

Durr, Clifford, 13

Durr, Virginia, 13

East Carroll Parish, 169

East St. Louis, 213

Economic Opportunity Act (EOA):
    Community Action Program,
    198; Concentrated Employment
    Program, 155; culture of poverty
    theory, 100; Green Amendment,
    100, 357n54; origins, 14, 44–49,
    58–59, 338n26; response to,
    73. *See also* Community Action
    Program (CAP); War on Poverty;
    and names of programs

Economic Security Act of 1935, 39,
    40, 228, 229; 1956 amendments,
    108; rise in OASDI payments,
    229; "standard of need" mandate,
    234

economy of New Orleans, 23–26

Edith Sampson Playground, 84

Edwards, Edwin Washington, 26–27,
    254; on Mark Essex, 294; 1971
    gubernatorial race and Acronyms,
    261; and self-definition, 264–65;
    Southern University shootings,
    287; "wizard under the sheets,"
    301

Edwards, Morris A., 106

Edwards, Tyrone, 278

Edwards, Winifred, 202

Egerton, John, 9, 337n14

Elie, Lolis, 34, 36, 280

Ellender, Allen, 198

Elloie, Charles, 57, 208, 254, 258, 283,
    391n22

Elloie, Pearlie, 57

Episcopal Church, 39

Erikson, Erik, 106

of Desire, 70, 275; on racial discrimination, 159; on white exploitation, 121. See also *Plain Truth, The*

Freiberg, Norma, 143, 269

Freidberg, Peter, 90–92

French Quarter, 133, 194, 252, 286, 290, 398

Freud, Sigmund, 106

Frey, Robert, 284

Gallatoire's restaurant, 166

Galvez Streeet, 123

Garden District, 3, 30, 71, 142

Gardner, Mrs. E., 117

Garrison, Jim, 207

Garvey, Marcus, 33, 92

Gayle, James, 79

General Taylor Street bridge, opposition to, 255–56

Gentilly, 253

Gertler, David, 262, 393n46

Gert Town, 120, 239, 243, 289

Gervais, Pershing, 269

"Ghetto of Desire," 70

Giarrusso, Clarence: Black Panthers, 272–80 passim, 285; Felony Action Squad, 286, 289; Mark Essex, 289, 294

Girarrusso, Joseph: Black Panthers, 275, 276; civil disorder, 134, 138, 143; jobs program, 156; on TCA, 140; Thugs United, 221

Glass, Robert, 280

God, 22, 26, 74; local invocation of, 79, 81, 294

Godchaux, Thomas, 46, 54, 140, 367n59

Goodwin, Richard, 42

Gracia, Karina, 116

Grambling State University, 287

Gravier Improvement Project, 194

Gravier Street, 292

Gray Areas Program, of Ford Foundation, 41, 198

Great Society: criticism of, 97; early programs, 54–58; end of, 20, 294; historical trajectory of, 11–13, 15, 167, 297; and hunger policy, 165–79; as an ideal, 8, 78; impact on racial inclusion, 15, 102, 338n29; introduced, 2–3; and *Kerner Report*, 148; legacies, 298–310; and manpower, 151–64; as marketplace, 150, 338n29; Moon Landrieu, 262, 264–66; and neighborhood political development, 86, 102, 179, 211, 251; 1969 mayoral race, 262; and political and therapeutic thought, 17–18, 19, 72, 104–20, 145, 217, 295; and politics of, 49, 75, 101, 177, 238, 247, 253, 259, 272; promises, compared to post-Katrina, 312–13; as racial management tool, 6, 15, 272; shifting power, 86; and southern liberalism, 7–8, 10; on the streets of New Orleans, 11; and struggle over, in Louisiana, 49–54; terms used by press, 337n12; visions of, 42–45, 78, 80, 127, 145–46, 148; welfare rights, 238. *See also* civil rights movement; Community Action Program (CAP); community organizing; Johnson, Lyndon B.; Soft State; War on Poverty

Green, Edith, 100, 357n54

Green, Lee, 123

gubernatorial campaigns, Louisiana: of 1959–60, 35; of 1963–64, 48, 265; of 1970–71, 253–54, 261, 273; of 1983–84, 27

Guillemet, Clarence, 383n83

Gulf of Mexico, 1, 4, 75, 277, 309, 312

Guste, William J., Jr., 189, 199, 262, 293

Guste Homes, 41, 68, 201

Guyton, Donald, Sr. (Malik Rahim), 275

Haas, Edward F., 27–28

Haley, Oretha Castle, 84, 93, 101, 224, 254–55, 259–61. *See also* Castle, Oretha

Haley, Richard, 34, 84, 254, 255, 308; assessment of SWPC board and War on Poverty, 96–97; as community organizing director, 68, 72, 96, 101; and difficulties of integration, 81–82; police incident, 91

Hall, Edward "Sticks," 221–22

Halloween, 37, 281

Hall v. Nagel, 248

Hamer, Fannie Lou, 2

Hampton, Fred, 274

Hampton, John, 236

Hannan, Philip, 135, 171, 235, 367n59

HANO. *See* Housing Authority of New Orleans

Hanrahan, Edward, 394n4

Harrell, Alfred, Jr., 289

Harrington, Michael, 42, 105

Harris, Alvin "Butte," 214

Haynesville, Louisiana, 274

Head Start, 47, 104, 338n26, 338n30, 347n6; compared to CEP, 153–

54; described, 54, 55–57; Xavier Teacher Corps, 243

Health Education Authority of Louisiana (HEAL), 194

Hébert, Edward F., 51, 98, 126, 185, 249

Heebe, Frederick, 283

Heier, Thomas J., Jr., 189, 192

Heller, Walter, 41

Help Desk, New Orleans HRC, 145

Henry, Anthony R., 233

Henry, Clarence "Chink," 248

Hensgen, Kathleen M., 104

Hernon, Peter, 290, 292, 295

Hessler, Ernest J., Jr., 250

Hibernia Bank, 25–26

Highlander Folk School, 13

Highway 90, 236

History, of New Orleans, 21–37

home-rule charter, 27

Hoover, J. Edgar, 273

HOPE VI, 310

Horton, Myles, 13

Hosli, Edwin, Sr., 289

House of Wisdom, 120

Housing Acts of 1937, 1949, and 1954, 182

Housing and Community Development Act of 1974, 181, 294

Housing Authority of New Orleans (HANO): Black Panthers (NCCF), 281, 283–84; civil disorder, 138; described, 183; on housing conditions, 33; mentioned, 53, 190, 339n30; number of residences, 183; outreach to black residents, 138; popularity within, 70, 339n34; racial discrimination,

Neighborhood Youth Corps (NYC)
(*continued*)
    156; role in empowerment,
    115–18
Nellie's Grocery Store, 277, 278, 279
Nelson, John, Jr., 35, 387n12
Newark, 62, 126, 133, 134, 137, 144
New Careers, 152, 155, 156, 163;
    assessment, 161; COUP, 391n22
New Deal, 11–13; and AFDC, 227;
    Democratic regime, 337n21;
    Food Stamp Program, 167–68;
    housing, 183; Jim Crow, 53, 183;
    labor market, 151–53; welfare
    state, 39, 40, 372, 73n42
New Federalism, 300
New Left, 42
New Orleans Athletic Club, 32
New Orleans Committee for the
    Economic Opportunity Program
    (NOCEOP), 46, 48
New Orleans Federal Savings and
    Loan Association, 190
New Orleans Health Corporation, 205
New Orleans Health Department, 91,
    268
New Orleans Legal Assistance
    Corporation (NOLAC), 35,
    339n30; Black Panthers (NCCF),
    280–83; described, 387n12;
    Desire area, 273; Thugs United,
    221; welfare rights movement,
    225, 230–31, 234, 237
New Orleans Philharmonic Orchestra,
    194
New Orleans Police Department
    (NOPD), 266; Black Panthers,
    271–80, 282–86; black political
    development, 209–10; civil
    disorder, 91, 130–33, 135, 137–

38, 140; dragging incident, 37,
    246; Felony Action Squad, 286,
    289; jobs program, 156; Mark
    Essex, 288–92, 295; SCEF, 37;
    shooting of Robert Lee Boyd,
    133; "stop and frisk" policy, 131,
    209; Thugs United, 221; VISTA
    surveillance, 90; welfare rights,
    232
New Orleans Public Belt Railroad
    Commission, 39
New Orleans Recreation Department
    (NORD), 84–86
New Orleans Saints, 297
New Orleans States-Item, 68, 222;
    civil disorder, 134; on conditions
    for black residents, 130, 145; jobs
    program, 155, 156; Mark Essex,
    292; Urban Renewal, 189
New Orleans Tenants Organization
    (NOTO), 225, 231, 236–38
New Orleans Times-Picayune: Black
    Panthers, 279; jobs program, 159;
    welfare rights march, 235
New Orleans Travelers Aid Associa-
    tion, 217
New Orleans Welfare Rights
    Organization (NOWRO), 224–39,
    245; entitlement thinking, 225;
    Food Stamp program, 165, 170,
    172–73; NOLAC, 273; origins,
    231–32
New Orleans Youth Enterprises, 221
Newsome, Betty, 116
Newton, Huey P., 273
New York, 56, 128; fiscal problems in,
    299–300; Food Stamp program
    in, 374n16; the Real Great Society
    in New York, 213
New York Daily News, 299

New Yorker, 30
New York Mets, 56
New York National Guard, discrimination against, 196
New York Times, 148, 337n12
Nineveh, 81
Ninth Ward, 4, 30, 137, 190, 250, 253, 258–59, 275, 277
Ninth Ward Citizen's Voters League, 249
Ninth Ward Civic Improvement League, 75–76, 79, 87, 192, 248
Nixon, Patricia, 290
Nixon, Richard: black power, 119; Boggs funeral, 290; expansion of conservatism, 10; Food Stamp program, 175; inauguration, 20, 294; law and order, 127, 142; "New Federalism," transformation of Great Society, 141, 179, 181, 203, 294
Nobel Peace Prize, 205
NOLA Express: Black Panthers, 275, 279; police brutality, 131; Urban Renewal, 192
North Carolina, 48, 89, 338n23
Novak, Robert, 291

Odom, Larry Sylvester, 130, 147
Odum, Howard, 9
Office of AMERICANISM vs. COMMUNISM Committee, 185
Office of Economic Opportunity (OEO), 14–15; analysis of jobs programs, 161; appropriation of, 47, 100; Black Panthers, 280–81; bypassing existing structures, 47, 50; Carrollton area, 244; Chicago gangs, 284n1; civil disorders, 140–41, 146–47, 232; controversy

with Louisiana governor, 49–54; criticism of, 97–98; Food Stamp program, 171, 173–74, 178; jobs programs, 152–53, 156–57, 160–64; League of Women Voters, 240; local oversight, lack of, 61–62; mentioned, 47, 53, 59, 94, 109, 130; NACW, 108; objectives of leaders, 99; rules of, 89, 92, 95, 98–100, 280, 281; Soft State expansion, 141, 339n30; spending and recommendations, 95, 102, 130; Youth Organizations United, 213. *See also* Community Action Agencies; Community Action Program (CAP); Louisiana OEO; maximum feasible participation (MFP); New Orleans Welfare Rights Organization (NOWRO); Social Welfare Planning Council (SWPC); Total Community Action (TCA)
Ohlin, Lloyd, 41, 48
oil prices and economic conditions, 24, 247, 297, 298, 304, 305
O'Keefe, Michael, 235
Old Age, Survivors, Disability Insurance program (OASDI), 228, 229
Old Regulars, 28. *See also* Regular Democratic Organization (RDO)
Old Testament, 81
"one-drop" rule, 4
Operation Feed the Babies, 229
Operation Shoe Shine, 221
Operation Upgrade, 54, 108
Opportunity Food Store, 123
opportunity theory, 41
Orangeburg, South Carolina, 287

Organization of American States (OAS), 28

Orleans Levee Board, 30

Orleans Parish Progressive Voters League (OPPVL), 28, 248, 249, 258

Orleans Parish School Board (OPSB), 45, 52, 53; elections, 249, 251; and Head Start, 55–56

Ortique, Revius, 137, 249, 257, 367n59, 392n29

Other Americans, 42

Our Paper, 113

Paris, peace talks in, 294

Parker, Mary Evelyn, 228–29

Peace Corps, 42

Pea Patch farm, 26

Pecot, Carlton, 235, 392n29

Pecoul, John, 145

Pennsylvania, 86

Pentagon, 142

People's College, 212, 218, 221

People's Defense League, 248

People's Methodist Community Center, 91

Persigo, Paul, 291

"personal politics," 22

Petre, John, 132, 392n46

Pezant, James N. "Jim," 178

Pickwick Club, 26, 29

Piety Street, 275, 277

Pigs' Eye, 286

Pinchback, P. B. S., 247

Plain Truth, The: black political disunity, 258; community life, 65; deprivation, 118; grocery boycott, 124; Moon Landrieu, 264, 270; racial discrimination, 159; Urban Renewal, 193; welfare

rights, 236–37; work ethic, 124

Plaquemines Parish, 69

Plessy v. Ferguson, 248

Poage, W. R., 376n45

Poitevent, Eads, 220

Police Association of New Orleans (PANO), 222

"politics of personal despair," 110

Pontchartrain Expressway, 186

Pontchartrain Park, 30, 253

Poor Law of 1880, 39

Pope, Betty, 76, 131–33

population statistics, New Orleans, 3, 5–6, 66

Populism, 11–13. *See also* Black Power populism

Portman, Robert, 280

Port of New Orleans, 21, 24, 26, 39, 135

poverty, 108–11, 300. *See also* War on Poverty

Powell, Adam Clayton, 146

Powell, Betty, 284

President's Committee on Juvenile Delinquency and Youth Crime (PCJD), 41

President's Council of Economic Advisers. *See* Council of Economic Advisers, President's (CEA)

Problem We All Live With, The (Rockwell), 19

Progressivism, 11–13

Project Enable, 54–55

Project Score, 54

Proteus, Krewe of, 29

Public Accommodations Ordinance, 195–97

Public Works Administration, 152

254; early programs, 55–58; employment, 85–85; Family Health Foundation scandal, 205; Food Stamp program, 171–72, 174–79; funding in 1969, 181; jobs program, 153–63; Mark Essex, 288; Model Cities, compared to, 178, 202; origins, 48, 53–54, 88, 367n59; as political alternative, 73, 88, 102–3, 139, 251, 255, 257; problems with, 77–78; and racial prejudice, 78; and recreation, 84–87; and scandal, 303; and small business development, 123, 203–4; three-pronged approach, 54; Thugs United, 215; Urban Renewal, 181, 185, 192; and VISTA, 88–89; welfare rights, 172, 232. *See also* community organizing; Social Welfare Planning Council (SWPC)

tourism, 196, 297

transportation in New Orleans, 25–27, 28, 32, 70, 122, 186, 202, 340n11

Travels with Charley, 19

Tremé, 101, 194, 252, 362n63, 391n22

Tremé Improvement Political Society (TIPS), 252

Tucker, Robert H., Jr., 203, 254, 280, 283, 286

Tulane University: area around, 3; Black Panthers, 282, 283; Family Health Foundation scandal, 204, 205; Gert Town, 239; historically segregated, 116; jobs program, 153; medical school, 194; mentioned, 54, 68, 95, 111, 255; Thugs United, 218; Urban Renewal, 185, 186

Tulane University Medical School, 194

Tulane University School of Social Work, 54, 90, 131, 239

Tupelo Avenue Canal, 193

Tureaud, A. P., 33, 248, 249

Twelfth and Oxford Film Maker Corporation, Philadelphia, 213

Uhuru no Umoja, 270

underclass, 359n13

"undeserving" v. "deserving" poor, 228

Union Railroad Terminal, 33

Unitarian Universalist Church, 35

United Clubs, 33

United Fund, 40, 47, 54; Thugs United, 216, 222

United Negro Improvement Association, 33, 92

University of Michigan, 42, 80

University of New Orleans, 269; and Black Panthers, 282, 283

University of Virginia, 290

Upstairs Lounge fire, 398n69

Upton, Milton, 37

Uptown, 30, 35, 143, 177, 263, 286, 393n46

Upward Bound, 54, 308n26

urban crisis, 3, 8; Acronyms, 257; described, 126, 128, 146, 209; end of Jim Crow, 125, 129; Great Society, 129; Soft State expansion, 16, 141; and the South, 17, 128, 142; Thugs United, 211, 216, 218. *See also* civil disorder; Great Society; violence

Urban League of Greater New Orleans (ULGNO), 14, 18; Black Panthers, 280; Carrollton area and Gert Town, 239–40; community action, 139; history

14; historically in Louisiana and New Orleans, 128–29, 308–9; 1980s and 1990s, 309; by whites against blacks, 102. *See also* Black Panthers; Essex, Mark James "Jimmy"; New Orleans Police Department (NOPD)

Vitter, C. E., 231

Volunteers in Service to America (VISTA), 47, 67, 338n26, 338n30; and alienation, 109; Carrollton area, 243–45; controversy and conflict, 84, 88–94, 96, 243; segregation issue, 81–82, 243

"Vote for the Crook" bumper sticker, 27

Voter Education and Registration Project, 92,

voter registration, 34, 211, 250, 251, 253; in Carrollton area, 240, 242; in Central City, 93–94; and COUP, 254; by DACC, 72–73; in Louisiana, 1950s and 1960s, 249; and Neighborhood Development Centers, 65; after Voting Rights Act, 250; white purge, 249

Voting Rights Act of 1965, 5, 14, 60, 208; antipoverty functions, 15, 62; LBJ reaction, 337n16; Moon Landrieu, 246; response to, 73, 105, 250

Wallace, George, 10, 50, 127
Wallace, Lurleen, 50
Wal-Mart, 9, 310
Walmsley, T. Semmes, 28
Walton, Ronald, 124
War and Industry Board, 141
Ward, Charles Ray, 269
Ward, Martha, 206

War on Drugs, 307

War on Poverty: anticommunism, impact of, 92–93; background to, in New Orleans, 39–41; Carrollton area, 239–40; civil disorder, 139–40, 226; civil rights movement, 14, 101–3, 150; conflict in Louisiana, 49–53; control over, 95–99, 179; criticism of, 85–90; declaration, 5; definition, 14–15; family and gender, 7; functions in New Orleans, 15, 272; legacies, 300–308; limits of, 77–82; localism, 64, 102; national leadership of, 42; police incident, 91; political development from, 7, 84, 86, 88, 99–103, 134, 145–46, 177, 212, 254–59, 263, 268, 272, 280, 302; Progressive Era influences, 12; Richard Nixon, 294; Ronald Reagan, 300, 307; second stage of, 149–50, 202; and Soft State, 15; spending in New Orleans, 15; therapeutic influence of, 15, 105–19, 121, 180–81, 216–17, 241; Thugs United, 212; vision for, 43–44, 59, 72. *See also* civil disorder; community action; community organizing; Family Health Foundation scandal; Great Society; individualism; maximum feasible participation; New Orleans Committee for the Economic Opportunity Program (NOCEOP); New Orleans Welfare Rights Organization (NOWRO); Social Welfare Planning Council (SWPC); target areas; therapeutic culture, impact